Language in Immigrant

Exploring the complex relationship between language and immigration in the United States, this timely book challenges mainstream, historically established assumptions about American citizenship and identity. Set within both a historical and current political context, this book covers hotly debated topics such as language and ethnicity, the relationship between non-native English and American identity, perceptions and stereotypes related to foreign accents, code-switching, hybrid language forms such as Spanglish, language and the family, and the future of language in America. Work from linguistics, education policy, history, sociology, and politics is brought together to provide an accessible overview of the key issues. Through specific examples and case studies, immigrant America is presented as a diverse, multilingual, and multidimensional space in which identities are often hybridized and always multifaceted.

DOMINIKA BARAN is Assistant Professor of English at Duke University, specializing in sociolinguistics and linguistic anthropology in transnational contexts. Her interest in language and immigration in the United States stems partly from her own background as a political refugee from Poland who settled in New York at age fifteen and spoke only minimal English. Her ongoing projects include a discourse analytic study of narratives of migration among Polish immigrants in Anglophone countries.

Language in Immigrant America

Dominika Baran

Duke University

CAMBRIDGE
UNIVERSITY PRESS

CAMBRIDGE
UNIVERSITY PRESS

University Printing House, Cambridge CB2 8BS, United Kingdom

One Liberty Plaza, 20th Floor, New York, NY 10006, USA

477 Williamstown Road, Port Melbourne, VIC 3207, Australia

4843/24, 2nd Floor, Ansari Road, Daryaganj, Delhi – 110002, India

79 Anson Road, #06–04/06, Singapore 079906

Cambridge University Press is part of the University of Cambridge.

It furthers the University's mission by disseminating knowledge in the pursuit of education, learning, and research at the highest international levels of excellence.

www.cambridge.org
Information on this title: www.cambridge.org/9781107058392
DOI: 10.1017/9781107415713

First published 2017

Printed in the United States of America by Sheridan Books, Inc.

A catalogue record for this publication is available from the British Library.

ISBN 978-1-107-05839-2 Hardback
ISBN 978-1-107-68981-7 Paperback

To my daughter, Salomé

Contents

Figures and Tables

Figures

Tables

Preface

As I completed this book in August 2016, the presidential election campaign in the United States was in full swing, and the derogatory comments about minorities, women, immigrants, and Muslims made by then-candidate Donald Trump were regularly making headlines. The discursive strategy of Trump's campaign was the familiar one of appealing to white voters by depicting all "others" as a threat. He described Mexicans as "criminals" and "rapists," asserted that "Islam hates us," called for establishing a Muslim registry, and frequently invoked an old racist stereotype that equates African American communities with crime-ridden inner cities. This rhetoric drew supporters as well as many outspoken critics. But then, on November 8, Trump was elected president. Soon afterwards, a white supremacist – so-called "alt-right" – conference got under way in a federal building in Washington, DC, focusing on celebrating the election results and on developing strategies for "expanding white privilege," in the words of leading alt-right activist Richard Spencer. And, as I write this preface in February 2017, two major events have taken place. On January 20, Donald Trump was sworn in as the country's forty-fifth president. The very next day, millions took to the streets in the historic Women's March on Washington, both in the US capital and in countless cities across America and the world, to protest the discriminatory attitudes that permeate the new administration's promised agenda, which targets numerous groups, including immigrants, refugees, people of color, Native Americans, Muslims, women, the LGBTQ community, and people with disabilities. This context contrasts profoundly with that invoked by Smedley and Smedley (2011) in the preface to their book *Race in North America*: "Finally, an extraordinary event has happened in American lives. In 2008 Americans elected as president Barack Obama, an African American, which has caused many to query what this means for 'race relations' . . . This election has opened up a wide range of opportunities for reflection on the meaning of race and the future of our racial ideology" (xiii). Today, in 2017, many worry that instead of thinking about the future, we will be fighting against going back to a troubled past.

One of this book's important themes is an examination of discourses surrounding immigration throughout American history, in which new immigrant groups are time and again portrayed as inferior to earlier, now assimilated ones. The language used to denigrate Latinos today is not much different from that used by early-twentieth-century nativists to disparage Southern and Eastern Europeans, or by late-nineteenth-century white Californians who fought to limit contact between their own children and those of Chinese immigrants for fear of physical and moral contamination. Furthermore, the language and policies that today discriminate against or disadvantage groups (such as women, Muslims, or the LGBTQ community) and that undermine public education or equitable access to healthcare have profound implications for immigrants as well, since immigrant issues intersect with those of gender, religion, sexuality, and many others. The fact that a candidate whose campaign was built on the rhetoric of fear of the Other succeeded in winning the presidency illustrates that the xenophobic sentiments and discourses that have historically fed the tensions between "immigrants" and "Americans" continue to be influential today. Just days after taking office, Trump issued executive orders to begin the construction of a border wall with Mexico and to suspend the entry of refugees from Muslim countries hit the hardest by ongoing humanitarian crises, thus revealing the very real consequences of the politics of fear. At the same time, however, the scale of the protests witnessed on January 21, 2017 demonstrates widespread opposition to these xenophobic discourses. In public discussion of current events one also often hears the explicit mention of Trump's racism, xenophobia, and sexism. This moment, perhaps, is another opportunity to confront our mainstream ideologies of discrimination and to meaningfully challenge our institutional prejudices.

This book presents immigrant America as a diverse, multilingual, and multidimensional space in which identities are often hybridized and always complex. It argues that any attempts to define what makes a "true" American that are rooted in exclusion and divisiveness, and in the reification of categories that are in fact fluid and changing social constructs, work only to exacerbate social injustice. They seek to reduce the complexity of the immigrant American experience to simplistic oppositions of "us" against "them," and they ignore the reality of privilege. They also erase the contributions of those who have been historically excluded from full American citizenship, such as African slaves, Asian railway and mine workers, and in recent years, undocumented Latino farm workers who are vilified as "illegals" yet absolutely essential to the functioning of American economy. Though the focus of this book is language, from a sociolinguistic perspective, language never exists in isolation from its social, cultural, and political context. It is through language that identities are negotiated and enacted, and it is also through language that inequalities are normalized and made to appear as inevitable. I hope that this book succeeds in helping to debunk some longstanding myths about immigrants, to challenge assumptions about American citizenship and identity, and to reimagine the relationship between the categories of citizen and immigrant.

Acknowledgments

This book could not have come to fruition without the invaluable support and input of numerous people. In the first place, I would like to thank my students who over the past six years have taken my course, Language in Immigrant America. This book was inspired by and took shape in response to the discussions we had in class and the ideas that these discussions generated. I would also like to thank the community partners in Durham, North Carolina, with whom my students work in the service component of this service-learning course and who make it possible for us to connect class discussions with real immigrant lives, as well as the Duke Service-Learning Program, in particular Kristin Wright, Bonnie McManus, and Joan Clifford. In addition, I would like to acknowledge the role of library archives in my research process, in particular the Rubenstein Special Collections Library at Duke University and the Jagiellonian Library of the Jagiellonian University in Kraków, Poland. Special thanks go out to Duke University librarians who assisted with bibliographies and special collections, in particular Linda Daniel, Greta Boers, and Elizabeth Dunn.

As this project moved from a proposal to a finished manuscript, my work on it benefited from extensive discussions with colleagues, mentors, and friends. Julie Tetel Andresen provided support and encouragement, as well as numerous practical tips for how to approach writing one's first monograph. Edna Andrews offered helpful comments on the proposal as well as invaluable moral support throughout this project. Both Julie's and Edna's work was also instrumental in influencing my thinking about the nature of language and multilingualism as it relates to this book. I also want to thank my colleagues Thomas Ferraro, Priscilla Wald, and Luciana Fellin for their support and for conversations that contributed to my analysis of immigration and migrant lives.

The inspiration to write this book came partly from the meetings of the Migration, Languages and Cultures Working Group, supported by the Franklin Humanities Institute at Duke, which I co-convened in 2011–2012 with my Duke colleagues Gareth Price, Luciana Fellin, and Hae-Young Kim. I would like to express my deepest thanks to my co-conveners, who helped organize the seminars and stimulate discussions that directly and indirectly influenced the ideas that inform this book, as well as to all the participants who came to our meetings and contributed to discussions. In addition, I am indebted to the guest speakers whose work had an impact on this book, both in their presentations at the working group meetings and in both formal and informal discussions afterwards; in particular, I would like to thank Anna De Fina and Adrienne Lo. In addition, big thanks go out to Erin Callahan, at the time a graduate student in Linguistics at Duke/NCSU, who was an integral part of the Working Group, whose research on the emerging Hispanic English in North Carolina inspired parts of this book, and whose intellectual input I benefited from in our discussions.

All shortcomings of this work remain, of course, my own.

A separate heartfelt thank you goes out to my colleague, intellectual partner, friend, and husband, Gareth Price. Our ongoing conversations and the inspiration of Gareth's extensive expertise in political sociology, sociolinguistics, and critical discourse analysis have been invaluable as I developed the theoretical approaches underpinning this book.

I thank my wonderful friends, who have helped me keep a healthy mind and a sense of humor, and my daughter, Salomé, who took to making her own books while still in preschool and thus motivated me to finish mine.

Last but not least, I would like to thank my parents, without whose decision in 1987 to leave their lives behind and take their chances in the United States I would not have become an immigrant American.

Introduction

The phrase describing America as "a nation of immigrants" was made famous as the title of President John F. Kennedy's book, published posthumously in October 1964. Almost exactly fifty years later, on November 20, 2014, President Barack Obama quoted this phrase when speaking about immigration reform: "My fellow Americans, we are and always will be a nation of immigrants. We were strangers once too."[1] Obama's assertion constructs a familial link, an imaginary continuation of a bloodline between the "strangers" of the past and the Americans of today, a spatial and temporal kinship-like connection through which "strangers" and "Americans" are all identified as immigrants.

There are those who oppose such representations. Samuel Huntington, in his final (2004) book *Who Are We? The Challenges to America's National Identity*, which views Latino immigration as a major threat to American identity and culture, argues that whereas today's newcomers are immigrants, *in*-migrating to the already established polity and society of the United States, the first Europeans were settlers, not immigrants. They did not come to join – and presumably assimilate to – an existing community or state with established territorial jurisdiction, government, laws, and customs. Rather, they came to settle in what they presumed to be *vacuum domicilium* ("uninhabited land," Anderson 2014: 42) and to develop from the ground up their own society, with their own institutions, physical structures, and way of life. In Huntington's words, "Settlers leave an existing society, usually in a group, in order to create a new community, a city on a hill, in a new and often distant territory ... Immigrants, in contrast, do not create a new society. They move from one society to a different society ... Before immigrants could come to America, settlers had to found America" (Huntington 2004: 39–40).

Huntington's argument rests on a number of problematic assumptions (cf. Newton 2008). It not only accepts the early settlers' claim to the American lands as based on a mandate from God to find and settle a new "Promised Land," not only ignores the fact that there *were* existing and

[1] www.whitehouse.gov/blog/2014/11/20/we-were-strangers-once-too-president-announces-new-steps-immigratio, accessed April 12, 2016.

developed societies and polities in North America and that the settlers *chose* not to assimilate to them but, instead, to destroy them – but it also seeks to justify an America in which present-day immigrants are expected to assimilate to the white, European, English-speaking, Christian, heteronormative mainstream (cf. Schmidt 2002; Schmidt 2000). Perspectives such as Huntington's, echoed every day by anti-immigration politicians, invent and propagate the fiction that early white English settlers had a "right" to American lands, and that today's often non-white, non-English-speaking immigrants form a different category of people, who should not be trusted with citizenship and who threaten the "American way of life."

Formulations such as Kennedy's and Obama's "nation of immigrants" seek to debunk these fictions by representing all Americans as immigrants and, by logical extension, all immigrants as Americans. But these alternative narratives are also problematic because they paint a harmonious picture of an America unified over space and time into a bonded immigrant family, sharing the same concerns and cares, and in so doing they gloss over the conflicts and battles produced by highly unequal power relations within American society. In reality, it is indeed impossible to establish a clear definitional boundary separating the immigrant from the American, but neither is it the case that immigrants and Americans are synonyms for one large category. Rather, the meanings of "immigrant" and "American" have always been contested, negotiated, and enacted discursively – as well as through violence and material control – on the frontier, on plantations, in battle, in factories, in mines, on railroad construction sites, in big-city tenements, in the courts and prisons, and in schools. The central theme of the present book is that language has been a crucial site for this contestation since the days of the first European settlements, and my aim here will be to explore language in America from this perspective, demonstrating that "immigrant" and "American" have been and continue to be overlapping, conflicting, fluid, and mutually constitutive categories. Furthermore, I aim to show that the complexity, fluidity, and hybridity of immigrant/American – or immigrant-American – identities has always been negotiated and enacted through hybrid language forms and practices, which in turn challenges the mainstream notions of languages as fully discrete, self-contained entities, and of clear dichotomies between monolingualism and multilingualism or between native speaker and language learner.

Language Ideology in the United States

In her discussion of Sudanese women refugees' experiences with learning English in America, Warriner (2007) makes the important point that discourses surrounding English and English learning invoke and naturalize assumptions about belonging and about rights to access material and nonmaterial resources in society. She writes, "Citizens and noncitizens are defined and constructed in relation to each other, often in ways that index (and further promote) ideologies of language, race, and difference" (Warriner 2007: 346). The African refugee women in her study have internalized the portrayal of immigrants who master English and are rewarded with a chance to share in the American dream: the women expend considerable energy on studying English even when they see no clear benefits to their own lives as a result.

The language ideology that sees English as intrinsic to Americanness, and English learning as a requirement for Americanization, has become deeply entrenched as part of America's national identity narrative. Proponent of assimilation Samuel Huntington argues forcefully that America's core culture is Anglo-Protestant and claims, incorrectly and misleadingly, that "until the appearance of large concentrations of Spanish-speaking immigrants in Miami and the Southwest, America was unique as a huge country of more than 200 million people virtually all speaking the same language [English]" (Huntington 2004: 60). The US English movement and legislation making English the official language of 32 states, as of March 2016, are based on similar assumptions (Citrin et al. 1990). The US English website outlines its position by invoking the English-as-path-to-success claim: "U.S. English believes that the passage of English as the official language will help to expand opportunities for immigrants to learn and speak English, the single greatest empowering tool that immigrants must have to succeed."[2] Pavlenko (2002) cites a study by Bigler (1996), in which Euro-American senior citizens "stated that their grandparents became full-fledged Americans by willingly assimilating, learning English, and restricting the native languages to the privacy of their homes, and that any other course of action would threaten national unity and culture" (Pavlenko 2002: 164). Pavlenko points out that this idealized story erases two centuries of relative tolerance towards multilingualism, the subsequent active construction of the American identity and spirit as embodied in the English language, the aggressive promotion of English monolingualism, and the forced nature of the language shift that took place in immigrant communities as a result.

In contrast to the dominant narrative, language, and English monolingualism in particular, came to be associated with Americanness relatively late, in response to the Great Migration of 1880–1924 and to the rise in xenophobic feeling surrounding World War I. Before that, as Pavlenko (2002) observes, "American national identity was historically founded on the assumption that whatever one's origin or native language, one could become an American by declaring a desire to do so and committing oneself to a set of liberal political principles, which include democracy, liberty, equality, and individual

[2] www.usenglish.org/view/3, accessed June 30, 2016.

achievement" (Pavlenko 2002: 165). This perspective, to be sure, requires some qualification, since the option to "become an American" was made available in the Naturalization Act of 1790 only to "free white persons," and was closed to slaves, free Africans, Asians, and Native Americans. And while African Americans became citizens after slavery was abolished, their treatment as *de facto* non-citizens continued. Other non-whites were formally barred from citizenship until well into the twentieth century. Restrictions based on race necessarily involved issues of language, since languages are closely bound up with ethnic categories and group identities. Accordingly, eighteenth- and nineteenth-century scholars developed theories that posited the polysynthetic features of Indigenous languages, often baffling to Europeans and absent from classical languages such as Greek or Latin, as evidence of Native Americans' supposed racial inferiority (Harvey 2015). Meanwhile, in popular culture, such as in minstrel shows, the Chinese-English pidgin spoken by Chinese migrant workers in the mid-nineteenth century was imitated, mocked, and became established as a marker of the Asian "perpetual foreigner" who was imagined to possess various undesirable, un-American qualities (Lee 1999; Leland 1892).

Nonetheless, Pavlenko (2002) is correct in observing that it was only in the early twentieth century that "English fluency – and eventually monolingualism in English – [became] a constitutive aspect of an American identity" (Pavlenko 2002: 165). As more immigrants from Eastern and Southern Europe arrived in the United States and settled in large urban and industrial centers, their presence sparked concerns over the changing ethnic makeup of the American population. Commentators, journalists, educators, and politicians began noticing and criticizing these new immigrants' relative poverty, low levels of education, non-Protestant religious practices, and supposed inability to grasp the principles that govern a democratic society (Schmid 2001; Willey 1909). While the pseudo-science of eugenics provided the basis for questionable classifications of peoples into hierarchically ordered "races," language quickly became the symbolic measure of racial superiority or inferiority. English was portrayed as a superior language that was especially well suited for expressing ideas of democracy, liberty, and the Protestant ethic (Pavlenko 2002; Schmidt 2002). Furthermore, English was constructed as a marker of native-born Americans, as opposed to the new immigrants, whose languages were often described as harsh and "barbaric" (Willey 1909). Immigrants were now expected to assimilate and to prove their willingness to do so by learning English and abandoning their native and heritage languages. In 1906, the first English-language requirement for naturalization was adopted "with the explicit purpose of limiting the entrance in the United States of southern and eastern Europeans" (Schmid 2001: 34–35), but with the outbreak of World War I, German speakers also came under intense censorship. A 1917 amendment to the Espionage Act required every foreign-language newspaper to provide Congress with English translations of all news articles relating to the war (Schmid 2001: 36). The previously robust German-language schools were often closed down, and many states adopted laws requiring English-only instruction in schools (Pavlenko 2002; Schmid 2001). Various local English-only initiatives also appeared: for example, "in Findlay, Ohio, the city council imposed a fine of $25 for speaking German on the streets" (Schmid 2001: 36).

English monolingualism thus became a central feature of true Americanness in government and popular discourses. The federal government proclaimed July 4, 1915 as "Americanization Day." A civics text published in 1918 for naturalization candidates asserted that "unity of speech will bring unity of thought, unity of feeling, unity of patriotism" (cited in Carnevale 2009: 66), and the Bureau of Naturalization appealed to prospective citizens with the slogan of "One language, one country, one flag" (66). Public schools and workplaces offered evening courses in English for immigrants, and some employers made attendance at these compulsory (Carnevale 2009: 67). Second-generation children were encouraged to teach English to their parents, while parents were pressured to give up speaking heritage languages at home. Pavlenko (2002), whose article provides a comprehensive analysis of how the language ideology of English monolingualism was produced, also observes this reversal of generational roles:

> Now it was no longer the children who had to learn the language of the parents, but parents who had to learn English in order to be able to communicate with their offspring, or in the words of Julia Richman, the district superintendent of New York's Lower East Side schools, "cross the bridge to join [their] child on the American side" (Pavlenko 2002: 181–182).

Simultaneously, bilingualism came under attack from researchers in education and psychology, who through various now-discredited tests "demonstrated" the intellectual inferiority of bilingual children (Schmid 2001). Even linguists were suspicious of bilingualism, viewing it as compromising a person's overall linguistic ability (Jespersen 1922). And even though linguists and other scholars have since reversed their assessment of bilingualism, a suspicion of using languages other than English outside the private sphere of the home persists among policy makers and the general population.

The myth that English has always been the language of the United States and that English monolingualism is necessary and desirable in America's public spaces has been thoroughly naturalized. While proponents of linguistic pluralism support immigrants' language rights, heritage-language maintenance, bilingual education, and bilingual ballots (cf. discussion by Schmidt 2002), the expectation that immigrants should learn English for the benefit of both themselves and of American society is almost never seriously questioned in mainstream debates. Proposals for immigration reform routinely make reference to immigrants' need for learning English. Thus, for example, at the start of President Obama's second term in office, various proposals for immigration reform – none of which resulted in legislation – included some version of a pathway to citizenship for undocumented immigrants, which in turn specified "learning English" as a prerequisite for qualification. This rather vague requirement is presented as a matter of course alongside such specific criteria as a criminal background check and paying a monetary penalty. The requirement is problematic on a number of levels: the path-to-citizenship proposals do not specify what "learning English" consists of or how it is to be facilitated, and the undocumented children and young people at whom such proposals are directed typically have spent the majority of their lives in the US and are fluent and sometimes monolingual in English. The fact that learning English is nonetheless specified as a criterion for potential citizenship eligibility reflects, on one hand, the persistent stereotype that undocumented immigrants do not speak English, and that immigrants in general refuse to learn it, and on the other hand, the assumption that one must learn English to become American (at the very least, one has to keep trying).

The rationale for the insistence that Americans must all speak English to each other is linked to the belief that a multilingual or plurilingual community is inevitably plagued by conflict (Schmidt 2002). This belief is rooted in the European nationalist ideology in which one people corresponds to one language. Speaking one shared language is an important step in constructing the imagined community of the nation state (Anderson 1982; Hall 1992). The reality that multilingual communities have existed peacefully for millennia all around the world – and if they were not at peace, it was not because of multilingualism – is ignored by English-language assimilationists. For example, a 1984 recruiting brochure published by US English unquestioningly invokes and links the assumptions that multilingualism is detrimental to a society's functioning, and that the United States is an English-speaking country:

> The United States has been spared the bitter conflicts that plague so many countries whose citizens do not share a common tongue. Historic forces made English the language of all Americans, though nothing in our laws designated it the official language of the nation. But now English is under attack, and we must take affirmative steps to guarantee that it continues to be our common heritage. Failure to do so may well lead to institutionalized language segregation and a gradual loss of national unity (citied in Schmidt 2002: 144).

Such strongly held beliefs have motivated the dismantling of bilingual education across the United States, the popular fears that the sound of other, especially non-European, languages in American public spaces will somehow de-Americanize US society, and the appropriation and caricature of the most visible non-English variety in performances of what Hill (2008; 2001) terms "Mock Spanish" (see also Zentella 2003).

As Schmidt (2002) observes, "far from being ethnically neutral and inclusive in its impact on racialized language minority groups, a mandatory assimilationist policy underlines and reinforces the social structure of racialized inequality" (Schmidt 2002: 154). He also points out that in the "new racism" described by a number of analysts (e.g. Bobo 1997; Goldberg 1993; Solomos and Back 1995), "specific cultural forms have come to signify racialized identities, particularly where traditional biologically-based racist attributions have become socially and politically disreputable" (Schmidt 2002: 154). Language has become one of the most readily targeted of such cultural forms. Discrimination at the workplace and in education based on real or perceived accents is common and often accepted as reasonable (Lippi-Green 2012). However, language forms – accents, languages, dialects, non-standard speech, bilingual practices, and so on – are frequently invoked as code for ethnicity and race. Urciuoli (1996), for example, analyzes the racialization of Spanish in New York, pointing out that "Bilingual neighborhoods are equated with slums, an equation familiar to people who live in them" (Urciuoli 1996: 26). The US Census has used mother-tongue data as an index of race since 1913. Because it doesn't ask which language a person or family speaks, but rather if they speak languages other than English, the census continues to construct English as the norm; moreover, if a language other than English is reported, the census asks for an assessment of its speakers' English competence (Leeman 2004). Assessing the dominant American language ideology that is currently reflected in and reproduced by the US Census, Leeman (2004) argues that language has become an acceptable stand-in for race:

> In the evolution of the current language ideology, language has taken on a dual role. On one hand, language continues to index racialized identities, in particular, Asian and Latino identities. On the other hand, the language-race link has been loosened, allowing language to be portrayed as a component of culture and thus largely as a question of personal choice. It is this duality of language as both a hereditary characteristic and a cultural behavior that permits linguistic discrimination to step in as a surrogate for racial discrimination; because language is constructed as a changeable attribute, discrimination based on language is portrayed as more benign than discrimination based on characteristics seen as unchangeable, such as race or gender. In turn, this portrayal is associated with judicial hesitancy to recognize linguistic rights or to rule in favor of bilingual plaintiffs forbidden from speaking non-English languages at work (Leeman 2004: 526).

The United States, however, is a multilingual, not an English-speaking, country, as can be demonstrated by various statistics of languages spoken by American families (Lippi-Green 2004; Bayley 2004; Medvedeva 2012; Schmidt 2002; Pavlenko 2002). While the dominant ideology is that of

English as the American language, the reality of many Americans' day-to-day lives is defined by multilingual encounters and practices. Furthermore, this situation is not a recent development, since multilingualism has always been a feature of American life. This book, in part, attempts to tell a small part of the story of this American multilingualism from the colonial times to the present day.

Theoretical Approaches

Of the several theoretical themes and concepts that inform the analysis presented in this book, in the remainder of this introduction I would like to outline three that appear most influential in structuring my discussion. The first of these is the view of identity as discursively produced in interaction, and also the relationship between this socially negotiated identity and an individual's internal sense of self. The second one is the notion of hybridity, including hybrid identities and hybrid languages. Finally, the third is the rejection of binaries such as monolingual/multilingual or native/non-native speaker in favor of a more fluid approach to language and languaging. This also applies to the larger theme of this book, which is the complexity and fluidity of immigrant-American identities that I discussed in the opening of this introduction. The overview below is necessarily very brief, as one cannot do justice to these complex concepts in only several pages, but it is intended to situate the book within the current theoretical landscape in sociolinguistics and linguistic anthropology.

Identity

The concept of identity employed in this book is rooted in recent tradition in sociocultural anthropology and cultural studies, which views identities as complex, fluid, relational, negotiated in social interaction, and enacted through sociocultural practices (e.g. Bucholtz and Hall 2004; De Fina 2007; Klein 2009; Kyratzis 2010; Riley 2007; Baran 2014; Baran 2013; Holliday et al. 2004; Barker 2000; Hall 1992; Cameron 1997; Butler 1990). This perspective stands in contrast to essentialism, which assumes that "those who occupy an identity category . . . are both fundamentally similar to one another and fundamentally different from members of other groups . . . [and] that these groupings are inevitable and natural" (Bucholtz and Hall 2004: 374). In the essentialist perspective, qualities associated with these groupings – for example, "femininity" or "Americanness" – are attributes of their members, and are reified as objectively definable and verifiable. When someone classified as a member of an identity category does not exhibit the qualities associated with it, they are defined as deviant or inauthentic. This essentialist view is related to "the

Enlightenment subject," who, as Stuart Hall explains, "was based on a conception of the human person as a fully centered, unified individual ... whose 'centre' consisted of an inner core which first emerged when the subject was born, and unfolded with it, while remaining essentially the same ... throughout the individual's existence" (Hall 1992: 275). Much of the debate surrounding immigration in the United States – as elsewhere – is built on essentialist assumptions, such as, for example, that a "true American" speaks "unaccented" English and conforms to white, Anglo-Saxon cultural norms.

Hall contrasts the Enlightenment subject with "the post-modern subject, conceptualized as having no fixed, essential or permanent identity. Identity becomes a 'movable feast': formed and transformed continuously in relation to the ways we are represented or addressed in the cultural systems which surround us ... Within us are contradictory identities, pulling in different directions, so that our identifications are continuously being shifted about" (Hall 1992: 277). Thus defined post-modern subject inspires the understanding of identities as produced and negotiated in social interaction, enacted in discourse, and situated in context (Holliday et al. 2004) by researchers in linguistic anthropology, sociolinguistics, and applied linguistics. Bucholtz and Hall (2004), for example, argue that "identity inheres in actions, not in people" (Bucholtz and Hall 2004: 376), and they develop the analytical framework of tactics of intersubjectivity, which they use to theorize how individuals and groups perform their self-identification with social categories. Similarly, De Fina (2007) argues that "ethnicity should not be regarded as an abstract attribute of the individual, but rather as an interactional achievement grounded in concrete social contexts and evolving with them" (De Fina 2007: 374). The present book also embraces this perspective.

At the same time, however, it is instructive to remember that, as Bucholtz and Hall (2004: 376) point out, essentialist views of identity can be very much real, relevant, important, and salient to members of a particular community. The analyst has to acknowledge that these views represent locally salient ideologies that structure community life and inform how individuals position themselves in relation to identity categories that are meaningful in their social networks. Thus, for example, the frequently encountered belief that Asian accents are difficult to understand relies on essentialism because, among other problems, it conflates people from a number of countries who speak a variety of unrelated languages into one uniform category, and it racializes their linguistic practices by linking "Asian" phenotypical features[3] with the foreign and the inscrutable (Young

[3] Ideologies of race reify categories such as "Asian" by reinforcing beliefs that certain physical features should be grouped together, and that as a group they can be used to identify members of a particular race. In reality, race is a social construct, not a real or objective attribute of people. I will say more on this in Chapter 2.

1982). As a result, European Americans have been shown to report difficulty with understanding Asian American speakers of Mainstream US English because they believe they hear an "incomprehensible" foreign accent (Lippi-Green 2012; Shuck 2006; Rubin 1992; Rubin and Smith 1990). This is so even though Asian Americans are native speakers of American English, and despite the fact that even when speakers do have foreign accents, the extent to which these accents impede comprehension and their aesthetic appeal are subjective interpretations, not objective facts.

On one hand, therefore, the analyst must remember that essentialism informs the intersecting discourses of language, race, gender, class, etc., that circulate in communities, while at the same time not allowing essentialist assumptions to become part of his or her own analysis. On the other hand, from the perspective of the individual, there exists a psychological need to maintain a sense of a coherent self. Stuart Hall assesses this need with skepticism: "If we feel we have a unified identity from birth to death, it is only because we construct a comforting story or 'narrative of the self' about ourselves ... The fully unified, completed, secure and coherent identity is a fantasy" (Hall 1992: 277). But while Hall appears to dismiss the "narrative of the self" as merely a "comforting story," his observation holds true: individuals develop such personal narratives to make sense of their lives. Accordingly, psychologists have described self-identity as "a self-narrative that integrates one's past events into a coherent story ... [and] the construction of a future story that continues the 'I' of the person" (Polkinghorne 1988: 107). Drawing on this perspective in their study of how people reconstruct their self-identities in a second language, Pavlenko and Lantolf (2000) write:

> The events that happen to people can only make sense if they can be fitted into an existing plot or if the plot itself can be reconfigured or replaced ... Failure to integrate new events into these systems of coherence or to alter the plot of a life story appropriately, frequently results in confusion, strangeness, and conflict, and can, on occasion, lead to deep cognitive and emotional instabilities that end tragically (Pavlenko and Lantolf 2000: 160).

This book employs the analytical perspective of identities as socially and discursively constructed, situated, and contextualized, as well as complex and fluid. Additionally, talking about the experience of a multilingual individual, as I do later in the book, entails engaging with the psychological perspective in which the individual's construction of a coherent self-narrative across different linguistic contexts takes center stage. I will also acknowledge and engage with essentialist views of identity that often structure the sociocultural reality in which immigrants in the United States must orient and position themselves.

Hybridity

The notion of hybridity, as in *hybrid identities* or *hybrid linguistic forms*, surfaces frequently throughout this book. I refer to hybridization when discussing the negotiation of hyphenated identities in Chapter 3, when describing multilingual practices or the emergence of new language varieties such as Spanglish or Polamerican in Chapter 5, and again when discussing how individuals resolve the conflicts of acculturation in Chapter 7. Consequently, it may be helpful in this introduction to say a few words about hybridity, since it is a concept that has gained wide currency in various fields that concern themselves with issues of identity.

The term *hybrid* comes from the Latin word *hibrida*, and while it can be applied today to anything from biology to automobiles, its dictionary definition emphasizes its reference to things "derived from heterogenous or incongruous sources."[4] Thus in biology, for example, hybrid life forms are created from the crossbreeding of two already existing forms. This concept of the confrontation of existing forms to produce something new became a useful metaphor for describing heteroglossic cultural forms (Bakhtin 1981; Kyratzis 2010; Easthope 1998) and for problematizing identity in post-colonial and diasporic contexts (Bhabha 1994; Anzaldúa 2012; Gutiérrez et al. 1999; Klein 2009). In literary and cultural criticism, hybridity is theorized by Homi K. Bhabha (1994) as a process through which the colonized elude becoming "knowable" to the colonizer, and come to exercise subjectivity and agency (McRobbie 2005; Mizutani 2013). As McRobbie (2005) explains, Bhabha is concerned with "the disruptive currents which make the practice of orientalism less unimpeded than Said suggests" (McRobbie 2005: 101). These currents emerge "when subordinated peoples are expected to copy the manners, behavior and education of the colonizer. Their mimicry unsettles the ruler, precisely because the space of translating from one culture to the other also provides a space for insubordination, or antagonism" (McRobbie 2005: 101). As a result, the colonizer's cultural identity is altered by the colonized subject. Hybridity challenges "the 'temporal dimension' of colonial discourse: its logic of permanent presence, or of never-changing identity" (Mizutani 2013: 36). Instead of the colonized assimilating to the dominating culture of the colonizer while the latter remains unaffected by this encounter, cultural boundaries are destabilized and blurred in the production of hybrid forms and identities (Barker 2000: 202).

While Bhabha's concern in particular is with colonial and post-colonial contexts, the notion of hybridity has been similarly applied to migrant communities and to those whose circumstances blend the colonized/immigrant distinction in ways different from the former British Empire (cf. Gutiérrez

[4] For example, in the Oxford English Dictionary or at www.dictionary.com.

et al. 1999). Gloria Anzaldúa (2012), for example, explores the negotiation of identities in the American "borderlands," where the local inhabitants were colonized and recolonized, first by Spain, and then, already as Spanish-speaking Mexicans, by the United States. At the same time, they are identified with Mexican immigrants due to their geographic proximity to, and an ethnic and sometimes familial relationship with Mexicans living across the border. They are people who live in their ancient homeland, but are marginalized and redefined as trespassers. In Anzaldúa's account, Mexican Americans in the US Southwest construct their national, ethnic, and linguistic identities through ongoing hybridization, and these identities are further structured by competing ideologies of gender, sexuality, religion, and family.

Similarly complex hybridization in the borderlands – figuratively if not literally understood – occurs among young Muslim Americans, who, as Sirin and Fine (2008) discuss, are subjected to ethnogenesis and moral exclusion from the "nation of immigrants" on the basis of their shared and often outwardly visible religious affiliation. Sikh Americans' religious practice also requires embodiment through physical performance, in this case involving men growing out their beards and hair, and wearing turbans. While the Sikhs' visible ethnicity is marked as Other because of these practices, they are also often mistaken for Muslims, which in post-9/11 years has made them targets of threats and violence (Klein 2009). Sikh Americans' metaphorical borderlands thus juxtapose and blur boundaries between various religious practices, ethnic affiliations, and physical attributes. As Klein (2009) explains, "In the United States, second-generation Sikh American experience is mediated partly through what R. Radhakrishnan (1996) refers to as 'ethnic hyphenation,' a notion that captures the integrative yet liminal process of negotiating the space between different ethnic experiences in immigrant populations" (Klein 2009: 112). Gutiérrez et al. (1999), on the other hand, apply hybridity to the their analysis of dual-immersion bilingual classrooms, in which hybrid spaces and hybrid linguistic practices open the way to new opportunities for discussion and learning.

Crucially, for scholars such as Sirin and Fine (2008), Klein (2009), or Gutiérrez et al. (1999), hybridity describes active and agentive processes of construction, negotiation, reinterpretation, and reinvention of identities and sociocultural meanings; it is what happens when subjectivities and intersubjectivities are negotiated through "working the hyphen" (Sirin and Fine 2008: 114). Hybrid identities, meanings, and language forms are continuously being created and recreated, rather than fixed or completed. Also, hybrids represent more than the sum of their parts; they are new forms that deconstruct boundaries between sociocultural categories that are assumed by mainstream discourses. In the present book, one such boundary is that between "immigrants" and "Americans." Others include, for example, boundaries between languages, between ethnic groups, between "native speakers" and "language learners," and between monolinguals and multilinguals.

Fluidity and Continua

Related to the notion of hybridity, which upsets and disrupts boundaries, is the rejection of binaries and dichotomies in favor of theoretical approaches that emphasize fluidity and see categories in terms of continua. In applied linguistics, language and education, and sociolinguistics, researchers have been replacing binary conceptualizations of speakers and of linguistic practices and forms with notions such as "emergent bilinguals" (Bartlett and García 2011; García and Kleifgen 2010; García 2009), "native-like speakers" (Andrews 2014; Pavlenko 2005), languaging and translanguaging (García and Wei 2014; Wei 2011; Canagarajah 2011a; Bartlett and García 2011; Andresen 2014; Alvarez 2014; Palmer et al. 2014), engaging with language (De Fina 2012), polylanguaging (Jørgensen 2012, 2008; Jørgensen et al. 2011), superdiversity (Arnaut and Spotti 2014; Blommaert and Rampton 2011; Silverstein 2013), "superdiverse repertoires" (Blommaert and Backus 2012), and "transnational literacy" and "continua of biliteracy" (Hornberger 1989, 2003; Hornberger and Skilton-Sylvester 2000; Hornberger and Link 2012). This perspective, which sees the relationships between language varieties and between different kinds of speakers as fluid and continuous, rather than categorical and oppositional, avoids such seemingly self-explanatory yet highly problematic designations as "mother tongue," "native speaker," "foreign accent," or "bilingual." As a result, it helps us to interrogate the assumptions behind these commonly used terms. And in the case of immigrant Americans, the perspective we adopt potentially impacts policy decisions, from bilingual education, to bilingual ballots, to employees' rights.

In the present book, binary approaches to other sociocultural categories that we, as a society, tend to take for granted, are also being rejected in favor of fluidity and continua. Thus, as I argued at the start of this introduction, the immigrant/American juxtaposition is an unhelpful way to think about American citizenship and belonging. Similarly, I argue that the hyphen in identifications such as Mexican American, Irish American, or Asian American is not a link conjoining two entities, but rather the site of the dynamic creation and negotiation of complex new meanings. This emphasis on fluidity and dynamic transformation, on hybridity and on complexity of identities, informs the story of language in immigrant America that this book seeks to tell: the story of language as the site of ongoing negotiation of immigrant-American identities.

1 Whose America?

In a 1906 article titled "Culdees & Irland It Mikla: The Irish in America One Thousand Years before Columbus," Martin John Mulroy, having presented various extant evidence, makes the following claim:

> From these three Irish documents, preserved by the Landnamabok, the Eyrbyggia, and the Saga of Thorfinn Karlsefne, it is proved that the Irish had discovered, in the West, a country, to which they gave the name of Irland It Mikla, or "Greater Ireland." That this other name of "Huitramannaland" or "Land Where Man Dressed in White" recalls the customs of the Culdees; that they had preserved the usages of the Celtic language, and remained faithful to their Celtic civilization; that they celebrated with processions and the singing of hymns; and finally that they were without pity for shipwrecked sailors, because, being themselves several times pursued and banished from their settlements, by the cruel Northmen, they wished to ensure future security, and for that reason concealed, as much as possible, all their discoveries. America, therefore, has been known and partly colonized by the Irish, and although the testimony from their own literature fails in precision owing to the immense quantity of their native books that were ruthlessly destroyed, still the existence of Irland It Mikla can and must be considered as an established historical fact (Mulroy 1906: 6).

Written at the turn of the twentieth century, when Irish immigrants were far from embraced as equals to "native" Anglo-Saxon Americans, this passage underscores the point that "America" has been a contested concept from its earliest days. The meanings of such fundamentally American principles as equality, freedom, and citizenship have been debated and negotiated through arguments seeking to validate or undermine the right to Americanness for particular ethnic and social groups – including the continent's Indigenous inhabitants – and revolving around complex questions. Who does American equality extend to? Does this equality apply differently to different areas of life? What liberties does American freedom protect? What are the rights and obligations of an American citizen? Are some people "inherently" better candidates for American citizenship? Does the enjoyment of equality and freedom depend on how "true" of an American one is?

The implications of these questions for the immigration debate may seem obvious, but this does not make them any less complicated and thorny. This is partly because we often imagine these questions to be debated by "Americans" with respect to "immigrants," as if these two categories were clearly distinguishable and self-explanatory, while in reality they are anything but. "American" and "immigrant" are continuous, overlapping, and intertwined notions, with numerous and frequently conflicting interpretations of who belongs to which category and why. Furthermore, "immigrants" are not passive objects of the debate. Rather, we can envision the generations inhabiting the territory known as the United States as active participants in the ongoing "conversation" (Gee 1999: 13) about the meaning of America and Americanness. The main distinction among them lies in their relative position with respect to social and political hegemony at various historical points.

One recurring theme in this conversation is the claim to "true" Americanness. This claim has been staked by different groups invoking arguments ranging from an inherent inclination towards American ideals possessed by the essentialistically imagined ethnic group, to historical precedent.

Thus, Thomas D'Arcy McGee's 1852 book titled *A History of the Irish Settlers in North America, from the Earliest Period to the Census of 1850* lists in detail the contributions of people of Irish origin or descent (either born in Ireland or of Irish parents) to the cause of America: whether it was in the expansion of "civilization" at the expense of Indigenous peoples, or in developing American economy, industry, arts, and so on; whether in colonial times, or later during the Revolutionary War or the War of 1812. The book's overarching theme is, quite clearly, to establish the Irish claim to being true, unquestioned Americans and, in this way, to counter nativist portrayals of the Catholic Irish as suspect and potentially disloyal. But this is not all. McGee opens his account by setting up America as uniquely and primarily Irish by connecting the pre-Columbian voyages to the West with the Irish people, much as Mulroy (1906) does in the passage above. McGee states that America was visited in the Middle Ages by Northern sailors who referred to it in their sagas as *Irland it Mikla*, or Great Ireland (McGee 1852: 18–19). Some of the Scandinavian figures mentioned appear to have lived in Ireland as well as Iceland for various stretches of time. And even before this time occurs the legendary voyage of Saint Bernard, mentioned in the Irish Annals (20). Since accounts of the Irish – e.g. the Culdees (Mulroy 1906) – reaching the shores of America and naming it Great Ireland (or Mulroy's Greater Ireland) exist in both Irish and Scandinavian sources, authors such as McGee and Mulroy interpret them as evidence that the Irish have a justifiable claim to American lands.

Other ethnic groups also make claims to true Americanness. For example, writing in praise of what he sees as Polish-American contributions to the antislavery cause, Wytrwal (1982) offers the example of Brigadier General Tadeusz (Thaddeus) Kosciuszko, a Polish general who fought in the Revolutionary War and who in his testament authorized Thomas Jefferson to sell his lands in Ohio and use the proceeds to liberate and educate slaves (29).

Wytrwal cites Kosciuszko and other Poles as critical of slavery on the grounds that it was the only "deformity" in American institutions (32). Viewed through the lens of Wytrwal's 1982 text and its pro-Polish-American agenda, these Poles become more American, in a sense, than their own contemporaries – committed to the American ideals and ready to both fight for them and to take them to their logical conclusion of equality for all men. Meanwhile, many nineteenth-century Polish immigrants to America, especially prominent intellectuals, saw the opportunity for creating in America an actual, physical New Poland, possibly by purchasing lands in one of the Midwestern states (Dziembowska 1977a and 1977b), an aspiration born out of the fact that at that point in time, Poland had been partitioned by its neighbors and did not in fact exist as a sovereign state (see Section 1.2). These examples highlight the diversity and complexity of perspectives on what America stands for and what it can offer, and of motivations for claiming it as one's own.

Consequently, in this chapter I wish to reframe the question "What does 'American' mean?" into "Whose America is this?" in order to highlight the diversity, the inequalities, and the power struggles among the various groups that have had a stake in the making of America, in its success as a nation, and in creating and pursuing the "American dream." This chapter thus sets the stage for the subsequent critical examination of which definitions of Americanness are legitimized, who becomes a privileged participant in the American project, and how immigrants at different historical moments have utilized the resources of language to negotiate their position within American society. As such, the chapter also previews the argument, to be expanded in later chapters and in the conclusion, that in contrast to dominant discourses (e.g. Wright 2008; cf. Kubota and Lin 2006 on racialized essentialist dichotomies), a multiplicity of identities and of multilingual resources presents a more useful model for viewing immigration in America than a dichotomy between the native and the foreign.

1.1 The Invasion of Indigenous America

In telling the history of the United States as a settler-colonial society from the perspective of Indigenous peoples and their experience, Dunbar-Ortiz (2014) writes, "Influences from the south powerfully shaped the Indigenous peoples to the north (in what is now the United States) and Mexicans continue to migrate as they have for millennia but now across the arbitrary border that was established in the US war against Mexico in 1846–48" (18). This statement reframes the relationship between the United States as a state and America's Indigenous peoples, and thus challenges the notions of "Mexican immigrants" or even "illegal aliens" by casting them in a drastically different historical light. Reading it, one might even wonder whether undertaking a project such as this one with "immigrant America" in the title is a valid cause at all, since "immigrant America" implies the existence of a non-immigrant America, a native America that is envisioned as anything but Indigenous. The presumed "native," non-immigrant America would be white, Anglo-Saxon, English-speaking, and mostly Protestant, reflecting the background of the first settlers from England. An accurate picture of non-immigrant North America, or Native America, however, is that by the time of European contact, it was the historical homeland of about 15 million people[1] who had, on their own, invented agriculture, grown indigenous crops, built diverse architectural structures from burial mounds of the Mississippian cultures to the multistory stone-carved settlements of the Southwestern Pueblos and the Hohokam irrigation canal systems, and lived in a variety of social arrangements from small nomadic groups to settled kingdoms with complex social and religious systems (Page 2004: 93). Through trade and other contacts with Central American empires, they had access to the scientific, artistic, and philosophical knowledge equivalent to that of ancient Greeks (Dunbar-Ortiz 2014: 18). They experienced ethnic, linguistic, political and religious diversity; alliances and schisms; and the rise, fall, and transformation of cultures (cf. Fixico 2009: 556). Prior to European contact, the Americas were a living place, full of culture, language, human achievements, and human strife. With these points in mind, Dunbar-Ortiz argues that the United States history as accepted by the dominant society today erases the existence as well as experience of Indigenous Americans, and, at best, presents the Indigenous person as "the gift-giving Indian helping to establish and enrich the development of the United States," in this way obscuring "the fact that the very existence of the country is a result of the looting of an entire continent and its resources" (Dunbar-Ortiz 2014: 5).

Nonetheless, from the perspective of later immigrants – those who came for a plethora of reasons to join the first settlers in their newly "claimed" land – their experience as immigrants to a white, Anglo-Saxon, Protestant colony – or, later, state – was one in which Indigenous peoples had been presumed as ordained by God to be vanquished. Succeeding waves of immigrants joined those already here in waging what was typically perceived as a just war against the Indians, first taking possession of their land and then defending it from being claimed back. Later, when the United States had succeeded in destroying or subjugating the Indigenous American nations, newly arrived European immigrants did not encounter or consider Indigenous people at all, except

[1] The population size in the Americas prior to European contact is a matter of much debate, since we have no direct records or evidence of it, and almost immediately afterwards the vast majority of Indigenous Americans (estimates claim as much as 75–95 percent of the population) died through exposure to European-brought pathogens such as smallpox, measles, and influenza. Estimates of the North American population size have ranged from the rather low 2 million to 18 million (Page 2004: 105).

perhaps in the most superficial way as the makers of dream catchers and indispensable characters in the classic American film genre of the Western. Native Americans have been erased from the dominant discourse on immigration and from the broader political discourse regarding the United States of America. At best, as Dunbar-Ortiz persuasively argues, they have been co-opted as quasi-willing contributors to the "Great American Tapestry" (cf. Dunbar-Ortiz 2014: 6).

Reflecting on the Indigenous history of the United States while thinking about immigration highlights the fact that early settlers did not come to an empty land and that American history neither begins with the establishment of the colonies, nor can it be neatly separated into self-contained pre-colonial and post-European-contact "periods." Understanding American history from the Indigenous perspective allows us to question assumptions we may have about those "crossing the border" from the south, about Spanish speakers and other linguistic minorities in the United States, and certainly about any claims that English is by default the American language. Thus, while the focus of discussion in this book is on language in the experience of immigrants to the United States of America – an "America" that was increasingly, and violently, becoming more European and less Indigenous – Indigenous America will be referred to and engaged with at various points (e.g. in the discussion of Spanglish in Section 5.3).

"Savage" Tongues in the Promised Land

From today's vantage point it is easy to forget that subjugating Indigenous Americans was not a peripheral or accidental matter in the colonies and early republic, but rather a primary concern perceived as a divinely ordained destiny. To the mind of Puritan settlers, Indians represented Biblical Canaanites: it was God's will that they be fought, vanquished, and pushed out of the Puritans' Promised Land (Csábi 2001). At the same time, the Puritan was called on to be "a civilizer and a Christianizer" (Pearce 1965: 19). Anderson (2014) also points out that under the leadership of John Winthrop, the Massachusetts Bay Colony passed legislation which permitted forcible purchase of uncultivated Indian lands, citing the Book of Genesis and the Psalms as justification (Anderson 2014: 42).

This sentiment was shared by settlers elsewhere. Reverend Samuel Purchas, writing in 1625, claims that the English colonization of Virginia is clearly God's will because the heathen Indians, living in a state of nature and not civility, are merely subsisting on their land instead of working and improving it as God had intended. Christian colonizers thus must carry out God's will, "God in wisedome having enriched the Savage Countries, that those riches might be attractive for Christian suters, which there may sowe spirituals and reape temporals" (Purchas 1614: 232; cited in Pearce 1965: 8). Accordingly, if the American "savages," as they were commonly referred to, accepted the gifts of Christianity and civilization, changed their ways so as to submit to the European forms of government and laws, gave up their traditional ways of life and with them rights to their land, and instead learned agriculture, trade, and the value of private property, then they may have been accepted as inferior and subordinate but good-natured charges of the civilized white man. Any rebellion, however – which is to say, any attempt on part of the Indians to deal with the settlers on an equal footing – was perceived as a challenge to God's will, a manifestation of the work of Satan, and thus a mandate for the killing, destruction, and removal of Indigenous people (Pearce 1965; Harvey 2015). Throughout much of United States' history, dealing with Native Americans remained at the forefront of foreign policy, and during this time the question was always how most efficiently to "civilize" and dispossess them, making room for inevitable and God-ordained white expansion.

Indigenous people's experience of encountering Europeans was similar in those parts of today's United States that were first colonized by non-Anglophone invaders. The Spanish crown placed strong emphasis on Christianization, sending Jesuits and Franciscans to establish missions in La Florida and in Nuevo Mexico as early as the middle of the sixteenth century (Page 2004; McCarty 2010). Indigenous land was claimed in the name of Spain, the Vatican, and Christ. As Page (2004) comments, referring specifically to the 1598 colonization venture into the lands surrounding the Rio Grande led by Don Juan de Oñate, "These would-be colonists were devout people who saw Spain as the most important power acting in behalf of the pontiff in Rome . . . For these people it was another crossing of the river Jordan, and there was holy work to be done" (Page 2004: 143). Christian Europeans of all denominations and persuasions saw themselves as fulfilling God's will by taking over Indigenous lands and converting the people, by force if necessary.

Meanwhile, language became and remained a focus in European Americans' debates about the "nature" of Indians and their potential for assimilation to civilized Christian ways. The first missionaries already observed the immense differences between English and Indigenous languages – which were from the beginning referred to as "American" languages – and questioned whether fundamental Christian concepts could ever be adequately or accurately expressed in an Indigenous language (Harvey 2015). Subsequent studies of American languages, from amateur etymologies to serious researches by people like Du Ponceau and Heckewelder, all ultimately revolved around the question of the relationship between "savage" language and "savage" people.

Early travelers, missionaries, and settlers often perceived the numbers and diversity of Native languages as a "diabolical plot to foil evangelization" (Harvey 2015: 20), or, at best, as a manifestation of ungodly ways and social disorder. The apparently drastic differences between Native and European languages convinced European Americans that Indians had completely different ways of thinking, since language was believed to shape thought (Harvey 2015).[2] Unable to make sense of Indigenous grammar, they concluded that it was disorderly and devoid of any set rules. Seventeenth- and eighteenth-century efforts at describing and learning Native American languages were all grounded in the assumption that Indo-European languages such as English, Greek, or Latin represent the superior, more advanced, and civilized modes of expression, suited to reason and abstract thinking as well as to Christian morality. Native languages were studied through the prism of Indo-European grammatical categories, and in this way found wanting. They were also judged as incapable of expressing "universal" ideas and claimed to lack terms for abstract concepts such as *time, space*, or *substance* (43), which was seen as stemming from, but also causing, their speakers' lack of civilization. Theories connecting linguistic structure with character, disposition and intellect abounded, such as Puritan John Eliot's mid-seventeenth-century explanation for Massachusett-speakers' "delight in *Compounding of* words": "*It seems their desires are* slow, *but* strong; / *Because they be utter'd* double-breath't, *and* long" (cited in Harvey 2015: 33). Jesuit Pierre Biard believed that the apparent lack of equivalents for European abstract or spiritual terms in Montagnais meant that "these miserable people ... will always remain in a perpetual infancy as to language and reason" (33), while Presbyterian David Brainerd in the mid-eighteenth century described the "defectiveness" of Delaware which would prevent the Delawares from being Christianized because they had "*no Foundation in their Mind to begin upon*" (33). Furthermore, European American missionaries and etymologists found the pronunciation of many Indigenous sounds difficult and struggled to represent them using European alphabets, which led them to develop theories about the distinctness – and inferiority – of the vocal organs of Indigenous Americans (Harvey 2015: 17).

Linguistic "deficiency" was seen as inextricably tied to Native Americans' inherent "savagery" (45). It was believed that cultivation and civilization led to a change in pronunciation away from "harsh" to "gentle" sounds, with the latter being, unsurprisingly, typical of European languages (45). Polysynthesis was interpreted as a primitive merging into one of what in "cultivated" languages were distinct parts of speech expressing a separation and ordering of concepts (151). "Savages" were bound to nature, and so was their language. Speakers

[2] The influential, though now largely discredited, Sapir-Whorf hypothesis stating that language fully determines thought and argued for on the basis of Whorf's ethnographic work among the Hopi Indians was not as revolutionary as it is sometimes presented. Rather, it had solid roots in centuries of thinking about Indigenous languages and about the relationships among language, thought, and civilization.

thus could express the immediate and the tangible, it was argued, and mixed up agents, actions, and objects into single words much as nature is spontaneous and disorderly before being tamed and controlled by people according to God's will (44).

These ideas led further to generalizations about all Native languages as sharing the qualities of natural and primitive disorder. Hugh Blair writes in 1783 that the "American and Indian languages" are, like all "savage" languages, powerful and poetic but imprecise, and "governed by imagination and passion, more than by reason" (cited in Harvey 2015: 44). Missionaries also raised fears that expanding the semantic scope of Native terms to include the Christian meaning of words such as *grace, blessing*, or *redemption* (32) would lead to a contamination of these sacred concepts with heathen notions. In this way, early motivations for replacing Native languages with English in the course of "civilization" were laid. Thomas Jefferson, committed to surveying and describing Native languages, was equally committed to civilizing the Indians, and this, to his mind, ultimately required rejecting traditional knowledge and traditional spiritual and social customs and roles, as well as the shift to English. As Harvey writes, "'Civilization' entailed the surrender of lands, spiritual transformation, and language loss" (89).

The undeniable marked differences between Indigenous and European languages also sparked the debate over Indigenous people's origins. In the monogenetic scheme enshrined in the Bible, all people descended from a single stock; their language, however, was confused as they were dispersed following the construction of the Tower of Babel. Students of Native languages thus began to consider how Indigenous people fit into this scheme. Some saw in them the descendants of the Lost Tribes of Israel (Harvey 2015; Page 2004; Pearce 1965). Consequently, questions arose as to whether the present state of Native languages represented a primeval pre-civilization stage of linguistic "development," or the opposite – a degeneration caused by separation from God and His laws. Harvey's (2015) detailed study of the central role of language in the story of conquest and dispossession in what became the United States traces the conflicting arguments advanced by a minority of scholars who appreciated and studied Native languages on their own terms as complex and satisfactory systems, such as Heckewelder and Du Ponceau, as well as those who discounted such "romanticizations" of "savage" speech and saw any unique and unusual features as merely proof of Native Americans' inherent inability to be assimilated into Christian civilization. As Harvey outlines, by the nineteenth century, elaborate studies of Native languages replaced earlier ad-hoc anecdotal accounts, but ultimately all such research remained profoundly Eurocentric in its assumptions.

Du Ponceau's ideas were squarely rejected by Lewis Cass, governor and superintendent of Michigan Territory and later the Secretary of War – a position which oversaw the Bureau of Indian Affairs – who was committed to the notion that Native American languages were fundamentally different from and inferior to English, making Indians unassimilable. Incapable of being "civilized," Native Americans need to be "removed" – ostensibly also for their own good – and placed away from the white settlers who now, by God's will, took possession of their land. Ignoring meticulous linguistic data collected and analyzed by specialists like Heckewelder and Du Ponceau, Cass insisted that the agents he sent out to survey Native languages focus on Native "savagery," arguing – rather vaguely – in his writings that "uncultivated" languages were "harsh in the utterance, artificial in their construction, indeterminate in their application, and incapable of expressing a vast variety of ideas, particularly those which relate to invisible objects" (Harvey 2015: 151). Similarly, Henry R. Schoolcraft, US Indian agent at Sault Ste. Marie from 1822, who, unlike his superintendent Cass, was a speaker and careful student of Algonquian thanks to his Ojibwe wife and her kinship network, also disparaged non-Indo-European linguistic features such as the use of participles or the animate-inanimate rather than male-female gender distinction, as typical of "rude languages" (150). He saw polysynthetic compounding and the Ojibwe pictographs as together somehow reflecting the limitations of "the Indian mind" and fostering superstition and idolatry (171–172). Not surprisingly, Lewis Cass became a crucial figure in the formulation and implementation of Indian Removal, while views such as Schoolcraft's were used to justify the obliteration of Indigenous languages for the sake of the progress of civilization.[3] Accordingly, by 1886 the Bureau of Indian Affairs mandated that Native children receive English-only instruction, following numerous recommendations, for instance by the Indian Peace Commission, that schools be established where "their barbarous dialects should be blotted out and the English language substituted" (180). Compulsory boarding schools set up for Native children prohibited any use of Native languages, purposely made such use more difficult by mixing together children from different tribes, instituted often violent punishments for speaking Native languages, and required instruction entirely in English (Harvey 2015: 15; Leap 1981; McCarty 2010). The result has been language shift, loss, and death.

[3] The "civilization" of many communities to be removed had already, in fact, been accomplished, which underscores the underlying motives for the Removal Act as deriving from the need for more land. Sean Teuton (2013) writes: "On the passing of the 1830 Removal Act . . . most Americans were unaware of the Westernized condition of these indigenous communities. In fact, by the end of the eighteenth century, groups such as the Cherokees already had consciously restructured their government from a traditional network of self-governing towns into a modern centralized republic, when they formed their National Council in 1794. In 1808, Cherokees wrote a code of law in English; in 1821, they created a written language. In 1826, they founded the capital city of New Echota, and in 1827, they ratified a constitution" (Teuton 2013: 38).

Language Loss, Death, and Revival in Indigenous America

During the 2014 Super Bowl, Coca-Cola caused a massive controversy by running an ad, titled "It's Beautiful," in which the patriotic song "America the Beautiful" is sung by Americans of diverse ethnic and religious backgrounds, many of them non-white and some clearly non-Christian as indexed by their clothing, in eight different languages. Immediately, extreme sentiments in support of or against the ad exploded all over social media. Tweets included "Hey @CocaCola This is America. English, please. #SB48" as well as "Thanks @CocaCola for reminding us that we are beautiful because of and not in spite of our linguistic diversity. #AmericaIsBeautiful." Coca-Cola's Facebook page included comments such as "Speak English or go home" and "Screwed up a beautiful song. No Coke for my family."[4] Comments below a YouTube video of the ad posted on February 2, 2014[5] included very explicit references to race, for example:

> America is a White country. Always has been. It's something that is not debatable. Unless you have no idea of who the American population really is and always has been. Like the top comment says: "America is White. End of discussion." Fully agree.

Or

> Hm . . . I like different languages and cultures, but only in the context of preparation to VISIT their countries. I don't want to LIVE with hearing 10 different languages every day. Great, we're multicultural. I can see too much of that becoming very bad for us in the future. How are we going to stay "one nation, indivisible" if people in one state can't understand the language/culture of people one state over? Is Islam compatible with the individual liberties this country was built on? Do third world immigrants understand the history of our nation and what it stands for, or do they simply bring the culture of the country they are from and transplant it here?
>
> For now it's "working". What happens when all the separate irreconcilable cultures get bigger? Will they continue to get along as space runs out and conflicts emerge?

These essentialist links made between the language and the people (and their skin color), as well as religion, reflect the dominant or at least very robust vision of America as white, Christian, and English-speaking. Americanness is racialized as white, and everything else is a departure from the norm; American identities are thus racialized and so are languages spoken in the United States. Certainly, these are not everyone's views, but such views are widespread, mainstream, socially acceptable, and believed by many to be righteously patriotic: an expression of "true" Americanness. In the case of the outrage at the Coca-Cola ad, these views were embodied in the hashtag via which they trended: #SpeakAmerican.

Against this Internet debate appeared a video, in which a non-white and non-African-American vocalist sings what sounds like "America the Beautiful" to the

[4] www.usatoday.com/story/news/nation-now/2014/02/03/coca-cola-ad-super-bowl-racism/5177463/.
[5] www.youtube.com/watch?v=443Vy3I0gJs.

graceful accompaniment of his guitar.[6] The language of the song is not easily recognizable, and may leave even those of us familiar with many of the world's languages somewhat perplexed. One of the first questions we have might be, "What *foreign* language is this?" or, "What *immigrant* language?" because we assume the video to be referring to the controversial Coca-Cola ad. But following the song, the artist looks at the camera, speaking his language, and the subtitles read: "Every single non-indigenous language IS FOREIGN HERE!!! They say, 'Speak American!' I can speak an 'American' language ... CAN YOU?!?!" The video ends with the hashtag #SpeakAmerican, followed by the credit: "By Cody Pata (*a Nomlaki Indian*)." As it turns out, the video *is* referring to the Coca-Cola ad, but in an indirect and subversive way. The response is to the *negative reactions* to the ad, through enacting the same storyline as the ad but subverting the relationship between the native and the foreign that is assumed both in the attacks on the ad and in the ad itself: the Nomlaki becomes the American, the white Anglophone becomes the foreigner. Furthermore, historically Native languages have been treated much the same way as immigrant languages – as subordinate to English and best replaced with it in the process of "assimilating" their speakers. In his YouTube performance, Cody Pata inverts this relationship by asserting that English and other non-Indigenous languages are in fact trespassers on American land. This is important because to some, views such as Pata's are preposterous: they believe that having arrived on the scene first does not give Native Americans any legitimate claim to their own land, as seen in some of the quotes cited above.

Cody Pata himself did not grow up speaking Nomlaki. Born and raised in Hawai'i, he came to California to take part in the revitalization of Nomlaki language and culture. Today, Nomlaki is spoken by the Paskenta Band of Nomlaki Indians (Nomlāqa Bōda), one of the two major divisions of Nomlaki Indians, in present-day Tehama and Glenn Counties, Northern California.[7] The tribe lost its official recognition in 1959, along with rights to their land, as did many other tribes during this time.[8] The pressure to "assimilate" had its effects: according to Golla (2011), there was only one speaker of Nomlaki left at the time of his research. Others who spoke it were afraid to admit it. Cody Pata recalls how, after first learning some Nomlaki words during the first Breath of Life conference at UC Berkeley, devoted to the revitalization of Native languages, he traveled to his grandmother's home to share his new knowledge and discovered that she was, in fact, a speaker: "To my amazement, she began correcting me. No one in my family

[6] www.youtube.com/watch?v=0gqwlggKwJ8 and also at www.facebook.com/IdleNoMoreCommunity/posts/10152090563566492, newsfromnativecalifornia.com/blog/in-our-languages-cody-pata/, and in a Huffington Post blog article at www.huffingtonpost.com/adrian-kamalii/speakamerican-how-about-b_b_4727036.html.

[7] http://paskenta-nsn.gov/about-us/history/, accessed March 15, 2016.

[8] www.gpo.gov/fdsys/pkg/BILLS-103hr5050rh/html/BILLS-103hr5050rh.htm, accessed May 4, 2016.

realized that she could speak our language. Lo-and-behold, a few other elders found the courage to speak our language openly once again."[9] Pata has now devoted himself to efforts at revitalizing his heritage language. As he puts it, "Our language has truly been resuscitated by the Breath of Life."

Nomlaki is but one example of a nearly extinct Native American language. McCarty (2010) estimates that 300 languages indigenous to the US were spoken at the time of contact, and of these 175 were still in use as of 1998 (47). Navajo (Diné), spoken in Arizona, New Mexico and Utah, has the most speakers out of all Indigenous languages at 178,000. It is followed next by Western Ojibwe, spoken in Montana, North Dakota, and Lake Superior region, which has only 35,000 speakers. Cherokee numbers 11,905 speakers in Oklahoma and North Carolina. Zuni, a Pueblo language of New Mexico, has 6,413. Meanwhile, as many as a third of Native American languages have only a few elderly speakers left (McCarty 2010: 47–48). But even an apparently robust language like Navajo or, less so, Ojibwe, faces extinction if it fails to be transmitted to future generations. And in 2006, as many as 72 percent of Native Americans five years old and over "were reported as speaking only English at home" (McCarty 2010: 56). Analyzing the age of their speakers, Krauss (1998) cautions that without a "radical change and success at reversal of language shift," all but 20 Native American languages will become extinct (11). Currently, all Native languages are considered endangered (47).

The fate of Indigenous languages is the direct product of the United States' settler colonialism, which was accompanied by a policy of "civilization" and "assimilation." This in turn was, as discussed above, justified by appealing to Euro-centric notions of "civilization," Christian beliefs and values, and an essentialist conceptualization of the "nature" of Native languages. By 1886, Native children were being forcibly removed from their families and placed in boarding schools whose express purpose was to precipitate a shift from Native languages to English. As McCarty (2010) writes, "Accounts abound of children being ridiculed, beaten, and having their mouths 'washed' with soap for speaking their mother tongue" (49; see also McCarty 2002; Reyhner and Eder 2004; Glenn 2011). It is not surprising – and, indeed, is typical of situations in other colonial contexts such as Australia or Siberia – that many children left boarding schools refusing to speak and pass on their language due to shame, fear, or simple pragmatic calculation. English was the language of the present and future.

In recent decades, revitalization efforts have begun in earnest in numerous Indigenous communities, motivated on one hand by the American Indian Movement and Red Power Movement (Shreve 2011; Deloria and Salisbury 2002; Teuton 2008) of the 1970s, and on the other by the global tendency of

[9] http://newscenter.berkeley.edu/2014/08/05/giving-the-breath-of-life-to-endangered-languages/, accessed March 15, 2016; similar cases are reported in the 2008 film *The Linguists*.

linguists to start paying more attention to endangered languages from the 1990s onwards. Some examples include the successful Hawaiian-medium education that began with Hawaiian "language nest" preschools in 1983 and now spans all levels of schooling through public high schools and university programs (McCarty 2010: 63); Navajo immersion schools that as of 2010 spanned K–8 with plans to expand to twelfth grade (64); the Master-Apprentice Language Learning Program (MALLP) in California (63); the Cherokee immersion school, New Kituwah Academy, established in 2010 in Cherokee, North Carolina, which currently serves preschool and elementary school children; and the Nomlaki revitalization program that Cody Pata is part of.

The establishment and some measure of success of language revitalization programs should not, however, be taken as evidence that Native languages are faring well or that Indigenous people's position in the fabric of Americanness has significantly improved. Rather, they testify to Indigenous people's agency in negotiating their own American identities. The demise of boarding schools and the American Indian Movement and Red Power Movement opened the way for a public discussion of ethnic prejudice against Indigenous people even as Native Americans continue to remain "invisible" to much of mainstream American society – more real as romanticized characters in historical films than as citizens and neighbors. Native American studies departments have produced a body of scholarship that addresses Indigenous issues from the Indigenous, not European-American, perspective – what Fixico (2009) refers to as "writing from home." Young people may not speak their tribe's languages very well, but neither are they ashamed of the language: more likely, they express shame and regret at *not* speaking it (Lee 2009). Alternately, they emphasize the importance of cultural practices that trumps mere linguistic knowledge: as one of Nicholas' (2009) research participants explains, "... a Pahaana (Anglo) can learn how to speak it, speak the language, but they don't know the meaning behind it, or the actual culture, the in-depth stuff; [so] then they're not Hopi" (321). While speaking Hopi is important to the young people in Nicholas' study, what really counts is "living" Hopi. In other cases, Indigenous groups and tribes have developed their own, unique varieties of English, such as, for example, Lumbee Indians in North Carolina. Features of Lumbee English, which set it apart from Southern English as well as from African American Vernacular English, have been documented by Dannenberg (2002) and Wolfram and Dannenberg (1999).

In their initial contact with the United States, as well as before with the colonial representatives of Great Britain, Spain, and France, Native Americans were treated as savages to be converted and civilized, to be sure, but they were also dealt with as sovereign peoples with whom negotiations were held and treaties signed. The Christian, Euro-centric discourse of "civilization" was eventually used to subjugate them and, with the coming on the scene of an independent United States, absorb their lands into the new state while "assimilating" their inhabitants. Native languages were explained away as primitive and destined for disappearance, and English-only boarding schools appeared not long before all public education was mandated to be in English, and the ideology of monolingualism pressured immigrant parents to raise their children as English-only speakers. Native Americans became foreigners in their own land, expected to assimilate to the dominant culture. The only thing setting them apart from immigrants from overseas was the fact that they had been here first. But they have not vanished, and their languages have not completely disappeared. From the beginning, Native peoples had a stake in the future of the United States, and continue to do so today. However, unlike the various immigrant groups, their populations have no chance of being replenished from abroad, and there are no other "home" versions of their languages spoken in other countries. In the case of Native Americans and their languages, "assimilation" has meant destruction.

1.2 American Expansion

The United States came into being as a polity through the medium of English, through the words of documents like the Declaration of Independence and the Constitution. This fact is not surprising, given that all the delegates to the Constitutional Convention were of English background, several of them having been born in England. They were all graduates of prestigious universities, including Harvard, Yale, College of New Jersey (later Princeton), College of William and Mary, College of Philadelphia (later University of Pennsylvania), and Dartmouth, all of which were modeled on English universities and used English as the means of instruction. Eight of them attended university in England.[10] Many – though not all – were sons of educated men, or came from wealthy families. Some had been active in the colonial government, for example John Blair Jr., who served as the governor of Virginia; Jacob Broom, who had been a member of the Delaware legislature and a burgess of Wilmington; or Nathaniel Gorham, who served in the Massachusetts legislature (Vile 2013). Benjamin Franklin had represented the colonies in England during the disputes leading up to the Revolutionary War (Vile 2013: 85). Not only were the Founding Fathers all of English descent and educated in English or English-style universities, but the colonial system against which they spoke out and ultimately fought was English as well. The institutions of the United States came into being through and in English because the states had been former English colonies, with English institutions and bureaucracies already in place (cf. Belgum 2015; Wiley 2014).

The English-language heritage of American political institutions reflects the dominance of English in the colonial government, the colonies' political ties to England, and the fact that English was the most widely spoken language among

[10] http://teachingamericanhistory.org/convention/delegates/education/, accessed March 10, 2016.

the colonies' residents (Wiley 2014). English was not, however, the majority language. American shores attracted also the Dutch, Scots, Germans, and the French, among others. According to Schmid (2001), in the late seventeenth century, Americans of all social classes were frequently bilingual, especially in New York, Pennsylvania, New Jersey, and Delaware. By the beginning of the Revolutionary War in 1775, of the 2 million European Americans in the thirteen colonies, 250,000 were Scots-Irish and 200,000 were German (Wright 2008). Schmid (2001) reports that "the first census in the United States showed that the English and their descendants constituted slightly less than half of the population" (18). It appears, therefore, that the new Republic was a linguistically diverse place, although English was the dominant language, both numerically and sociopolitically. This reality was reflected in the Founding Fathers' active engagement with the non-English-speaking population: Pavlenko (2002) reminds us that "during the years of the War of Independence ... the Continental Congress published several documents, including the Articles of Confederation, in English and German, and at times even in French" (Pavlenko 2002: 167).

Immigration from around the world from the middle of the nineteenth century onwards further shaped the ethnolinguistic makeup of America. Early on, non-English immigrant languages were often relatively isolated, as their speakers settled in their own, mostly rural, ethnolinguistic communities, such as those of Poles and Czechs in Texas. Non-English immigrants often started their own schools and newspapers, and while English remained dominant and continued to be used in national politics, local affairs were often conducted in the language of a given community (Schmid 2001). Anti-immigrant sentiments began to flare up, not surprisingly, in response to large-scale migration of non-Anglo-Saxon groups, in particular the Irish in the East and the Chinese in the West, in the middle of the nineteenth century (see Chapter 2). But despite suspicion and discrimination towards and within immigrant groups, aggressive promotion of English as synonymous with Americanness and coupled with suppression of immigrant languages did not begin in earnest until the turn of the twentieth century, perhaps as the large-scale migration from vast regions of Europe and expanding industrialization brought together natively born, English-speaking Americans with multilingual European communities in the emerging urban and industrial centers (cf. Pavlenko 2002).

Crucially, while the official business of the United States was from the beginning conducted in English, no official language was formally established for the country by the Founding Fathers. They tended to believe that giving English official status in the Constitution would interfere with states' rights, and that a multilingual approach was crucial for national unification (Pavlenko 2002: 167). In addition, although the authors of the Constitution generally assumed that English would become the common and unifying language in the United States, they held diverse and conflicted views regarding language minorities (Schmid 2001). Benjamin Franklin, for example, on a number of occasions decried the presence of so many German speakers in Pennsylvania, believing that holding on to their language and traditions would prevent German immigrants from embracing the political culture and values of the colonies and the emerging republic. In a 1753 letter, he wrote,

> Not being used to Liberty, (they) know not how to make modest use of it ... Advertisements, intended to be general are now printed in German and English; the Signs in our Streets have inscriptions in both languages, and in some places in only German: They begin of late to make all their Bonds and other legal Writings in their own Language, which (though I think it ought not to be) are allowed good in our Courts (letter to Collinson, May 9, 1753, cited in Schmid 2001: 15).

The same Franklin, however, was the founder of one of the first German newspapers in America in 1738, and later in his life supported German-language higher education (Schmid 2001: 16). In 1787, he was involved in the establishment of the "first German-language institution of higher learning, now known as Franklin and Marshall College" (Pavlenko 2002: 168).

Other Revolutionary leaders shared Franklin's concern that immigrants coming from continental European absolutist monarchies would preserve their languages, which in turn would prevent them from adjusting to American freedom and democracy. We might note that these same concerns were voiced again a century later, in reaction to immigration from Eastern and Southern Europe (see Chapter 2). America's political structure and ideals were derived from British constitutional monarchy and were thus perceived as embodied in the English language. In this vein, in 1807, Thomas Jefferson "proposed settling thirty thousand Americans in the newly acquired Louisiana Territory to prevent the area from retaining the French language and legal code system" (Schmid 2001: 16). At the same time, Jefferson believed in the importance of language learning. Another member of the Continental Congress, Benjamin Rush, encouraged the maintenance of non-English languages and supported the establishment of a German college in Pennsylvania, believing that by learning in their own language, Germans would more easily acquire English (Schmid 2001: 16) – a view advocated today by bilingual education researchers (see Chapter 6). Overall, as Schmid puts it, "During the nation's first century there was, in general, a laissez-faire attitude towards language issues" (19). The government did not interfere much with parochial or public education being conducted in languages other than English and as a result, "in the eighteenth and nineteenth centuries immigrant communities enjoyed a vibrant cultural life" (Pavlenko 2002: 168).

At the same time as the young nation was being formed on the East Coast, other parts of the continent witnessed their own ethnolinguistic development. Large swathes of what today is the United States were not English-speaking at the time of the Revolution and long after. In addition to Indigenous languages discussed in the previous section, major local languages included Spanish in the Southwest and Florida, and French in Louisiana (as witnessed in Thomas Jefferson's concern described above).

The linguistic picture briefly outlined above suggests that, while English has always been the dominant language in the United States, a dichotomy between English-speaking Americans and non-English-speaking immigrants is an unhelpful and inaccurate representation of America's linguistic history. Rather, the relationship among language, identity, belonging, and citizenship was complex and full of ambiguities throughout the eighteenth and nineteenth centuries, and has remained so even as the dominant ideology of English as the essential marker of Americanness took shape in the early decades of the twentieth century. Furthermore, non-English-speaking settler and immigrant groups have since the beginning contributed to the making of the American society. Pavlenko (2002) argues that "immigrants have always assumed a very active role in shaping the America around them – transforming school districts and curricula, opening native language schools, editing native language newspapers, speaking to larger audiences, and recording their experiences in a substantial body of autobiographic writing" (186).

The aim of this section is therefore to challenge the mainstream discourses that naturalize the status of English as America's *de facto* national language – discourses which, it has to be noted, are reproduced not just in politics, media, and popular culture, but also by some academics such as Samuel Huntington (2004). In the rest of the section, I will discuss examples of non-English-speaking stakeholders in the American project, focusing specifically on non-English-speaking Europeans and on the residents of the Southwest and of the Louisiana Purchase.

European Immigrants at the Frontier

Much as some Irish authors described stories of early Irish visits to North America, which they called *Irland it Mikla*, framing them as evidence of the long-standing Irish claim to America, similar stories found in Icelandic sagas tell of Scandinavian explorations in the same region, referred to as Vinland. Linguist Einar Haugen (1967) writes, "Leif Ericson, who discovered Vinland in the year 1000, was born in Iceland of a Norwegian father and lived in Greenland most of his life; the Norwegians like to claim him as the first Norwegian immigrant to America" (2; see also Peterson 2011). Ericson, also written Erikson or Eiriksson, may indeed have reached North American shores, but the precise circumstances of this journey remain unclear.[11] Nor was he an

[11] www.bbc.co.uk/history/historic_figures/erikson_leif.shtml, accessed March 15, 2016. Also, www.history.com/topics/exploration/leif-eriksson, accessed March 15, 2016.

immigrant or a settler; in fact, while archaeologists have found remnants of a likely Viking base camp in northern Newfoundland, no lasting Scandinavian settlements were ever established there.[12] Nonetheless, the story provides a mythical link between Norwegian immigrants to the United States and their distant Norse ancestors' first steps on the North American continent. Additionally, Norwegian Americans invoked their Viking ancestors to claim a genetic connection to English settlers, through the Viking conquest of Britain (Peterson 2011: 6). They also aligned themselves with Anglo-Americans by claiming the ownership of values such as liberty and democracy, "postulat[ing] that it was actually Norwegians who had signed the great democratic document, the Magna Carta, which had been an inspiration for the American Constitution" (6). At the turn of the twentieth century, Norwegian organizations and publications actively promoted the image of Norway as a bastion of progress, democracy, equality, and freedom, and insisted that "Norwegian Americans who came to the United States should use the opportunity to implement [these] Norwegian ideals in America" (8). Much like Polish Americans who, through the legacy of Kosciuszko's aversion to slavery, claimed to be more committed to American ideals than Anglo-Americans, Norwegian immigrants constructed their Americanness around similar principles. Norwegian Americans' commitment to progress also found expression in their fight for women's suffrage, which I will return to in Section 7.3.

Meanwhile, the exploits of Leif Ericson notwithstanding, the first bona fide Norwegian immigrants, a group of fifty-one religious dissenters, landed in New York on October 9, 1825 (Haugen 1967: 2–3), and eventually settled in Fox River Valley, Illinois. One of them, Cleng Peerson, who first headed West from their initial stop in New York to search for desirable land, was said to react in the following way when he saw Illinois: "Almost exhausted from hunger and fatigue, he threw himself on the grass and thanked God for having directed his steps to such an attractive land. In his enthusiasm he temporarily forgot his hunger and weariness and his thoughts turned to Moses and the Promised Land" (Blegen 1931: 61). This imagery is strikingly similar to the claims of the Puritans and other English settlers that America was their God-given Canaan.

The Norwegians kept making the journey to America: by the outbreak of the Civil War, there were 70,000 Norwegian immigrants in the country, at a time when the total population of Norway was about a million people (Haugen 1967). Most of them were farmers and were among the first settlers in the Midwest: in Illinois, Wisconsin, Iowa, Minnesota, and the Dakotas. Some of their earliest settlements formed a stretch of Norwegian communities across these states between 1835 and 1890. They often settled in clusters of family

[12] www.history.com/topics/exploration/leif-eriksson, accessed March 15, 2016.

members who may have come from the same neighborhood or family back in Norway. They preserved the Norwegian language, but it underwent contact-induced change, mixing in English words and grammar structures to produce a distinct American-Norwegian variety (Haugen 1967: 14; see Section 5.4). Meanwhile, a lasting Norwegian contribution to American culture was the popularization of skiing (Haugen 1967).

The Norwegians were also eager to move forward; according to Haugen, "Settlement of the Dakotas did not begin in earnest until the 1870's, but Norwegians had already entered immediately after 1859, when the new lands were thrown open to settlement" (Haugen 1967: 9). Based on this history, Norwegian Americans have a long-standing claim as some of the first American pioneers. Haugen, himself the son of Norwegian immigrants who came to the US in the late nineteenth century, assesses Norwegian Americans' investment in their adopted homeland with pride:

> In the earliest years of immigration, conditions were so hazardous that one can wonder how people ventured to risk their lives on the journey to America. Sailing vessels were slow and dangerous, often crowded and unsanitary. The American reception was rough and ready, with emigrants often fleeced at the ports of entry and stowed like cattle in the boats and trains that took them west. Once they were there, everything had to be worked up from the beginning. There were epidemics, pests, landsharks, and storms to be overcome. But the Norwegians came – and made an important contribution at this early stage of American life, especially in the Middle West. They were used to hard work and willingly gave of their strength and devotion to the building of America (Haugen 1967: 4).

Another Scandinavian group with claims to early roots in America, and who also settled in the Midwest, are the Swedes. The first small expedition established a colony they called New Sweden in the Delaware River valley in 1638, which came under Dutch rule less than twenty years later (Stasiewicz-Bieńkowska 2011: 43). After that, Swedish pioneers who ventured into the forests and prairies of Minnesota, Illinois, Iowa, Michigan, Wisconsin, Kansas, and Nebraska, started to arrive in America in the 1840s. By the outbreak of the Civil War, their number reached over 17,000. Swedish immigration continued to grow after the war, with as many as 295,000 Swedes arriving in the United States in the 1880s alone. Their communities, similarly to the Norwegians, had the support of ethnic organizations such as churches, schools, newspapers, associations, hospitals, orphanages, and hospices (Stasiewicz-Bieńkowska 2011: 43–44).

The maintenance of the Swedish language was an important priority of Swedish American associations and presses, one of which, the church-affiliated Augustana Book Concern whose establishment dates back to 1855, is the subject of a study by Stasiewicz-Bieńkowska (2011). The author focuses specifically on how the Augustana Book Concern sought to shape the Swedish-

American identity of US-born Swedish children and youth, promoting their dual heritage as an asset rather than a burden and encouraging young people to embrace it. At the same time, authors of articles and books published by the Concern criticized language mixing and hybrid forms known as *svengelska*. They venerated the Swedish language, praising it as the most beautiful of all languages and a unique embodiment of the "Nordic spirit" (161). Stasiewicz-Bieńkowska writes, "Preserving the language, both by the immigrant generation and among their children, was presented in terms of a moral duty. Neglecting this issue was said to represent great spiritual losses for Sweden and for Swedish Americans, as well as for America itself . . . Some even went as far as to claim that not only Swedish Americans, but every resident of America should learn the Swedish language, poetry, and prose, since these represent the heritage of those who discovered the American continent" (163).[13] These arguments, appearing in publications at the turn of the twentieth century, portrayed the Swedish immigrant as an integral and indispensable actor in the process of America's formation and growth, and framed the Swedish language as an invaluable part of American cultural heritage. In claiming the "discovery" of America for the Swedes, these writers and editors may be recalling the 1638 landing of the Swedish ship in Delaware – but, more likely, they refer to the Scandinavian ancestry of the Swedes, constructing a genealogical link between Swedish Americans and the legendary Viking explorers.

If nineteenth-century America was defined in part by its people's willingness to take on the challenge of Westward expansion – what is sometimes referred to as the "pioneering spirit" – then the earliest immigrants showed themselves to be Americans par excellence. Newcomers from various countries became pioneers: if we were to accept Huntington's (2004) distinction between settlers and immigrants, they resembled the former, venturing out into new territory, undertaking enormous risks and backbreaking work, in places where there was as yet no society, culture, or dominant language to assimilate to (with the exception of Indigenous people as discussed above). The communities they built were, in this respect, no less American than the Plymouth colony, even though their members spoke languages other than English: Norwegian, Swedish, Polish, Czech, German. Some of them settled in the frontier lands just as these became part of the United States, or even before. One such region is Texas.

Panna Maria, which means "Virgin Mary," located in Karnes County, Texas, southeast of San Antonio, is the oldest Polish settlement in the United States. It was established at the end of 1854 by a group of about 300 farmers from Upper Silesia, led by a Franciscan priest, Reverend Leopold Moczygemba (Kruszka 1905).[14] Brożek (1972), in his history of Polish settlements in Texas,

[13] All quotes from Polish original texts are translated by me.

[14] Some have this figure at 800 people, while others at 100 families (Brożek 1972).

cites an extensive excerpt from the memoirs of Reverend Adolf Bakanowski, the priest in Panna Maria between 1866 and 1870, who in turn recounts vivid depictions of the settlement's early days as told by his parishioners, such as the following one by a man named Wawrzyniec:

> What sufferings we went through here in our beginnings! We had no huts, only fields, brush, and trees for shelter. We came here, together about a hundred families. It was 1854. We set up camp in this place, where today is Panna Maria, but there was no church which they had promised us in Europe, not one house, not even any people. Sometimes an American showed up. We couldn't communicate with them, and they marveled at us, laughed . . . and left. The grass was so tall everywhere that we could barely see one another from just a few steps away. At every step we would see several rattlesnakes. Oh, we did suffer great misery in those days! People were nearly dying of starvation. Although we had money, there was nothing to buy . . . A few also died from snake bites . . . We lived in dug-out burrows, covered with thatch and sticks (Bakanowski, cited in Brożek 1972: 104).

Despite the hardships, the settlers persevered, and eventually cleared the land, adjusted to life in the hot, arid climate, learned how to grow crops unknown in Poland, and built a church. This first group was soon followed by others from the same region who came to join relatives, neighbors, and friends. Two decades later, a second town, named Czestochowa, was founded five miles away from Panna Maria (Olesch 1970; Brożek 1972), after the city that is home to the most revered, centuries-old sanctuary of the Virgin Mary in Poland. Life in isolated farming communities such as Panna Maria centered around a Polish church, which had Catholic priests from Poland and which typically also established an elementary school for Polish children where all instruction was in Polish. As a result, these settlements maintained their ethnic identification, cultural traditions, and language for many generations (see Section 5.4).

At the same time, Poles were also settling in established towns such as San Antonio or Bandera, where they became part of multilingual and multiethnic communities. Brożek (1972) cites the following contemporary description of Catholic life in San Antonio: "San Antonio, which is the central hub of activity for Franciscan Friars, has a German and a Polish parish. Father Moczygemba gives sermons in both German and Polish, and he has to hear confession in several languages because this is where Spanish and English populations meet" (28).

Not only could the Poles count themselves among the original American pioneers, but their investment in a future in the United States was bound up in specific ways with their past and present in Poland. From 1795 to 1918, Poland did not exist as a sovereign country, since it had been partitioned by its powerful neighbors, Russia, Prussia, and Austria, who took advantage of the country's internal conflicts and weakness. Poland's history of self-government dating back to the tenth century, and of constant warfare with its Russian and German neighbors, contributed to an especially strong effort at preserving the Polish language, cultural distinctiveness, and a sense of ethnic identity during the partitions. The gentry and intellectuals, in particular, focused their efforts on promoting Polish nationalism through literature and art. But Poland was also at this time essentially a feudal society. Consequently, among Polish immigrants there were on one hand large groups of uneducated, poverty-stricken peasants who left for America in search of work, and on the other hand, intellectuals who saw America as an opportunity to nurture Polish cultural traditions freely, especially in light of numerous failed attempts at regaining independence in the nineteenth century. Some even suggested the possibility of collectively purchasing a large swath of land somewhere in a state like Arkansas and settling it as "New Poland" (Dziembowska 1977a and 1997b). Thus, the Poles had a dual stake in the American project: they were both real American pioneers, and they saw American liberty as their chance to protect their Polish heritage in ways that they could not back in their homeland.

Interestingly, in Texas the Poles found themselves among their neighbors – and enemies – from the Old World: Czechs, Slovaks, and Germans. The Germans in particular formed a large part of local immigrants. By 1850, the total number of German speakers in Texas is estimated at about 5 percent of its overall population, and in some counties, they far outnumbered non-German settlers. In these areas, they mostly lived in isolated and relatively homogeneous towns and villages, much like the speakers of Polish described above, forming a stretch of settlements that Boas (2009) refers to as the "German Belt." They had their own German-language newspapers, schools, churches, and social organizations spread throughout central Texas.

Significantly, German presence in Texas predates its annexation by the United States. The first permanent German settlement in Texas was established in the 1830s, when Texas was part of Mexico and its official language was Spanish (Boas 2009: 33). This was a situation quite different from that encountered during colonial times by German immigrants to Pennsylvania, which had already been mostly settled by English-speakers and was under British rule. From the beginning, Texan Germans did not perceive English as a majority or dominant language to which they needed to assimilate. Moreover, once Texas gained independence from Mexico in 1836 and English became the language of trade and administration, German's importance was also officially recognized: in 1843, the Texas legislature mandated that its laws should be published in German as well as in English, and in 1844 it granted a charter to a German university (Boas 2009: 39). Kloss (1998, cited in Boas 2009: 39) argues that Texas Germans felt themselves to be equal to English-speakers as an ethnolinguistic group because they were "old established settlers" joining the Union, rather than new immigrants.

"The Border Crossed Us": Mexican Americans as Outsiders in Their Ancestral Lands

"We didn't cross the border, the border crossed us" is a common slogan in the Latino immigrant rights movement (Cisneros 2013: 1). It refers to the historical fact that Mexicans, for decades constructed in mainstream discourses as the threatening "illegal aliens," synonymous with crime and lawlessness (Chavez 2008; Weber 2003), who "invade" America but "refuse" to learn the "American" language, English, had been established residents of today's Southwestern United States long before the first Anglo-Americans reached the North American continent.

Spain encouraged the colonization of the northern reaches of its American territory, establishing religious missions "to Christianize and civilize the natives" (Chanbonpin 2004: 301), promoting agriculture, and handing out land grants to both Spanish-speaking and Anglo settlers. Anglo-Americans started to arrive in these regions in the beginning of the nineteenth century, but compared to Spanish colonizers and, more importantly, to local Indigenous peoples, they were latecomers.[15] By this point, Spanish colonization had also produced a local population that was ethnically diverse and mixed, since intermarriage between Spaniards and Indigenous people was common, unlike in the British colonies where it was shunned (Weber 2003). Anglo-Americans noticed and disdained the Mexican "racial mixture": according to Weber (2003), "American visitors to the Mexican frontier were nearly unanimous in commenting on the dark skin of Mexican mestizos who, it was generally agreed, had inherited the worst qualities of Spaniards and Indians to produce a 'race' still more despicable than that of either parent" (59–60). The beliefs in Anglo-American racial superiority were used to justify the takeover of Mexican lands.

Mexico won its independence from Spain in 1821, and quickly opened its borders to American trade. Mexicans harbored mixed feelings towards the United States: on one hand, they admired its early struggle against British colonial rule and its success as an independent republic; on the other hand, they were apprehensive about American expansion (Weber 2003: 55). But slowly, more and more Anglo-Americans settled in northern Mexico – California and New Mexico – often accepting Mexican citizenship. Even more settled in Texas, becoming a majority there by 1836, the year Texas became an independent republic. During the next ten years, the United States provoked a war with Mexico, invading it in 1846, which led to the 1848 Treaty of Guadalupe-Hidalgo that forced Mexico to cede its northern lands, including present-day California, Utah, Nevada, Arizona, and parts of Colorado and New Mexico.

[15] Interestingly, according to Chanbonpin (2004), "Historical records suggest that as early as 1767, Benjamin Franklin had designs on Mexico and Cuba as sites for future U.S. colonization" (303).

Texas, which included parts of today's New Mexico, had been annexed by the United States in 1845. Mexican and Indigenous inhabitants of these vast territories, speakers of Spanish and of Indigenous languages, suddenly found themselves living in the United States. They constituted the majority of the population in New Mexico (until the 1940s) and in Arizona (until the 1870s) (Weber 2003: 143–144). Half of California's 15,000 residents in 1848 were Mexican, although they were soon outnumbered thanks to the Gold Rush (Schmid 2001: 27). In New Mexico, 43 percent of the population consider themselves Mexican according to the 2000 US census, while some estimates place the state's Latino population at over 50 percent (Lipski 2008: 192). In addition, according to Lipski (2008), "Central and northern New Mexico are home to a Hispanic population that dates its origin to the Juan de Oñate expedition of 1598, and who regard themselves as direct descendants of Spaniards" (Lipski 2008: 192).

The government-sponsored dominance of English in the newly acquired territory was not a priority at first. The original California State Constitution, for example, was debated at the 1849 Monterey Constitutional Convention in both English and Spanish with the aid of an official translator, and the final document was not only published in both languages, but also provided that all laws would be published bilingually (Schmid 2001: 27). But as California's Anglo-American population increased, these earlier bilingual provisions were dropped. English became the sole language of school instruction and government proceedings, and an 1894 amendment to the California constitution "restrict[ed] the vote to those who could read and write English" (Schmid 2001: 28). Even in New Mexico, which remained predominantly Mexican American, an 1891 statute mandated that all education be conducted in English (29). In California, Mexican landowners were also routinely dispossessed, and their land transferred to Anglo-American settlers (Weber 2003; Chanbonpin 2004). Although the Treaty of Guadalupe-Hidalgo guaranteed US citizenship and equality under the law to all Mexicans living in the ceded territory, in practice the original inhabitants of these lands were quickly being disenfranchised and relegated to the status of outsiders (Chanbonpin 2004: 300).

Furthermore, to Indigenous peoples of the region the new US-Mexico border was an arbitrary line cutting through their ancient homelands and migration routes, as mentioned above in Section 1.1, and discussed at some length by Dunbar-Ortiz (2014). Luna-Firebaugh (2002) points out that as these borders were established, "little if any regard was given to the separation of native villages, and native nations were not consulted. The lines imposed by the colonizers ignored traditional hunting lands, areas of resource procurement, and religious sites" (161). The southern US border affected numerous

Indigenous peoples, including the Tohono O'odham, the Cocopah, the Yaqui, the Kickapoo, and the Kumeyaay (Luna-Firebaugh 2002).

As Josue Cisneros (2013) observes, the US takeover of Mexican territory under the Treaty of Guadalupe-Hidalgo gave birth to the "border problem" that is still at the forefront of immigration debates, as witnessed most recently in the 2016 presidential race rhetoric among Republican candidates, and in the determination of President Trump to build a border wall aimed at keeping Mexicans out. But the much-maligned Mexican-immigrant and Mexican American presence in the Southwest can be convincingly reframed as local people traveling within their own homeland, which has been occupied and colonized by a foreign power – the United States. Spanish, which is often represented as the primary threat to English – as evidenced, for instance, by the passage of anti-bilingual-education laws in California and Arizona (see Section 6.1) – has deep historical roots in the Southwest. Cisneros further argues that the American anxiety over the Southern border extends to the "contestation over the meaning and potential pliability of the borders between 'citizen' and 'foreigner'" (2013: 1). These ideas echo Gloria Anzaldúa's (2012[1987]) theorizing of Chicano/a identity as borderland identity, born from the dispossession and dislocation of the Mexican/Mestizo/Indigenous inhabitants of the American Southwest. The case of Mexican Americans exemplifies perhaps most clearly that such designations as "citizen," "American," "foreigner," or "immigrant" represent sociopolitical constructs that are continuously challenged and reframed, rather than any absolute categories.

Louisiana Purchase

The Louisiana Purchase, acquired in 1803, included lands stretching from the mouth of the Mississippi River out to the North and Northwest, encompassing present-day Midwestern states as far as Montana, Wyoming, and Colorado, and leaving the border in Texas in dispute until 1819 (Weber 2003: 53). At the time, European presence in the plains and mountains region was limited (Antieau 2003), but New Orleans had already developed into an important entry port, through which barges, boats, and eventually steam-powered ships traveled up and down the Mississippi. Despite its hot and wet climate, which for a city its size meant yearly outbreaks of yellow fever and cholera, New Orleans attracted immigrants from diverse backgrounds, and by 1800, at 17,000 inhabitants, it was the sixth largest city in North America (R. Bailey 2003). Furthermore, New Orleans was home to one-third of Louisiana's European American population, making it a much more regionally dominant metropolis than, for example, New York City, whose residents accounted for only 10 percent of New York State's population (R. Bailey 2003: 364).

A newcomer to New Orleans shortly after the completion of the Louisiana Purchase would have encountered a diversity of cultures, ethnic groups, and languages unrivaled by any other city on the eastern seaboard. African Americans made up 63 percent of the city's population, and many of them were free. People spoke Indigenous, African, Caribbean, German, Spanish, French, and English languages, among which English was far from dominant (R. Bailey 2003: 365). There were several varieties of French in use in the area: European French dialects spoken by migrants from France, "Acadian" (later Cajun) French spoken by exiles expelled by the British from Acadia, Canada, in 1755, and Kreyól spoken by refugees from the revolution in Haiti (365–366). There were also different Spanish dialects, including that of immigrants from the Canary Islands, whose descendants, according to Richard Bailey (2003), have "retained [their] distinctive variety of Spanish, though now markedly influenced by English and Louisiana French" (370). Hybrids of all sorts were common, if not exactly appreciated by visitors, as evidenced by observations such as this one regarding local riverboat men's language, cited by Bailey (R. Bailey 2003: 370): "This is a breed of animals that neither speak French, English, nor Spanish correctly, but have a jargon composed of the impure parts of these three." New Orleans' robust multilingualism grew upon the foundation of language diversity and mixing that predated European arrival. The area around the mouth of the Mississippi had been, as Bailey points out, "multilingual before any Europeans appeared in the Western Hemisphere" (368), likely because of its strategic location and resultant importance for commercial and cultural exchange.

English did, eventually, come to dominate Louisiana, but it did not succeed in extinguishing other varieties completely, as evidenced for example by Louisiana French, as well as by Cajun influence on local English (Wolfram and Schilling 2016). New Orleans is another example of an area that is decidedly part of today's America both politically and culturally, but whose linguistic heritage is not rooted in English. It is another reminder that as the United States expanded, claiming ever more territory, the English language brought by American settlers encountered existing linguistic ecologies in which Indigenous, African, and European languages already had their established roles. English may have been the dominant – though not the only – language of the thirteen colonies that first formed the Union, but as Americans colonized the continent, it became the language of the colonial power, imposed on others through oppression and discrimination, and not, as it is often portrayed today, the inevitable American language.

1.3 African American Language

One cannot discuss language and immigration in America without acknowledging the contribution of Africans and their languages to what America is today, both linguistically and socioculturally. As is often pointed out, race in the United States is one of the most powerful aspects of social organization, and its rise and reproduction as a relevant identity category is due directly to the trans-Atlantic slave trade and the establishment of racial slavery on American soil (see Section 2.3). Today, we witness African American Vernacular English (AAVE) as a powerful identity marker, an influence on Mainstream US English (MUSE), and the site of expressions of resistance and of oppositional youth identities, as seen for example in hip-hop (Morgan 2002). As pointed out by Alim and Smitherman (2012), in his 2008 campaign then–presidential candidate Barack Obama frequently relied on features of AAVE and sociocultural meanings associated with it, as well as on his ability to code-switch between MUSE and AAVE, to establish legitimacy and a sense of community with racially diverse audiences. At the same time, AAVE is a resource for cultural crossing by European American youth who seek to inhabit the sort of hyper-masculinity that they associate with African American men (Cutler 1999; Bucholtz 1999). AAVE expressions and other features have long been appropriated by members of mainstream culture as symbols of "coolness" and nonconformity. Furthermore, minority youth from neither white nor black backgrounds, who do not fit neatly into America's traditional white-versus-black racial scheme, also rely on AAVE and various cultural practices linked with it to construct their identities as Asian Americans, Indian Americans, Latino Americans, or Muslim Americans. I will be returning to these points throughout the book, and especially in Chapters 3 and 5.

It is beyond the scope of this book to attempt to do justice to the exceptional impact that the forced migration of Africans by kidnapping and enslavement had on the United States' sociocultural, political, economic, and linguistic development. Interested readers can turn to the vast research on AAVE in sociolinguistics and linguistic anthropology – as Wolfram and Schilling (2016) report, "more than five times as many publications [have been] devoted to AAE [African American English] than any other American English dialect" (217). In this section, I aim to highlight in brief the crucial role of African Americans in the story of language in the United States, as well as the fact that the ancestors of many Americans came to America's shores against their will (Wright 2008; Wood 2003). Wright (2008) describes African slaves as "involuntary immigrants" and even as "the first 'illegal immigrants'" (4), but such terminology is deceptive because it erases the violence and trauma of slavery by framing it as just another kind of immigration. At the same time, examining the stakeholders and participants involved in the making of America, as this chapter seeks to do, is not possible without acknowledging that major contributors to the development of America include victims of slavery and their descendants. I would like to reinforce this point while at the same time rejecting the term "involuntary immigration."

African slaves' linguistic situation was different from free immigrants because, as a means of control, they were deliberately deprived of the opportunity to form ethnically homogeneous groups where they could easily communicate and assist each other (cf. Daniels 2002). They also lacked access to a systematic way of learning English and were kept from becoming literate. Their predicament was shared with victims of the slave trade elsewhere in the Americas, and its linguistic consequences included the emergence of creoles, especially in plantation contexts. Gillian Sankoff (1979) offers a poignant assessment of this situation:

> The plantation system is crucial because it was unique in creating a catastrophic break in linguistic tradition that is unparalleled. It is difficult to conceive of another situation where people arrived with such a variety of native languages; where they were so cut off from their native language groups; where the size of no language group was large enough to ensure its survival; where no second language was shared by enough people to serve as a useful vehicle of intercommunication; and where the legitimate language was inaccessible to almost everyone (Sankoff 1979: 24).

The formation of creoles with various European lexifier languages occurred in many places where plantation slavery was dominant, including the Caribbean (e.g. Jamaican Creole, Haitian Creole, Papiamentu, Kweyol) and the northern Atlantic coast of South America (e.g. Sranan, Berbice Dutch, Saramaccan). Recently, some linguists have questioned the notion of "creole exceptionalism," arguing that the traditional view of creoles as unique in their development positions them as anomalous among languages, and is ultimately rooted in the colonial discourses of language and race (see Section 1.1) that imagine and elevate linguistic/racial "purity" while disparaging mixed heritage (Wolfram and Schilling 2016; DeGraff 2005, 2003; Mufwene 2008). Wolfram and Schilling argue that in fact, "most languages reflect the mixing of quite different languages" (2016: 228), while Mufwene (2001, 2008) observes that far from being drastically different, creole languages are products of the same restructuring processes – including language mixing and hybridization – as all human languages. Some, therefore, have chosen to abandon any structurally motivated definitions of creoles, shifting instead to a sociohistorical and "strictly atheoretical" (DeGraff 2003: 391) definition. Thus, DeGraff writes,

> For me, "Creole" is an ostensive label that, in the Caribbean case for example, points to certain speech varieties that developed between Europeans and Africans during the colonization of the so-called New World. In a related vein, the term "creolization" refers to the sequence of sociohistorical events that led to the formation of these languages known as Creoles (DeGraff 2003: 391).

While this is an important perspective,[16] we must nonetheless emphasize that the "sequence of sociohistorical events" referred to by DeGraff consisted, in the context of plantation societies and slavery, of the capture, enslavement, sale, forced transportation, and horrific abuse of human beings, including purposeful breaking up of ethnic groups and families. Given these facts, it is certainly reasonable to assert that the development of creole languages occurred under traumatic conditions, much like those described by Sankoff, that are not shared by free immigrant groups. These traumatic circumstances have produced language change that, while not "anomalous," is characterized by a rapid development of new language forms out of contact among many unrelated languages; furthermore, these new forms served as "counterlanguages" (Morgan 2002) that helped the enslaved people survive, and have become important community-building and identity-making resources for historically oppressed and disenfranchised groups, such as African Americans.

Present-day AAVE is not a creole, but a distinct dialect of American English. Linguists have differed on its origins, however, with some claiming that AAVE developed from the same British English sources as European American dialects, and others arguing that it developed out of an earlier creole language that was related to other English-lexifier creoles spoken in West Africa and the Caribbean.

The former view is supported by data such as recorded narratives of former slaves collected by the Works Project Administration (WPA) between the 1930s and 1970s (G. Bailey et al. 1991), mid-nineteenth-century letters by semi-literate slaves, and other materials containing transcripts of interviews with African Americans from the first half of the twentieth century (Wolfram and Schilling 2016: 229), as well as by studies of English varieties spoken by descendants of African American expatriates (Poplack and Sankoff 1987; Poplack and Tagliamonte 1989; Wolfram and Schilling 2016). These records and studies suggest that early African American speech was in fact more similar to other dialects of English than it is today, calling into question the creole origins hypothesis. Evidence shows that AAVE has been diverging from white American dialects, and, while it exhibits internal variation, it has also developed supra-regional traits shared across the United States (Wolfram and Schilling 2016: 230). After their large-scale migration from the rural South to Northern cities in the mid-twentieth century, African Americans found themselves living in greater practical segregation than had been the case in the South (Wilkerson 2011). This racial separation and the shared experience of

[16] The argument against creole exceptionalism is far more complex than the scope of this section allows me to discuss. Mufwene (2008), for example, challenges such long-standing assumptions as the progression from pidgins to creoles, or the Bickertonian theory of creolization as a window onto the evolution of human language. For more on this topic, see DeGraff (2003, 2005) and Mufwene (2000, 2001, 2008).

discrimination on part of white society contributed to AAVE's separate development. Moreover, it has been pointed out that unlike in typical plantation contexts (e.g. the Caribbean),[17] in the American South "over 80 percent of all slaves were associated with families that had fewer than four slaves per household" (Wolfram and Schilling 2016: 229).[18] Such an arrangement is not conducive the the birth of a creole because African slaves would have significant contact with white speakers of English rather than interacting predominantly with large numbers of speakers of African languages.

Linguists have also argued, however, for a creole-origin theory of AAVE's development (Dillard 1972; Rickford 1998), citing as evidence the features that AAVE shares with English-lexifier creoles such as Krio in West Africa or the Caribbean creoles of Barbados, Jamaica, or St. Thomas. These include copula absence (e.g. *You ugly*), absence of third-person present tense *-s* (e.g. *Mary go*) or possessive *-s* (e.g. *Mary hat* for *Mary's hat*), and consonant cluster reduction (Wolfram and Schilling 2016: 227). And of course there is also the Gullah (Geechee) creole still spoken by African Americans on the Sea Islands in South Carolina and Georgia, which suggests that a similar language may once have been spoken more widely by slaves across the American South. Proponents of the creolist hypothesis argue that over time, this early creole underwent gradual decreolization through contact with the surrounding English dialects, resulting in modern-day AAVE. Rickford and Rickford (2000) also note that contemporary observers described the speech of slaves in the eighteenth century as "a wild confused medley of Negro and corrupt English," "a mixed dialect between the Guinea and the English," or "a new creole language ... combining the vocabulary of several African languages common among the immigrants, African linguistic structures, and the few English words needed for communication with the master" (Rickford and Rickford 2000: 136). Crucially, these and other data supporting the existence of an early creole or mixed language date back to the eighteenth century, which is well before the former slaves recorded by the WPA project (Wolfram and Schilling 2016) were born.

Regardless of whether AAVE was once a creole or not, however, African influences in it are unmistakable (Smitherman 1998). On this point, AAE researcher Sonja Lanehart writes, "When I tell people outside the field about AAE, they seem dumbfounded that anyone would believe that AAE is not historically rooted to Africa, since the people who speak it are ... Ultimately, I do not feel the evidence exists that can support either side beyond reasonable doubt. And besides, it does not matter what the outcome of this storied debate may be" (2007: 133). For Lanehart, the

[17] In Jamaica, for example, Africans constituted 92 percent of the population by 1746.

[18] At the same time, blacks constituted a large proportion of the population in the South: 69 percent in South Carolina and 45 percent in Georgia by 1776, and 27 percent in North Carolina, 31 percent in Maryland, and 44 percent in Virginia by 1750.

focus should be on the future rather than the past. For our discussion in this section, what matters is not so much how AAVE came to be, but rather the African elements in it that have also influenced American English more broadly. And the distinctiveness of AAVE is not debatable. As Rickford and Rickford put it, "The fact is that most African Americans *do* talk differently from whites and Americans of other ethnic groups, or at least most of us can when we want to. And the fact is that most Americans, black and white, know this to be true" (2000: 4). Studies also support this claim: listeners have been shown to identify African American speakers accurately over 80 percent of the time when presented with audio recordings devoid of any culturally-specific content (Wolfram and Schilling 2016: 220).

Structural linguistic influence of African languages on AAVE is found in its phonology, morphology, and syntax. Wolfram and Schilling (2016) and Wolfram (2003) argue that persisting substrate effects have always distinguished AAVE from other American English varieties, including white Southern English. Some of these features, common to AAVE across the US and found also in historically isolated African American enclaves in coastal North Carolina and Appalachia, include copula absence, third-person present tense -*s* absence, possessive -*s* absence, and simplification of final consonant clusters (e.g. *lif'* for *lift, ches'* for *chest*). Wolfram and Schilling point out that these effects are common in contact situations, and indeed they are found in English lexifier Atlantic/Caribbean creoles. Some other features unique to AAVE (i.e. not found elsewhere in American English) include (adapted from Wolfram and Schilling 2016; Rickford and Rickford 2000; Morgan 2002):

- habitual be: He **be** talkin' with this lady every day.
- plural -*s* absence: *some dog* for *some dogs*
- stressed remote time marker *BEEN (BIN)* – describes a state that came into being a long time ago: "She ain't tell me that today, you know. She ***BEEN*** tell me that." (Rickford and Rickford 2000: 118)
- *had* + verb for simple past tense: *They* ***had*** *went to the store.*
- ain't for didn't: He **ain't** go there yesterday.
- *skr* for *str* in initial clusters: *skreet* for *street*
- [f] and [v] for final *th: toof* for *tooth*

Aside from the structural features, AAVE contains a large repertoire of particular discourse practices, verbal performances, verbal play, and storytelling styles, many of which have roots in Africa or in the time of slavery. Rickford and Rickford (2000) and Morgan (2002) describe many of these in some detail. Morgan, in a chapter titled "Forms of Speech: Verbal Styles, Discourse, and Interaction," discusses verbal practices and traditions such as indirectness, reading (one speaker denigrating or accusing another to his or her face), signifying, and playing the dozens (see also Smitherman 1986; Morgan 1998;

Spears 1998; Alim and Smitherman 2012). Crucially, to engage in these the speaker needs both a target and an audience. Describing indirectness in African American culture, Morgan (2002) makes the following observations:

> The array of hearers, overhearers and passersby that are part of the fabric of African American interaction are common throughout Africa and the diaspora. They function in ways similar to the intermediate or instrumental agents that have been reported to be central in interactions and formal talk throughout many African cultures . . . [N]umerous African societies practice social and verbal indirection through intermediaries who protect the public "face" of chiefs. For example, in African societies where audiences must confirm the leader's right to lead, those in power often use a spokesperson to deliver a message and mediate for them in case the audience finds fault in the message . . . Within African American community in the US, verbal acts also function to save face as they address multiple audiences, some aware and some unaware, through ambiguity and camouflaging (Morgan 2002: 46–47).

Rickford and Rickford (2000), in their chapter on writers writing in AAVE, bring up Zora Neale Hurston's "love affair with black speech [that] extended to a passion for folktales" (25). They continue: "Passed on through generations from elders – descendants of African griots who held the wisdom of nations on their tongues – to youngsters, the various genres of African American folklore serve both to entertain and educate" (25). One example of an African tradition continued in African American folktales is the trickster, who emerges as the hare Brer Rabbit or the spider Anansi (32). Other verbal traditions particular to African American culture that Rickford and Rickford discuss include the prayer and preaching style of black preachers, which they describe as chants and performances (43), or the use of direct quotation in narratives, folktales, accounts of real events, and comedy. Both Morgan (2002) and Rickford and Rickford (2000) also describe features of African American prosody. Meanwhile, Smitherman (1998) argues that "[t]he Traditional Black Church has been the single most significant force in nurturing the surviving African linguistic and cultural traditions of African America" (209). She makes this point come to life in the following vivid description: "In the spirit-getting, tongue-speaking, vision-receiving, Amen-saying, sing-song preaching, holy-dancing Traditional Black Church, the oral tradition is *live!* 'exciting, lively, high-spirited'. This is so because the church has not been pressured to take on Eurocentric culture and language. As the only independent African-American institution, the Black church does not have to answer to white folk!" (Smitherman 1998: 210).

Morgan (2002) also draws attention to the African and slavery roots of African American verbal culture in her discussion of counterlanguage. She argues that the system of plantation slavery represented what Goffman (1961) calls a total institution, in which the subordinates' lives are totally controlled in every aspect by those in charge. Under slavery and later under segregation, until the Civil Rights movement in the 1960s, African Americans' lives, including their talk and interaction practices, were regulated by rules determined by whites. In black-white interactions, for example, blacks were expected to talk only when granted permission, avert their gaze, avoid using educated speech, always give the expected answer, never contradict a white person, bow, and respond with "Yes sir/ma'am" (Morgan 2002: 24). But the antisociety and the counterlanguage that bonded it together permitted for the communication of coded messages, which flouted the norms set out by whites. As Smitherman (1998) puts it, "enslaved Africans had to devise a system of talking to each other about Black affairs, and about *The Man* (the White man) right in front of his face" (Smitherman 1998: 222). An African American speaker's words addressed to a white person could also carry another, indirect meaning for the black audience that may have been present (Morgan 2002: 22–25). For example, in a narrative a black speaker might say that his daddy moved their sharecropping family "to a farm near Cobb's Store," but to a local black listener, "Cobb's Store" indexes other "significant, yet indirect, local knowledge," such as that the store was owned and frequented by whites, and this meant the speaker's father "was under constant surveillance and scrutiny" (Morgan 2002: 27). Morgan also argues that "though based on norms of African interaction, the counterlanguage developed in ways that reflected the social, cultural, and political experience of African Americans" (Morgan 2002: 24). AAVE thus is a hybrid that enacts a blend of African tradition and American experience, which in the case of slaves was traumatic.

Rickford and Rickford (2000), Morgan (2002), Smitherman (1998), and Alim and Smitherman (2012) all show that the counterlanguage – the verbal practices built on indirectness – helped African slaves survive, and later helped connect and strengthen the African American community. They show how it found its way into many forms of cultural expression, such as music, from blues and jazz to house and hip-hop. Meanwhile, the immense influence that African American culture, and music in particular, has had within American culture as a whole is undeniable. Simultaneously, African American language has had a great influence on general American English. AAVE slang, word coinages, expressions, even aspects of pronunciation and grammar, are continuously being borrowed by non-black speakers, both whites and the mainstream society they represent, and other minority groups – albeit for different communicative aims.

Collections and dictionaries of African American language, including but not limited to slang (e.g. Major 1994; Smitherman 2000), present a large range of words, phrases, and expressions, some of which are used exclusively in the African American community and others that have been borrowed into mainstream culture. As Rickford and Rickford (2000) point out, many of these "refer to unique aspects of the black experience, including the physical attributes, social distinctions, and cultural practices and traditions of African Americans" (94). Many also have African origins. For example, Smitherman (2000) offers the following definitions (cited in Rickford and Rickford 2000: 94):

BAD:	Good, excellent, great, fine. [In] the Mandingo language in West Africa, *a ka nyi ko-jugu* [is] literally "It is good badly," meaning "It is very good."
JUNETEENTH:	The day, usually in mid to late June, when African Americans celebrate emancipation from enslavement; originally June 19, 1865, the date Africans in Texas learned they had been freed.
KITCHEN:	Hair at the nape of the neck, inclined to be the most curly (*kinky*) and thus the hardest part of *straightened* hair to keep from *going back.*

Some expressions are literal translations from West African languages into English, such as *suck-teeth* (the action of clenching one's teeth and sucking in air, producing a "sucking" sound in an expression of annoyance or anger), *bad-eye* (evil eye, threatening glance), and *bad-mouth* (to speak ill of someone) (Rickford and Rickford 2000: 95). For example, and *bad-mouth* is *da-jugu* in Mandingo and *mugum-baki* in Hausa (95). Similarly, Holloway and Vass (1993), in their book *The African Heritage of American English*, outline the African etymologies of words and expressions in Gullah, AAVE, and general American English. A few examples quoted and/or adapted from their lists include:

Bad-eye	Threatening, hateful glance, cf. Mandingo *nyejugu* "hateful glance" (lit. "Bad eye") and similar phrases in other West African languages (Holloway and Vass 1993: 137).
Bug	Mandingo *baga* "to offend, annoy, harm" (someone); Wolof *bugal* "to annoy, worry" (139).
Chigger	Wolof *jigs* "insect, sand flea." Recorded 1743, via Caribbean. Originally pronounced and spelled *chigo, chego*, or *chi ego* (139).
Goober	Bantu *nguba* "peanut," use recorded 1834 (141).
Hep, hip	Wolof *hepi, hopi* "to open one's eyes, be aware of what's going on" (142).
Kill	To affect strongly, as in "you kill me!" Similar usage in a number of West African languages, including Wolof and Mandingo, of verbs meaning lit. "to kill" (144).
Mojo	Fula *mica*, to cast a magic spell by spitting. Mainly used today in sense of something working in one's favor: "I got my mojo working!" Cf. Gullah *mock* "witchcraft, magic," Jamaican Creole *majoe, mojo* "plant with renowned medicinal powers" (145).
Ruckus	Bantu *lukashi*, sound of cheering and applause (147).

The above expressions are common in general American English today, as are numerous others (cf. Rickford and Rickford 2000; Lee 1998, cited in

Rickford and Rickford 2000: 240). This linguistic influence came, as mentioned above, as part of larger cultural influence, starting in the earliest days of the slave trade. According to Wood (2003), many foods made their way into the American diet through a combination of African and Native American culinary practices. For example, Wood writes, "Black newcomers in South Carolina and Georgia found an abundance of shrimp (a delicacy well known to many Africans but foreign to Europeans) in the waters surrounding the coastal Sea Islands. They wove casting nets and hauled in schools of tasty shrimp just as they had done in West Africa" (52). Of the cultural contact between Africans and Native Americans, he notes, "Such African foods as okra, yams, peanuts, and sesame seeds made their way into Southern cooking. Often they were combined with traditional Indian delicacies, as in gumbo, the famous specialty of Louisiana cuisine. The thick base is made by cooking sliced okra (an African dish) or powdered sassafras (a Choctaw Indian staple) in slowly heated oil" (55).

The cultural and linguistic contribution of African Americans to general American language and culture is not only extensive, but also rooted in the very beginnings of the United States' history. In the first century of North American settlement, from 1675 to 1775, more than 400,000 Africans were forcibly brought to the colonies as slaves, and a further 200,000 arrived in the newly established United States between 1776 and 1807, when the importation of slaves was outlawed (Wood 2003: 36).[19] Reflecting on these statistics, Wood makes a powerful observation: given that the largest migrations of Europeans to the United States began in the late nineteenth century, and increased even more in the twentieth century, the average African American's ancestry in the United States goes back much further than that of the average white American's (35). This realization certainly puts in perspective the notion of whiteness as the American norm, and the claims to European "roots" of American society and culture.

It is to these notions and claims, and their evolution and present-day manifestations, that I turn to in the next chapter.

[19] This is not to say that the import of slaves ceased completely: Wright (2008) estimates that as many as 50,000 slaves were smuggled into the United States illegally between 1808 and the 1850s (Wright 2008: 4).

2 The Alien Specter Then and Now

The term "alien" emerges in American political discourse surrounding statehood and citizenship at least as early as the Alien and Sedition Acts passed by Congress in 1798 during the presidency of John Adams. Among other provisions, they gave the president the authority to deport non-citizens suspected of subversive activity (Alien Friends Act) or who came from a hostile nation (Alien Enemies Act) (Wright 2008: 35). "Aliens" were thus defined in opposition to "citizens" as Others, as non-belonging, as not part of the American community. But although on the surface, the term "alien" appears neutral and equally applicable to all non-citizens, in reality it invokes a racially, ethnically, and culturally specific image of the immigrant/foreigner that is produced through currently circulating discourses. These discourses and the "alien specter" they construct have morphed and recombined over time, but the unmarked, default citizen that they assume as the "quintessential" American has always been the Anglo-Saxon white male. A manifestation of this assumption is the early limitation of citizenship eligibility to "free white persons" (Wright 2008: 33). Over time, the interpretation of what constitutes "whiteness" changed, but although eventually the racial restriction was dropped from legislation, the assumption that "problem" immigrants are not white persists.

This chapter examines, on one hand, how the alien has been constructed and represented throughout the United States' history, and where the lines among citizenship, potential citizenship, and perpetual foreignness have been drawn. It focuses on the discursive production of difference between what is alien and what is American, which engages the intersubjective tactics of adequation and distinction (Bucholtz and Hall 2004). The chapter examines the history of the process through which the fear of the "alien" has been naturalized and reproduced with each generation of immigrants. On the other hand, the chapter explores oppositional self-classifications by immigrant groups that have ignored, challenged, subverted, or reinvented the more mainstream categories.

2.1 The Melting Pot?

To hear America described as a "melting pot" has become, by the twenty-first century, commonplace to the point of cliché. At the same time, the metaphor has been imbued with contested meanings. Some have argued that the "melting" of ethnicities and cultures is what America should aspire to be. Others reject the desirability of such "melting," or challenge the metaphor's accuracy, proposing alternatives such as "salad bowl" or "mosaic." My own students have suggested that perhaps America is a "stew," in which some degree of melting together and blending takes place, but individual ingredients can still be discerned, albeit having influenced and changed each other. And for ethnic minorities whose distinctiveness has been historically viewed with suspicion as un-American, the metaphor of the melting pot can underscore their otherization and exclusion. Racialized attributes such as skin color, in particular, cannot be easily melted into the uniform American alloy, which has always been envisioned, more or less explicitly, as fundamentally white. This is illustrated, for example, in the efforts of nineteenth-century Californians to segregate public schools in response to increasing Chinese immigration. Chinese children were excluded from public education on the basis of their alleged "disease and immorality" (Jorae 2009: 114), and bills were passed introducing separate schools for non-white children. In one famous case, the parents of Chinese student Mamie Tape sued the Spring Valley School in San Francisco for refusing to admit their daughter because of her Chinese heritage, and in 1885 the California Supreme Court ruled in their favor. But since education had to be segregated as long as an appropriate public school existed, local officials opened a school for "Mongolians" (115), insisting that this is where Mamie Tape must enroll. Her mother Mary then penned the following letter to the San Francisco Board of Education:

> Do you call that a Christian act to compel my little children to go so far to a school that is made in purpose for them. My children don't dress like the other Chinese. They look just as phunny amongst them as the Chinese dress in Chinese look amongst you Caucasians ... Her playmates is all Caucasians ever since she could toddle around. If she is good enough to play with them! Then is she not good enough to be in the same room and studie with them? You had better come and see for yourselves. See if the Tape's is not the same as other Caucasians, except in features. It seems no matter how a Chinese may live and dress so long as you know they Chinese. Then they are hated as one (cited in Jorae 2009: 115).

It is clear from Mary Tape's letter that her Chinese family sought to assimilate to the religious and cultural mainstream so that they could be "the same as other Caucasians." If they had been European immigrants, their daughter could likely have claimed an American identity without being challenged. She could have "dissolved" into the melting pot. As Mary Tape points out, however, the family's racialized appearance marked them as unassimilable, and Asian Americans continue to face the otherizing categorization as "perpetual foreigners" to this day (cf. Lippi-Green 2012). Examples such as that of the Tapes demonstrate that groups physically standing out from the unmarked European norm cannot simply choose or strive to assimilate. The melting pot metaphor excludes them.

Possibly in response to this observation, recently the phrase "America is a melting pot" has been included on the list of racial microaggressions published as reference guides for faculty at institutions including the University of Wisconsin and the University of California.[1] Such guides are based on Sue et al.'s (2007) and Sue's (2010) work on microaggressions. Sue et al. (2007) include "America is a melting pot" in a table listing examples of racial microaggressions, explaining that the phrase's message is "assimilate/acculturate to the dominant culture" (276).[2] Not only does the "melting pot" imply the expectation of assimilating, but it also excludes racial minorities because in an America that is assumed to be by default white, they have little hope of achieving such assimilation, regardless of whether they aspire to it or not.

To be sure, not everyone today understands "melting pot" to mean complete assimilation. In his 2015 State of the Union address, President Barack Obama invoked the phrase to describe his native Hawai'i, and from the context of his words, it is apparent that he takes "melting pot" to mean mixture and diversity:

> You know, just over a decade ago, I gave a speech in Boston where I said there wasn't a liberal America or a conservative America; a black America or a white America – but a United States of America. I said this because I had seen it in my own life, in a nation that gave someone like me a chance; because I grew up in Hawaii, a melting pot of races and customs; because I made Illinois my home – a state of small towns, rich farmland, one of the world's great cities; a microcosm of the country where Democrats and Republicans and Independents, good people of every ethnicity and every faith, share certain bedrock values.[3]

However, despite the frequent popular use of "melting pot" to refer to diversity and multiculturalism,[4] the original meaning of the phrase was precisely the

1 www.washingtonpost.com/news/volokh-conspiracy/wp/2015/06/16/uc-teaching-faculty-members-not-to-criticize-race-based-affirmative-action-call-america-melting-pot-and-more/, accessed August 28, 2015; www.thecollegefix.com/post/23135/, accessed August 26, 2015.

2 Sue et al. (2007) define racial microaggressions as "commonplace verbal or behavioral indignities, whether intentional or unintentional, which communicate hostile, derogatory, or negative racial slights and insults" (278). Other examples include "You speak good English" when addressing Asian Americans or Latino Americans; "I'm not a racist. I have several Black friends"; and "You are so articulate" (276). The last example is explored at length in Alim and Smitherman's (2012) book *Articulate While Black: Barack Obama, Language, and Race in the U.S.*

3 www.whitehouse.gov/the-press-office/2015/01/20/remarks-president-state-union-address-january-20–2015, accessed August 26, 2015.

4 Such uses are many; for example, a simple Google search yields an August 17, 2015 article on the CBS news site, titled "Sharon, Massachusetts ranked 3rd among 'Best Places to Live in

opposite: complete and total dissolution of differences into a new, homogenous alloy. As early as 1782, J. Hector St. John Crèvecoeur, in his *Letters from an American Farmer*, writes, " ... they are mixture of English, Scotch, Irish, French, Dutch, Germans, and Swedes. From this promiscuous breed, that race now called Americans have arisen . . . Here individuals of all nations are *melted* into a new race of men, whose labours and posterity will one day cause great changes in the world" (cited in Vought 2004: 2, emphasis mine),[5] a claim that sounds like a harbinger of the notion of Manifest Destiny. Crèvecoeur further states, "He is an American, who, leaving behind him all his ancient prejudices and manners, receives new ones from the new mode of life he has embraced, the new government he obeys, and the new rank he holds" (2).

These ideas are reflected in the play that popularized the phrase, British Jewish immigrant Israel Zangwill's *The Melting Pot: The Great American Drama*. The play opened on October 5, 1908, in Washington, DC, before an audience that included President Theodore Roosevelt (Kraus 1999). Its plot centers around a love story between a Russian Jew, David, and a Russian gentile, Vera, who meet in America and only later discover that Vera's father was the official responsible for killing all of David's immediate family during a *pogrom* in Russia[6]. David himself is a composer who is writing a symphony to celebrate the idea of America, which he passionately explains to Vera and to his uncle Mendel in a frequently quoted passage:

> . . . America is God's Crucible, the great Melting-Pot where all the races of Europe are melting and re-forming! Here you stand, good folk, think I, when I see them at Ellis Island, here you stand [*Graphically illustrating it on the table*] in your fifty groups, with your fifty languages and histories, and your fifty blood hatreds and rivalries. But you won't be long like that, brothers, for these are the fires of God you've come to – these are the fires of God. A fig for your feuds and vendettas! Germans and Frenchmen, Irishmen and Englishmen, Jews and Russians – into the Crucible with you all! God is making the American (Zangwill's *The Melting Pot*, cited in Kraus 1999: 13).

Zangwill's melting pot is not some exciting culinary experiment, a mixture of diverse ingredients all harmoniously complementing each other's traits. Rather, it is the site of violent destruction and remaking, entailing a complete erasure of all that came before. Zangwill's protagonist speaks of "the fires of God," and his description of America as "God's Crucible" is almost

America'." In it, we read that the ranking "calls the town a small melting pot with residents that have embraced community building and diversity." http://boston.cbslocal.com/2015/08/17/best-places-to-live-massachusetts/, accessed August 26, 2015.

5 Also available online at http://xroads.virginia.edu/~hyper/CREV/letter03.html, accessed September 9, 2015.

6 The play is available to read for free at www.gutenberg.org/files/23893/23893-h/23893-h.htm, accessed August 31, 2015, and at http://archive.org/stream/themeltingpot23893gut/23893.txt, accessed May 10, 2016.

Figure 2.1 Cover for the theater program of Israel Zangwill's play *The Melting Pot*, 1916. Source: University of Iowa Libraries Special Collections Department

threatening. The melting pot is the site of violent purging. Those who come to America must be stripped of everything that distinguishes them from each other, and while their traits might contribute to the structure of the final product, quite like the properties of different metals in an alloy, the individual ingredients themselves are to become indistinguishable. The alloy is envisioned as a uniform entity. This theme continues throughout Zangwill's play in David's other pronouncements: for example, " . . . the real American has not yet arrived. He is only in the Crucible, I tell you – he will be the fusion of all races, perhaps the coming superman"; "Not when one hears the roaring of the fires of God? Not when one sees the souls melting in the Crucible?"; or, especially "Those who love us *must* suffer, and *we* must suffer in their suffering. It is live things, not dead metals, that are being melted in the Crucible."[7] So strong is David's belief in the melting pot that when, upon discovering who Vera's father is, he wavers in his commitment to marry her, he blames himself for being too weak to submit himself to the "fires of God." And ultimately, the two lovers come together, solidifying Zangwill's overall message: that the fate of America is to be the melting pot that mercilessly purges all prior distinctions in a great violent act. In the final lines of the play, embracing Vera and watching the fiery sunset over New York harbor, David proclaims: "It is the fires of God round His Crucible . . . There she lies, the great Melting Pot – listen! Can't you hear the roaring and the bubbling? There gapes her mouth . . . – the harbor where a thousand mammoth feeders come from the ends of the world to pour in their human freight. Ah, what a stirring and a seething! Celt and Latin, Slav and Teuton, Greek and Syrian, – black and yellow."[8]

When it appeared in Washington, New York, Chicago, and the West Coast in 1908 and 1909, Zangwill's play received mixed reviews: some critics noted its political critique, while others detested its heterogeneity and sentimentality; it is not coincidental, however, that Theodore Roosevelt was one of its biggest fans (Kraus 1999: 3). The image of the melting pot as presented by Zangwill was in line with mainstream political thought of the time. As I discuss further in Chapter 3, Roosevelt had no time for ethnic diversity or hyphenated identities, and demanded of every citizen an unquestioned loyalty to America, including its language and customs. According to Vought (2004), Roosevelt "was an imperialist who believed in the superiority of the White race, but he believed it was a historical rather than biological superiority" (27). Consequently, he argued that everyone was capable of Americanization. In his 1894 article in *The Forum* titled "True Americanism,"[9] he criticized racially or

[7] Available at http://archive.org/stream/themeltingpot23893gut/23893.txt, accessed May 10, 2016.

[8] http://archive.org/stream/themeltingpot23893gut/23893.txt, accessed May 10, 2016.

[9] Available online at http://teachingamericanhistory.org/library/document/true-americanism-the-forum-magazine/, accessed September 8, 2015.

religiously based anti-immigrant attitudes, labeling them "utterly un-American." Instead, he called for efforts to "Americanize [the newcomers] in every way, in speech, in political ideas and principles, and in their way of looking at the relations between Church and State," but also, crucially, for the immigrants to embrace America and assimilate into it. His words are not much different from Zangwill's:

> ... where immigrants, or the sons of immigrants, do not heartily and in good faith throw in their lot with us, but cling to the speech, the customs, the ways of life, and the habits of thought of the Old World which they have left, they thereby harm both themselves and us ... [the immigrant] must not bring in his Old-World religious race and national antipathies, but must merge them into love for our common country, and must take pride in the things which we can all take pride in. He must revere only our flag; not only must it come first, but no other flag should even come second. He must learn to celebrate Washington's birthday rather than that of the Queen or Kaiser, and the Fourth of July instead of St. Patrick's Day.

In the same article, Roosevelt also called for making English the sole language of instruction in all schools, and criticized churches that remain "foreign, in language or spirit." Assimilation for him clearly entailed learning English as well as, crucially, giving up one's heritage language. It also required adopting various aspects of American cultural norms – or, as Roosevelt puts it, "conviction, and thought" – which are closely bound up with English political traditions and with Protestant Christianity (Vought 2004). Roosevelt was clear about this: in a 1900 letter to Robert J. Thomspon, he explains that "the English, and especially the Puritans, made the mold into which the other races were run" (Vought 2004: 34). Roosevelt did advocate for regulating immigration in favor of more easily assimilable groups, but he appeared to define these more along socioeconomic than ethnic lines. For example, he demanded the respectful treatment of the Japanese and Chinese, as long as they were "gentlemen," students, merchants, and professionals, and simultaneously argued for a ban on all working-class immigration, including from Europe (Vought 2004). It was education and upper-class upbringing that, for Roosevelt, made complete assimilation more easily attainable.

Yet ultimately, the America into which Roosevelt expected all immigrants to assimilate was (and remains today) more open to some ethnic groups than others, for both cultural and phenotypical reasons. European immigrants, and those from Northern Europe in particular, already shared many norms and ideals that were long dominant in America. Vought (2004) writes, "Although the revolutionaries could not exclusively identify themselves with their British heritage, they never disowned it. The founders spoke the English language, they believed in English political ideals, and they expected those of different nationality to do the same" (2; see Chapter 1). In response to the third wave of immigration (Linton 2009),

Southern and Eastern Europeans were commonly portrayed as incapable of assimilating because of their distinct political traditions. They were seen as enslaved to tyrannical rule and corrupt religious institutions (Willey 1909; Pavlenko 2002). Non-Europeans were even further alienated from Americanness. Despite Roosevelt's expressed admiration for Eastern, and particularly Japanese, civilization, Chinese and other Asian immigrants were commonly seen as a moral threat because of their unfamiliar customs and religious beliefs deemed as pagan (Jorae 2009). If immigrants were to assimilate completely, they needed to become as much like Anglo-Saxon Americans as possible: English-speaking, dressed in Western clothes, following American customs, and preferably Christian. This fact was not lost on some immigrants, such as Norwegian American journalist Waldemar Ager or German American politician Richard Bartholdt, who criticized the "melting pot" ideal from the beginning, arguing that it was in fact "Anglo-conformity in disguise" (Pavlenko 2002: 188).

And, as we saw on the example of Mrs. Tape in San Francisco, linguistic and cultural assimilation was often not enough to be accepted as American. Human beings are obviously not metals, and they can become an alloy only metaphorically. In reality, it is not possible to dissolve one's physical appearance into the mainstream, even if one were to accomplish all other aspects of assimilation. Thus race easily constituted, and still does, a certain barometer of Americanization. Specifically, non-whiteness has often been represented as evidence of foreignness, sometimes directly, and sometimes as an index of unassimilable "culture." In fact, physical appearance, place of origin, and other attributes such as religion, customs, dress styles, and language, were frequently invoked interchangeably and linked to imagined moral and intellectual characteristics. Such representations were unremarkable in the context of mainstream popular and academic discourses of the early twentieth century that saw each ethnic group in essentialist terms as endowed with specific inherent qualities, but as we will discuss in Sections 2.3 and 2.4, they still appear in the political discourse of today, decades after the Civil Rights Movement and the popularization of post-structuralist thinking about identity.

Thus, for example, author and journalist Kenneth Roberts, a frequent contributor to the *Saturday Evening Post* on the subject of the evils of "new" immigration from Southern and Eastern Europe, expressed the following sentiment:

> If the United States is the melting pot, something is wrong with the heating system, for an inconveniently large portion of the new immigration floats around in unsightly indigestible lumps. Of recent years, the contents of the melting pot have stood badly in need of straining in order that the refuse might be removed and deposited in the customary receptacle for such things (Simon 1985: 83).

In this image, we see not just the inevitable violence of the melting pot, but also the argument that some groups of people are impossible to "melt down" and should therefore be rejected like useless garbage. Their Southern and Eastern European origins are linked with their moral character. As Suárez-Orozco and Suárez-Orozco (2001) explain, "The immigrants of the time were viewed as intellectually inferior, lazy, crime-prone, and altogether unassimilable" (39). Similarly, Ellwood Cubberley, superintendent of San Francisco schools and historian of American education, wrote in 1909 that the new immigrants are "illiterate, docile, lacking in self-reliance and initiative, and not possessing the Anglo-Teutonic conceptions of law, order, and government, their coming has served to dilute tremendously our national stock, and to corrupt our civic life" (cited in Pavlenko 2002: 175).

The ideal of American homogeneity built around Anglo-Saxonization (Pavlenko 2002) was equally embraced by Woodrow Wilson, who seems to have expressed a rather openly racist perspective on assimilability. For example, Wilson publicly defended the Chinese Exclusion Act, and the California Alien Land Bill of 1913, according to which Chinese and Japanese immigrants could not be naturalized or own land. In a published telegram to San Francisco's mayor, James Duval Phelan, Wilson writes:

> The whole question is one of assimilation of diverse races. We cannot make a homogeneous population out of people who do not blend with the Caucasian race. Their lower standards of living as laborers will crowd out the white agriculturalists and will in other fields prove a most serious industrial menace ... Oriental coolieism will give us another race problem to solve and surely we have had our lesson (cited in *The Independent* magazine on October 10, 1912;[10] see also Vought 1994: 29; Hobson 2012: 175).

Wilson's political opponent and sponsor of the literacy test for immigrants, Sen. Henry Cabot Lodge, supported the ideal of America as a homogeneous society, but he especially emphasized the superiority of Anglo-Americans, and the need for all other groups to abandon their ethnic heritage (Vought 1994: 37). Wilson, meanwhile, focused on unity and on the spiritual concept of America as the "city on a hill," the new Jerusalem, and of Americans as "a people set apart by God to be an example and inspiration to all the world" (Vought 1994: 40). Thus, despite the constitutional separation of church and state, the Puritan idea of America as a Christian nation remained central to much of the political thinking about immigration and assimilation. Ethnic groups perceived as difficult to Christianize, such as the Chinese, were seen as unassimilable,

[10] Available in a free e-book online at https://play.google.com/store/books/details?id=kDMPAQAAIAAJ&rdid=book-kDMPAQAAIAAJ&rdot=1, accessed September 9, 2015. The book is a collection of the magazine's seventy-third volume, including issues from July to December 1912.

morally corrupt, and thus dangerous – a topic we will return to in the following sections.

As the above discussion demonstrates, the idea of the melting pot has its historical roots in colonial and revolutionary times, and specifically in the early notions of America as the refuge for those seeking to escape old oppressions, to shed old ways, and to come together and blend into a new – Christian, homogeneous, democratic, and preferably Caucasian – people (see also Vought 2004). In response to the third wave of immigration, which spanned from the end of the nineteenth to the first decades of the twentieth century, which brought mainly immigrants from Southern and Eastern Europe, and which included Catholics, Orthodox Christians, and Jews, the ideal of American homogeneity was revived and actively promoted by political leaders and in mainstream political discourse. It was further popularized through Zangwill's image of the melting pot. However, this ideal homogeneity was obviously not achievable, and instead it inspired discrimination and prejudice against those who stood out as too different to "melt" and blend in. With time, the phrase "melting pot" has come to be used as a synonym for diversity and multiculturalism – precisely the opposite of its early-twentieth-century meaning. As we saw above, efforts have also been made to recognize the phrase's historically exclusionary implications, designating it as a racial microaggression. Nonetheless, the discourses that envision America as fundamentally a white, Christian, English-speaking country continue to circulate today. Thus, in the name of preserving American values, non-white and non-Christian immigrants are constructed as a threat, and so is the desire to preserve heritage languages or to celebrate multilingualism.

2.2 Good and Bad Immigrants

In his five-volume 1902 book *A History of the American People*, Woodrow Wilson, whose ideas we have already encountered, wrote the following critical assessment of "new" immigrants:

> Throughout the century men of the sturdy stocks of the north of Europe had made up the main strain of foreign blood which was every year added to the vital working force of the country, or else men of the Latin-Gallic stocks of France and northern Italy; but now there came multitudes of men of the lowest class from the south of Italy and men of the meaner sort out of Hungary and Poland, men out of the ranks where there was neither skill nor energy nor any initiative of quick intelligence; and they came in numbers which increased from year to year, as if the countries of the south of Europe were disburdening themselves of the more sordid and hapless elements of their population . . . (cited in Vought 1994: 29).

Wilson's harsh words landed him in trouble with various ethnic groups and organizations, such as the United Polish Societies of Manhattan and the

Italian-American Civic Union of New York (Vought 1994: 30), and even with the Roman Catholic Church, which objected to Wilson's unfavorable comments about Catholics (31). Nevertheless, his views reflected the dominant discourse of the day, spanning from around the 1890s to the 1930s, in which Southern and Eastern Europeans were constructed as undesirable immigrants, unfit to become Americans. In fact, from the earliest days of American settlement until today, some immigrants have been seen as more desirable than others. Typically, the rationale for this prejudice has been rooted in the various ethnic groups' perceived potential for assimilation (Suárez-Orozco and Suárez-Orozco 2001), and thus intimately bound up with prevailing ideologies of America. Those viewed as "unassimilable" become targets of xenophobic attacks and discrimination. They tend to be marginalized and excluded from the hegemonic definitions of Americanness.

This section offers a historical look at the constructs of the desirable and undesirable immigrants, emphasizing three themes. The first is the ongoing reproduction of the construct of the wrong kind of immigrant who poses a threat to America. As Wright (2008) points out, throughout American history, established citizens have tended to resent and look down upon new arrivals, who found themselves ostracized for their cultural practices and inability to speak English. As these groups assimilated, they or their descendants in turn adopted the same prejudiced views towards immigrant groups that followed later. Tensions between American citizens and new immigrants are not a new phenomenon, but rather an ongoing feature of America's social reality. The second theme in this section is how similarly the undesirable and threatening immigrants have been represented over time. Although the targeted groups have changed – from the Germans in revolutionary times, to the Irish and the Chinese in the nineteenth century, to Poles and Southern Italians in the early 1900s, to Mexican and other Latin American immigrants more recently – the discourses of fear rely on similar imagery: the newcomers are portrayed as alien and strange, their presence is seen as a threat to the prevailing social order, and their customs and ways of life are linked with laziness, uncleanliness, disease, dangerous ideas incompatible with American values, ungodliness, and criminality. Finally, the third theme in this section is the role language has played in constructing an immigrant group's desirability or undesirability.

Germans as Un-American

Although the bulk of early settler population in the colonies came from England, other European countries were also represented. The second largest group of settlers were Germans, who, as pointed out in Section 1.2, numbered 200,000 out of the total two million European Americans, or 10 percent of the white population. In Pennsylvania, German speakers accounted for as much as one-third of the population (Schmid 2001: 15). As a relatively noticeable group, Germans drew some negative attention, with Benjamin Franklin as a particularly well-known, outspoken critic of German immigrants. Franklin, in fact, did not consider Germans to be as "white" as the English and saw this as evidence of their inferiority. In 1751, in a document titled "Observations Concerning the Increase of Mankind, Peopling of Countries, etc.," he praised the "lovely" white race in contrast to black, "tawny," and "swarthy" ethnicities like the Germans, and he compared the latter's inability to acquire white complexion with their unwillingness to learn the English language:

> And since Detachments of *English* from *Britain* sent to America, will have their Places at Home so soon supply'd and increase so largely here; why should the *Palatine Boors* be suffered to swarm into our Settlements, and by herding together establish their Language and Manners to the Exclusion of ours? Why should Pennsylvania, founded by the *English*, become a Colony of Aliens, who will shortly be so numerous as to Germanize us instead of our Anglifying them, and will never adopt our Language or Customs, any more than they can acquire our Complexion.[11]

I will return to Franklin's ideas about race and racial hierarchies in the next section. For now, we can observe that already in 1751 – several decades before the founding of the independent United States – Franklin's suspicion of German settlers in Pennsylvania manifests itself through the discourse of desirability and undesirability of particular ethnic groups. Franklin's choice of words in constructing the image of German immigrants is reminiscent of the language employed by immigration critics today: they are portrayed in dehumanizing and homogenizing terms as "swarming" and "herding," much like pests or cattle, and thus pose a threat to English settlements; they are referred to as "boors," underscoring their inferior culture; and their language and customs are presented as bound to push out English ones if nothing is done to stop them. This discourse also naturalizes the problematic notion, discussed in Chapter 1, that America is fundamentally an English-speaking land built on English customs and that these customs are inherently superior. Finally, one's potential for assimilating is explicitly linked to one's skin color.

Despite sentiments such as Franklin's, German immigration continued, and, while the German language retained a strong presence in the life of German American communities, it did not push out or replace English. And with time, German immigrants came to be viewed as exemplary when compared with those who followed.

[11] In his "Observations Concerning the Increase of Mankind, Peopling of Countries, etc.," available at www.historycarper.com/1751/09/01/observations-concerning-the-increase-of-mankind-peopling-of-countries-c/, accessed September 18, 2015.

Nativism versus the Catholic Irish

Between 1820 and 1930, about 4.5 million Irish immigrants came to the United States, not counting those who first went to Britain or Canada, and were thus listed as British or Canadian in American statistics (Daniels 2002: 127). During much of this time, the Irish constituted the largest proportion of immigrants. For example, in the 1840s, they accounted for 45.6 percent of all immigrants, while in 1860, they made up 38.9 percent of the four million foreign-born people in America (127). Between 1847 and 1854, at the peak of Irish immigration following the potato famine, 1.2 million Irish came to America (Tracy 1988: 1). Due to various reasons, including opportunities for trans-Atlantic passage via Canada and demand for labor, the Irish tended to settle in New England. In 1860, New England was home to 20 percent of all the Irish-born in the United States, as compared with only 2 percent of all the German-born – a large difference given the similar size of the two immigrant groups (129). Boston – the city founded by Puritans – was home to 50,000 Irish by 1855 (Osofsky 1975: 889), and Bean (1934) even refers to "the Celtic invasion of Puritan Massachusetts" in his historical account (70). The response to the growing Irish presence in New England and elsewhere combined a reliance on them for doing the work shunned by native-born Americans with resentment and discrimination – both themes that, as I will discuss below, are common in today with regards to Latinos. Daniels (2002) explains that young Irish women were "often reluctantly . . . accepted, and by midcentury 'Bridget' had taken an essential role in thousands of northeastern homes" (131). He also points to "[t]he great reluctance of native-born Americans – and this, of course, included second-generation children of immigrants – to work as servants ('I'd starve first')" (131). At the same time, anti-Irish prejudice was common, as evidenced in the infamous "NINA" or "No Irish Need Apply" specification in job ads that has become part of Irish American immigrant lore. As various historical documents demonstrate, the Irish were stereotyped as unclean, uncouth, and prone to drunkenness, crime, and disease (Daniels 2002; Tracy 1988; Sessions 1987; see also Lewis 2008: 189–247).

The anti-Irish sentiment at the time of the largest wave of Irish immigration, in the 1830s through 1850s, was intricately bound up with several domestic political discourses, the most prominent of which were abolitionism, nativism, and mistrust of Catholicism and the papacy. Social reformers such as William Lloyd Garrison, a founder of the American Anti-Slavery Society and the editor of the abolitionist newspaper *The Liberator*, actively campaigned for the Irish American support of the abolitionist cause, arguing for the parallels between the enslavement of American blacks on one hand, and the oppression suffered by the Irish at the hands of Britain and their impoverishment and stigmatization in America, on the other (Osofsky 1975). In this, Garrison and his followers found some prominent Irish allies, most notably London-based Daniel O'Connell, who issued many addresses urging Irish Americans to join the abolitionist cause. Among the Irish community in the United States, however, feelings were divided. Many simply did not see blacks as their equals. Some, incredibly, believed that the Irish in America were in a worse condition than the slaves (Osofsky 1975: 902). Their socioeconomic status also brought them into conflict with free working-class blacks in Northern cities, leading not infrequently to violence (900).

Meanwhile, Irish Roman Catholicism became a target for nativist attacks. The American Republican party, formed in the 1840s, later rebranded as the American Party and known commonly as the Know-Nothings, was especially aggressively opposed to Irish immigration on ostensibly religious grounds (Kurtz 2014; Tracy 1988). Catholicism was seen as contrary to American institutions and values of freedom and democracy (Daniels 2002; Osofsky 1975; Bean 1934). It implied an allegiance to a foreign power – the pope – that took precedence over that to the United States (Osofsky 1975), and an inherent inability to appreciate and adopt democratic values (Sessions 1987; Bean 1934; Willey 1909). Thus, Protestant-Catholic tensions escalated during the Mexican War, when loyalty to the Republic could be tested against the loyalty to the Church in the face of fighting a Catholic country (Kurtz 2014).

Openly accused of disloyalty, Irish immigrants were first and foremost invested in proving their commitment to the United States, and their legitimacy as Americans. As Osofsky (1975) aptly puts it, "The working-class, Roman Catholic, poverty-stricken,[12] and much-abused Irish immigrant could not afford the luxury of political radicalism" (905). And in the 1840s, abolitionism was politically radical. Consequently, Irish-Americans distanced themselves from the anti-slavery cause in the name of allegiance to the Constitution. As the newspaper *Irish American* asserted in 1954, "The Irish do not stand for slavery . . . They do not hate slavery less, but love the Union more" (cited in Bean 1934: 88). This position, however, was in turn represented by nativists such as the Know-Nothings as evidence of the Catholic affinity for enslavement, and thus as justification for anti-immigrant, and anti-Irish in particular, policies (Bean 1934). To complicate matters, Irish Catholicism was also believed to be a matter of national pride more than faith, since, as some claimed, "Irish Catholics were often restless under English or French priests" (Bean 1934: 70). In the end, most Irish-Americans who fought in the Civil War did so on the side of the Union. However, despite their efforts in both the Mexican and Civil Wars, anti-Catholic and anti-Irish nativist sentiments

[12] Writing about the history of Irish settlement in the village of Northfield, Vermont, Sessions (1987) refers to "the Irish underclass identity" (76). In a meticulous account, he demonstrates the abysmal poverty in which Irish immigrants were forced to live. Northfield is but one of many examples of these conditions.

persisted even after the disappearance of the Know-Nothing party (Kurtz 2014; Wright 2008).

The Irish were the first immigrant group in the history of the United States to arrive in a short span of time in numbers large enough to provoke a response of fear that the Protestant, Anglo-Saxon sociocultural order governing the country could be shifted or displaced (Tracy 1988). However, the discourses invoked to justify prejudice against them, while reinvented, were certainly not new, and they would be revived again and again when positioning subsequent waves of immigrants as un-American. These discourses are called upon each time groups of Americans seek to construct distinction between themselves and immigrant groups. They have included discourses of religious difference and thus moral weakness, of criminality, of strangeness and thus a lower level of civilization, of pollution and disease, and of the need for assimilation. We can observe all of these when we examine how antipathy towards the Irish was framed.

The Roman Catholic religion of the Irish was viewed by devout Protestants as false Christianity. It appeared full of sinful practices, such as image-worship and following the directives of the authoritarian church hierarchy rather than seeking a direct relationship with God. This mistrust of Catholic practices could be invoked when constructing the Irish as untrustworthy and morally weak. We find many references to Catholic affinity for enslavement and their unquestioning allegiance to the pope (Bean 1934; Sessions 1987), or to their devotion to the papacy and likelihood of voting according to their priests' instructions (Willey 1909). Osofsky (1975) writes: "These were years of intense nativism in America, and one of the key tenets of the nativist stance was that Roman Catholic immigrants were especially prone to foreign dictation and were literally agents of the papacy in America" (900).

The narrative of religious and moral inferiority of the Irish was extended to other representations. The Irish were frequently portrayed as drunks, trouble-makers, simpletons, and criminals. In Northfield, Vermont – a small town whose newly built railroad attracted Irish immigrants looking for employment in the 1840s and 1850s – the influx of newcomers prompted local newspapers to describe the Irish as a "foreign, aggressive, and uncongenial element," to complain of their "strange dress, and stranger language," and to ridicule the "Hibernian simplicity" of Irish girls (cited in Sessions 1987: 78). The town's citizens worried about threats to law and order posed by the "drunkenness, pauperism, and criminality" (79) associated with Irish immigrants. The accusation of pauperism stirred fears that these newcomers would be supported by the state and also that they would be willing to work for little money, thus becoming unfair competition for the native workers and depressing the wages (Tracy 1988). Similarly, writing his historical piece in 1934, Bean observes, "This increased Celtic immigration was thought to be accompanied by a train of pauperism, crime, and insanity" (Bean 1934: 71).

And finally, those willing to accept Irish immigrants at the time were equally vocal about the need to Americanize them and convert them to Protestantism (Sessions 1987: 81). Edward Everett Hale, author, historian, and Unitarian minister, explicated his ideas for the policy of Americanization towards the Irish in the *Boston Daily Advertiser* in the early 1850s. These included allowing the immigrants to settle among local Americans in the maximum ratio of eight Irish to every one hundred natives, arguing that such "distribution would prevent the congregation of the Irish in the large cities and might lead also to their being Protestantized" (Bean 1934: 70). As we will see, similar discourses were involved in constructing the immigrant as Other in reference to the Chinese, Southern and Eastern Europeans, and Latinos.

The Chinese as the Embodiment of Immorality

In California, religion and race intertwined in the anti-immigrant rhetoric aimed at the Chinese. Initially, the overwhelming majority of Chinese who came to work in the mines and factories of California were male (Jorae 2009). They were quickly exoticized and portrayed both as a moral threat to the Christian American family and as an economic threat to the American worker. The single Chinese men were represented as sojourner laborers who sent their earnings back home, as argued for example by the California Congressman Thomas J. Geary in 1893: "They establish no domestic relations here, found no homes, and in no wise increase or promote the growth of the community in which they reside" (Jorae 2009: 16).

In fact, the first settlers coming to California from the East coast were also mostly men, so much so that by the 1850s San Franciscans nostalgically mused about the old "steamer days" when "seraped natives chased the wild bullock over the surrounding hills . . . when a Chinese was a *lusus naturae* [freak of nature], and a woman on the street . . . an absolute and unmitigated wonder" (cited in Lee 1999: 21). But while women slowly joined the growing white population of San Franciscans in what was to become, by the 1860s, one of the fastest-growing cities in the United States and its sixth busiest port (23), the Chinese, despite their increasing numbers, continued to be constructed as "freaks of nature" or, at the very least, cultural and moral aberrations. They were racialized as "Orientals," and the resulting construct of the "yellow race" eventually came to include other Asians as well, a topic which will be addressed more fully in the next section. But the relatively low numbers of Chinese women and families in late nineteenth century California led to the depiction of Chinese immigrants as alien, deviant, engaged in immoral lifestyles, and consequently unassimilable. The fascination with the alleged moral depravity of Chinatown life in turn led to intensified scrutiny of any Chinese women who did arrive in San Francisco since they were viewed as potential prostitutes.

I chose the term "fascination" because nineteenth-century white Americans were at the same time appalled by Chinatown brothels and opium dens, and attracted by this exoticized image of the morally corrupt Orient. Most Chinese immigrants did not take part in sex trade or lounge around smoking opium; rather, they worked in mines and on railroad construction, and when those jobs ended, moved into factory work or domestic service. Some opened their own small businesses such as shops or laundries. Many lived in Chinatown, but many did not. It is true that the sale of young girls into service as *mui tsai* (servant girls) in wealthier Chinese households, or into sexual slavery at Chinatown brothels did take place. Jorae (2009) reports that "San Franscico census enumerators in 1870 listed sixty-six Chinese girls age sixteen and under as prostitutes (20 percent of all Chinese girls in San Francisco)" (141). Prostitution in early Chinatown was prominent, including both low-priced working-class brothels that catered to a racially diverse clientele and more upscale parlor houses frequented exclusively by wealthy Chinese men that featured expensive opium pipes as part of their furnishings and equipment (142–143). Nonetheless, prostitution did not represent the majority of Chinese immigrant lives, and it certainly was not an "illness" with which the Chinese were "infecting" Christian America. Rather, Chinese prostitution involved a "complex homosocial exchange between Chinese men and white men that made possible the profitable exchange of Chinese women's bodies as a commodity" (Lee 1999: 90).

But, although white Americans were active participants in the Chinese sex trade, they were portrayed as victims of a uniquely Chinese vice that implicated all Chinese immigrants. For example, in 1877 Dr. Hugh H. Toland, a local health board member, "insisted" that "young white boys had contracted syphilis from frequenting Chinese brothels," and he blamed Chinese prostitutes "for seducing boys, spreading syphilis, and, consequently, corrupting American families" (Jorae 2009: 143). Simultaneously, white America's racializing and exoticizing gaze was drawn to these aspects of Chinatown life. Well-meaning charity activists, in particular white women, labored to locate and rescue enslaved Chinese girls, moving them out of brothels and into mission schools where they would be Christianized and educated to become proper American ladies. The same activists also vocally attacked Chinese sex slavery and Chinatown prostitution, perpetuating the image of the heathen and morally corrupt Oriental. At the same time, tour guides led sensation-hungry visitors to San Francisco through the supposed underbelly of Chinatown, peeking at staged brothel scenes and paying local Chinese to gamble and smoke opium for the tourists. Jorae (2009) recounts photographer Arnold Genthe's description of the home of an old opium addict:

Tour guides would bring visitors to his living quarters and announce, "If we are fortunate you will see a rare sight – a Chinaman smoking opium." After observing the old man laying on a pile of rags and puffing away on his pipe, the visitors would depart satisfied that they had observed a genuine scene of "Oriental depravity," and the guides would pay him a few nickels for his effort (178).

These practices drew protests of Chinese American entrepreneurs and other wealthier Chinese who wanted to promote a positive image of Chinese immigrants (184).

The commodification of Chinatown "vices" contributed to the representation of the Chinese as dirty and diseased, both physically and morally. Although the Chinese were criticized for not establishing families and migrating as single male sojourners, at the same time Chinese women were viewed with suspicion. According to Jorae (2009), dominant "scientific" theories held that "Chinese women presented a particular medical threat to American society because of their less moral and more animalistic tendencies" (21). The 1875 Page Act placed strict control on Chinese females entering the United States. Consequently, women and girls arriving in California had to demonstrate that they were not being smuggled as prostitutes, and as little as being observed conversing with men or a condemning testimony of a fellow white passenger was enough to deny a Chinese female entry to the United States. Such restrictions placed severe limitations on the viability of Chinese American family life. Still, many families did establish roots in California and elsewhere (41), but they endured constant scrutiny and criticism. Their children were portrayed as unclean and morally deficient, and thus unfit for associating with white children, leading to the segregation of schools. In response, wealthier Chinese emphasized their children's Americanization in order to combat these prejudiced attitudes. The efforts expanded by these parents lay part of the groundwork for the later construction of Asian Americans as the "model minority" – a point I will return to later in this chapter.

Southern and Eastern Europe

In towns like Northfield, Vermont, animosity towards Irish immigrants had abated by the 1890s and had sometimes been replaced by acceptance as Irish immigration slowed down, and the children of Irish immigrants established themselves as displaying the "American" characteristics of "thrift, industry, and self-reliance" (Sessions 1987: 83). At the same time, immigration trends were changing. So-called old immigration from Northern and Western Europe was giving way to so-called new immigration from Southern and Eastern Europe. The first year in which more new than old immigrants arrived in the United States was 1896, and by the year 1907, the United States had seen the peak of these "new" immigrants at 1.285 million (Wright 2008: 75). Another useful comparison is that in 1882, old immigrants made up 87 percent of all immigrants, while in 1907, new immigrants made up 81 percent (75).

These immigrants became the new target of anti-immigrant feeling. Meanwhile, as Suárez-Orozco and Suárez-Orozco (2001) point out, "The pseudoscience of eugenics of the early decades of [the twentieth] century gave deep anti-immigrant sentiment a cloak of rationality" (39). The essentialist belief that people hailing from different nations possessed intrinsic "national" characteristics that were physically, intellectually, and morally evident, and that races were biologically defined and hierarchically ordered categories, was accepted as fact in the early 1900s. And, not surprisingly, the most desirable mental and moral qualities were assumed to accompany lighter skin and Northern European features.

Speaking from this perspective, Dan Allen Willey wrote in a 1909 issue of *Putnam and the Reader* that just as the South had its "Southern problem" of "trying to decide the future of the negro" (Willey 1909: 456), and the West had its fear "that the states beyond the Rockies may be Asiaticized" (457), the people of New England faced their own problem of the new immigration. This problem, according to Willey, is more urgent than any other, because it pertains to "the future of the American people themselves, whether they are to be Americans – or something else" (456). Willey observes that "the Yankee is fading from his ancestral land" (457), and offers as evidence the growing numbers of Southern and Eastern European immigrants settling in New England, which he perceives as the bastion of traditional America. He observes, "In Connecticut valley you frequently see hamlets comprising perhaps a half-dozen families of Bohemians or Hungarians . . . the Italians and Poles have come by thousands. There are even Greeks, Portuguese and Armenians who turn up the New England soil for subsistence" (459). These new immigrants are then contrasted with immigrants of old – the good immigrants who assimilated more easily to Puritan America:

> In the early days of immigration to the United States, it may be needless to say, most of the home-seekers were from Northern Europe; but the majority of those who have recently crossed the ocean into the Eastern States are a part of the more recent movement from Southern Europe. They have no apprehension of that view of man which is the organizing principle of American life, and having never enjoyed true political freedom, they misunderstand the nature of civil liberty and are unqualified for its responsibilities . . . They settle by themselves in compact communities; they set up their own type of home, retain their old standard of living and adhere to their own institutions of religion, which they conduct in a foreign tongue and spirit, perpetuating a low order of life, obstructing to progress and at variance with the genius of American institutions (Willey 1909: 460).

In this passage, as in the rest of his article, Willey constructs the new immigrants as a threat because of their inability and unwillingness to assimilate.

Implicated in this threat are the immigrants' tendency to stick together, as well as their religion, language, and cultural practices, all of which are seen as incompatible with American life. Willey then praises schools and colleges designed specifically for immigrants, which he terms "character factories" and "in which young men and young women are trained to become apostles of Americanism among those of their own blood" (462). The emphasis in these schools is on learning English: "From the time the student signs the roll until he gets his graduating parchment, the importance of English is pressed upon him till he speaks and reads it fluently and accepts its importance as the mother-tongue of his adopted country" (462). Other important lessons involve American patriotism and customs, and the lives of American heroes. Crucially, Willey voices a similar concern over non-English languages as Benjamin Franklin did with regards to German-speaking settlers in Pennsylvania in the 1750s, and, like Franklin, he identifies the American language as English.

Rita Simon's (1985) meticulous analysis of the public opinion regarding immigrants as represented in print media from 1880 to 1980 includes numerous examples of the same discourses that Willey (1909) invokes, in publications including *North American Review, Saturday Evening Post, Literary Digest*, and *Atlantic Monthly*, among others. For example, Cornelia James Cannon writes in 1923 in *North American Review*, " . . . they come in far greater numbers, vermin infested, alien in languages and in spirit, with racial imprints which can be neither burned out nor bred out . . . " (cited in Simon 1985: 75). Another contributor, economics professor Ray Garis, wrote in 1924:

> According to every test made in recent years and from a practical study of the problem, it is evident beyond doubt that the immigrants from Northern and Western Europe are far superior to the ones from Southern and Eastern Europe. The vital thing is to preserve the American race – build it up with Nordic stock: intelligent, literate, easily assimilated, appreciating and able to carry on our American institutions (cited in Simon 1985: 76).

Similarly, author Kenneth Roberts, the frequent writer for *Saturday Night Post* cited in Section 2.1, explains in a 1920 editorial that whereas "the old immigrants came from England, Ireland, Scotland, Wales, Denmark, France, Germany, Holland, Norway and Switzerland . . . [t]he new immigration is made up of people from Eastern and Southern Europe . . . More than a third of them cannot read and write; generally speaking they have been very difficult to assimilate" (cited in Simon 1985: 83). In a 1923 issue of the *Post*, Secretary of Labor James J. Davis described incoming immigrants as "the dregs of humanity" (cited in Simon 1985: 85). Another *Post* contributor Marcus Eli Ravage wrote in the same issue, "Given two individuals of equal intelligence, one from Eastern Europe and the other from Western Europe, there cannot be a moment's doubt as to which one will be the first to fit into the American scheme of things: the person from Western Europe" (cited in Simon 1985: 85). Twenty years earlier, in 1900, we read in the *Literary Digest*, "The swelling tide of immigrants from Southern Europe and the Orient who can neither read nor write their own language and not even speak ours, who bring with them only money enough to stave off starvation but a few days, is a startling national menace that cannot be disregarded with safety" (cited in Simon 1985: 107). And as early as 1892, Professor Francis Walker thus opined in the *Yale Review* about Poles, Bohemians, Hungarians, Russian Jews, and Southern Italians: "Ignorant, unskilled, inert, accustomed to the beastliest conditions, with little social aspirations, with none of the desire for air and light and room, for decent dress and home comfort, which our native people possess and which our earlier immigrants so speedily acquired" (cited in Simon 1985: 102). The recurring themes here, as in the case of the Chinese, revolve around dirt, infestation, disease, pollution, and moral inferiority.

The Latino Threat in Current Political Discourse

The language used to discuss immigration in the mainstream print and other media today does not typically invoke such explicit prejudice or appeal to racial hierarchies, as was the case when eugenics was taken seriously as a science. Nonetheless, present-day discussions center around many of the same discourses as those surrounding Irish or Southern and Eastern European immigrants. For example, we hear politicians linking immigrants with criminality, talking about their refusal to assimilate, and emphasizing the need to learn English as a prerequisite for becoming American. Despite the increasing popularity of Spanish or Mandarin dual-immersion programs among white, middle-class parents, immigrants speaking non-English languages continue to be constructed as a threat to traditional American ways of life.

Thus, for example, President Donald Trump had this to say on his official campaign web page while running in the primaries:

> For many years, Mexico's leaders have been taking advantage of the United States by using illegal immigration to export the crime and poverty in their own country (as well as in other Latin American countries) . . . The impact in terms of crime has been tragic. In recent weeks, the headlines have been covered with cases of criminals who crossed our border illegally only to go on to commit horrific crimes against Americans.[13]

Or compare, for example, this quote from the aforementioned Kenneth Roberts' 1929 editorial in the *Saturday Night Post*, and the now infamous quote from Donald Trump's presidential candidacy announcement on June 29, 2015, below it:

[13] www.donaldjtrump.com/positions/immigration-reform, accessed September 27, 2015.

Instead of being a great melting pot which it was prior to 1880 because of the similarity of the early Nordic immigrant, America has largely become the dumping ground for the world's human riffraff, who couldn't make a living in their own countries (Roberts in 1929, cited in Simon 1985: 88).

The US has become a dumping ground for everybody else's problems . . . When Mexico sends its people, they're not sending their best. They're not sending you. They're not sending you. They're sending people that have lots of problems, and they're bringing those problems with us (sic). They're bringing drugs. They're bringing crime. They're rapists. And some, I assume, are good people (Trump in 2015).[14]

Both Roberts and Trump use the phrase "dumping ground" to describe America as the place where all other countries dispose of their undesirable citizens. Trump goes on to accuse Mexican immigrants of being criminals, even drug traffickers and rapists, for which he was vociferously attacked by left-wing media and which annoyed other Republicans. Despite this, Trump became the Republican presidential nominee after winning nearly all primary contests, and eventually won the presidency. This suggests that many Americans recognize and accept his framing of the immigration question just as nineteenth and early twentieth century Americans accepted the portrayal of the Irish and of Eastern and Southern Europeans as threats (Lakoff 2004).

Undocumented immigrants in particular tend to be represented as criminals, which is often argued to be self-evident because by staying in the US without appropriate visas, they are breaking the law. The use of the term "illegal immigrants" or "illegal aliens" to refer to undocumented immigrants further naturalizes the notion that they add to the crime problem in the United States (cf. Chavez 2008). In 1994, California voters passed Proposition 187, dubbed the "Save our State" initiative, which would prevent undocumented immigrants from receiving public services, including public education (Suárez-Orozco and Suárez-Orozco 2001: 40). The language introducing the proposition on the ballot invoked the connection between undocumented immigrants and crime, and positioned California residents as victims of unspecified criminal activities conducted by undocumented immigrants: "[The People of California] have suffered and are suffering economic hardship caused by the presence of *illegal aliens* in this state. That they have suffered and are suffering personal injury and damage caused by the criminal conduct of *illegal aliens* in this state" (cited in Suárez-Orozco and Suárez-Orozco 2001: 40; emphasis mine). Similar representations of undocumented immigrants as criminals appeared in the discussion about the DREAM Act in 2010, which was ultimately defeated in Congress. On December 6, 2010, Jeff Sessions, then a US Republican senator from Alabama and now US Attorney General, made a speech on the Senate

[14] www.bostonglobe.com/arts/television/2015/06/29/what-did-donald-trump-say-about-immigrants/ForaqpQHjwgeKRdVUdYrdM/story.html, accessed September 27, 2015.

floor condemning the DREAM Act, in which he used the term "illegal aliens" and contrasted the American values of law and order with various criminal activities supposedly perpetrated by undocumented immigrants, as evidenced in the following excerpts from his speech:

> One of the fundamental things that separates America from other nations of the world is our commitment to the rule of law . . . Yet we have allowed our borders to descend into chaos and lawlessness. For decades, we have failed to uphold the rule of law; we have failed to protect the integrity of American citizenship. Even now, in a post 9/11 world, we still lack control over who or what comes into our country. Every day guns, drugs, and unknown people unlawfully pour across our broken border . . . Ranchers living on US soil must confront this chaos as a reality of daily life. They are denied the peaceable possession of their private property. Phoenix, the capital of Arizona, is now known as one of the kidnapping capitals of the world . . . Democrat leaders are now pushing a reckless proposal for mass amnesty known as the DREAM Act. At a time when our nation is struggling with high unemployment and runaway government spending, this bill would authorize millions of illegal workers . . . those eligible for the DREAM Act amnesty include illegal aliens with criminal records . . . Americans want us to enforce our laws. But we are considering a bill that would reward and encourage their violation.[15]

Sessions offers no evidence to support his claims regarding undocumented immigrants' criminality, but repeatedly frames their presence in the US as illegal in itself, as linked with guns, drugs, and even terrorism – which he does by referring to the "post 9/11 world" – and as undermining the American ethos of law-abiding citizenship. Chavez (2008) argues that the construction of Mexican Americans in particular as criminals and "illegals" dates as far back as the 1920s, which also "witnessed a profound new importance placed on the territorial imperative of national borders . . . new techniques of surveillance, the creation of the Border Patrol, and immigrant health examinations" (23) – issues that have been resurrected and placed at the forefront of Donald Trump's 2016 campaign and subsequent presidential agenda. The latest incarnation of this rhetoric is Trump's "Border Security and Immigration Enforcement Improvements" executive order of January 25, 2017, which focuses specifically on the "Southern border," commands the Secretary of Homeland Security to begin the construction of the border wall, increases the number of Border Patrol agents by 5,000, and expands definitions of criminality to facilitate deportations.[16] Meanwhile, in present-day anti-immigrant discourse, "Mexican" is often used as a stand-in term for all Latinos (cf. Dick 2011b, 2010).

Another theme that emerges in the public discourse surrounding Latino immigrants is the idea that they do not assimilate and as such that they threaten

15 http://blog.al.com/pr/2010/12 transcript_of_us_sen_jeff_sess.html, accessed September 28, 2015.
16 http://i2.cdn.turner.com/cnn/2017/images/01/28/border.security.and.immigration.enforcement .improvements.pdf, accessed February 17, 2017.

American national identity and, by extension, Western civilization as a whole. Racist language in this discourse is less explicit than in the past, but the fears are the same and the feared populations are not white. As Suárez-Orozco and Suárez-Orozco (2001) put it, "whereas in earlier times concern was over postulated biological and racial inferiority, in more recent times ... we are witnessing the use of so-called cultural differences as the banner of those who are against immigration" (39). And indeed, since the 1990s there has been a proliferation of books by anti-immigration activists and politicians, all of which invoke the threat posed by large numbers of Latinos in the United States (Chavez 2008: 30). Some telling titles include Peter Brimelow's (1995) *Alien Nation*, Georgie Anne Geyer's (1996) *Americans No More*, Patrick Buchanan's (2002) *Death of the West: How Dying Populations and Immigrant Invasions Imperil Our Country and Civilization* and (2006) *State of Emergency: The Third World Invasion and the Conquest of America*, Victor Davis Hanson's (2003) *Mexifornia*, and Samuel Huntington's (2004) *Who We Are: The Challenges to America's National Identity*. Chavez (2008) points out that these various texts all rely on the imagery of invasion, whereby America is being invaded and overrun by Latino – which usually means Mexican – immigrants who are plotting a re-conquest of lands north of the border. The irony is, of course, that, as I discussed earlier, from the Mexican and Native American perspective, the US-Mexico border is an arbitrary line drawn rather recently across their ancient homelands and migration routes (see Chapter 1).

Throughout these Latino-phobic discussions, the issue of language is frequently raised in ways that, again, reinforce the idea that English is the American language and that immigrants are a threat when they do not speak it. For example, during one Republican primary debate in 2015, Donald Trump criticized Jeb Bush for speaking Spanish when answering a Spanish question during a campaign appearance: "We have a country where to assimilate you have to speak English ... To have a country, we have to have assimilation ... This is a country where we speak English, not Spanish."[17] Along similar lines, former Alaska governor and vice-presidential candidate Sarah Palin remarked while speaking to CNN on September 6, 2015, "I think we can send a message and say, 'You want to be in America, (a) you'd better be here legally or you're out of here, (b) when you're here, let's speak American ... Let's speak English, and that's a kind of a unifying aspect of the nation is the language that is understood by all.'"[18] And the DREAM Act itself posited that undocumented immigrants would have to demonstrate that they have learned English if they

[17] Transcribed by me while watching the debate on September 16, 2015.

[18] http://gawker.com/sarah-palin-says-if-you-want-to-be-in-america-you-bette-1729025305, accessed September 28, 2015.

were to be considered for a path to citizenship, despite the fact that the legislation was geared at those who were brought to the US as children and are therefore likely native speakers of English.

The Fear of Islam

On March 18, 2015, Pine Bush High School in upstate New York sparked a massive controversy by having the Pledge of Allegiance recited in Arabic during its morning announcements. The school's idea was to recite the pledge in different languages throughout the week to honor the National Foreign Language Week, and the reading in Arabic was to be followed by Japanese, Italian, French, and Spanish. As the school district explained in a statement, the point was "to celebrate the many races, cultures and religions that make up this great country and our school district . . . The intention was to promote the fact that those who speak a language other than English still pledge to salute this great country."[19] Significantly, this school's efforts engage with an alternative representation of American identity – one that emphasizes plurality, diversity, and multilingualism – demonstrating that, as is always the case, the discourses that focus on immigration as threat, and that invoke the idea of English as the national language, coexist with and are challenged by oppositional discourses.

However, the reaction to the school's Foreign Language Week activity demonstrates the continuing acceptance by many people of the fear and suspicion of both multilingualism and of non-Christians within the physical and conceptual borders of America. Immediately after the event, the school and the district's superintendent began receiving complaints. There were angry students, parents calling the district office, residents complaining to local news outlets, and angry comments online. The next day, a number of cars in the school's parking lot were flying American flags, and a few had the words "We live in America. Speak English" scrawled on their back windows.

Residents described the event as disrespectful. Comments reported in the news included, as reported by CBS news, "Judging [from] what the country is dealing with now with extreme Muslims and all the war and stuff over there, I wouldn't have started off with Arabic" and "I think it should be spoken in English. This is America."[20] To be sure, there were also voices of support, such as one resident who said "Everybody should be welcome. Everybody should be free."[21] In local news outlets' comment sections, discussion went back and

19 www.washingtonpost.com/news/post-nation/wp/2015/03/19/pledge-of-allegiance-reading-in-arabic-sparks-controversy-at-new-york-school/, accessed September 29, 2015.

20 http://newyork.cbslocal.com/2015/03/19/upstate-n-y-school-apologizes-for-reciting-pledge-of-allegiance-in-arabic/, accessed May 11, 2016.

21 http://newyork.cbslocal.com/2015/03/19/upstate-n-y-school-apologizes-for-reciting-pledge-of-allegiance-in-arabic/, accessed May 11, 2016.

Figure 2.2 A Pine Bush High School student's car the day after the Arabic Pledge of Allegiance, March 2015. Photo credit: Times Herald-Record, Middletown, NY

forth. Some expressed criticism of the school, at the same time reproducing the discourses of the English language and American values being under threat:

> Thanks to the illegal invasion and the concept of "celebrate diversity," English is becoming a foreign language in America.
>
> The Pledge of Allegiance isn't a "salute" to America . . . It's a promise to be loyal to it. Part of that loyalty should be to learn English and integrating into our culture.

Others disagreed:

> This story has nothing to do with Islam just because the Pledge of Allegiance was said in Arabic, which is a language, not a religion.
>
> The school shouldn't have to apologize for anything. Arabic is a language, and shouldn't be affiliated with terrorists . . . just like how English shouldn't be affiliated with wealth. Did parents freak out when the pledge was done in French? This is absolutely ridiculous.[22]

[22] www.recordonline.com/article/20150318/NEWS/150319327, accessed September 29, 2015.

And just two years earlier, in February 2013, a similar decision to recite the Pledge in Arabic at Rocky Mountain High School in Colorado provoked a heated debate, including both angry and supportive tweets such as:

> Another reason to pull your kids out of public schools- Pledge of allegiance in Arabic? One Nation under Allah?
>
> Over my dead body, and I don't die easy. RT @VeronicaCoffin: Islam in Public Schools but Christianity is OUT?
>
> Pathetically Stupid Principal allows Arabic Pledge of Allegiance Recitation at Co HS-Pledge One Nation Under Allah.
>
> This is what America's all about! Proud of this school and their principal, Tom Lopez.
>
> One of my students lead the entire school in the pledge of allegiance today . . . in Arabic. I am damn proud of her.
>
> Somebody correct me if I'm wrong, but doesn't the Pledge say " . . . with liberty and justice for all?" So, it says that everyone has liberty, but not the liberty to speak another language?[23]

It is clear from these comments that the definition of American as monolingual in English and culturally Christian is not universally held, but rather there is a multiplicity of opposing discourses. At the same time, however, the fear of non-English languages on one hand, and of Islam on the other, creates a powerful discourse in which Arabic and its speakers are particularly vilified as un-American – or, even, anti-American. The anti-Muslim sentiment is another incarnation of earlier religious prejudices, which we saw in the example of the Catholic Irish and the non-Christian Chinese in the nineteenth century, and it has been successfully reinforced in political discourse by equating Islam with terrorism and the events of 9/11. Comments such as "Pledge of allegiance in Arabic? One Nation under Allah?" or "Islam in Public Schools but Christianity is OUT?" underscore the discursive conflation of the Arabic language and Muslim religion. As several comments pointed out, there had not been the same uproar over Spanish and French versions of the pledge. Arabic in particular has been, in recent years, iconized (Irvine and Gal 2000) as a threat to American values and nationhood. Another example of this fear of Arabic as the icon of anti-Americanism was the protest in Houston, Texas, over the opening of an Arabic immersion program in the Houston Independent School District in September 2015. Angry protesters stood outside the school on its opening morning holding signs with anti-Muslim slogans: for example, "Everything I needed to know about Islam I learned from Muslims on 9-11-2001."[24] Again, texts such as this one discursively identify the Arabic language with Islam, and Islam with terrorism. Meanwhile, the perception of Islam as fundamentally anti-American is common enough to have produced

[23] http://stream.aljazeera.com/story/201302010235–0022519, accessed May 11, 2016.

[24] http://thinkprogress.org/immigration/2015/08/24/3694686/hisd-arabic-immersion-program/, accessed September 29, 2015.

relatively widespread concern among conservative Americans that Barack Obama, the country's first African American president, may have been a Muslim. What is crucial in these accusations is not whether they were fabricated or not, but that a Muslim president is so completely inconceivable. In fact, even Obama himself accepted this frame when he defended himself by claiming a strong Christian faith in speeches dating as far back as 2008, as for example in Sumter, South Carolina, where he denied being a Muslim by forcefully claiming, "I've been a member of the same church for almost twenty years. Praying to Jesus. With my Bible."[25]

Islam, it seems, has become the newest most feared Other. President Donald Trump's anti-Muslim rhetoric, as well as his controversial executive order banning travel from predominantly Muslim countries, capitalizes on and perpetuates this fear. Significantly, "Islam" also becomes yet another code word for "non-white," since many Muslim immigrants and Muslim Americans come from ethnic minority backgrounds. It is therefore not surprising that the anti-Muslim attacks – much like the anti-Mexican ones – that have defined Trump's candidacy and presidency have been accompanied by the rise of white nationalism and have encouraged white supremacists to bring their message into the larger public arena.

2.3 Race in America

Race, as has by now been much discussed in academic work, is both a sociocultural construct and a lived experience (cf. e.g. Helms 1994; Gregory and Sanjek 1994; Wood 2003; Smedley and Smedley 2012). The first of these notions – that race is a sociocultural construct rather than a biological fact – implies that the ideas around race (e.g. who counts as white or how the hierarchy of races is arranged) can vary and shift by region, cultural context, and historical period; and that sociocultural practices, such a language use, can be racialized. It also means that socio-politically dominant groups – which in America means those of European descent – can construct and propagate a racially based hierarchy that on one hand is scientifically unsupportable, and on the other is invoked to justify oppression. The second notion, that race is a lived experience, implies that people are treated by others and thus experience the reality of their everyday lives in part through how others classify them according to their perceived physical characteristics. These classifications are made in reference to the contextually specific construct of race, namely, where the lines between black and white, or between white and non-white, are drawn. As Smedley and Smedley (2012) write, "race originated as the imposition of an arbitrary value system on the facts of biological (phenotypic) variations in the

[25] www.youtube.com/watch?v=gh69Zi2rV-U, accessed May 11, 2016.

human species" (20). Race as a scientific classification is meaningless – and, indeed, nonexistent – but it is meaningful as a social, political and cultural idea because of the ways in which it structures sociopolitical hierarchies and inequalities, and access to crucial resources such as economic and educational opportunities, the right to political representation, and fair treatment by the justice system. For these reasons, the lived experience of race is particularly relevant for the oppressed groups – in other words for those who are classified as non-white. And a shared history of sociopolitical oppression in turn reinforces a sense of common racial identity (Helms 1994: 296; Smedley and Smedley 2012: 17–20).

Throughout the history of the United States and the various waves of immigration, people who fit within the predominant paradigm of unmarked racial characteristics – specifically, whiteness – have found assimilation possible, or at least possible to claim. They have been able to authenticate themselves as Americans. For those outside the "white" sphere or those on its outskirts, however, performing or crossing into Americanness has been much more complicated, if not impossible. Their claim to American identity and allegiance to the United States is always up for questioning, always open to challenge. As Helms (1994) accurately points out, "since Whites are the dominant racial group, they can choose to expel from their ranks individuals who do not look White" (296) and continues, "Group-defining racial characteristics generally are selected by the dominant or sociopolitically powerful group. Thus, in the United States, White people specify the relevant racial traits and use themselves as the standard or comparison group" (297). These "relevant traits" include visible aspects of a person's appearance, such as skin color, hair texture, or facial features. Helms refers to these as "quasi-biological race," meaning that while the traits themselves are observed to exist, they are arranged into groups that are in fact extremely diverse and do not form coherent categories, and they reveal nothing about the rest of the person: their personality, morality, strength, or intelligence.

In America, however, race has been reified and reinforced as possibly the most visible and important aspect of social identity. Despite evidence to the contrary – for example, the shifting boundaries of who counts as white – Americans tend to believe in the existence and relevance of race. They also continue to reproduce, more or less explicitly, the long-standing racial hierarchies, in which whites are at the top and African Americans at the bottom (Helms 1994: 299), with the other races evaluated with respect to this dichotomy. Smedley and Smedley (2012) observe, "The strange, often contradictory, ways in which US courts have historically assigned, or not assigned, white identities to various immigrants is indicative of the arbitrariness of racial categorization and the hierarchical nature of *race*. 'Whiteness' has positive meanings in our culture; any change in the valorization of whiteness would clearly signify a change in the meaning of race" (Smedley and Smedley 2012:

xi). Accordingly, I will now turn to the idea of whiteness is America, and how it has been imposed and reinforced by European Americans.

Whiteness in America

As authors such as Smedley and Smedley (2012), Wood (2003), and Sanjek (1994) observe, the modern concept of race is a relatively new phenomenon. Wood, for example, points out that early in the days of the trans-Atlantic slave trade, the justification for enslaving a person was typically based in religion. Europeans, and in North America, the English in particular, enslaved African people – as well as Native Americans – because they were "heathen." It was only with time and because of complex sociopolitical and economic circumstances, that white Americans came to view themselves as "white," and successfully implemented the institution of racially defined and hereditary slavery. By the end of the seventeenth century, blacks were seen as justifiably enslaved based on their African heritage and phenotype, the words "*Negro*" and "*slave*" were used interchangeably,[26] slavery was a lifetime condition, and it was passed from mother to child (Wood 2003: 33).[27]

In keeping with these changes, we see the emergence of discourses linking race with personality traits, intellect, morality, and other characteristics. Soon, we see whiteness recognized as a category, elevated to a superior status, and linked with the most favorable attributes. Benjamin Franklin's 1751 piece that was briefly mentioned in the previous section includes the following paragraph:

> [T]he Number of purely white People in the World is proportionably very small. All Africa is black or tawny. Asia chiefly tawny. America (exclusive of the new Comers) wholly so. And in Europe, the Spaniards, Italians, French, Russians and Swedes, are generally of what we call a swarthy Complexion; as are the Germans also, the Saxons only excepted, who with the English, make the principal Body of White People on the Face of the Earth. I could wish their Numbers were increased. And while we are, as I may call it, Scouring our Planet, by clearing America of Woods, and so making this Side of our Globe reflect a brighter Light to the Eyes of Inhabitants in Mars or Venus, why should we in the Sight of Superior Beings, darken its People? why increase the Sons of Africa, by Planting them in America, where we have so fair an Opportunity, by excluding all Blacks and Tawneys, of increasing the lovely White and Red? But perhaps I am partial to the Complexion of my Country, for such Kind of Partiality is natural to Mankind.[28]

[26] As observed in 1680 by a Christian minister, Reverend Morgan Godwyn, cited in Wood (2003: 32).

[27] To be sure, the development of the concept of race in America occurred within the larger context of colonialism and European expansion, where a hierarchy of several racial categories began to be developed from the 1400s onwards (Sanjek 1994). I will return to this point a little further in this section.

[28] In his "Observations Concerning the Increase of Mankind, Peopling of Countries, etc.," available at www.historycarper.com/1751/09/01/observations-concerning-the-increase-of-mankind-peopling-of-countries-c/, accessed September 18, 2015.

Franklin's intense focus on skin color down to its various shades, and his assumption that white skin is both aesthetically superior and indexes a superiority of character, may seem unsettling to us today given Franklin's status as one of the Founding Fathers.[29] However, his views accurately reflect the dominant discourse of his time. The Naturalization Act of 1790 stipulated race as a determining qualification for citizenship, offering it only to free whites (Lee 1999: 107). And another revered American, Thomas Jefferson, wrote an extensive analysis of the "nature" of the "African Race" in his book *Notes on the State of Virginia*. Here are some excerpts from this text:

> The first difference [between whites and blacks] which strikes us is that of color . . . The difference is fixed in nature, and is as real as if its seat and cause were better known to us . . . Are not the fine mixtures of red and white, the expressions of every passion by greater or less suffusions of color in the one, preferable to that eternal monotony, which reigns in the countenances, that immoveable veil of black which covers all the emotions of the other race? . . .
>
> They are at least as brave, and more adventuresome. But this may perhaps proceed from a want of forethought, which prevents their seeing a danger till it be present. When present, they do not go through it with more coolness or steadiness than the whites. They are more ardent after their female: but love seems with them to be more an eager desire, than a tender delicate mixture of sentiment and sensation . . .
>
> Comparing them by their faculties of memory, reason, and imagination, it appears to me, that in memory they are equal to the whites; in reason much inferior, as I think one [black] could scarcely be found capable of tracing and comprehending the investigations of Euclid; and that in imagination they are dull, tasteless, and anomalous.[30]

Race in the eighteenth and nineteenth centuries was being constructed as a scientifically observable and objective phenomenon. An influential figure in these "scientific" studies was polygenist Samuel Morton, who relied on craniometry, which was believed to indicate brain size, to argue for the superiority of whites over other races. Typical divisions of humankind into racial groups resembled the one posited in 1795 by Johann Friedrich Blumenbach, which included Caucasian, Mongolian, Ethiopian, American, and Malayan races (Sanjek 1994: 5). As we saw in Section 1.1, language scholars supported these types of studies by arguing for the inferiority of non-European – and in the case of North America, Indigenous – languages, further cementing the construct of rigid racial divides. Polygenists typically believed that different

[29] It has to be noted that it is only the explicitness of this assertion by a national leader that may appear surprising. In reality, the perception of lighter skin as more beautiful, better, and associated with greater intelligence and grace, and of darker skin as less desirable, especially in women, persists today and is openly voiced by many. An informative discussion of this topic is offered in the 2011 documentary *Dark Girls*, directed by D. Channsin Berry and Bill Duke, and available on Netflix.

[30] www.historytools.org/sources/Jefferson-Race.pdf, accessed October 2, 2015. See also Franklin 1991 (in Helms 1994).

races were more akin to different species. Such ideas contributed to the fears of miscegenation, despite the fact that mixing among groups had been and continued to be a fact of life in the New World (Harvey 2015; Morales 2002; Anderson 2014). A logical next step was the infamous "one-drop rule" whereby "one-thirty-second of known African ancestry was considered sufficient to classify a person as Black" (Helms 1994: 296): from the perspective of scientific racism, even a minute amount of non-white blood would produce an inferior human being. This idea was echoed in the early twentieth century by eugenicist Madison Grant, author of *The Passing of the Great Race* and a fierce opponent of race mixing, who claimed that "the cross between any of the three European races and a Jew is a Jew" (cited in Sacks 1994: 81). In 1920, Grant's protégé, Lothrop Stoddard, published his own racist manifesto, *The Rising Tide of Color*, which argued that the white race was under threat of destruction primarily from the impact of immigration from Asia (R.G. Lee 1999: 136–139).

Scientific racism and eugenics were both embraced and promoted by affluent Protestant Americans of "old" immigrant heritage in the face of "new" immigration (Sacks 1994). Pseudo-scientific work was directed at producing evidence for distinctions and hierarchies among the imagined few "major" human races, but also within the white racial group. We saw examples of the discourse motivated by this racist thinking in Section 2.2. In fact, this discourse was so mainstream that politicians with otherwise opposing views, such as Roosevelt and Wilson, recognized and reproduced it. Kenneth Roberts, a staunch eugenicist, proclaimed, "The American nation was founded and developed by the Nordic race, but if a few more million members of the Alpine, Mediterranean and Semitic races are poured among us, the result must inevitably be a hybrid race of people as worthless and futile as the good-for-nothing mongrels of Central America and Southeastern Europe" (cited in Sacks 1994: 78; Carlson and Colburn 1972: 312). In thus dividing white or European people, Roberts follows Grant's "discovery" that "there were three or four major European races ranging from the superior Nordics of northwestern Europe to the inferior southern and eastern races of Alpines, Mediterraneans, and, worst of all, Jews" (Sacks 1994: 80). The pioneer of "intelligence testing," Robert Yerkes, was also a eugenicist who argued for immigration restriction based on the notion, supposedly "proved" by his tests, that Southeastern Europeans were "feeble-minded," much like African Americans and Native Americans: "For the past ten years or so the intellectual status of immigrants has been disquietingly low. Perhaps this is because of the dominance of the Mediterranean races, as contrasted with the Nordic and Alpine" (1923; cited in Sacks 1994: 81; Carlson and Colburn 1972: 333–334). It is not clear what precisely is meant in these statements by the "Alpine" race, but historically the term referred to an imagined subgroup of Caucasians located around Central and Southeastern

Europe. As such, it may have included the French and Northern Italians, and while Grant considered Alpines to be inferior to Nordics, Yerkes groups these two together as superior to Mediterraneans. The dominant view in the 1920s and 1930s was, as Sacks (1994) aptly puts it, "that real Americans were white and real whites came from northwest Europe" (81). As one of many examples, Stave (2010) reports that at the end of the 1930s, in response to the arrival of large groups of Jewish, Italian, and Eastern European immigrants, residents of New Haven, Connecticut, expressed views such as "this is a white man's country, and God willing, it will continue to be" (Stave 2010: 205).

Later, when eugenics and discrimination among the European "races" fell out of favor after World War II, the previously maligned "inferior" races were gradually accepted into the fold of whiteness. Sacks (1994) describes how a combination of the post-war turn away from open anti-Semitism and anti-European racism, the stimulus provided by the GI Bill of Rights, and the mushrooming suburbanization of mainstream American life contributed to the ascendancy of Jewish, Southern European, and Eastern European Americans into the white middle class. To be sure, anti-Semitism did not disappear in America, but it was no longer built into mainstream public discourse or justified on the basis of eugenics. Instead, Jews, along with Poles, Italians, Greeks, Portuguese, and other Euroethnics (Sacks 1994: 86–87) secured home mortgages, moved into the suburbs, sent their children to college, and became another "kind of white folks" (78) in addition to the WASP prototype. However, the same measures that helped expand whiteness to include previously disqualified groups also reinforced the strict separation between whites and non-whites. African Americans, in particular, were targeted: builders of new suburban developments refused to sell to them, and the FHA (Federal Housing Association) "underwriting manuals openly insisted on racially homogenous neighborhoods, and their loans were made only in white neighborhoods" (Sacks 1994: 94; see also Wilkerson 2011).

As the above discussion illustrates, the boundary between whiteness and non-whiteness is a shifting one, with some previously shunned groups being allowed in, while the more noticeably different-looking and culturally distinct groups continue to be kept out, or when new groups appear and become a challenge. With time, certain "less white" groups – for example Franklin's Swedes and Germans, whom he describes as "swarthy" – came to be permanently included in the definition of whiteness. Indeed, Franklin's description of whiteness would most definitely exclude a large percentage of people who today identify as Caucasian or European American. Furthermore, some of the groups that Franklin excludes – such as Swedes and Germans – became, in later times, the very paragon of the desirable immigrant of the past, juxtaposed with the undesirable and not-quite-white Irish, Poles, or Italians. And in time, once the descendants of the Irish, the Slavs, and the Southern

Europeans Americanized, they in turn became the immigrant ideal: the kind of immigrant who, by virtue of skin color, features, and shared cultural reference points (e.g. the Judeo-Christian and Greco-Roman traditions), are likely to assimilate successfully to Anglo-Saxon, Protestant "native" Americans – in contrast to the much more clearly non-white Latinos, Africans, and Asians.

Americans of Color

In 1923, an immigrant from India, in *US* v. *Bhagat Singh Thind*, argued that he should qualify for naturalization under the 1790 Naturalization Act that made US citizenship available to "free white persons" (later amended to include "persons of African nativity and descent"; Lee 1999: 108), on the basis that since Indians belonged to the Aryan/Caucasian group, they were therefore white (Sacks 1994: 81). The Supreme Court ruled against Thind, stating:

> [The words "free white persons"] imply as we have said, a racial test; but the term "race" is one which, for the practical purposes of the statute, must be applied to a group of living persons *now* possessing in common the requisite characteristics, not to groups of persons who are supposed to be or really are descended from some remote, common ancestor, but who, whether they both resemble him to a greater or less extend, have, at any rate, ceased altogether to resemble one another. It may be true that the blond Scandinavian and the brown Hindu have a common ancestor in the dim reaches of antiquity, but the average man knows perfectly well that there are unmistakable and profound differences between them today.[31]

Interestingly, the court conceded that "The various authorities are in irreconcilable disagreement as to what constitutes a proper racial division ... The explanation probably is that 'the innumerable varieties of mankind run into one another by insensible degrees,' and to arrange them in sharply bounded divisions is an undertaking of such uncertainty that common agreement is practically impossible."[32] Nonetheless, the court also made it clear that there exists a category of "free white persons" as intended by the Founding Fathers and as can be "interpreted in accordance with the understanding of the common man."[33] Furthermore, referring to the common origins of Indo-European – and thus also Northern Indian – languages, the court argues, "Our own history has witnessed the adoption of the English tongue by millions of Negroes, whose descendants can never be classified racially with the descendants of white persons notwithstanding both may speak a common root language."

[31] http://historymatters.gmu.edu/d/5076/, accessed October 6, 2015.
[32] http://historymatters.gmu.edu/d/5076/, accessed October 6, 2015.
[33] http://historymatters.gmu.edu/d/5076/, accessed October 6, 2015.

Admittedly, the justices avoided any reference to intrinsic characteristics of different races or their hierarchies, and even admitted that Thind as an individual met the qualifications for naturalization; rather, they argued that racial distinctions are real, and that Asian immigrants, regardless of their character, are not eligible to become American citizens because they are not white in the popular understanding of this term. It would be naive, however, to assume that the court decision's wording meant that despite the racist naturalization policy, white Americans viewed Asians as equals. The opposite was quite clearly the case. The *US* v. *Bhagat Singh Thind* decision reinforced the notion that the most significant racial distinction in America is that between whites and non-whites. Smedley and Smedley (2012) point out that a unique feature of the American race system is its binary opposition between whites and blacks. Although as we have seen, the discourse on race recognizes and evaluates many shades and gradations of people's skin color and other physical features, conceptually there is no category for someone of a multiracial background as there is, for example, in South American countries or in South Africa (Smedley and Smedley 2012). This is reflected in legal and official terminology, for example on census questionnaires or various other forms where a person must declare themselves as one of a set of possible racial designations. And although these designations typically include categories such as Hispanic or Latino/a, Asian American, Pacific Islander, Native American, and even "Other," the most significant opposition that has structured the conversation about race in the United States is that between whites and blacks. The other groups have usually been constructed in relation to these two oppositional categories and variously located in the space between them. Moreover, one unchanging aspect of the American race system is that one cannot be both white and black, and that whites are at the top and blacks at the bottom of the racial hierarchy (Smedley and Smedley 2012; Sanjek 1994; Helms 1994; Dick 2011a).

The American race system developed in the context of European expansion in the "age of discovery" and colonization (Sanjek 1994). This global construction of races and racial hierarchies always placed Europeans at the top. When Willey (1909) compares the "Northern problem" of "new" immigration to the South's post-slavery relations between African Americans and whites, and to the West coast's problem of "the little brown man," he establishes a relational system in which African Americans, Asians, and Southeastern Europeans all present a "problem" for the "real" American: the white man, descended from inhabitants of Northwestern Europe. Similarly, as we saw in Section 1.1, Indigenous Americans were, soon after the initial encounter, constructed as racially inferior on the basis of their language structure, among other "evidence."

Asian immigrants and Asian Americans have been positioned at various points between white and black. George Washington, for example, while he was a slave owner and while the 1790 Naturalization Act was passed during his presidency, reportedly expressed surprise that Chinese were not "white" (Lee 1999: 107; Miller 1969). And the first significant encounter between white Americans and Chinese immigrants took place in mid-nineteenth century California. Consequently, Asians were not one of the groups targeted by early racist legislation in the United States, and their status was unclear. According to Robert G. Lee's (1999) *Orientals: Asian Americans in Popular Culture*, the treatment of Asian immigrants applying for naturalization between the 1850s and early twentieth century was marked by inconsistency, with policies differing by state and by the nationality of the applicants (107). But Asians were also, simultaneously, fetishized as the feared (when male) yet desired (when female) "Orientals." Lee argues that since the first Chinese arrived in California, Asians have been racialized as "Orientals" in mainstream American discourse, expressed especially clearly in yellowface representations that emphasize specific features "such as 'slanted' eyes, overbite, and mustard-yellow skin color" (2). Lee emphasizes that "Only the racialized Oriental is yellow; Asians are not. Asia is not a biological fact but a geographic destination" (2).

According to Lee, the racialization of Asians and Asian Americans as "Orientals" found its earliest expression in popular culture including the use of yellowface and popular songs or ballads published widely in the nineteenth century. These songs were important for the construction of solidarity and common identity because they were sung at gatherings rather than simply heard as performance by others (Lee 1999: 17). They were an embodied practice, and the stories told in them reflected and constructed a shared narrative. And a number of them published between 1855 and 1882 focused on "the Chinese immigrant as an agent of economic decline and social disorder for free white workingmen and their families" (17). Over time, six distinct images of the racialized Oriental have shaped the mainstream American perception of Asians as aliens: "the pollutant, the coolie, the deviant, the yellow peril, the model minority, and the gook" (8). Lee's book is structured around the detailed analyses of these six images in American popular culture and mainstream discourse.

Lee argues that California in the 1850s was imagined as "a place sufficiently distant to destabilize personal histories, a space for rehabilitation if not redemption . . . a place where a lost American organic community could be reconstructed" (15). California was even represented as yet another incarnation of the City on the Hill (18; see Chapter 1). The Chinese quickly came to be seen as a serious threat to this idealized version of California life. As the California gold rush attracted merchants and immigrants, San Francisco became a major center of international trade, on route between Asia and the East Coast, as well as of immigration both from the American Northeast, and from Europe,

Latin America, and Asia (23). In 1860, half of all San Franciscans were born abroad, as compared with 10 percent of all Americans (23). California was the site of the first encounter among white Anglo-Americans from the States, white immigrants from Europe, Asians – particularly the Chinese – and groups today classified as Latinos. The Chinese and Latin Americans were quickly identified as racially non-white. Of these, the Chinese appeared especially foreign and were thoroughly otherized. In addition, the Chinese were not Christian, and their religious practices were categorized as "heathen" (Jorae 2009).

Given the world order in which Europeans were the colonizers, a global race system where whiteness ranked at the top of the racial hierarchy that the Europeans invented and imposed, and the naturalized racist perspectives and beliefs consequently held by both white Americans and European immigrants who arrived in California, the Chinese – and later other Asians – were readily constructed as representatives of the inferior "yellow" or "brown" race. In 1854, the California Supreme Court ruled that Chinese witnesses were prohibited from testifying in cases involving a white person, on the grounds that the Chinese belonged to a "race of people whom nature has marked as inferior, and who are incapable of progress or intellectual development beyond a certain point" (cited in Knapp 1997: 747–748).

The exoticization of the Chinese in nineteenth century California, much of which centered, as discussed in Section 2.2, on their alleged deviant and morally deficient nature, ultimately contributed to the construction of Asians as a racial threat to white Americans. In Lee's (1999) terms, Asians were racialized as potential pollutants. The anxiety over the potential effects of "Oriental" contamination manifested itself in the anti-miscegenation law passed in California in 1880, which prohibited the marriage of a white person with a "Negro, Mulatto, or Mongolian" (Jorae 2009: 44). In lobbying Congress for the continuation of the Chinese Exclusion Act of 1882, Californians wrote, "It is well established that the issue of the Caucasian and the Mongolian do not possess the virtues of either, but develop the vices of both" (cited in Jorae 2009: 45). Chinese Americans would thus always be kept apart, and consequently would never assimilate. Although those born in the United States were American citizens, Asians were barred from naturalization until 1952, when racial and ethnic restrictions on naturalization were removed in the McCarran-Walter Act (Wright 2008: 98).

Asian Americans' responses to the prejudice against them included efforts at successful assimilation, thereby aligning themselves with white Americans and against those long defined as not "white persons," that is, African Americans. We saw an example of this in Section 2.1, in Chinese immigrant Mary Tape's argument that her daughter should be allowed to enroll in regular public school because the family was Americanized and did not follow Chinese customs. Similarly, in 1922 – just one year before *US* v. *Bhagat Singh Thind* – another case regarding Asians and US citizenship, *Takao Ozawa* v. *US*, was built around Ozawa's claims to Americanization. Ozawa had arrived in the US as a teenager, and twenty-eight years later he was being denied citizenship because he was deemed not white. In his own brief documenting his assimilation, Ozawa wrote:

> In name I am not an American, but at heart I am a true American . . . I do not have any connection with any Japanese churches or schools . . . I am sending my children to an American church and American school in place of a Japanese one . . . Most of the time I use the American (English) language at home, so that my children cannot speak the Japanese language . . . I chose as my wife one educated in American schools (cited in Lee 1999: 141).

The Supreme Court ruled against Ozawa, claiming that his degree of assimilation was irrelevant because he, like Thind, did not represent "a person of what is popularly known as the Caucasian race,"[34] citing as reference a number of federal and state court decisions to the same effect. Asians continued to be classified as "of a race which is not Caucasian and therefore belongs entirely outside the zone [of eligibility for naturalization] on the negative side"[35] even as many of them continued to make efforts to assimilate and avoid being targets of discrimination. With World War II came a change to the US immigration policy: fighting against Nazi Germany made it difficult to justify discrimination based on supposedly biological or genetic race. However, the race discourse shifted instead to focus on cultural rather than genetic differences (Lee 1999). As racial barriers to citizenship were lifted in legislation, Asian Americans were constructed as, and encouraged to live up to, the "paragon of ethnic virtue" (Lee 1999: 145). The wartime rounding up and internment of Japanese Americans could be framed in political and cultural rather than genetically racial terms, and, importantly, it also served as a warning to Asian Americans more generally of the potential consequences of not cooperating with white Americans' expectations of them.[36]

The "model minority" construct in which Asian Americans are the exemplary minority group because they readily and successfully assimilate presumes and expects Asian Americans' participation in reproducing the American race structure. As Lee (1999) explains, this representation extols virtues of "stoic patience, political obedience, and self-improvement," and when it began to form at the outset of the Cold War, it became "a critically important narrative of ethnic liberalism that simultaneously promoted racial equality and sought to

[34] http://caselaw.findlaw.com/us-supreme-court/260/178.html, accessed October 23, 2015.

[35] http://caselaw.findlaw.com/us-supreme-court/260/178.html, accessed October 23, 2015.

[36] Lee (1999: 151–153) discusses this issue at some length, pointing for example to the risks faced by noncompliant Asians of being identified as communists and deported. Such course of action was legislated in the 1950 Emergency Detention Act, which was passed when the Korean War broke out.

contain demands for social transformation" (145). Significantly, when it "emerged explicitly during the civil rights movement in the 1960s" (Reyes 2009: 44), the model minority image was held up as an example of self-reliance and self-improvement to other minority groups, most notably African Americans. It served to support the doctrine of a "colorblind" society in which everyone was meant to be judged on their merit while the state did not have to be involved in assisting disadvantaged groups (Lee 1999: 160). Crucially, of course, the norms used to measure performance in the "color-blind" society continued to be dictated by whites. As Reyes (2009) aptly points out, "the model minority myth upholds the American ideologies of meritocracy and individualism, diverts attention away from racial inequality, sustains whites in the racial hierarchy, and pits minority groups against one another" (44).

Not all Asians, however, are as readily included in the model minority or, one could say, "close enough to white" category. Southeast Asian Americans, for example, are often positioned "as problematic immigrants who are dependent on government assistance and are the sources of an array of social ills" (Bucholtz 2009: 22; see also Song et al. 1992). Bucholtz argues that the US racial discourse constructs a two-tiered hierarchy of Asian Americans, with "honorary whiteness" (Tuan 1999) conferred on middle-class, mostly East and South Asians, while working-class Southeast Asians are stigmatized with negative racial profiling (Bucholtz 2009: 22). Southeast Asian American youth are forced to situate themselves on the racial map of the United States in relation on one hand to whiteness and blackness, and on the other to the Asian model minority stereotype and expectations. Many, as for example in Lee's (1994) study of high school students, choose to identify in opposition to the model minority image. Lee reports that in contrast to the Korean student group, who identified as Korean rather than Asian and looked to educational success to secure their future, Southeast Asians who formed the group of "new wave Asians" rejected school success and in doing so subverted the Asian nerd and model minority stereotypes. Regardless of their intelligence and abilities, they did the bare minimum of work in order to pass their classes, and oriented away from school-centered social structures and towards independent peer networks (cf. Eckert 1989; Willis 1977).

Bucholtz points out that Asian Americans are evaluated in terms of their approximation to whiteness or to blackness: for example the high school girls in her research in California were routinely described in terms of how "white" or "black" they acted (Bucholtz 2009: 27; See Section 3.2). And in mainstream American discourses, East Asians such as the Chinese, Japanese, and Koreans, are perceived as relatively close to whites compared with Southeast Asians, such as the Vietnamese or Filipino, who are more often grouped with African

Americans. In terms of the model minority stereotype, East Asians are praised for assimilating "successfully" because they are seen as assimilating to American white culture. Associated mainly with East Asians, the "model minority" image portrays an "ethnic" group successfully "whitening" (Tuan 1999: 31). Southeast Asians, however, are perceived as failing to do this, and so they continue to be seen as visible ethnics. Looking thus to situate themselves on the racial map in the US, Southeast Asian youth often identify and affiliate themselves with American black culture (see also Section 3.2). This also constitutes assimilation, but such assimilation is erased in dominant discourses that are built around the idea that African Americans themselves ought to assimilate to mainstream, white-dominated cultural norms, values and practices. Lee (1999) argues that "[t]he elevation of Asian Americans to the position of model minority had less to do with the actual success of Asian Americans than [with] the perceived failure – worse, refusal – of African Americans to assimilate" (145). From the perspective of white America, Southeast Asians affiliating themselves with African American culture are rejecting assimilation.

While the model minority stereotype emphasizes assimilation, however, it is accompanied by the contradictory image of the "perpetual foreigner." Asian Americans are on one hand expected to shed as much of their "color" as possible in order to affirm their model minority status, and on the other are constantly reminded that their claim to Americanness is always open to challenge. Although, according to Tuan (1999), some "even argue that [Asian Americans] may be undergoing 'whitening' processes similar to those experienced by southern, central, and eastern European immigrants earlier in the [twentieth] century," thus "earn[ing] Asian-Americans the curious designation of 'honorary whites'" (31), at the beginning of the twenty-first century it appears very clear that in popular mainstream discourse, the racial category of whiteness does not include Asian Americans. The "perpetual foreigner" construct keeps their integration in check, so to speak. They remain racialized and Orientalized as non-white Others, a point that comedian Margaret Cho invokes in her stand-up routine when she describes a TV network's manager asking her to address the audience "in [her] native language," to which she responds by speaking in native-speaker, mainstream US English (MUSE), thus denaturalizing the identification of Asians as foreigners who speak English as a second language. We will return to the image of the Asian "perpetual foreigner" in Chapter 4, where I discuss discourses surrounding foreign accents.

Through the model minority myth, East Asian and South Asian youth come to be associated with scholastic aptitude and social awkwardness, as evidenced in the stereotype of the East or South Asian nerd who is either very quiet or oblivious to social "coolness," but is always extremely gifted at math and science, as for example the character of Ravi Ross in the Disney Channel's show *Jessie*. Paradoxically, the model minority myth has also had the effect of side-lining Asian Americans in discussions of race in the United States (Takagi 1994: 232), thus further perpetuating the issue of race as that between whites and blacks. Takagi (1994) points out that the "squeaky-clean image of Asian Americans as good minorities led to their being dropped from most university affirmative action programs during the 1970s" (232), which would have adversely impacted the "lower tier" of Asian Americans – namely the Southeast Asians – discussed by Bucholtz (2009).

The above discussion illustrates that, with whiteness firmly maintained at the top of the racial hierarchy in the United States, Asians of various backgrounds have been accepted as "honorary whites" provided that they, as Takagi (1994) puts it, succeeded in "outwhiting whites" (232). Southeast Asians, however, have often been grouped with other "problem minorities." In addition, some groups have been racialized as non-white because of adherence to practices that mark them not just as different from, but a potential threat to, the dominant understanding of Americanness. Sikhs, despite being ethnically South Asian, practice their religion in embodied, outwardly visible ways. As I discuss further in Section 3.2, Sikh men in turbans and with naturally growing facial hair tend to arouse suspicion because of their resemblance to the prototypical image of the terrorist, especially after 9/11. Insisting on maintaining a cultural practice that positions them in this way can be read as defiance in the face of mainstream American norms, and as rejection of assimilation.

Similarly, Muslim Americans are, since 9/11, a group that has been subjected to what Sirin and Fine (2008) call "a forced *ethnogenesis*, or creating one people out of many" (59, emphasis original). Sirin and Fine argue that American identity has been constructed on a "foundation of exclusions," starting with the specification of "whiteness" as the prerequisite for citizenship in the 1790 Naturalization Act (59). They see Muslim Americans as the most recent in a series of groups to be excluded from the national body of "true" Americans. Muslims in America are homogenized, reduced to the most extreme interpretations of their religion, and depicted as a threat not just to American culture, but to America's very existence. Adherents of Islam include Arabs, Iranians, South Asians, Southeast Asians, Africans, and Europeans. Given this great diversity, it seems impossible to consider Muslims as a racial group given the prevailing emphasis on physical features in American race discourse. Yet, most Muslims are marked as Other in America, and are not accepted as white. The stereotypical Muslim is envisioned as dark-haired and brown-skinned, is identified as Middle Eastern, and little distinction is made between significant regional differences such as between Arabs and Iranians, or within the Arab group itself. Section 3.2 takes a closer look at Muslim American identity.

The process of ethnogenesis as discussed by Sirin and Fine (2008) in reference to Muslim Americans applies also to Latinos in the United States. The widespread use of the terms "Hispanic" and "Latino/a" – as, for example, in discussions of presidential candidates appealing to "Hispanic voters" – gives the impression that these terms refer to specific, clearly defined categories that share a number of significant characteristics. But if there is one common feature to people commonly described as Hispanic/Latino, it is their ethnic, cultural, national, and linguistic diversity. I will return to this diversity in Section 2.4.

According to Morales (2002), "Latino – derived from Latin America, originally coined by Napoleon-era France as a public relations ploy to explain why a French emperor was installed in Mexico City – was a mid-'70s incarnation of the term meant to allude to a separate identity from Spain" (2). Morales also claims that the term "Hispanic" was invented by the Nixon administration and "designed to allow the lighter-skinned to claim a European heritage" (2). Meanwhile, sociologist G. Cristina Mora (2014) argues that the term "Hispanic" was popularized in the 1970s by grassroots activists, Spanish-language broadcasters, and federal officials. Mora points out that previously, the US Census Bureau classified Latin Americans – and specifically, Mexicans, Cubans, and Puerto Ricans – as white/Caucasian, listing their specific national origins. After 1980, the Census included the supposedly inclusive category "Hispanic," which, however, does not extend to Portuguese-speaking Brazilians.

The annexation of large areas of Mexico and Texas, which I discussed at some length in Section 1.2, placed Mexican Americans in a racially ambiguous category. As Chavez (2008) explains, "The 'whiteness' of Mexicans was a legal definition that was a by-product of Mexico's signing of the Treaty of Guadalupe Hidalgo at the end of the U.S.-Mexican War. Mexicans living in what was now U.S. Territory were allowed to become U.S. Citizens, a privilege reserved for 'white' immigrants at the time. Despite such legal definitions, Mexicans were still considered 'not-white' in the public imagination" (24). While Mexicans who had been "crossed by the border" were accepted as Americans citizens, at least officially, Mexican immigrants in the early twentieth century began to be constructed as "illegal aliens," and, according to Chavez (2008), were thus "legally racialized" (24). This construct of the "illegal alien" has by now been extended to all Latinos, who are imagined according to a set of homogenizing stereotypes. These are built around the themes of criminality, drug trafficking, menial jobs in cleaning, construction, and farm work, refusal to assimilate culturally or linguistically, the "encroachment" of Spanish on English-speaking America, an out-of-control Latina sexuality and fertility (Chavez 2008), and culturally reductive images of tacos, sombreros, mustaches, and piñatas.

Chavez emphasizes that Latinos are a *racialized* group because they do not represent any ethnically unified category, but rather are socioculturally constructed as such based on perceived characteristics imbued with social meaning. This, as I have sought to demonstrate in this section, is the case with all racial categories. Latinos, however, are, as a group, both highly diverse and representing a mixing of other racialized categories, namely Caucasians, Africans, and American Indians. Smedley and Smedley (2012) point out that in Latin America, there has historically existed a range of official and conceptual categories classifying one's racial background. In colonial Mexico, for example, the various categories included mestizo (child of a Spaniard and an Indian), *castizo* (child of a Mestizo man and a Spanish woman), mulatto (child of a Spanish woman and an African slave), *morisco* (child of a Spaniard and a mulatto woman), *albino* (child of a morisco woman and a Spaniard); in addition, it was also possible to "raise" one's racial status by appropriate mixing: the child of a castizo woman and a Spaniard was seen as a Spaniard, as was the child of a Spaniard and an albino woman (Vigil 2012: 105).

In the United States, however, such fine distinctions have not been prominent, although they existed and were even included in nineteenth century censuses (Leeman 2004). While lighter skin has been typically granted higher social status because of its proximity to whiteness, the two dominant racial categories have always been white and black. As discussed above, Native Americans were placed on the spectrum somewhere between the two, but were definitely not considered white. Meanwhile, the Mexicans who were granted US citizenship as a result of the US-Mexican War were largely descendants of people who had occupied and settled in the "Spanish borderlands," spanning present-day New Mexico, Texas, California, and Arizona, and who included representatives of all the mixed-race types that Spanish colonialism produced. As an example, "the pueblo of Los Angeles, known then as the Indian community of Yang-na, was settled in 1776 by two Spaniards, one mestizo, two Africans, eight mulattos, and nine Indians from Mexico" (Vigil 2012: 87). Similar mixing took place elsewhere in Latin America, resulting in what has been referred to as *mestizaje*: a complex racial, ethnic, linguistic, and cultural mixing that is characterized by diversity rather than homogeneity (see also Section 5.3). The umbrella-term "Latino/a," however, erases this rich diversity by implying a unity, while at the same time constructing the image of Latin American immigrants as distinct from whites. The term "Hispanic," meanwhile, racializes also the language associated with this group of immigrants, namely Spanish – despite the fact that while a large proportion of Latin American immigrants are Spanish speakers, many also speak other languages, including Portuguese, French, Indigenous languages such as Maya, Quechua, and Aimara, and a number of Spanish, French, and English-lexifier creoles. Some Indigenous

Mexican immigrants, in fact, either do not speak Spanish at all or have a limited knowledge of it as a second language. Some only begin to learn Spanish post-migration, in the Latino communities in the United States.

Racialized Language

When Spanish is used in the United States outside the context of a Spanish class in school, it is consistently constructed as both a symbolic and actual threat to American identity. Symbolically, Spanish represents the prototype of the "illegal alien," who is usually envisioned as a homogenized, racialized Latino, and in popular discourse often conflated with the ethnic label "Mexican." Spanish is also represented as an actual threat by those who see the English language as inherently linked with Americanness. At the same time, "Spanish holds a unique role in the United States that places it nearer to an indigenous language than to an immigrant language . . . Spanish was spoken in about one-third of what would become the United States long before the Pilgrims arrived on its eastern shores" (Gándara et al. 2010: 21). Spanish, therefore, comes to be seen as a threat since it can be linked with the feared prospect of *reconquista*, of a reclaiming of the Chicano homeland of Aztlan (See Section 1.2; Anzaldúa 2012). And unlike Native American languages, Spanish is not disappearing from the American linguistic landscape any time soon.

In a society like the United States in which race is a highly salient category, language becomes readily racialized along with other sociocultural practices. Thus in America, "unaccented" English – which is to say, Mainstream US English (MUSE) that is loosely based on the speech of white, middle-class Midwesterners (Lippi-Green 2012) – comes to represent whiteness, and becomes the prerequisite for educational and professional success. Fought (2006) points out that "ideologies concerning the social correlates of being white that we find in the discourse of societies like the USA follow directly from the dominant social position of white speakers" (115). Consequently white speech is associated with using features such as standard (MUSE) or superstandard grammatical forms and sophisticated vocabulary (Fought 2006; Lippi-Green 2012). These, in turn, are bound up with other sociocultural correlates, such as a higher education level, but also a certain lack of "coolness" or an ethnic "invisibility" (for a more detailed discussion of this, see Fought 2006).

Whiteness in America is also the default, unmarked category. Bucholtz and Hall (2004: 372–373), in discussing the relationship between power and markedness, argue that powerful identities often acquire an unmarked status through the operation of supralocal as well as local ideologies. Unmarked categories come to represent the norm, while markedness indexes deviation from this norm. And, as Bucholtz and Hall emphasize, "[w]hen one category is elevated as an unmarked norm, its power is more pervasive because it is masked" (372).

Unmarked identities are associated with unmarked language, while linguistic forms used by marked groups are racialized, ethnicized, or otherwise singled out as deviant (e.g. "having an accent," "sounding gay," "speaking street slang," "sounding black," etc.). In the American immigrant context, groups that gradually became accepted as white also witnessed their sociocultural practices included in a broader conceptualization of mainstream, unmarked Americanness. In this way, the Irish and Italians were once excluded from whiteness, and their Catholic religion was viewed with suspicion and even hatred. As I discussed in the previous section, in the case of the Irish, their ethnicity or "race" and their Catholicism were closely interwoven in the discourses that produced anti-Irish feeling. But with time, these groups were recognized as legitimately white, and Catholicism has also become an acceptably American religion. Judaism has also been included in the greater set of legitimate American religions, as evidenced for example by the ubiquity of "Happy Hanukkah" greeting cards and other visible cultural symbols that appear in major shopping outlets at winter holidays' time alongside Christmas trees. And one can argue that the speech characteristics of these "newly white" groups are also recognized as white. New York Jewish or Italian American accents are certainly not unmarked. They are stigmatized, otherized, and exploited for the purposes of entertainment as in, for example, the numerous mafia-themed films. They are not, however, identified as non-white, or non-American. Catholicism and Judaism are also somewhat marked when compared with Protestantism, but have been firmly established as American, in contrast to Islam or Sikhism.

The fact that the practices, norms, and values associated with whites in America become the unmarked default that other groups are compared to produces what anthropologist Jane Hill (2001) refers to as "white public space." White speakers tend to feel entitled to appropriate linguistic forms of other groups, sometimes to claim affiliation with them (Cutler 1999; Bucholtz 1999), and sometimes to produce a humorous effect while simultaneously disparagingly stereotyping non-whites, as in the case of Mock Spanish (Hill 2001). As Hill argues, white speakers, because of their dominant social position and resultant claim to norm-setting, are able to engage in such appropriations without risking their privileged status. White Americans can speak Spanish with a strong American English accent and even distort its forms – as in, for example, *no problemo* – without repercussions for their status in American society, but Latino speakers risk negative cultural stereotyping and serious socioeconomic disadvantages when they speak English with a Chicano, Puerto Rican, or other Hispanic accent (see Chapter 4).

Immigrants arriving in the United States are inevitably evaluated against the American racial hierarchy, as are their children and descendants. They in turn need to respond to the way they are read as racialized subjects. While seeking groups that they both wish to belong to, and feel will accept them, they begin their identity-making work, employing resources such as orientation towards educational performance, musical and other stylistic preferences, attitudes towards official authority, orientation towards heritage norms, values, and traditions, and – crucially – linguistic practices. And not surprisingly, they do not all choose to align with American whiteness. For some, it is socially more advantageous and personally more meaningful to affiliate with non-white groups (Mendoza-Denton 2008; Chun 2001; Lee 1994). Although MUSE is accorded higher status as the unmarked language variety in mainstream American society, Bucholtz and Hall (2004) point out that at the local level, "unmarked identities may be reproduced as well as challenged and reinscribed with identity markings" (372). Over time, these localized alternative readings of unmarked identities can spread across communities and become widely recognized as challengers to the dominant identity discourses, so that "sounding white" can be deemed socially undesirable in various communities and contexts (Fought 2006: 119–121). Minority immigrants, and youth in particular, face the challenge of navigating this American landscape of racialized identities that is not an issue for their white peers.

2.4 Similarity and Distinction within Immigrant Communities

By inventing, adopting, and propagating terms such as Hispanic, Latino/a, and Asian American, white Americans participate in and reproduce mainstream discourses that otherize and racialize immigrant communities, simultaneously homogenizing very complex and diverse groups. Similarities among Asians or Latin Americans are emphasized, while distinctions within these groups are erased (Bucholtz and Hall 2004). Often, as we have already seen in this chapter and will return to again, these mainstream discourses treat these imagined racial groupings reductively and essentialistically, and evaluate them against the American (white) norm. Upon first arriving in the United States, immigrants may be unfamiliar with and bemused by American racial categories, as well as their own apparent positioning within these. Those coming from European countries encounter a completely new understanding of whiteness, and have to choose which kind of American "white person" they will seek to align with, assuming that they have the cultural and linguistic resources to do so. Those who arrive in the US and find themselves racialized as non-white have to respond to their placement in a category – such as Hispanic, Latino, or Asian American – that they do not necessarily understand or identify with. In this way, being a "Latina" or an "Asian American," despite its newness to the immigrant who might instead see him or herself as Mexican, Mayan, Cuban, Argentinian, Korean, or Filipina, becomes his or her lived experience.

At the same time, however, immigrants resist these homogenizing classifications, and draw alternative boundaries of similarity and distinction that may be based on the ones brought along from their regions of origin, or may arise locally in America in response to pressures relevant to specific immigrant groups. The ideologies that inform these alignments may be completely unrelated to ones that are relevant in racial and ethnic discourses in the United States, but highly relevant to the immigrants themselves.

American Catholics

The tensions, contestations, and animosities within the Catholic community at the turn of the twentieth century provide an instructive example of these processes. As discussed earlier in the chapter, the Irish arrived in the United States in the nineteenth century in unprecedented numbers, only to encounter rejection on the basis of both "race" and religion. Catholicism was seen as superstition and enslavement. When Polish immigrants began to arrive in large numbers in the late nineteenth century, like other immigrant groups, they settled in groups of kin and friends, often from the same place in the home country (Panek 1898; Brożek 1972; Dziembowska 1977a and 1977b). Once they had a viable Polish community, Poles recruited a Polish priest and soon they built a local Polish church, even if there already was an Irish or German Catholic church in the area. Polish priest, the Reverend Wacław Kruszka, in his extensive work on Polish Americans published in 1905, devotes many pages to describing the central role of churches in Polish American life. Another early author, P. Panek, published an account titled *Polish Immigrants in the United States of North America* in 1898, having returned from spending five years among Polish American communities in Chicago, Detroit, Buffalo, Cleveland, Boston, New York, Philadelphia, and the mining areas of Pennsylvania. He points out that the farmers who emigrated from the impoverished Polish countryside had been used to a village life that was rich both socially and religiously. In America, settling together and establishing a Polish church provided the familiar comfort of sermons and confession in their own language, and of regional traditions such as the Polish food-blessing ceremony at Easter (see also Platt 1977; Jozefski 2008). It also provided the logical center for community life to the deeply religious Poles. Immigrants whose memoirs were collected in the interwar period and published later by Dziembowska (1977a and 1977b) expressed similar sentiments.

Poles gave their hard-earned money towards the building of Polish churches and supporting them not only in order to have an ethnolinguistic community, but also because they felt unrepresented in the existing

American Catholic church hierarchy. One would perhaps expect that, given the commonality of their Catholic religion and the antagonistic attitude towards Catholicism on part of "native" Protestant Americans, Catholic immigrants would stick together and support each other. However, the opposite was very often true. Polish immigrants resented the dominance of Irish American and German American clergy in positions of influence – as bishops and other high officials in the diocese. Crucially, by this point the Germans and the Irish had already been accepted as white Americans, whereas the Slavs – along with Southern Europeans and Jews – were the new otherized and excluded groups. Poles were routinely kept from advancing in the church hierarchy, and Polish Catholics felt that the Irish and German bishops did not care about their needs, and in fact discriminated against them (Orzell 1979). Panek, for example, opines: "Americans believe that the surest means towards regularizing relations between Poles and Americans in the church is the total Americanization of the Poles, which is what they seek and do not pretend otherwise" (Panek 1898: 42; cf. Orzell 1979: 8). And indeed, when in 1912 Polish American priests lobbied for the American Catholic church to supplicate the Pope to appoint bishops of Polish descent in the United States, their requests were met with what Platt (1977) describes as a "typical response" on part of the Archbishop of Milwaukee, Sebastian Messmer:

> The longer I think it over the more it seems to me a dangerous experiment at this stage to give the Polish people a bishop, for the very reason he will be considered the bishop for all the Poles of the United States. I know it. Wherever a bishop would have any difficulty with a Polish parish, their bishop would be appealed to. The Polish are not yet American enough and keep aloof too much from the rest of us (cited in Platt 1977: 475).

In the memoirs edited and published by Dziembowska (1977a and 1977b), the Polish church emerges as an important component of Polish American life, and there, too, one finds frequent complaints about the unchecked dominance of *Ajrysze* within it. *Ajrysze*, pronounced [ɑjrɨʂɛ], is the Polamerican ethnic term for the Irish. Like many other hybrid words that will be discussed in Section 5.3, the word *Ajrysze* was a blend that uniquely expressed the Polish American experience. In place of the Polish term *Irlandczycy*, the authors of the memoirs are borrowing the English word "Irish" and polonizing it by rendering it in Polish phonology, morphology, and orthography. But while the word may sound Polish, it is in fact incomprehensible to Poles living in Poland. In the memoirs, it was used pejoratively when commenting on and resisting perceived discrimination of Polish Catholics in the American Catholic church. *Ajrysze* thus was a term imbued with locally relevant sociocultural meanings, and denoted not just the Irish, but the Irish in America as relationally positioned against the Poles in America.

Thus the Catholic community in the United States, despite being uniformly the target of white Protestant Americans' prejudice, did not coalesce around their shared religion. Instead, it was characterized by rivalries along ethnic and political lines that played out within the church structure as well as outside of it. Stave (2010) comments on the intense rivalry between the Irish and the French Canadians in 1880s Connecticut: "Irish and French-Canadian schoolchildren taunted each other with chants such as, 'Corn beef and cabbage make the Irish savage,' which usually earned the response, 'Pea soup and Johnny cake makes a Frenchman's belly ache.' Ultimately, the two groups witnessed a sea change in immigration to their adopted state; one that made their rivalry pale" (203). Poles and Italians were the most significant new Catholic groups, and, as discussed earlier in this chapter, they were being classified among Europe's inferior races. The established, already "white" Irish and French-Canadian Catholics' attitude towards Slavs and Southern Europeans must have produced some tensions, judging from discourse such as in the following complaint by one of the memoir authors in Dziembowska (1977a):

> In the first few years of my stay [in America], I experienced a constant yearning to return to my little village, even though here I had a better quality of life, and I lived with my sisters and brothers-in-law, with whom I got along very well. We lived in a neighborhood inhabited mostly by Poles ... I couldn't get used to this buzz of machines in the factory, to this screeching of the tramways that passed by our house at 1 a.m., and then this dislike of Poles on the part of most of the Irish in those days. [The Irish] would instigate fights with the Poles in saloons in order to arrest the latter and put them in jail, and then they paid [the police] five dollars for each lash and broke sticks hitting Polish heads (214).

The author acknowledges all the advantages of living in America that he should be grateful for, yet continues to feel nostalgia when thinking back on his native village in Poland. These feelings intensify when he encounters unfamiliar circumstances: the noise of industrialization, and the confusing ethnic prejudice. Whether the story he tells of the Irish provocations of Poles in order to get them beaten up by the police is true or not, it testifies to his own experience and interpretation of Irish American animosity towards Polish immigrants, which was taking place at a time when the Irish were already part of white America, but the Slavs were not. Such tensions between immigrant groups were not uncommon: for example, Lee (1999) writes about anti-Chinese attitudes among Irish Americans in California (see also Wright 2008).

Some Polish Americans responded to the complex negotiation of roles within the Roman Catholic church, in which they saw Poles as definite losers, by exiting the argument altogether. In 1895, the Reverend Anton Kozlowski of St. Jadwiga's parish in Chicago broke away from his unpopular rector and organized an independent parish of All Saints, which was subsequently joined by twenty-two others (Platt 1977: 477; Orzell 1979: 7) in Buffalo, Chicago,

Cleveland, and Detroit.[37] At the same time, in 1897, Polish American parishioners in St. Mary's parish in Scranton, Pennsylvania, asked the German-speaking rector for "some representation in parochial affairs" since they "had contributed toward the building of a new church" (477). As Panek (1898) explains, Poles in America often felt that, because they support their local parish financially, they "own" it and should have a say in its workings, including having the priest accountable to them (see also Orzell 1979: 8). This, however, is not how the strictly hierarchical Roman Catholic organization is run. Accordingly, St. Mary's rector rejected his parishioners' request for representation, which in turn led a large group of them to stage protests that turned into riots, complete with police intervention and arrests. The protesters, whose demands met with disapproval of the Irish American bishops O'Hara and Hoban (Orzell 1979), established an independent parish of St. Stanislaus, under the leadership of the Reverend Franciszek Hodur (Platt 1977; Orzell 1979). Hodur eventually travelled to Rome and attempted to negotiate a reconciliation with the Holy See. In response, however, he was excommunicated. In 1904, the various independent Polish parishes formed the Polish National Catholic Church (PNCC) with Hodur at its helm. The Church's doctrine emphasized elements borrowed from American Protestant values, such as tolerance of varying doctrinal views, pluralism of religious bodies, and the rejection of the Roman Catholic "claim of exclusive revelation" (Platt 1977: 480). Liturgy was conducted in Polish, not in Latin. Furthermore, as if responding to the longstanding mainstream American criticism of Catholics as slavishly subservient to centralized papal authority, Francis Hodur, now leader of the new Church, declared, "Our Polish National Catholic Church in America, a country of the free, must be free. Ecclesiastical autocracy in a democracy is an anomaly, a contradiction" (cited in Platt 1977: 483).

The PNCC's *raison d'être* relied on the ideology of Polish nationalism (Orzell 1979; Jozefski 2008), which was fueled by the growing independence movement in then partitioned Poland. Its split from Vatican-led Roman Catholicism highlighted at the same time conflicts along ethnic boundaries within the American Catholic church, and political and religious divisions within the Polish American community. Not all Poles gravitated to the PNCC, and those who did not, became its staunch opponents. Many belonged to the Polish Roman Catholic Union of America,[38] and the Polish National Alliance[39], organizations supportive of the Roman Catholic Church. Several memoirs in Dziembowska's (1977a and 1977b) collection describe mutual animosity between the two groups of Polish American Catholics.

[37] www.pncc.org/?page_id=6, accessed November 10, 2015.
[38] www.prcua.org, accessed November 10, 2015.
[39] www.poloniawchicago.com/ap/pna.htm, accessed November 10, 2015.

The Reverend Wacław Kruszka, who as I mentioned above writes extensively and with great praise of the crucial role of Polish churches for the Polish American community, unequivocally condemns the PNCC: "The picture of our church relations contains some holes which are the 'independent' congregations" (1905: vol. 5, p. 6), he writes in his introduction to the lengthy section of his Polish American history that deals with religious life. Crucially, not only does he place the word *independent* in quotation marks, but he uses the word *zbór* – which I translate here as "congregation," but in Polish, it is used specifically to refer to Protestant churches – rather than *kościół*, which means "church," and the Roman Catholic Church in particular. He then refers to Franciszek Hodur as the leader of a "sect" (*sekta*), rather than "church" or "parish" (1905: vol. 5, p. 50). At the same time, Kruszka acknowledges that Polish Catholics are not represented among American bishops, and believes that Poles should be supported in maintaining their linguistic and cultural traditions within the church. In response to Irish American bishops' call for Poles to Americanize before receiving a Polish bishop, he writes:

> But, for God's sake, we Poles have long since become Americans! The only difference between us is that they are Americans of English, Irish, and German descent, whereas we are Americans of Polish descent. So what is it they want? Not to Americanize, but to Anglicize us! They want us to deny our Polish roots and become – not Americans – but **Yankees!** And will we do it? God save us from it! (1905: vol. 5, p. 58; emphasis original).

Notwithstanding, Kruszka believes that the correct action is supplication with Rome, not splitting from the Roman Catholic Church.

Latino Identities: Linguistic Encoding of Non-Mainstream Group Boundaries

Latinos in the United States tend to be homogenized into one racialized category in mainstream discourses, as I discussed in the previous section. In her discussion of undocumented Mexican immigrants' narratives, De Fina (2000) writes:

> Like other Latin American immigrants, Mexicans realize as soon as they enter the USA, that they are "US Hispanics" ... This kind of identification presents them with many dilemmas. First, they need to accept the idea of using and applying ethnic categorizations to themselves, although other properties of their definition as human beings, such as social class or occupation, for example, might be more salient to them. Second, they need to build specific connections between what they feel they are as individuals, and the categories socially available to them (De Fina 2000: 136).

De Fina observes that in their narratives, Mexican immigrants "resist an easy self-identification with Hispanics by making their own national distinctions, but they also talk about Hispanics and Latinos as people who have much in common and should help each other" (136). Acceptance and resistance of these classifications are not mutually exclusive, but simultaneous and contextualized. In one example, a Mexican woman named Raquel elaborates on her and her friend's claim that Central Americans are difficult to get along with. She invokes regional and national designations such as "Central American" and "Salvadoran" to refer to specific individuals who, in her experience, have been difficult or unpleasant. She supports this with a personal story in which she and her sister encountered a group of Salvadorans who were making offensive comments about Mexicans on a bus. While in the story itself, specific Salvadorans are reported as disrespecting Mexicans, the story serves to justify Raquel's dislike of Central Americans as a group. Raquel asks: "I mean, you start thinking how is it possible that the others ... the **Central Americans** sometimes start, how is it possible that people who speak our language (.) start insulting us" (De Fina 2000: 142; emphasis original). Here, she moves from "Salvadoran" as referring to specific people to "Central American" as a generalized category. At the same time as she draws this distinction between people like herself – Mexicans – and other Central Americans, she also appeals to their common identity as speakers of the same language and as Latinos, and to their shared experience as immigrants in the US. She concludes, "I mean, they behave in a racist way with us (.) and with other **Latinos** – how can they do that! Because one would expect that if they didn't help, they would at least find something in common (with us)! Listen, an **American** at least is in his own country, (.) but from someone who speaks our language!" (142, emphasis original). In her narrative, Raquel uses ethnic and racial terms both to describe individuals and to construct generic categories; she emphasizes distinctions between Mexicans and Salvadorans (Mexicans have respect for the Latino community, Salvadorans do not; De Fina 2000: 144), and points out similarities between them (shared language, Latino identity). Her construction of ethnic categories exemplifies the complexity of immigrant identities beyond the homogenizing labels that are salient in mainstream discourses, as well as the way immigrants, in this case Latinos, position themselves with respect to these labels and categories.

De Fina (2000) lists the number of times various ethnic terms appear in the narratives she collected. Among these, the are eight instances of Hispanic and one of Latino, and three instances of *moreno* ("colored") and four of *negro* (black). One of De Fina's participants, Laura, uses the term *morena* to refer to a supervisor at work in a story discussing Americans' prejudice towards Mexicans immigrants (De Fina 2000: 148). De Fina translates *morena* as "colored," explaining that "'negro' is usually used for 'black.' For Mexican immigrants, 'moreno' is the politically correct version of 'negro'" (De Fina 2000: 155). In this example, Laura is drawing on American racial categories while constructing her story, but she denotes them with Spanish terms that do not strictly correspond to their English equivalents in terms of cultural meaning. As I discussed above, racial categories in Latin America are numerous and not easily mapped onto the black-white dichotomy salient in the United States. Latin Americans themselves represent great racial diversity, including complex patterns of racial mixing. In the United States, however, they are on one hand homogenized and racialized in the discursive construction of Latino/as and Hispanics, and on the other hand they are evaluated in terms of their approximation to whiteness or blackness. Responses to these racial categorizations vary, as we have already seen in De Fina's study. Other examples include Baquedano-López' (2001) study of *doctrina* narratives, religious stories told in Mexican American Catholic religion classes in Los Angeles. Baquedano-López discusses how the Virgen de Guadelupe's dark skin color is invoked to construct the Catholic God as validating non-whiteness and caring for the needs of dark-skinned people.

Caribbean Latinos, such as Dominicans, Puerto Ricans, and Cubans, are a racially diverse group including many who have African ancestry and find themselves classified as black in the United States. Araujo-Dawson (2015), in a study based on the Latino National Survey containing 8,634 interviews, finds that lighter-skinned Caribbean Latinos are "less likely to perceive Latino/a as a racial category than their darker skinned counterparts" (251). Citing her own research as well as previous work, Araujo-Dawson shows that lighter-skinned Latinos are more likely to identify as white than as Hispanic or Latino/a, and that conversely, those Latinos who are darker-skinned, who experience more racial discrimination in the US, and who are perceived as black, are more likely to reject American racial categories and identify themselves as Latinos.

An example of how Caribbean Latinos negotiate their identities in response to mainstream categories is Bailey's (2001) work with second-generation Dominican American teenagers in Providence, Rhode Island. Bailey writes: "Up to 90 percent of Dominicans have sub-Saharan African ancestry . . . That would make them African American by historical US 'one-drop' rules of racial classification . . . Dominican Americans, however, do not think of themselves as 'black,' but rather as 'Dominican,' 'Spanish,' or 'Hispanic,' and their Spanish language makes this ethnolinguistic identity situationally salient to others" (190). Crucially, Bailey's research participants are aware that they are considered black by non-Dominicans, and they neither uniformly reject nor accept this classification. Rather, they simultaneously align themselves with African Americans as a minority group because they do not see themselves as white, and construct a distinct identity based around speaking Spanish and Dominican national origin. One participant observes, " . . . in America, there's only white and black, that's the only colors we have. Spanish people are considered black, that's the way they consider us, black" (199). Another one reports her own process of reinterpreting a fellow student's identity: "I would know who's Dominican. Actually, no, there was this guy, he's Dominican, and I thought he was black. And then when I heard him speak Spanish, I was like, 'He's Spanish! He's a Dominican'" (204). Code-switching into Spanish is a crucial marker of these teenagers' distinction from African Americans. However, Spanish is also relevant for intragroup boundaries: second-generation Dominicans sometimes perceive new immigrants as "hicks," an identity category that is encoded partly by speaking "too much" Spanish (209–211). I return to Bailey's study in my discussion of code-switching in Section 5.1.

In addition to responding to racial and ethnic classifications, Latino Americans also construct local identities that bring together categories of belonging based on national and regional origin, ethnicities salient in their home countries, linguistic repertoires, and sociocultural practices such as religion or gang membership. In her linguistic ethnography of *el bloque* ("the block") in the Puerto Rican neighborhood in New York, Zentella (1997) emphasizes the community's characteristic language diversity, "a diversity that reflected the community's varied regional, class, and cultural identifications with Puerto Rico's past and New York City's present" (41). According to Zentella, *el bloque*'s "bilingual/multidialectal repertoire" included Popular Puerto Rican (PR) Spanish, Standard PR Spanish, English-dominant Spanish, PR English, African American Vernacular English (AAVE), Hispanized English, and Standard NYC English (41). No single individual knew and spoke all these varieties, but they all constituted the repertoire of this particular speech community, and were crucial in producing locally relevant social categories – categories erased in mainstream discourses and thus invisible to the mainstream non-Latino majority.

Another example of locally salient Latino identities is found in Farr's (2006) study of the transnational community of *rancheros* who migrate between their Mexican hometown of San Juanico in Michoacán, and their immigrant community in Chicago. In mainstream discourse, "Mexican" is frequently used as a generic term for all Latinos, and it is both homogenizing and associated with negative stereotypes (Chavez 2008). To the immigrants, however, not only does "Mexican" refer to an ethnic group that can be distinguished from other Central Americans, as shown by De Fina (2000), but among Mexican Americans and Mexican immigrants themselves, there are various salient social identities, based on regional origin and socioeconomic class, but also on local factors. Farr (2006) emphasizes this when she explains: "I am writing about a specific group of families, especially the adult women in these families, from a particular village in Mexico, many of whom have lived or now live in Chicago" (Farr 2006: 4).

Rancheros constitute a specific group of rural Mexicans, originating in the nineteenth century. Their socioeconomic circumstances can range from relative poverty to middle class or "rural bourgeoisie" (43). Farr explains that those in her study "could be described as a community with such rural middle-class roots and with a potentially middle-class future . . . their status is clearly midway between the indigenous P'urhepecha (and 'de-Indianized' campesino Mestizos) and the urban, professional, and upper-class elite" (43). They are thus situated as a distinct group in terms of their economic circumstances, social status, regional affiliation with Michoacán, and racial background, descending from the "lower orders of Spanish conquerors – soldiers, miners, sailors, farmers, and other working-class and peasant colonists" (43) who historically "did not identify with local people of color" and "valued *pureza de sangre*" (48). Racial categorization features prominently in these rancheros' discourses of identity and belonging. Although they acknowledge the ubiquity of race mixing in Mexico,[40] and their resultant Mestizo heritage, they explicitly discuss their distinctiveness from Indians living in neighboring villages, and "identify nonequivocally as nonindigenous" (131). They construct and maintain ethnic boundaries between themselves and indigenous people through an array of practices, including clothing style, food choices (e.g. emphasis on wheat flour as preferable to corn meal), religious practices such as avoiding the November 1 Day of the Dead celebration because of its Indigenous roots (118), and overt talk otherizing Indians such as "The indigenous are very hardworking . . . They know [how to make] pottery, woodwork, furniture . . . " (143), as well as their language which is portrayed as difficult for Spanish speakers to pronounce (142).

Racial distinction is also reinforced through linguistic practice. The rancheros "make a display of not knowing" the *p'urhépecha* (Indigenous) language, or, if they know some, frame it as the language of others, not part of their own repertoire (142). Furthermore, their Spanish is characterized by specific ranchero speech styles. One of these is the verbal style of *franqueza*, "frankness" or "directness," which according to Farr "enacts a self-assertive, proud stance that indexes the individualist ideology deeply ingrained in ranchero identity" (142) and which they contrast with the rancheros' perception of indigenous people as "shamefully humble" (143). Farr argues that the rancheros' individualist ideology stems from their historical isolation as a group, living in the countryside away from urban centers, and in conflict with local Indians because they were taking Indigenous land. These living conditions fostered an emphasis on self-reliance, courage, and hard

[40] Farr (2006) points out that this is due as much to the high likelihood that interracial coupling took place in these rancheros' family history, as to the official promotion of the *mestizaje* or "mixed race" Mexican heritage as central to Mexican national identity that the rancheros would have encountered in school and other government-sponsored outlets.

physical work, as well as the development of dense and multiplex social networks (161–162). *Franqueza* as a speech style is believed to correspond to these values: it is "direct, straightforward, candid language that goes directly to a point . . . [it] can be blunt and rude (according to more 'cultured' people), sometimes peppered with obscenities. It is a direct, 'no bull' approach to communication" (162). On one hand, *franqueza* constructs an identity based on personal strength, independence, and rugged toughness. On the other, it emphasizes the egalitarian and intimate nature of interpersonal relationships, in which "open, candid communication can occur" (178).

Another ranchero speech marker is "indirect playful speech" and the high value placed on various forms of "playing with language" (121). These include sayings, proverbs, jokes, double meanings, stories, riddles, and personal anecdotes, and their prevalence demonstrates the importance of "the aesthetic potential of language" (122) to the rancheros. These playful genres are used to perform *relajo*, which is the opposite of the serious *franqueza* and which Farr defines as "a way of speaking which is framed as play" (226). *Relajo* can be simple teasing or fooling around, but it can also be used to diffuse tension (224–226) and challenge existing social norms. It is characterized by social transgressions, such as subverting norms of deference to others, swearing, or talking about sex, all framed as verbal play and thus permissible. For the rancheros, *relajo* is a way of affirming group identity. Crucially, examples of *relajo* documented by Farr (2006) in Chicago include "talk about previous talk in Mexico" (251). Farr comments that *relajo* "among the families in this study affirms their Mexican identity and transforms places into Mexican spaces, even in Chicago" (236). She also contrasts *relajo* among the San Juanico rancheros with a related style of *relajo* among Puerto Ricans.

Linguistic practices including *franqueza* and *relajo* occur both in the San Juanico rancho, and in the Chicago migrant community. They reinforce group cohesion, and contribute to the production of the community's transnational identity, which Farr expresses with the hybrid term Chicagoacán (58). Mobility and relocation are part of ranchero tradition, as they have migrated for work back and forth to the United States since the late nineteenth century, including to the Chicago area. Farr describes this process with Roger Rouse's term "transnational migrant circuit" (Rouse 1988, cited in Farr 2006: 56–57), because the migrants establish "daughter" communities in the United States, with relatives, neighbors and friends from the home village traveling back and forth and participating in work, education, and family activities in both locations. San Juanico's growing prosperity is due to the transfer of US-earned dollars. Children are sent to school in Chicago to learn English and acculturate in America, and in Mexico to learn Spanish and obtain what is perceived as superior education. They move back and forth and live with relatives. They travel to the rancho to celebrate events like first communion or *quinceañera*.

People temporarily out of work in Chicago go back to San Juanico to help with farming or construction, renting their Chicago houses out to friends and relatives in the meantime.

While in reference to Mexican racial categories, the rancheros identify as non-indigenous or as white (*blancos*, Farr 2006: 132), in the US context they often resist being classified as non-white under the racialized category of "Hispanic" or "Latino." The term "Hispanic" is avoided, while the term "Latino" is applied in ways that challenge mainstream assumptions, for example by using it to refer to Italian Americans (151). At other times, the rancheros differentiate themselves from other Latinos through their discursive practices, such as talking about differences in values between themselves and Puerto Ricans (152). Some of the San Juanico rancheros appear phenotypically European and are perceived as white, but even they do not see themselves as easily fitting into the black-white dichotomy, nor do they accept the American racial hierarchy and Latinos' place within it. Rather, they identify according to their nationality as Mexicans, but more importantly, specifically as rancheros.

As a final example of locally salient identities and boundaries that are not in line with mainstream categories, and that are encoded linguistically, I will mention gang-related affiliations. Dietrich (1998) and Mendoza-Denton (1997, 2008) both study Latina adolescents and their relationship to gangs, as well as their positioning within the social structures of school, of immigrant communities, of racial categories, and of gender roles. Dietrich's study focuses on Chicana adolescents in the Varrio Granos housing development in the multiethnic town of Westhills, located between San Diego and Los Angeles. Mendoza-Denton writes about female members of Latino youth gangs in the San Francisco Bay Area. In both cases, young Latinas' social identities are structured less around homogenizing categories such as "Latinos" versus "whites," and more around orientation towards gang-related activities. Some girls identify positively with school, stay away from gangs, and pay attention to their studies. For others, membership in specific gangs becomes the most relevant social identity marker.

Mendoza-Denton (1997, 2008) discusses the dichotomy between Norteña and Sureña gang members, who are engaged in strict rivalry and employ a number of social practices to produce oppositional gang identities. Norteñas are relatively Americanized, often second-generation Chicanas, in contrast to the Mexican or Latin-American-oriented Sureñas. Accordingly, Norteñas are English-dominant, and typically speak Chicano English and African American Vernacular English varieties, whereas Sureñas tend to speak Mexican Spanish and some Chicano English. The two groups' gang affiliation is marked by hair styles (feathered hair for Norteñas versus vertical ponytails for Sureñas), clothing colors (red and burgundy versus blue and navy), makeup (deep red lipstick versus brown lipstick), and choice of music

(Motown oldies versus Mexican Banda music). These distinctions and regional orientations parallel global political, socioeconomic, and cultural divisions. Mendoza-Denton argues that these youth gangs "are actively negotiating the contradictions of migration, language, globalization, and citizenship in the border regions between the 'Global North' and the 'Global South'" (Mendoza-Denton 2008: 59).

Furthermore, gang members distinguish themselves from non-gang affiliated Latinos by adopting particular features of Chicano English. For example, they are more likely to engage in the raising and tensing of the [ɪ] vowel so that it sounds more like [i], especially in Th-Pro lexical items such as *nothing, anything, everything, something*, and *thing*. By contrast, Latinos who are not affiliated with gangs draw on other varieties of Spanish, such as rural Mexican Spanish or "urban, middle-class Latin American Spanish varieties" (Mendoza-Denton 2008: 230). The identity categories that these Latina girls align with, and the resources that they draw on to do so, relate to categories meaningful both in Latin America (e.g. different dialects of Mexican Spanish, middle-class Latin American Spanish, regional Latin American identities), and locally among Latinos in California (e.g. specific gang membership). These are much more salient than mainstream categories that group them together as "Latinas" or "Hispanic."

These are just a few examples of how boundaries of similarity and distinction are drawn in immigrant communities in ways that do not correspond to mainstream American classifications. Linguistic practices are a key resource in establishing and negotiating these boundaries, oftentimes in ways that are either overlooked or erased by mainstream society. Newly arrived immigrants have to position themselves with respect not just to mainstream categories and expectations, but also those that are salient and meaningful in their particular communities. These can often be in conflict, especially for young immigrants who must choose paths of acculturation while negotiating the demands of their families, peer networks, ethnic communities, and society at large. Naturally, the scope of this section does not allow for a comprehensive discussion of this topic. I have by necessity left out important distinctions and dichotomies, such as between documented and undocumented immigrants, or within the extremely broadly defined Asian American community. In subsequent chapters, I will return to this topic while discussing sociocultural and linguistic practices through which immigrants negotiate their place in American society.

3 Hyphenated Identity

The hyphen that conjoins the two halves of designations such as Mexican-American, Chinese-American, or Polish-American has over time become an iconic representation of immigrant identities that straddle two worlds and realities, one based in the home country and one in America. Whether it is written out graphically or implied (e.g. Mexican American), the "hyphen" is an example *par excellence* of Bakhtinian heteroglossia, for it is inhabited by contested and conflicting meanings that refer to each other synchronically, as well as back in time to the early uses of the notion – and the graphic symbol – of hyphenation in talking about immigrant-American identities. The hyphen is both a characteristically American phenomenon and a source of controversy. It has been both rejected as an insult and embraced as a source of pride. It has stood to refer to the numerous ways in which one experiences an immigrant life and to one's definition of what constitutes "American." By examining this issue, this chapter focuses on immigrant identity as *American* identity. It considers the ongoing debates around the hyphen as negotiations of the balance between loyalty to one's heritage and country of origin, and commitment to the current American homeland, but it also challenges the prevalent understanding of the hyphen as centered around choice, in-betweenness, or balance; in other words, it argues that hyphenated identities need not be perceived as binary.

The hyphen has been frequently, and especially when it first emerged as a concept, assumed to symbolize dichotomy. Initially, as I will discuss below, it was believed to signify an inability to choose between one's past and one's new life in America, and thus a failure, or a refusal, to assimilate. More recent rejections of the hyphen include this assessment by Eric Liu, former White House speechwriter and policy advisor, and author of several books, including one on American identity (See Liu 1999):

> I call myself "Chinese American" – without a hyphen. American is the noun, Chinese the adjective. Or, rather, Chinese is one adjective. I am many kinds of American, after all: a politically active American, a short American, an earnest American, an educated American . . . The hyphenated form, "Chinese-American," to me signifies a transaction

between two parties, as in Chinese-American diplomatic negotiation or Chinese-American commerce and trade. The hyphen implies a state of interchange across nations. It does not name a person, much less a citizen (Liu 2014).

Liu rejects the graphic symbol of the hyphen as well as what it could potentially represent, which in his interpretation is an exchange between two separate entities. He also interprets the term "Chinese American" in a very specific way, with the primary category centered on "American" as a noun and "Chinese" as one of its many modifiers. As such, he makes it very clear that for him, the unhyphenated "Chinese American" does not contain an implied hyphen. He reads the hyphen as dichotomizing and does not identify with it. But even a more fluid interpretation of the hyphen as a spectrum would represent a linear phenomenon, a movement from "more heritage" to "more American" and back, with two distinct and opposing reference points.

A different way to think about the hyphen is to view hyphenated identities as hybrid identities, while taking the "hyphen" itself as the site at which the process of hybridization occurs. The hyphen is no longer just a symbol of something already pre-formed or shorthand for linking two competing categories. Through hybridization one can be simultaneously "very Chinese" and "very American" – or perhaps neither. Furthermore, one does not need to settle into some balanced combination of or compromise between one's immigrant and American selves. It is possible to perform and emphasize various aspects of one's multifaceted identity at different times, for different purposes, and for different audiences.

This process of hybridization, the negotiation of identity that takes place "in" or "at" the hyphen is what Sirin and Fine (2008) refer to as "working the hyphen" (114). They discuss "the psychological labor of 'working the hyphen'" based on interviews and focus groups with young Muslim Americans. Interestingly, Sirin and Fine do not use the graphic symbol of the dash anywhere in their book, choosing "Muslim American," rather than "Muslim-American." Yet, although the hyphen is not visually present in their book, its subtitle refers to "hyphenated identities,"[1] and much of the discussion explicitly centers around the hyphen. And in their work, the hyphen is seen as a site of activity. Sirin and Fine explain, "These youths take up residence in the middle of the hyphen, where they play with multiple allegiances to, and experience multiple stresses from, both their Muslim communities and the mainstream U.S. society ... [they generate] *hyphenated identities*, that is, rich, complex, and highly salient identities cutting across borders and going beyond the fixed, geographic, nation-bound binaries" (Sirin and Fine 2008: 131, emphasis original). An illustration of this process of "working the hyphen"

[1] The book's title is *Muslim American Youth: Understanding Hyphenated Identities through Multiple Methods.*

can be found in the following explanation offered by Xuan, a high school student of Vietnamese background who self-identifies as Asian American:

I have experiences that are similar to other Asians that live in America: that my culture is not all Asian and it's not all American. It's something entirely different. And it's not like some people say, that it's a mixture. It's like a whole different thing. When I say I'm Asian American, I feel like I establish a root for myself here. [My] parents think of themselves as Vietnamese because their roots are in Vietnam. Being Asian American is like a way to feel I belong (interviewed by Lee 1994: 427).

While the perspective adopted here is that the hyphen can be seen as the site of hybridization, the hyphen remains a contested concept. Mainstream discourses and immigrants themselves have often viewed it as undesirable and divisive. Accordingly, I will now turn to the early history of hyphenated identities.

3.1 "Only Part of Them Has Come Over": Early Days of the Hyphen

On May 23, 1914, the newspaper *The Gaelic American* published a scathing response to Woodrow Wilson's speech from a week earlier in which the president contrasted Commodore John Barry, a "true" American despite his Irish background, with the half-hearted Americans with hyphenated identities. Wilson gave his speech at the unveiling of a monument to the commodore, and he took that opportunity to underscore his own commitment to American neutrality in European affairs and to George Washington's policy of "No Entangling Alliances," implying that a hyphenated "name" betrays foreign allegiances. Wilson argued:

John Barry was an Irishman, but his heart crossed the Atlantic with him. He did not leave it in Ireland. And the test of all of us – for all of us had our origins on the other side of the sea – is whether we will assist in enabling America to live her separate and independent life, retaining our ancient affections, but determining everything that we do by the interests that exist on this side of the sea. Some Americans need hyphens in their names, because only part of them has come over. But when the whole man has come over, heart and thought and all, the hyphen drops of its own weight out of his name. This man was not an Irish-American; he was an Irishman who became an American. I venture to say if he voted he voted with regard to the questions as they looked on this side of the water and not on the other side and that is my infallible test of a genuine American – that when he votes, or when he acts, or when he fights, his heart and his thought are nowhere but in the centre of the emotion and the purposes and the policies of the United States (cited in The Gaelic American, May 23, 1914, p.1).

The authors of *The Gaelic American* article, titled "Molasses for Irish Flies," take Wilson's statements to be an attack on and an insult to Americans born in Ireland and those of Irish descent: "He praised John Barry as if he was the only Irishman who had ever done anything creditable for the United States, and he implied that all the rest were actuated by unworthy motives." They criticize

Wilson for failing to recognize not just Barry but "the race to which Jack Barry belonged" for its contributions to the causes of the American Revolution, the War of 1812, and the Civil War, as well as "the development of the Republic from the Revolution to the present day." This omission is seen as an implicit accusation that other "Irishmen and sons of Irishmen" see themselves as hyphenated. This is insulting, the authors explain, precisely because of the dedication that the Irish have historically shown to the American cause. Outraged, they reject any suggestion that the hyphenated identity is something Irish immigrants would ever claim, simultaneously accepting the definition of the hyphen as a mark of disloyalty: "No Irishman and no German who comes to this country uses the hyphen to describe his status: the appellation 'Irish-American' and 'German-American' was invented by Americans to describe them."[2]

The anti-hyphen sentiment was shared by many of Woodrow Wilson's contemporaries. The term "hyphenated American" was used in a derogatory way at the turn of the twentieth century, and such use is even reported in publications outside the United States. For example, in the January 3, 1904, issue of the Westminster Gazette we find a reference to "American politics, where men who call themselves Irish-Americans, German-Americans, Dutch-Americans, and so on, are contemptuously referred to as 'hyphenated Americans.'"[3] According to *The Gaelic American* article, "The 'hyphen' epithet was invented by the Knownothings," but it is difficult to find substantiation of this claim in other historical documents. William Safire in *Safire's Political Dictionary* credits Theodore Roosevelt with the propagation of the phrases "100% American" and "hyphenated American" (Safire 1978: 18). In his October 12, 1915, address to the assembly of the Knights of Columbus at Carnegie Hall in New York City, the former president focused squarely on condemning "hyphenated Americans" as nothing short of traitors of the United States:

> There is no room in this country for hyphenated Americanism. When I refer to hyphenated Americans, I do not refer to naturalized Americans. Some of the very best Americans I have ever known were naturalized Americans, Americans born abroad. But

[2] The article then proceeds with a critique of Wilson's perceived affinity for Anglo-Saxons and, by implication, for England. The Irish are represented as in contrast to "Anglos." The author goes on to explain how the Irish who distinguished themselves in America all "hated England as intensely as any Irishman who ever lived." The author portrays Wilson as one of the "men who are steeped in English prejudice, or have English interests to serve and who always take the English side in Anglo-American controversies … Irish citizens … have never asked the United States *to do anything for Ireland, or against England:* they have simply warned the American people against entanglement in the wiles of British diplomacy, which they understand better than any people on earth" (emphasis original). The Irish are thus being depicted as more American than Wilson himself or anyone else who places trust in Great Britain.

[3] Cited by Patricia T. O'Conner and Stewart Kellerman in a January 27, 2012, post on their blog Grammarphobia, www.grammarphobia.com/blog/2012/01/hyphenated-americans.html, accessed March 7, 2015.

a hyphenated American is not an American at all. This is just as true of the man who puts "native" before the hyphen as of the man who puts German or Irish or English or French before the hyphen. Americanism is a matter of the spirit and of the soul. Our allegiance must be purely to the United States. We must unsparingly condemn any man who holds any other allegiance. But if he is heartily and singly loyal to this Republic, then no matter where he was born, he is just as good an American as any one else. The one absolutely certain way of bringing this nation to ruin, of preventing all possibility of its continuing to be a nation at all, would be to permit it to become a tangle of squabbling nationalities, an intricate knot of German-Americans, Irish-Americans, English-Americans, French-Americans, Scandinavian-Americans or Italian-Americans, each preserving its separate nationality, each at heart feeling more sympathy with Europeans of that nationality, than with the other citizens of the American Republic. The men who do not become Americans and nothing else are hyphenated Americans; and there ought to be no room for them in this country . . . For an American citizen to vote as a German-American, an Irish-American, or an English-American, is to be a traitor to American institutions; and those hyphenated Americans who terrorize American politicians by threats of the foreign vote are engaged in treason to the American Republic.[4]

Despite being his political opponent, Woodrow Wilson echoed Roosevelt's sentiment regarding the hyphen, which testifies to its mainstream appeal at the time. Wilson's beliefs were rooted in his conviction that an efficient and honest government required the support of a committed and unified public. To this end, he hoped "to unify all classes and ethnic groups into a homogeneous middle class, socializing them through education to accept American political, social and economic ideals" (Vought 2004: 94). The notion of the hyphen was anathema to the ideal of such a homogeneous populace, melted down into a uniform alloy in what Zangwill calls "God's crucible" (cited in Kraus 1999: 13; see Section 2.1). To paraphrase Roosevelt's words, there was no room for the hyphen in the melting pot. And, as we have seen, the melting pot, in its most literal and almost violent sense, increasingly became the preferred metaphor for what America should aspire to be, particularly at the dawn of what promised to be "a century of American glory" (Vought 2004: 98). American greatness could not tolerate divided loyalties, which was what the hyphen unequivocally represented.

From the perspective of European nation-state ideology of the time, one nation was embodied in one language, and multilingualism was viewed with suspicion (Romaine 1995). The dominant anti-hyphen discourse thus finds its expression also in American attitudes towards languages other than English and towards multilingualism. We have seen in earlier chapters how the early ambivalence towards the language issue in the United States transformed into

[4] The speech is cited in its entirety on the website called "Unhyphenated America" (http://unhyphenatedamerica.org/2014/05/05/teddy-roosevelt-unhyphenated-america-speech/) as an example of positive thinking about the United States. Its authors oppose progressive politics, and believe that ethnicity and race should be "invisible" in all areas of American life.

support for English monolingualism at the turn of the twentieth century, solidifying around the formulation of the "melting pot" metaphor, with English as an essential feature of the final alloy. Roosevelt, in the Knights of Columbus speech cited above, included a clear condemnation of promoting non-English languages in the United States, which he linked with the promotion of foreign loyalties: "It has recently been announced that the Russian Government is to rent a house in New York as a national centre to be Russian in faith and patriotism, to foster the Russian language and keep alive the national feeling in immigrants who come hither. All of this is utterly antagonistic to proper American sentiment."[5] Three years later, in an August 26, 1918 speech delivered in Springfield, Illinois, Roosevelt attacks multilingualism as un-American more explicitly in this often-cited passage: " . . . if we permit our people be split into a score of different nationalities, each speaking a different language and each paying its real soul homage to some national ideal overseas, we shall not be a nation at all, but merely a polyglot boarding house" (Roosevelt 1919: 957).

In keeping with this political discourse, the first half of the twentieth century saw research on bilingualism focus on its potentially detrimental effect on intelligence and cognition (Romaine 1995; Hakuta 1986). In Europe, nationalist ideology was bolstered by claims of distinguished linguists such as Otto Jespersen, who wrote, "It is, of course, an advantage for a child to be familiar with two languages: but without doubt the advantage may be, and generally is, purchased too dear . . . the brain effort required to master the two languages instead of one certainly diminishes the child's power of learning other things which might and ought to be learnt" (Jespersen 1922: 148). In the United States, scholarly interest in the negative aspects of bilingualism reflected the prevailing political and social climate in which certain types of immigrants were perceived as undesirable and a threat to the fabric of American society (Hakuta 1986). Research was geared to demonstrate that immigrants from Southern and Eastern Europe are of inferior "stock," and various dubious arguments to prove this proposition were advanced. Romaine (1995: 109) reports, "Many studies followed which indicated a negative relationship between amount of English used at home by various immigrant groups and IQ (intelligence quotient). In other words, the more English used at home, the higher the IQ." Romaine cites Goodenough (1926), who explained such findings as showing either the negative influence of using foreign languages in the home, or "that those nationality groups whose average intellectual ability is inferior do not

[5] Cited in *New York Times* article "Roosevelt Bars the Hyphenated." October 13, 1915. Available at http://query.nytimes.com/mem/archive-free/pdf?res=9901E0DD1239E333A25750C1A9669D946496D6CF, accessed March 11, 2015.

readily learn the new language" (1926: 393). The "indigestible lumps" (Suárez-Orozco and Suárez-Orozco 2001; Section 2.1) in the melting pot were thus identifiable in part by their competence in languages other than English (see also Hakuta 1986). And, as Pavlenko (2002) explains, the hegemony of English monolingualism was supported by "the discourse of the superiority of English, which allowed politicians and educators to posit English as a language of high moral and intellectual value" (Pavlenko 2002: 180).

In light of such attitudes, it is not surprising that the immigrants themselves frequently frowned upon the hyphen, as we saw in the case of *The Gaelic American* article whose authors took umbrage at the suggestion that the Irish consider themselves to be "hyphenated Americans." Not all may have been equally explicit in their rejection of the hyphen, but the commitment to embracing American identity wholeheartedly is a recurrent theme. In her famous memoir *The Promised Land*,[6] Belarusian Jewish immigrant Mary Antin writes in 1912:

> The public school has done its best for us foreigners, and for the country, when it has made us into good Americans. I am glad it is mine to tell how the miracle was wrought in one case. You should be glad to hear of it, you born Americans; for it is the story of the growth of your country; of the flocking of your brothers and sisters from the far ends of the earth to the flag you love; of the recruiting of your armies of workers, thinkers, and leaders. And you will be glad to hear of it, my comrades in adoption; for it is a rehearsal of your own experience, the thrill and wonder of which your own hearts have felt (Antin 1912: Chapter 11).

Antin speaks proudly of her own transformation from a foreigner into a "good American," and she sees it as the unquestioned goal for all immigrants, past and present. While the first chapters chronicle with nostalgic affection her childhood in her hometown of Polotsk, Antin's book is ultimately the story of Americanization as a triumph or even salvation: becoming worthy of inheriting "the promised land" of the United States of America.

This emotional transformation is also a linguistic one. Antin writes:

> I shall never have a better opportunity to make public declaration of my love for the English language. I am glad that American history runs, chapter for chapter, the way it does; for thus America came to be the country I love so dearly. I am glad, most of all, that the Americans began by being Englishmen, for thus did I come to inherit this beautiful language in which I think. It seems to me that in any other language happiness is not so sweet, logic is not so clear. I am not sure that I could believe in my neighbors as I do if I thought about them in un-English words. I could almost say that my conviction of immortality is bound up with the English of its promise. And as I am attached to my prejudices, I must love the English language! (Antin 1912: Chapter 10).

[6] Available at http://digital.library.upenn.edu/women/antin/land/land.html; accessed March 11, 2015.

Coming from precisely the part of Europe despised in mainstream discourses for producing "inferior" immigrants, and Jewish to boot,[7] Antin defies any suspicions or criticism by successfully achieving Roosevelt's and Wilson's ideal of the "unhyphenated" naturalized immigrant who "became an American," a transformation made complete by her unequivocal acceptance of the English language.

Antin is not alone. For the next several decades, immigrants were encouraged to speak English to their children at home, and many did so in the hope of aiding their children's assimilation into the American mainstream (Schmid 2001). This was the experience of another author of a well-known memoir, Richard Rodriguez. In *The Hunger of Memory*, Rodriguez recounts how nuns from his Catholic school pressured his parents into giving up speaking Spanish in the home. This took place in the early 1950s, and in his book, published in 1982, Rodriguez is still fully committed to the need for separation between the "private" heritage language and the "public" language, which is English. He believes that assimilation and Anglicization are essential to an immigrant's success. He writes:

> The bilingualists insist that a student should be reminded of his difference from others in mass society, his heritage. But they equate mere separateness with individuality . . . Only when I was able to think of myself as an American, no longer an alien in *gringo* society, could I seek the rights and opportunities necessary for full public individuality. The social and political advantages I enjoy as a man result from the day that I came to believe that my name, indeed, is *Rich-heard Road-ree-guess* . . . I celebrate the day I acquired my new name . . . Those middle-class ethnics who scorn assimilation seem to me filled with decadent self-pity, obsessed by the burden of public life. Dangerously, they romanticize public separateness and trivialize the dilemma of the socially disadvantaged (Rodriguez 1982: 26–27).

Rodriguez clearly believes in the binary choice: assimilate or remain an alien, choose Americanization or choose your heritage, embrace English or keep your language. Although he does not invoke the concept of hyphenation, his views align with the perception of the hyphen as undermining the assimilation effort: if Americanization is the goal, the hyphen is best abandoned. Unlike Antin, who professes her wholehearted love for America, Rodriguez frames his argument in terms of what benefits the immigrant. He acknowledges one's affection for one's heritage culture and mourns his own loss of family intimacy that had been enacted in Spanish, but ultimately dismisses attachment to these as "decadent self-pity" and a hindrance in claiming one's rights in American society. But both Antin and Rodriguez speak in favor of adopting a new identity, a new name, and a new language. For them, like for the American

[7] See Goddard (1917) for an IQ test–based study in which he concluded that twenty-five out of thirty adult Jews in his sample were "feeble-minded" (Romaine 1995: 109; Goddard 1917: 251).

critics of hyphenated immigrants, the choice is between the old and the new. The hyphen at worst embodies loyalty to the old, and at best reveals the failure to adapt.

It has to be remembered, however, that attitudes towards the hyphen have not been uniform. Even during America's most openly anti-immigrant mainstream stance – informed by discourses of racial difference and hierarchy, and of the superiority of the English language and undesirability of bilingualism – immigrant communities continued to maintain their cultural and linguistic customs and separateness. There continued to be ethnic churches with their own rituals, languages, and priests; and groups such as Poles, Swedes, Norwegians, and others continued to maintain their linguistic vitality in America (see Chapter 1).

At the same time, the sentiments expressed by Roosevelt and Wilson continue to be invoked today. Sometimes this is done implicitly, without referring to hyphenation. The US English movement's website makes reference to "the unifying role of the English language in the United States" on its home page. In a post titled "Bilingual Ballots Send Wrong Message to Immigrants," US English chairman Mauro E. Mujica criticizes both bilingual ballots and any other voting-related information produced in another language in addition to English: "As an immigrant myself, I have experienced firsthand the challenge of learning English. But I have also seen the opportunities that open when one does learn the common language of America … The government is only hurting non-English speakers by providing translations in other languages and perpetuating the myth that this is an English-optional society."[8] Mujica invokes the same argument as Richard Rodriguez, which posits that failure to embrace English fully is detrimental to an immigrant's future.[9] Others, in particular in the most conservative circles, explicitly invoke the hyphen while bemoaning the alleged demise of American unity. Writing on the American TEA Party blog in a post titled "The Hyphen That Destroyed a Nation," J.D. Longstreet refers to Roosevelt's Knights of Columbus speech:

> As we see today, Teddy was absolutely right. We have become the very thing he warned we *would become* if we did not drop the hyphen – both mentally and physically … At no time is it more obvious than during an election cycle when the politicians begin their pathetic pandering to every hyphenated group of so-called Americans in the country … *both legal and illegal* (emphasis original).

8 www.us-english.org/view/884, accessed March 12, 2015.

9 Both Rodriguez and Mujica speak from their own position as successfully assimilated immigrants who feel they benefited from the opportunity to learn English; however, their well-intentioned but paternalistic recommendations deny agency to other immigrants by speaking out against bilingual education or bilingual materials, and positing only one acceptable path for immigrant identity (more on this in Chapter 7).

Longstreet continues:

> Since Teddy made his remarks we have embraced the hyphen ad infinitum. Now we have: African American, Arab American, Asian American, European American, Latino American, Native American, Chinese American, English American, Filipino American, Greek American, German American, Irish American, Indian American, Italian American, Japanese American, Jewish American, Korean American, Mexican American, Norwegian American, Azerbaijani American, Polish American, Russian American, Spanish American, Swedish American, Ukrainian American, Vietnamese American, and the list just continues to grow. America is more divided today than she was during The War Between the States. We each seem to have our own little tribe to which we belong. The once famed "American culture" no longer exists. We have submerged it in a sea of multiculturalism and it has become the victim of something called "diversity" . . . We are drowning in a sea of hyphens![10]

Such explicit anti-hyphen views, once mainstream and backed by open prejudice and racism, are seen as more extreme today, but they continue to be part of the conversation about immigration and about America. The US English movement's success in getting official English legislation passed in thirty-one of the fifty states[11] testifies to this, illustrating also how the question of the hyphen is bound up with that of multilingualism. As Romaine (1995: 108) argues, "In the United States and many parts of western Europe, bilingualism has not been seen as a learned achievement, but more often as a stigma of recent immigration." At the same time, immigrants have countered the dominant narrative of assimilation with their own interpretations of immigrant-American identity that include the acceptance and negotiation of multilingualism and of hyphenation. For example, in Portes and Rumbaut's (2001) study, conducted in the 1990s, second-generation children and youth were asked to fill in their ethnic self-identity in an open-ended question, without any categories provided. In 1992, the seventh- and eighth-graders wrote in a "hyphenated American" designation (40.2 percent) or a "panethnic" designation such as Latino, Chicano, or Asian American (15.8 percent) more frequently than unmodified "American" (12.6 percent). In a 1995–1996 follow-up survey, the same respondents, now in high school, identified themselves as hyphenated less (30.6 percent) and as panethnic more (26.5 percent) than before, but especially infrequently as "American" (3.5 percent) (Portes and Rumbaut 2001: 154–155). The children were also more likely to self-identify by their country of origin in 1995–1996 (34.6 percent) than in 1992 (27.5 percent). Interestingly, in 1992 when the children were younger, "hyphenated American" was the most popular category, followed by the "national origin" category. In 1995–1996, however, these two are still the most popular, but in a reversed order.

[10] Longstreet, J.D. (2012) "The Hyphen that Destroyed a Nation." http://teapartyamerica.blogspot.com/2012/01/hyphen-that-destroyed-nation.html, accessed March 13, 2015.

[11] www.us-english.org/view/9, accessed March 13, 2015.

Meanwhile, self-identification as "panethnic" increased from 15.8 percent to 26.5 percent, while that as "American" decreased dramatically from 12.6 percent to 3.5 percent. These statistics suggest that self-identification does not reflect a straightforward process but rather an ongoing negotiation that likely involves numerous issues, for example family dynamics, peer influence, friendship networks, gender norms evolving throughout adolescence, reactions to the dominant culture encountered in schools, and teacher attitudes and expectations. In the next section, I will discuss the negotiation that takes place around and at the hyphen, repositioning hyphenation as a dynamic process and focusing on the construction of hybrid identities through linguistic practices.

3.2 Negotiating Hyphenated Selves

Serbian Americans in the early twentieth century counted among the suspicious and potentially "unassimilable" immigrants from Eastern and Southern Europe who were singled out by critics as representing a threat to Americanism. The representation of migrants from the Balkans – non-Anglo-Saxon, non-Protestant, and oftentimes with darker features – as the bizarre, not-quite-European Others speaking with heavy accents, observing peculiar customs, and being accompanied by large, loud and overbearingly involved families has been invoked in the media as late as the 1980s, in the sitcom *Perfect Strangers*, and in the 1990s, in the film *My Big Fat Greek Wedding*. Nonetheless, the Serbian diaspora in America tracing their roots back to the large waves of peasant migration from the Austro-Hungarian Empire has by now for the most part integrated into the American mainstream. As Simić (2007) points out in a study of Serbian American ethnic identity, "in the case of Euro-Americans, ethnicity is not an overarching or ubiquitous sign marking the individual in virtually all aspects of private and public life" (41). Rather, the process of accomplishing ethnic identity for the descendants of early-twentieth-century European immigrants is informed by choice in self-identification and in the extent of one's adoption of ethnic markers such as language competence, religion, traditional foods, holidays, and other cultural practices. Thus, for the Serbian Americans in Simić's study, ethnic identity is "an achieved status" and "a matter of personal predilection which theoretically has little or no role in public life" (Simić 2007: 38). Claiming a Serbian American identity involves negotiating the meaning of the hyphen with respect to various sociocultural dimensions.

One such issue is the meaning of genetic descent for one's ethnic self-identification and affiliation. Questions such as "how should we categorize a person with a Serbian father and an Irish mother?" (Simić 2007: 39) highlight the multiplicity of categories available and competing in the hyphenated space. They are not mutually exclusive, but rather can coexist and build on each other.

Beyond a claim to a reified bloodline, performing a Serbian ethnicity involves some degree of proficiency in the Serbian language, however minimal and limited to single culturally significant lexical items this knowledge may be. It also involves the celebration of Serbian holidays, participation in the Serbian Orthodox Church and associated organizations, and maintenance of a more or less extensive Serbian American social network. Crucially, however, Serbian American ethnicity is not a reproduction of Serbian culture in America. Rather, it is a reinterpretation, adaptation, and extension of this culture, and as such, it is an American product. Simić (2007: 44–45) gives the examples of the *tamburitza* orchestra and of *kolo* dancing, which stem from specific regional musical traditions in the Balkans, but have been adopted as emblems of "being Serbian" by immigrants from the entire area and their descendants. At the same time, these traditions have evolved in America into new forms, contributing to "a generic Serbian-American culture, one which has drawn not only upon a variety of traits from diverse areas in the original homeland, but also upon characteristics borrowed from both mainstream American life and other ethnic groups as well" (Simić 2007: 45). Serbian American identity is thus a dynamic hybridization, a process negotiated and accomplished at and through the hyphen.

Engagement in this negotiation of hyphenated identity is, however, "periodic and contextual" for Serbian Americans (Simić 2007: 41), and as Simić argues, it oftentimes takes on the characteristics of "symbolic ethnicity" (Simić 2007: 46; Gans 1979). A similar claim can be made about descendants of other European groups who have the choice to take up either American or hyphenated American subject positions, with the possible exception of European-American Muslims (e.g. from Bosnia), whose religious affiliation can make them visible in mainstream society through embodied religious practices. But for the most part, by the second generation, white immigrants can choose to present themselves as ethnically unmarked, without concern that their claim to Americanness will be challenged. This choice is not available, however, to immigrants from non-white groups, whether they are first generation, 1.5 or second generation, or ones with decades-old roots in the United States.

Thus, for example, Chacko (2003) examines ethnic identities of children of first-generation Ethiopian immigrants in Washington, DC. Her study is based on interviews conducted in 2002–2003 with ten 1.5-generation and ten second-generation Ethiopian Americans, aged 18–27. Emerging or having recently emerged from adolescence, part of which involves secondary socialization in the American education system, these young people have had to confront the demand to situate themselves within America's race structure, which is still dominated by the white-black dichotomy (Bucholtz 2009; Section 2.3). But race as it is understood in the United States is not a salient or even accessible category for recent Ethiopian immigrants, who come "from a country where the taxonomy of populations is based largely on linguistic, religious, and tribal affiliations" (Chacko 2003: 497). Faced with the need to classify themselves racially in American society, they are aware that "black" is perceived as the appropriate category, but they do not identify with it. They differentiate themselves from native-born descendants of African slaves, and in Chacko's interviews "all but one person claimed that becoming American did not mean becoming African American" (497). And, when asked to give their preferred ethnic identity, all of the second-generation immigrants said "Ethiopian American," while 80 percent of the 1.5 generation said "Ethiopian" (Chacko 2003: 500–501). The Ethiopian American hyphen involves negotiating one's relationship to Ethiopianness and to Americanness, but also to African Americanness. What is not available to them is assimilation into the mainstream, because they are classified by others as black. This experience is similar to that of Dominican American teenagers participating in Bailey's (2001) study, who likewise differentiate themselves from African Americans despite being typically grouped with them, and rely on the resources of Spanish-English bilingualism to enact this distinction.[12] However, the Dominican Americans in Bailey's study also distinguish themselves from white Americans and, like many other non-white groups, appropriate elements of African American Vernacular English (AAVE) to produce this distinction. But since phenotypically they resemble African Americans, their use of AAVE invokes and produces different sociocultural meanings than it does for Asian Americans (Chun 2001; Reyes 2005).

Similarly, Ethiopian Americans in Chacko's study adopt elements of black culture, including music, with reggae in particular being strongly associated with Ethiopia through Rastafarianism (Chacko 2003: 498). But their relationship with African American identity is complex and conflicted. Those in the 1.5 generation become more aware of race and phenotype the longer they stay in the United States. One interviewee reported: "During the first couple of years [after arriving in the United States], I considered myself only Ethiopian. Then I started thinking of myself as African. As time passed . . . I interacted more with [native] Blacks and other Americans. This country made me more aware of my race. I was Blacker than I thought I was!" (498). Others described feeling upset when treated as outsiders by black Americans. They explained that newly arrived immigrants speak English with Ethiopian accents, which are not always met with approval by their African American peers. Chacko quotes one young man as saying, "When you spoke, they would act like they didn't understand. They'd say, 'Speak English, man'" (Chacko 2003: 498). At the same time as they negotiate their relationship with blackness, Chacko's interviewees experience and practice a strong identification with Ethiopian history and culture.

[12] I discuss Bailey's (2001) study in Section 5.1.

They are proud of their connection to reggae music. They participate in local Ethiopian organizations and events. They emphasize Ethiopia's ancient civilization, the history of its Orthodox Church as one of the oldest churches in the world, and Ethiopia's status as the only black African state that did not become a Western colony. This latter point reinforces the Ethiopian immigrants' sense of separateness from African Americans, since they take pride in having been "never subjugated as a people" (Chacko 2003: 501). Yet by the second generation, there is a language shift away from Amharic, Oromo, or Tigrinya to English. Chacko reports that many families use language in non-reciprocal alternation (Zentella 1997: 86), with the parents speaking an Ethiopian language and the children responding in English (Chacko 2003: 502). The hybrid identities constructed by these immigrants at the site of and through hyphenation are complex, contextual, and always changing. Unlike Serbian Americans, however, Ethiopian Americans cannot assume an unmarked American identity. Their relationship with the hyphen is always a public and visible one.

The "new hybrid spaces" (Sirin and Fine 2008: 125), where the ongoing negotiation of identities occurs, are sites where race, ethnicity, class, gender, age or life stage, culture, religion, and other aspects of sociocultural life and identity intersect. For Muslim Americans, religion is a prominent axis in these intersections. Unlike the Ethiopian Americans described by Chacko, Muslim Americans do not constitute a single visible ethnic group, but rather they are characterized by a diversity of backgrounds, and "many 'appear' to be white" (Sirin and Fine 2008: 4). For example, the backgrounds of the 204 participants in Sirin and Fine's (2008) multi-method study included South Asia (Pakistan, India, Bangladesh), Arab countries (Palestine, Egypt, and others), as well as Turkey, Bosnia, Kosovo, Iran, Afghanistan, Azerbeijan, and West Indian nations, while their home languages besides English included Urdu, Arabic, Farsi, Bengali, Turkish, and others (16). The authors argue that in dominant discourses, Muslims in America have been subjected to ethnogenesis: "creating one people out of many" (59). People with backgrounds ranging from Africa to the Middle East to Central and South Asia, and with a corresponding diversity of religious and cultural practices, are ideologically constructed as if they were one entity, the marked Other targeted by moral exclusion, a point I will return to below. But contrary to this prevailing mainstream construct, only sometimes are Muslim Americans identifiable by their physical features or Arabic-sounding names. Often, their affiliation with Islam is made visible by outward religious practices such as attending mosque, praying, and wearing skullcaps or scarves. Girls and women who wear the *hijab*, in particular, become visible and identifiable as Muslim. In this way, a personal religious practice is reinterpreted in mainstream society as an "ethnic" marker in the ethnogenesis process. Sirin and Fine find that among their participants, girls who wear the *hijab* experience more discrimination than Muslims who can "pass" (95). And yet, many choose to express their religious commitment in this way, oftentimes in contrast to their relatively more secular parents or even against their objections (108). In Sirin and Fine's study, a recurring theme is young Muslim Americans' desire to educate non-Muslims about Islam in order to counter narrow-minded stereotypes. This has been especially relevant since the terrorist attacks of 9/11, when dominant sociopolitical discourses started to increasingly envision Muslims not just as outsiders, but as the enemy.

"Working the hyphen" (Sirin and Fine 2008: 114) for Muslim American youth thus involves positioning themselves in a context where on one hand they are targets of moral exclusion, and on the other they feel themselves to be both Muslims and American citizens. Following Opotow (1990, 1995), Sirin and Fine describe moral exclusion as the designation of a specific, otherized group as somehow failing the accepted moral standards, as less beneficial or even harmful to society, and thus as unworthy of equal justice. Consequently, the group is "ejected from the national 'we'" (Sirin and Fine 2008: 7; see also Chapter 2, Sections 2.1 and 2.2). Their research participants describe numerous instances of being targeted with aggression or ignorance: hearing racial slurs, being spat at, or being expected to speak authoritatively about terrorism. In light of this, it might seem that young Muslim Americans are stuck between two mutually exclusive choices – their religion or their Americanness – which is the message in the "clash of civilizations" discourse perpetuated in the media as well as by some academics (Huntington 2004; Sirin and Fine 2008: 125).

But it turns out that rather than a simplistic clash, Muslim American youth are able to create and negotiate hyphenated Muslim American identities characterized by blending and hybridity. At the hyphen, "they struggle to construct meaningful narratives of themselves" (Sirin and Fine 2008: 123) in which integration as opposed to assimilation is the goal and the main theme. One girl describes this process as fusion: "You're like a new culture. It's like those new restaurants that mix . . . you're like a *fusion* . . . a new fusion" (137). Such "hyphen work" is often marked by conflict and contradiction: fusion does not need to imply harmony. Rather, the fusing process is dynamic and vibrant. Some young Muslims find that as they negotiate their hyphenated selves, they come into conflict with their parents and relatives, either for being "too American" (101) or too religious (98, 108). Many speak and act from the position of American citizens, unafraid to critique American politics and speak out against the ignorance of their peers in what Maira (2004) calls dissenting citizenship (Maira 2004, Sirin and Fine 2008: 90). Some report feeling betrayed as Americans by religious profiling, whereas others, also as Americans, feel themselves to be under terrorist attack, simultaneously dissociating themselves from terrorism as Muslims. Yet others feel that living in America allows them to experiment with the practice of their religion in a relatively open climate of freedom of expression. The narratives and perspectives emerging in interviews, focus groups, and identity map sketches in Sirin and Fine's research reveal a complex and dynamic process of working out hyphenated identities around the axis of religion.

Sikh Americans are another group for whom religion is a visible identity marker: practicing Sikhism involves bodily practices of not cutting or shaving one's hair and wearing a turban. Some Sikhs choose to give up the turban, either in order to obtain employment or, as is more likely with second-generation immigrants, because the practice does not reflect their self-perception as a member of American society. These choices meet with evaluation and judgment from other Sikhs, whether approving or disapproving. Other young Sikhs, meanwhile, choose to stop cutting their hair and to start wearing the turban after having been brought up with short hair, often together with other male family members of their generation. For them, as Klein (2009) explains, "the collective sense of kin affiliation is embodied in the practice of wearing a turban" (117). Klein argues that Sikh Americans' narratives about the turban reveal three trends in how the practice is constructed discursively. One is the ties to family and to the Sikh community. The second is the donning of the turban as a transformative experience. One young man explains that "it makes you (have) strong will, strong power, and *tol*erance. To- to take- just- everything. Everything. Racial slurs, um getting up in the mornings . . . on time, everything" (Klein 2009: 118). Another says, "It really helps me figure out who people are, what they're about. It's really weird but I know what people are thinking just by their reactions, facial expressions, body language, I know what's going on now because I've seen it so many times" (118). The third theme is that of the turban as a situated practice. Some Sikhs' perspective on the turban is that it needs to be seen and practiced in context, and that it does not unequivocally determine one's authenticity as a Sikh. These young people "self-identify as Sikh but see themselves as broadening the definition of what it means to be a Sikh in regard to physical appearance" (119). The practice of wearing the turban has implications for those close to the turbaned men as well. One young woman, for instance, describes her own vigilance to other people's reactions when she is out with her turbaned husband (122). This awareness of non-Sikh reactions has become especially relevant since the events of 9/11, because Sikhs' traditional outward appearance is readily confused by the mainstream American public with the popularized image of the terrorist. The Sikh religion is racialized through the meanings attached to its outward expression in American mainstream discourse, and Sikh Americans are thus positioned as a confusing racial category, not fitting easily into the dominant stereotypes of Asian Americans as either the model minority, nor into the problem group of low-income Southeast Asian refugees associated with African American culture (Reyes 2005).

By contrast, other South Asians are readily placed in the model minority category, which has implications for their own negotiation of the hyphen. Asher (2008) explores hyphenation as the process through which "hybrid identities emerge in the interstices between different cultures" (Asher 2008: 13). She analyzes narratives of ten New York City high school students from Indian immigrant families, focusing on how they negotiate the dynamic intersections of class, gender, ethnicity, race, family relationships, and culture.[13] Asher argues for the relevance of postcolonial perspectives for the study of the experience of immigrant students, especially in the field of education where issues of "marginality, oppression, difference, identity, and representation" are significant (13). The Indian American teenagers in Asher's study "work the hyphen" to assert their American selves at home and their Indian selves at school. The hyphen is an in-between space and the site of struggle, contradiction, and creativity. One of Asher's participants explains: "I mean I've even heard a kid, . . . when we had this discussion about being hyphenated Americans, like, Indian-American, 'Why do you have to say that? Why can't you just say American?' And you can't bring out the argument that I am half Indian. I am not a whole American" (Asher 2008: 12). Another reports being chastised by her parents for speaking to them in what they see as a disrespectful tone and finding this problematic: " . . . they say, 'you're being too American.' I consider myself American. I was born and raised here" (12). The teenagers' hybrid culture includes elements of other minority cultures, in particular African American culture, such as the blending of hip-hop with South Asian pop music (15). Some adopt dress styles associated with hip-hop culture, which is not necessarily well received by their families and peers. One boy comments on his parents' disapproval of his baggy pants: "Like, you are turning Black or something," while another student's parents warned her sister that if she dresses like African Americans, her "grades are gonna match theirs and go down" (16). While situating themselves in the American race and class hierarchy, children of Indian immigrants are faced with the pressure to fit the stereotype of the "model minority" both within their community from their parents and outside of it from their teachers and classmates. The ongoing negotiation of their identities at times includes expressing oppositional attitudes towards both their families and the dominant culture through practices associated with minority counterculture, such as wearing baggy pants. At other times, it involves aligning with Indian cultural norms when explaining to their non-Asian peers the importance of acquiescing to their parents' wishes (17). Such negotiations are informed by multiple factors and are always contextualized.

[13] Asher's use of the concept of interstices refers to Homi K. Bhabha's (1994) work on in-between spaces and hybridization.

Southeast Asian immigrants are typically left out of the model minority typecasting, which tends to apply only to East and South Asians (Bucholtz 2009), not coincidentally because of the latter's overall more advantageous socioeconomic positioning. Instead, Southeast Asian Americans are often positioned "as problematic immigrants who are dependent on government assistance and are the sources of an array of social ills" (Bucholtz 2009: 22). In Bucholtz's (2009) paper, two Laotian girls are shown as producing identity relations through habitual linguistic practice, and specifically through their orientation to AAVE and African American youth cultural practices. Significantly, Bucholtz finds that Latino, Native American and Asian American high school students in her research, while themselves operating outside the black-white racial dichotomy, are typically perceived by the dominant groups in terms of "acting black" or "acting white" (27). In this context, Southeast Asian students draw on African American cultural resources but reinterpret them to produce new forms. For example, "many Southeast Asian American students wore baggier jeans than other students, and unlike other groups they ironed their pants and stapled or taped the cuffs under" (Bucholtz 2009: 39).

The girls in Bucholtz's study choose two distinct ways of navigating the racial structures at the high school. Nikki aligns herself with African American youth culture, which is also seen in local ideologies as being associated with youth gangs. She is a former gang member, wears gang colors, dresses in a style associated with hip-hop and youth gang culture, and uses numerous features of AAVE. Interestingly, Bucholtz points out that Nikki's speech style combines distinctly non-AAVE features (e.g. vowel quality) and some non-native English characteristics with a range of AAVE phonology and grammar much broader than that typically observed in the speech of European Americans (Bucholtz 2009: 31; Bucholtz 1999a; Cutler 1999). Since Nikki is a refugee who arrived in California at the age of five, and who is bilingual in Lao and English, it is possible that her home interactions are conducted in Lao and that she acquired AAVE features alongside Standard English (MUSE) during her second language learning process. While she may not be a fluent or native-like speaker of AAVE, her command of a broad range of features may be a product of her particular language learning experience, similar to that found among Latino children in North Carolina as described in Chapter 4 (Section 4.4). Nikki employs her knowledge of AAVE in constructing an identity linked to black youth culture as representative of cross-ethnic urban youth style for students of color, but also as an assertion of her own affiliation with gang membership.

By contrast, the other Laotian girl, Ada, aligns herself with school and specifically with a group of mostly European American girls who construct their identities around nerdiness and in opposition to trendiness and coolness

(Bucholtz 2009: 33; Bucholtz 1999b). At the same time, Ada dissociates herself from other Laotian students because of their interest in gangs, and her friendship network includes European Americans and Asian Americans of Chinese and Vietnamese backgrounds. Ada, like the nerd girls, wears loose T-shirts and jeans rather than either form-fitting clothes associated with the popular white girls or the baggy pants associated with urban youth styles. She also avoids youth slang and speaks mostly MUSE. Ada was nine when she arrived in California, and Bucholtz describes her as having many non-native features in her English that mark her as less fluent than Nikki (Bucholtz 2009: 34–35). And while Ada's English includes some features that could be AAVE, such as zero copula and habitual *be*, they are limited compared with Nikki's usage. Bucholtz argues that these are likely due to Ada's non-native English rather than AAVE influence, although this could be difficult to assess with certainty. The key point is, as Bucholtz points out, that "simply by aiming for Standard English rather than another variety as a language learner, Ada semiotically marked her social identity as different from students like Nikki" (2009: 35).

Similar negotiations of identity using the resources of AAVE are described by Reyes (2005). Her research participants are second- and 1.5-generation refugees from Cambodia, Laos, and Vietnam who live in lower-income urban areas of Philadelphia. Reyes points out that these Southeast Asian immigrants do not assimilate to "the dominant white majority in the United States," but instead they follow the path of "acculturation to socially and economically marginalized minority communities" (Reyes 2005: 515). This trajectory fits these students' socioeconomic reality: having few economic resources and thus having settled in poor urban areas, they live and go to school in predominantly non-white, largely African American neighborhoods, and they identify with the experiences of low-income African Americans more than with those of mainstream white students. These experiences include on one hand shared living and educational environments, and on the other similar struggles in the mainstream culture in terms of being typecast as a "problem" minority. Southeast Asian Americans in Reyes' study are thus seen adopting practices linked to African American urban youth culture, including clothing, accessories, make-up, hairstyles, practicing graffiti and rapping, and active participation in hip hop culture. They also draw on linguistic resources of AAVE. However, Reyes stresses that they do not speak AAVE systematically: "it is more accurate to characterize the speech of the majority of the teens as a hybrid variety that frequently incorporated features of AAVE as well as features of Mainstream American English (MAE) and of Vietnamese, Khmer (Cambodian), Lao or other home languages of the teens" (Reyes 2005: 515). Like the Laotian high schoolers in Bucholtz's study who iron their baggy pants and fold the cuffs under, Southeast Asian American teens in Philadelphia adopt elements of African American cultural and linguistic practices and reinterpret and recombine them to produce their own style. Southeast Asian Americans also engage in linguistic performance (Bucholtz 2009, Bucholtz and Hall 2004) when self-consciously adopting specific slang terms that originate in AAVE in order to assert identification with African Americans and distinction from Chinese, Japanese, and Korean Americans: as one Cambodian American teen explains, "we don't identify with Asians so we identify with blacks" (Reyes 2005: 519). At the same time, these linguistic choices index the teens as cool and tough, reproduce the association of African Americans with deviant social behaviors, and racialize slang as "belonging to African Americans" (520). But it turns out that slang is also invoked by these teens as a marker of urban youth culture to authenticate themselves as its members and in opposition to adults unfamiliar with slang terms (522). Identities negotiated at the hyphen are again not limited to race, ethnicity, and immigrant/American status, but involve many other aspects of social relations such as gender, age, generation, geographic location, and so on.

3.3 *Chan Is Missing* and *Fresh Off the Boat*: Immigrant American Subjectivities in Motion

Wayne Wang's 1982 film *Chan Is Missing* is a provocative examination of the heterogeneous, dynamic process that Feng (1996) describes as "becoming" (rather than "being") Asian American. In his paper, Feng interrogates hyphenated identity – which he terms "hyphenate identity" – and arrives at the conclusion that in contrast to the frequently encountered attempts at fixing or stabilizing some specific identity perceived as located at or created by the hyphen, in fact hyphenation is a dynamic process without an end: a becoming. Feng argues "that Asian American subjectivity cannot be founded upon any notions of stability, for such notions arrest the process of becoming and are not true to the fluidity of hyphenate identity" (1996: 110).

The plot of *Chan Is Missing* centers around two second-generation Chinese American cab drivers in San Francisco's Chinatown, Jo and his nephew Steve, as they search for Jo's missing friend, Chan Hung, who seems to have vanished with $4,000 of the men's money. Shot over ten consecutive weekends and produced on the low budget of $22,500 (Feng 1996: 97–98), the black-and-white, grainy, unpolished, eighty-minute film was well received by critics following its release[14]. It has been variously described as one of Wayne Wang's "brilliant, patient, edgy meditations on the well-worn theme of the immigrant experience" that "celebrated and reveled in the profound shapelessness of identity" (Hsu 2006) and "a small, whimsical treasure of a film that

[14] See, for example, the New York Times review on April 24, 1982, available at www.nytimes.com/1982/04/24/movies/chan-is-missing.html, accessed March 27, 2015.

gives us a real feeling for the people of San Francisco's Chinatown" (Ebert 1982). It has been seen as an art-house film, an Asian American film, and an experimental film playing with features of detective movies and film noir (Feng 1996). It seems that the film itself, as an artifact, is in the process of "becoming," its identity as dynamic an activity as that of its title character, who is at the same time central to the film and altogether absent from it.

In their quest to find Chan Hung, Jo and Steve follow various clues throughout Chinatown. Jo is worried about Chan's well-being, while Steve is more motivated by the desire to recover his money. They talk to numerous people who knew Chan, but none of them know where Chan might be. They all, however, have a hypothesis based on their individual interpretations of who Chan is as a person. As Feng argues, "everyone who offers an opinion of Chan Hung first . . . defines his/her own identity – and then depicts Chan as he best complements that identity . . . Each person sees Chan as the thing that s/he is not, or does not want to be" (Feng 1996: 105). And at the end of the film, having recovered their money through Chan Hung's daughter, but still not having located Chan himself and being no closer to knowing even where he might be, Jo reflects on all the different interpretations of Chan Hung that he has heard:

> Mr. Lee says Chan Hung and immigrants like him need to be taught everything as if they were children. Mr. Fong thinks anyone who can invent a word processing system in Chinese must be a genius. Steve thinks that Chan Hung is slow-witted, but sly when it comes to money. Jenny thinks that her father is honest and trustworthy. Mrs. Chan thinks her husband is a failure because he isn't rich. Amy thinks he's a hot-headed political activist. The old man thinks Chan Hung's just a paranoid person. Henry thinks Chan Hung is patriotic, and has gone back to the mainland to serve the people. Frankie thinks Chan Hung worries a lot about money and his inheritance. He thinks Chan Hung's back in Taiwan fighting with his brother over the partition of some property. George thinks Chan Hung's too Chinese, and unwilling to change. Presco thinks he's an eccentric who likes mariachi music (Quoted in Feng 1996: 102).

Not only, then, is Chan's identity elusive and fleeting, but as Feng argues, each character tries to fix and stabilize it, simultaneously also attempting to stabilize his or her own identity (106). In doing so, the characters invoke various discourses on immigration and on the Chinese American and Asian American experience, such as the obligation to learn English, the need to assimilate, the benefits of blending two cultures, or even the impassable rift between the Chinese and American worlds. The result is a confusing picture of a man who represents a different thing to each person that knows him, but who never actually appears. We never meet Chan Hung. According to Feng, "*Chan Is Missing*'s lack of closure is a manifestation of the process of becoming which the narrative describes" (102). If Chan had been found, and the process of becoming thus had been accomplished, the product would be a finalized state of "being," which is not how identity operates. Feng states that "Asian American subjectivity cannot be founded upon any notions of stability, for such notions arrest the process of becoming and are not true to the fluidity of hyphenate identity" (110). He takes his analysis further, suggesting that by deconstructing and de-centering the notion of a stable Chinese American identity in the person of Chan Hung, the film opens up the space for the emergence of something new: the Asian American subjectivity (110).

Reframing Feng's argument in the context of the discussion in this chapter, we can interpret the new Asian American subjectivity as the fluid, flexible, dynamic, and ongoing process of hyphenation and hybridization. *Chan Is Missing* represents the process of "working the hyphen" discussed by Sirin and Fine (2008). New subjectivities that emerge in the American context respond to but also participate in ethnogenesis, producing Asian Americans, Muslim Americans, African Americans, and Native Americans (Sirin and Fine 2008). But whereas Feng sees specific, nationally defined hyphenated labels – such as Chinese American – as attempts to fix hyphenated identities as definable combinations of their two components, reinterpreting the hyphen as a site of dynamic identity work allows for the formation and reformation of multiple and constantly shifting hyphenated selves. Asian Americanness is one of these, but it can co-emerge with a flexible Chinese Americanness, and the two can be sometimes complementary, sometimes parallel, and sometimes in conflict. Asian Americanness is certainly a subjectivity in motion, or in the process of becoming, but it is one of many such subjectivities.

Language is a key resource for the negotiation of hyphenated selves in *Chan Is Missing*, indexing multiple domains of belonging and establishing adequation and distinction (Bucholtz and Hall 2004). Since Chan Hung never appears, he cannot speak for himself. He has neither his own voice nor his own language. Those who talk about Chan, however, employ a range of linguistic forms to enact their own identities, and by the same token to index what Chan is not. Sometimes, their linguistic choices work to authenticate their claimed identities, and sometimes they denaturalize them (Bucholtz and Hall 2004).

Steve, the younger partner in the would-be detective duo, who at one point comedically introduces Jo and himself by saying, "That's Charlie Chan, and I'm his Number One Son – The Fly!," with "fly" pronounced as [fla:::::::], frequently crosses into AAVE. At the beginning of the film, while discussing Chinatown politics with his wife Amy and with Jo, he teasingly interrogates Jo's political loyalties: "What kind of CHINESE-Chinese are you, huh? PRC? Huh? Taiwan, pro-Taiwan?," with the diphthong in "Chinese" again emphasized and monothongized in keeping with AAVE features: [tʃa::ni:z]. Steve's strategy of performing an African American speech style is much like the linguistic practices of Asian American teenagers described by sociolinguists several decades after the release of *Chan Is Missing*, for example in work of Bucholtz (2009), Reyes (2005), and Chun (2001). And whereas the participants in Bucholtz's (2009) and Reyes' (2005) studies are Southeast Asian Americans whose use of AAVE is partly a response to being excluded from the "model minority" and stereotyped as a "problem" group, the Korean American young man named Jin discussed by Chun (2001) adopts certain superficial features of AAVE in what appears to be an assertion of tough heterosexual masculinity. Significantly, the "model minority" stereotype operates in tandem with the perception of Asian American males as weak and asexual. By contrast, African American masculinity is seen as tough and hypersexual in mainstream American discourses (Chun 2001; Cutler 1999; Bucholtz 1999), and Jin draws on this representation as he constructs his own masculine persona in talk with his Korean American friends. His efforts to resist and remake stereotypical depictions of Asian American masculinity rely on and reproduce dominant ideologies surrounding African Americans, demonstrating that identity negotiation is always dialogic and complex.

Steve in *Chan Is Missing* is shown as similarly employing AAVE in identity performances that invoke cultural stereotypes: the streetwise inner city male, and the comedic sidekick (cf. Lippi-Green 2012). And at times, his performance is rejected as inauthentic. Feng (1996) writes: "While shaking [Chan Hung's daughter's] hand, Steve adopts the posture of a streetwise ghetto kid, clasping her wrist and rapping, 'What's happening!' He then goes on a riff about Mrs. Chong's mah-jongg club, to which the girls reply, 'Who do you think you are, anyway, you think you're Richard Pryor, something like that?'" (105). By contrast, Chan's daughter Jenny, while dismissing Steve's identity claim, also speaks with some AAVE features, but these are not exaggerated and appear as linguistic practice rather than performance (Bucholtz 2009; Bucholtz and Hall 2004). Jenny is a second-generation Chinese American teenager who asserts her independence by disrespectfully defying her mother's repeated requests for silence in the presence of guests and instead blasting loud Cantonese pop music at full volume from her room. At the same time, she has a job and appears mature and assertive. Her consistent speech style authenticates the identity she is constructing for herself.

Meanwhile, Jenny's mother and Chan Hung's wife, Mrs. Chan, who is highly critical of her husband's inability or unwillingness to assimilate and to try to strike it rich in America, speaks in fluent English but with a Chinese accent – unlike Jo whose English sounds American – and engages in Chinese cultural practices such as giving fruit as gifts. Mrs. Chan's linguistic and cultural practices denaturalize her critique of Chan's failure to assimilate by clearly marking her as a first-generation immigrant, at the same time emphasizing the contested meaning of concepts such as assimilation. Finally, Henry, the cook at the Golden Dragon restaurant, who believes that Chan Hung left for the mainland for patriotic reasons, marks himself clearly as a first-generation unassimilated immigrant by speaking primarily in Chinese. He is in fact the only character in the film to do so. When Jo comes to ask him about Chan, Henry talks at length about the impossibility for Asian immigrants to assimilate in the United States. "We have been here over a hundred years, but they still treat us like foreigners," he says in Chinese before switching to English: "You are a *foreigner* here, you know that? You don't belong here."[15] But although Henry appears to speak for Chan Hung as well as to be proposing a sense of shared experience between himself, Chan and Jo, he is speaking in Beijing-accented Mandarin. Not only is Jo, who is American-born and who never utters a word of Chinese, unlikely to understand him – although it is never made clear whether Jo is familiar with any variety of Chinese or not – but Chan Hung's Taiwanese citizenship is foregrounded in the film on a number of occasions, including an important reference to a fight between Taiwanese and PRC immigrants over flags to be displayed at a Chinese New Year's parade. Henry's construction of a unified Chinese identity, which is incompatible with an American identity, is denaturalized by the very diversity of Chinese backgrounds, experiences, and relationships that is indexed by his use of Beijing Mandarin while talking to Jo. Which is not to say, of course, that Henry is not making a valid sociopolitical observation: that Asian Americans are viewed by mainstream society as perpetual foreigners. The complexity and diversity of voices and linguistic forms encountered in *Chan Is Missing*, combined, as Feng (1996) points out, with a lack of any kind of closure to the film's quest, highlight the ongoing "becoming" of Asian American subjectivities, and the dynamic hybridity of hyphenated identities more generally.

Thirty-three years after the release of *Chan Is Missing*, on February 4, 2015, the ABC channel launched *Fresh Off the Boat*, the first sitcom about an Asian American family since the short-lived *All American Girl*, starring Margaret Cho, aired on the channel for two seasons in 1994–1995. The sitcom is based on Eddie Huang's 2013 memoir of the same title. In it, Huang tells the story of his and his family's immigrant life, with all its gritty, messy complexity: his early childhood in New York, his parents' family background as Mainland Chinese immigrants in Taiwan and then as Taiwanese immigrants in America, his father's gangster past in Taipei, the family's move to Orlando in search of better prospects, the intimacy and dysfunction of his home life, his contentious relationship with education, negotiating his place within networks of peers of various ethnic backgrounds, running afoul of the law, drug dealing, his identification with hip hop and his cultural and personal resistance, and finally his success as an acclaimed chef running his own restaurant on New York City's Lower East Side. Quotes from reviews on the book cover describe the memoir as "bawdy," "brash," "hilarious," and "provocative," much of which is likely

[15] As heard in the film.

due to its unapologetically graphic and foul language, and the open discussion of taboo topics like drugs, sex, and violence.

The language of *Fresh Off the Boat*, however, is more than a provocative, superficially sprinkled special effect. Eddie Huang's style includes frequent crossing into what Bucholtz (1999) terms Cross-Racial AAVE or CRAAVE: the use of AAVE "as a symbolic marker of African American youth culture" that can be appropriated by "urban-identified" youth (445). Bucholtz further explains that "CRAAVE is not a unified speech style; different speakers draw on different features of AAVE phonology, syntax, and morphology, and their speech does not correspond to most African Americans' linguistic patterns," and she distinguishes it from cases where cross-racial AAVE is used "without commodification or appropriation, the difference being that the white speakers . . . were fully integrated into the African American speech community" (445–446). Huang's use of AAVE features throughout his book varies depending on register and on the role Huang inhabits: whether he speaks as the narrator telling his story to the wider audience, or as the protagonist interacting with other people in various social networks. He also uses elements of AAVE to represent the speech of others in constructed dialogue (Bucholtz 1999, Tannen 1989). AAVE features thus serve as crucial elements in constructing double-voiced discourse in Huang's memoir (Bakhtin 1981; Bucholtz 1999: 446). Eddie Huang's crossing into AAVE is more consistent and self-conscious than Steve's in *Chan Is Missing*, and it appears strongly motivated by Eddie's in-depth familiarity with and passion for hip-hop and basketball, as well as by his openly stated feelings of alienation from mainstream America.

Huang's use of AAVE features is always marked, as is the case with CRAAVE (Bucholtz 1999). Huang the narrator uses them to establish stance (Chun 2015), which most often emerges as disalignment from any manifestations of what he perceives as "whiteness." Thus, when commenting on cultural insensitivity exhibited by white Americans, he says, " . . . as soon as I opened up about it, everyone had a story about white people *talkin'* out the side of *they mouths* at work . . . That's what I loved about New York: even white people hated white people. No one wanted the stereotype of an ignorant white dude to represent them . . . " (Huang 2013: 213; emphasis mine). Here, in orienting himself in opposition to white privilege, which is consistent with his rejection of the "model minority" role throughout the memoir, and as he criticizes racism born out of ignorance, Huang uses the AAVE form *they* for the third-person plural possessive pronoun, *their* (Morgan 2002). Meanwhile, Huang the protagonist draws on AAVE features for interactional negotiation of identity, as well as for emphasizing aspects of his public persona and of his social relationships to the reader. Mostly, he does this when highlighting his orientation towards African American cultural practices such as hip-hop and basketball, or towards issues of race. For example, in showing his dismay that his "first

Asian homie" Joey Vano (Huang 2013: 82) loves surfing and alternative rock, he exclaims, "Damn, son, you Filipino, you should be the b-boy, rockin' snap-backs, listening to Pac, not me!" (83), with features such as copula deletion in "you Filipino," -ng > -n' and "son" as a form of address. Huang's AAVE features include vocabulary items, frequently those linked with hip-hop slang, such as *crib* ("house"), *mad* ("very"), *bitch* and *ho* to refer to women,[16] *to rock* ("to sport" in the sense of "to wear"), *cat* ("guy"), *naw mean* ("do you know what I mean?"; see Reyes 2005) and numerous references to hip-hop lyrics which mark Eddie's claim to insider status in the subculture. In addition, he uses morphological syntactic features, for example double negation, third-person singular *don't*, habitual *be, -ink* > *-ank* in "I woke up stankin'" (Huang 2013: 187; cf. *thing* > *thang* in Morgan 2002; Chun 2015), and the stressed *BIN* indicating remote past (Rickford and Rickford 2000). The latter form appears when two other sneaker collectors ask Eddie about his shoes: "'Where'd you get those Send Helps, though?' 'I been had them. I got all the SBs, Air Max, Jordans, etc., before they come out'" (Huang 2013: 218). Eddie is using *been had* to emphasize that he has had the sneakers for a long time before their official release date. This feature stands out because it has been described as not commonly borrowed in crossing into AAVE (Rickford and Rickford 2000), so it may be interpreted here as Huang's assertion of insider status and of strong orientation towards African American culture. Such grammatical choices contrast with Korean American Jin's AAVE use in Chun's (2001) study, which exhibits "primarily elements of AAVE 'slang' that have been appropriated by MAE speakers often through popular culture" (Chun 2001: 54) such as *boody, bro*, or *representin* (55).

Huang's most interesting uses of AAVE features, however, occur when he is speaking about topics linked to Asian American identities, contexts, and experiences. In Chapter 3 of his book, he describes his trip to Taiwan at age twelve, which changed his childhood hatred of being Chinese (Huang 2013: 53). He writes, "For the first time, I started seeing [my dad] and Taiwan as part of me. It wasn't a country full of kids with salad bowl haircuts and TI-82s. There were bosses in stretch Benzes, bad bitches selling betel nut, and master chefs making Dan-Dan Mian" (53–54). The phrase "bad bitches selling betel nut" draws on hip-hop slang to describe Taiwanese *binglang xishi* or "betel nut beauties": young women scantily dressed in provocative outfits, who sell betel nuts to the mostly working-class, male motorists. The women typically sit perched on high stools inside small stands with glass doors and walls, located on street corners and along highways. The shops are often open twenty-four hours, and at night they are brightly lit up with neon lights. In many ways, the

[16] These are discussed by Cecelia Cutler in her appearance in the PBS program *Do You Speak American?*

image of the *binglang xishi* might be read as the Taiwanese representation of hyper-sexualized and objectified women that appear in American hip hop videos, and Huang's mention of them using CRAAVE invokes that similarity. Elsewhere, Huang introduces the readers to his partner in drug dealing – "this Chino named Allen . . . That cat was a futuristic Chinaman with gold fronts and a pit bull named Jade" (164) – or reveals "The thing that my dad's employees, American friends, and associates didn't know is that my dad was a motherfucking G in Taiwan" (47), using the slang term *G* for "gangster." The use of "motherfucking" indexes not just hip-hop slang, but African American discourse more generally, if we accept Alim and Smitherman's (2012) argument that *muthafucka* in AAVE is an intensifier with historical roots in the days of slavery (120–125), and that it is best understood as "uncensored mode" (UM) rather than obscenity (110–111). Eddie Huang's bringing together of Asian and Asian American themes, hip-hop and African American themes, and elements of AAVE constructs a hybrid discourse in which the Asian American experience is reinterpreted and retold through CRAAVE.

Huang makes numerous other references to American popular culture when discussing his family or his struggles with being Asian in America. He describes one of his parents' many fights: "Then he flipped the table. Food went flying everywhere. Plates broke. That's when Mom went Connie Corleone" (Huang 2013: 17), with a reference to Francis Coppola's film *The Godfather*. He writes about a bonding experience with his dad: "My dad and I always watched *Married with Children* together and this was my Bud Bundy moment. Instead of beer and strippers, we had nachos and Run TMC" (36). When his new European American friend Dave who wears no shoes comes into his house with dirty feet, Huang asks, "Everyone knows to take their shoes off in an Asian home, but the fuck you're supposed to tell Huckleberry Finn when he rolls in barefoot?" (68). And, commenting on the "goofy" clothes worn by the ABC (American Born Chinese) peers he meets at the Taiwanese government–sponsored Study Tour in Taipei, he writes, "On one hand, I had childhood photos of me wearing the same uniform and it cracked me up, but once I decided I didn't want to be the Taiwanese Balki Bartokomous, I made money to buy Nike and 'Lo" (188). In this reference to Balki from the 1980s sitcom *Perfect Strangers*, Huang distances himself from mainstream American expectations of a naive and goofy immigrant, and from those Asian Americans who reproduce such stereotypes; at the same time, he demonstrates, again, his familiarity with American pop culture, positioning himself as both an insider and otherized outsider. Throughout the memoir, Huang tells his story "in American," both linguistically and culturally, producing a hybrid immigrant American discourse through which his own hybrid identity is constructed. The memoir is, one might say, told at the hyphen.

Huang's hyphenated identity is a process, a becoming, a dynamic and ongoing interplay of sociocultural moves. He describes complex and often conflicting feelings and experiences. He wants to participate in Debate Club in school but refuses to conform to its standards and eventually turns to violence and drug dealing. He describes Christianity as "weird" (27) and cheese as "nasty" and stinking "like feet" (40), thus reversing the otherizing gaze and fixing it on what is normatively considered as unremarkable aspects of American culture (cf. Chun 2009). He rejects authority and the school institution but has a passion and curiosity for learning. As a young boy, he wishes he were white, but then proclaims his hatred of "whiteness," specifically as a lifestyle and attitude: "[Warren] didn't understand that I didn't hate white people. I hated *whiteness*" (114, emphasis original). He shows pride in his ethnic heritage, but also pokes fun at it. He orients towards African American culture and experience, particularly as expressed in hip-hop, because "there wasn't anything else that welcomed us in" (60) and because of his inability to identify with white America: "It's the age-old problem for Asian Americans. You dig and reach and beg for anything that was made for you, but it's just not around" (115). He speaks bitterly about racism and being the victim of racist "ching chong" jokes. He talks about rejecting assimilation and the model minority stereotype, much like Jin in Chun (2001) who exclaims, "*forget conformity man. DOWN WITH WHITEY*" (Chun 2001: 59); at the same time, however, he has friends from various ethnic backgrounds, including white Americans, and he does not claim blackness. Rather, he negotiates his own subjectivity in relation to blackness, frequently orienting towards it and away from whiteness (Chun 2015). He does, however, claim belonging to multiple geographic and cultural communities: he is well versed in hip-hop as well as in Chinese traditions such as ancestor worship; he talks with equal fluency about basketball and Taiwanese street food; he sees himself as a Floridian, saying "we Southerners . . . love grits, boiled peanuts, and fried okra" (Huang 2013: 159); and he asserts his exercise of US citizenship: "We all had a part in it and when Obama got elected, I told myself, Today, you're an American motherfucker" (226).

Huang's identity is complex and dynamic, and he is aware of this. For instance, he reflects on feeling most at home at an international airport, and he loves playing football despite his poor performance because being in the game erases his ethnic markedness: "Instead of being singled out and laughed at for being Chinese, I was being laughed at for totally sucking at football. It was a relief" (71). And Eddie Huang's story, despite being a memoir centered on Asian American identity, makes it clear that ethnicity is interwoven into other aspects of life. Huang talks at length about issues that are not based in ethnicity at all: his father's gangster past in Taiwan, his parents' fighting, being physically and emotionally abused at home and yet feeling love and loyalty to his family, dealing drugs, becoming an acclaimed chef, acting on civic responsibility. Huang's memoir is the story of hybrid identity, in the sense described by Sirin and Fine (2008) in reference to Muslim Americans. It is in many ways a twenty-first-century response to *Chan Is Missing*.

The ABC sitcom version of the book, however, remakes Eddie Huang's story almost completely, pulling it back into the more familiar and – for mainstream viewers – more comfortable terrain of a mild and relatively uncontroversial revision of stereotypes. The sitcom Huangs are, by and large, a classic model minority family: self-made, morally sound, hardworking Asians trying honestly to make it in America while being endearing in their naiveté. Eddie Huang is shown as a good kid with a bit of a hip-hop attitude, a mischievous troublemaker who is unquestioningly adorable and always makes the right choices in the end. The Huangs are an all-American family, which simultaneously normalizes Asians as all-American and erases the tensions and complexities of the Asian American experience. The show attempts to present the all-American family with an ethnic bend: a bit quirky, sometimes speaking another language, eating "exotic" foods, and having just enough cultural dissonance to produce harmless confusion essential for situational comedy. The Huangs speak American English at home. Eddie has some features of AAVE, his brothers speak MUSE, and his parents both have some features of an Asian accent. There is even a wisdom-dispensing, Mandarin-speaking grandma, who does not feature in the book and who in the show is a solidly one-dimensional character providing a bridge to the old China. Grandma is shown to understand English, but never to speak it.

Eddie Huang, the memoir's author, narrates the voiceover in the show, which from the producers' perspective helps the audience "get into the mind of Young Eddie" (Huang 2015). Since Huang is playing himself, he appears to present the story to the viewers as his own. Yet, he is also deeply critical of the ABC network's interpretation of his memoir, emphatically denouncing it in numerous blogs, in interviews, and on social media, and even claiming that he does not watch the sitcom. Before the show's premiere, Huang complained, "They've made my dad into a neutered tourist in a fanny pack and stonewashed khakis" (Fan 2015). Elsewhere, he critiques the show, referring to the characters by the actors' names, Randall Park who plays Eddie's father, and Constance Wu who plays Eddie's mother: "Randall was neutered, Constance was exoticized, and Young Eddie was urbanized so that the viewers got their mise-en-place"; but then he adds, "People watching these channels have never seen us, and the network's approach to pacifying them is to say we're all the same. Sell them pasteurized network television with East Asian faces until they wake up intolerant of their own lactose, and hit 'em with the soy" (Huang 2015). Then on April 8, 2015, Huang sent out a series of tweets distancing himself from the show: "For the record I don't watch #FreshOffTheBoat on

@ABCnetwork"; "I'm happy that people of color are able to see a reflection of themselves through #FreshOffTheBoat on @ABCnetwork but I don't recognize it"; "I had to say something because I stood by the pilot. After that it got so far from the truth that I don't recognize my own life"; and "My grandma had bound feet, my grandpa committed suicide, HRS tried to take us from my parents. That shit was real" (Huang 2015).

Huang's intense and conflicted reaction to the sitcom on one hand reflects a critique of the way a "real" Asian American story has been remade to fit an existing stereotype, complete with an emasculated male – Eddie's sitcom father – which is both the image many Asian American young men reject in part by orienting towards African American culture (Chun 2001), and the opposite of Eddie's real father's tough, dominating, and violent personality. On the other hand, however, Huang recognizes that including Asian Americans as central figures in prime-time entertainment on ABC is a step towards involving Asian American voices in the conversation about Americanness. Furthermore, in the show, the immigrant story – the Taiwanese-Chinese-American story, as Huang describes it in several online outlets – enters a dialog with the genre of situational comedy, which is, in the form that it takes on prime time TV on networks such as ABC, a specifically American TV genre rooted in a style of comedy that follows shows such as *I Love Lucy* – which, incidentally, also incorporated a stylized and stereotyped immigrant figure, Ricky Ricardo (Morales 2002). It remains to be seen whether ABC's version of *Fresh Off the Boat* will lead to a revision of mainstream American entertainment or whether it will do nothing more than contribute to the reproduction and naturalization of ideologies surrounding Asian Americans.

According to Chun (2009), Korean American comedian Margaret Cho's routines that appear to center around stereotypes and draw on Mock Asian English, in fact frequently work to denaturalize assumptions about Asian Americans. Similarly, Eddie Huang's memoir denaturalizes the mainstream idea of Asian Americans as a uniform group with a predictable and easily categorizable set of characteristics. The book presents readers with a complexity of identities and human experiences that are not reducible to stereotypical molds. There is the gangster father, the experience of being Taiwanese-Chinese in America, the intergenerational conflict, the localized group identities relevant in Orlando, complex family relationships filled with both love and anger, and linguistic and cultural crossing as a reaction to public discrimination and private pain. Eddie feels a connection with hip-hop in part because of his alienation from white America – but also because it is his way of coping with domestic violence that is not a matter of culture or ethnicity. The Asian American characters in the book engage in hyphenation as a dynamic, ongoing, dialogic process. The ABC sitcom version, however, reverts to ethnic reductionism and racializes Eddie Huang's story by setting race up as the point of departure and an explanation. Huang himself passionately critiques this adaptation of his story: "From the Chinese Exclusion Act to *Yick Wo v. Hopkins* to your favorite talking head's favorite 'ching chong' jokes, America never ran out of the shadows to defend the honor of their obedient Chinamen. Despite being the 'man's' preferred lapdog of color, everything Asian-American immigrants have was fought for" (Huang 2015). Nonetheless, we might still argue that the dialogue taking place among the various texts – Huang's memoir, the ABC show, Huang's critique of the show, and various media responses to the show and to his critique – is in itself an ongoing, conflicted, public negotiation of the meanings of Asian American identities and of their relationship with mainstream American culture.

4 Foreign Accents and Immigrant Englishes

Race, as we have seen in the last two chapters, is a powerful construct in the United States, one that has long functioned as a marker of alienness. Asian Americans, Latinos, and Muslim Americans – in whose case physical appearance may be more or less salient than outward expressions of religious affiliation, such as the *hijab* – continue to be positioned in mainstream American discourses as "perpetual foreigners," whose status as non-white somehow legitimizes the question "Where are you *really* from?"[1] (Lippi-Green 2012; Cheryan and Monin 2005; Wu 2002). Another marker of alienness that persists in popular imagination and everyday encounters is the "foreign accent." I put the phrase in quotes intentionally, to emphasize that although foreign accents represent something concrete to many Americans who may believe that they can easily identify and define a foreign accent, in reality they, too, are a social construct. Foreign accents are positioned as the opposite of "native speaker accents," or, as envisioned in popular language ideologies, of American English "without an accent" (Lippi-Green 2012). But, as has been persuasively argued in recent scholarship, the notion of a "native speaker" is a highly problematic one since first and second language acquisition proceed simultaneously and throughout one's lifetime rather than occurring as separate events (Andrews 2014). The very recognition of a "foreign accent" is highly subjective: in my own ongoing research, I have found that the same speakers of American English as a second language may be evaluated by different interlocutors as having a very "strong" or "thick" foreign accent, or as not having one at all. Furthermore, such speakers are sometimes successful in convincing their American-born conversational counterparts that their accent is really from

[1] This phenomenon has been for some time the target of critique in popular culture and everyday discourse, as demonstrated in the short YouTube parody "What Kind of Asian Are You?" in which a young Asian American woman is thoroughly otherized by a white American man who cannot accept that she is, in fact, from San Diego. In response, she insists on finding out where his "people" are "really" from, and, once he finally says that his grandparents were from England, she proceeds to invoke various stereotypes of Britishness, ending with "I think your people's fish and chips are amazing," to the young man's utter dismay. Despite the circulation of such critiques, the "perpetual foreigner" experience continues to be part of non-white Americans' lives. www.youtube.com/watch?v=DWynJkN5HbQ, accessed January 11, 2016.

another part of the United States.[2] Thus, while accents are, as Urciuoli (1995) points out, key sociolinguistic resources available for the establishment of ethnic boundaries and of national belonging, they are also continuously negotiated social constructs. Differences in pronunciation and variations in grammatical features are perceived and evaluated as either "from here" or "from elsewhere," and some of these differences are designated as "foreign" in the sense of "not American."

Bolonyai (2015), in her study of the "Where are you from?" or "WAYF?" question as experienced by first-generation Hungarian immigrants in North Carolina, argues that "the 'WAYF?' question triggered by a nonnative accent is a boundary-making practice of ritualized Othering" (3). Whether the accent is evaluated as offensive, as a failure to assimilate ("You have been here twenty years and you still have such a heavy accent?!"), as a curiosity, or as charming or sexy, the very process of dissection and evaluation of the accent establishes a binary distinction (Bucholtz and Hall 2004) between the American-born "native speaker" and the foreign-born outsider. The accent becomes a legitimate target of questioning and comments, which, as Rosina Lippi-Green (2012) points out, is not the case to the same degree of overtness with physical features such as skin color (e.g. "Wow, how come you are black if you are from France?").[3] Crucially, regardless of the intentions behind the question – which may often be as innocuous as simple curiosity – the effect is one of otherization and of positioning the accented speaker as not from America. Furthermore, due to the abundant reliance on foreign accents to embody various characteristics and personality types in film and other media, and to produce comedic and other effects, the accent-triggered "WAYF?" question constructs the accented speaker as available for association with any of the foreign-accent stereotypes circulating in mainstream discourses (e.g. difficult to understand, sneaky, impenetrable, romantic, sexy, aggressive, etc.). Nonstandard accents that can be located as originating within the borders of the United States may be stigmatized and disparaged, but they do not serve as justification for questioning their speaker's belonging or loyalty to America. As Bolonyai (2015) puts it, "Such public Othering through the 'WAYF?' question positions local vs. foreign accents unequally, authorizing those on the home turf to patrol and reinforce boundaries between those who belong to the nativist chronotope and those who are out of place" (13). The paradox that emerges here is that there are plenty of American-born speakers of

[2] Bolonyai (2015) discusses the example of one of her research participants, who, while speaking with a Hungarian accent, insists that he is from Northern Virginia when questioned about his origins. Surprisingly, he claims that his American-born interlocutors believe him, commenting simply that they have not heard this particular dialect before.

[3] For example, one does not find popular critiques of accent-based otherization similar to the YouTube video "What Kind of Asian Are You?"

English who continue to have a "foreign accent," either because of growing up in non-English-dominant environments such as the border towns in Arizona and New Mexico, or because they learned a variety of American English that was born out of language contact and has features of the non-English input (see Section 4.3).

The goal of this chapter is to challenge assumptions about "foreign accents" and their relationship to Americanness. By examining the multiplicity of stereotypes, the conflicting representations, and the contested social meanings associated with foreign accents, I hope to highlight that, as any social construct, the "foreign accent" is not a stable entity but rather it is continuously negotiated and reinvented. However, as I will discuss in Section 4.2, not all foreign accents are treated as equal, and being identified as someone who speaks with an undesirable foreign accent can have serious repercussions for a person's social acceptance or employment opportunities (Lippi-Green 2012). Therefore, I hope that the discussion presented in this chapter contributes to a reconceptualization of accented English from some entity that stands apart from "native-speaker English" or "American English" to an integral part of a hybrid and constantly evolving repertoire of American Englishes (cf. Makoni and Pennycook 2005).

The most comprehensive study of accent in America to date is Rosina Lippi-Green's (2012) book *English with an Accent.* In it, Lippi-Green tackles the numerous manifestations of the "standard language myth" in the United States: the reproduction of the "standard English" ideology in schools and in children's programming; the effects of discrimination against non-standard English in the workplace and in the courts; the stigmatization of AAVE, of Southern English, of Hawai'i Creole, and of other non-standard varieties; the fear surrounding the use of Spanish in America; and the stereotyping of Asian Americans as speakers of incomprehensible English and thus as inauthentic Americans. Lippi-Green's work mounts a formidable challenge against accent-based discrimination, and succeeds at dismantling various myths that surround the concept of "accent." However, Lippi-Green builds her argument in part on the idea that phonology is an aspect of one's linguistic competence that is virtually impossible to modify past a certain point in one's life, which produces "accents" in second-language learners of any language – or, for that matter, learners of a different dialect of their first language.

Lippi-Green illustrates this point with two metaphors. One compares language to physical attributes such as height, which cannot be altered at will and over which we do not have control. Lippi-Green's point is that a person's linguistic repertoire such as the first language and the resulting regional and foreign accents is far less a matter of choice than is often assumed, and that requiring speakers to "give up" their accent is unrealistic and about as fair as requiring them to alter their height. Lippi-Green's second metaphor is that of the "Sound House," which she envisions as a structure we build as infants and young children from the "blueprints" that are only available to us up until a certain point. Once the blueprints are gone, we can continue to learn new languages, but we will never get their "Sound House" structures quite right. Again, the point is that language and dialect learners cannot change their accented pronunciation no matter how hard they try after a certain age. This, according to Lippi-Green, is a powerful argument against accent-based discrimination.

Lippi-Green's language-as-physical-attribute and "Sound House" metaphors rely on the assumption that there is a critical period for first and second language acquisition. However, recent research shows that such a critical period, which has typically been assumed to span from birth to puberty, does not in fact exist; rather, neuroscientists believe that critical periods in brain development are better described as continua with periods of greater sensitivity or susceptibility, whose beginning and end points are flexible and can be influenced by environment (Andrews 2014: 20). Birdsong (2006), in his extensive review of studies focusing on critical periods in language acquisition, finds that "the behavioral data are generally inconsistent with either a period of peak sensitivity whose end coincides with the end of maturation or with a leveling off of sensitivity whose beginning coincides with the end of maturation" (19). He also points out that age effects in native-like L2 acquisition interact with factors such as degree of similarity between L1 and L2, amount of L2 use, tasks L2 is used for, education in L2 as opposed to in L1, and others. While it has been suggested that acquisition of L2 phonetics/phonology is especially affected by a critical period – the assumption underlying Lippi-Green's "Sound House" metaphor – Birdsong cites studies showing that "[i]n the area of pronunciation, those learners who are taken for natives by native judges tend to be those with high levels of L2 practice, motivation to sound like a native, and L2 phonetic training" (Birdsong 2006: 20).

These findings seem to undermine Lippi-Green's argument that accent-based discrimination is similar to that based on physical features such as skin color or height, because they suggest that speakers have some control over the success of their L2 acquisition even in the area of pronunciation. However, although a rigid critical period for L2 phonetics/phonology acquisition may not exist, native-like acquisition is not always possible, depending on a range of factors. More importantly, however, studies cited by Andrews (2014) and Birdsong (2006) allow us to focus our attention on the ideologies that inform prejudice against foreign accents. Rather than trying to prove that L2 learners of English cannot "lose" their foreign accents, we may instead ask the question, *why should they?* The expectation that immigrants should strive to "overcome" their accents, and the praise offered to those who seem to have succeeded (Maulucci 2008: 38), point to the language ideology that envisions foreign accents as a badge of alienness. The "foreign accent" becomes a justification for the incessant WAYF? questions, for suspicions regarding one's loyalty to America, for stereotyping and profiling, and for rejection from employment opportunities. Moreover, accent is closely tied to race: as the discussion below will demonstrate, some foreign accents are believed to be less attractive and more difficult to understand than others, and the former are typically attributed to non-white speakers.

4.1 "I Just Can't Understand Them": Perceptions and Stereotypes of the Accented Other

Rubin and Smith (1990) employed the matched guise technique to study the connections among accent, ethnicity, and teaching ability as perceived by undergraduate students. The students listened to lectures given with a strong or a moderate Chinese accent, produced by the same speaker, while viewing a photograph of either a Caucasian or Asian female "instructor." The two photographs depicted individuals of similar dress, age, height, and hairstyle. Results showed that the photograph of the Caucasian instructor paired with a moderate accent was perceived as "less Asian/Oriental" than the same photograph paired with a stronger accent. In other words, high-accented guises were judged as "more Asian" than moderately accented ones, although the image remained the same and depicted a Caucasian female. Furthermore, when the students judged the instructor's accent to be stronger, they gave her lower teaching ratings, regardless of the actual degree of the speaker's accent. By contrast, actual comprehension was not significantly affected by actual or perceived level of accent. Rubin (1992) builds on these findings in a similar matched guise study, in which lectures read by a US-born speaker of American English were paired with photographs of Caucasian or Asian "instructors," again showing women of similar dress, age, height, and hairstyle. This time, students not only tended to perceive a foreign accent when looking at the Asian instructor, but their actual listening comprehension was negatively affected. These findings, which corroborate earlier research (e.g. Brown 1988), suggest that merely looking at an Asian face leads listeners to "hear" a foreign accent whether or not one is present, and to actually comprehend less of what they hear.

Given the long history of the racialization of Asians and Asian Americans as the "Oriental" threat, which I discussed in Chapter 2 (see Lee 1999), it is not surprising that the physical characteristics that are discursively grouped as racially Asian invoke, on one hand, the stereotype of a perpetual foreigner and, on the other, the perception of an incomprehensible accent, with the two reinforcing each other. Rubin and Smith (1990) and Rubin (1992) recognize this, interpreting the results of their studies as evidence that more ought to be done to educate American students about non-native accents by increasing exposure and countering stereotypes. They argue against the common assumption that it is the international instructors who should bear the onus for successful classroom communication and who should work to minimize their accents and "undergo transformation in the North American mold" (Rubin 1992: 512). Yet at the same time they admit that changing these attitudes is a daunting task that cannot be tackled at a superficial level. Indeed, the discriminatory attitudes of undergraduate students reflect dominant language ideologies that are rooted in a long history of racism that has been part of the national discourse surrounding immigration. At the heart of these ideologies is the assumption that a true American is a white, native (and preferably monolingual) speaker of American English.

Foreign Accent Ideology

In her analysis of linguistic discrimination in America, Lippi-Green (2012) develops the concept of the "standard language myth." According to this myth, there exists an identifiable "standard language" – in our case, Standard American English – which is not marked by regional characteristics, which can be most easily found in the Midwest or Far West, which is easily understood by all, and whose users are well educated, careful about their speech, possibly educators or broadcasters, and reliable arbiters of "proper" English (Lippi-Green 2012: 60). This imagined ideal (Milroy 1999; Crowley 2003) is promoted through schooling, the media, and other institutions as the correct form of the language, against which all others – whether regional, sociocultural, written, or vernacular – are evaluated. Lippi-Green calls this a myth, while Milroy (1999) describes standard languages as idealizations, since in reality even speakers whose language most closely resembles the "standard" diverge from it in various ways. He also discusses "standard language cultures" in which "the standard ideology" (Milroy 1999: 18) promoting the standard language's superior status is manufactured through naturalizing discourses. Lippi-Green describes the operation of these cultures as the "language subordination process" (Lippi-Green 2012: 70). Not surprisingly, so-called Standard American English is not typically associated with low-prestige regions such as the South or the New York boroughs of Brooklyn and Queens (Preston 2011), or with racial minorities. The standard language ideology associates "correct" English with whiteness and with the middle class. Those aspiring to middle-class status are expected to shed any regional and lower-class features, thereby demonstrating that they have received requisite education. There are exceptions, however. Powerful public figures are permitted to retain some of their non-standard features, which are then reinterpreted as "authentic," "charming," or "quaint." President Bill Clinton's

Southern accent, for example, did not detract from his political career, which was likely also helped by his privileged position as a white male.

"Foreign accent" ideology operates in similar ways, but centers on the notion of Americanness and its purported linguistic attributes. Like standard language ideology, it invokes the argument of comprehensibility as justification for prejudice. As Lippi-Green points out, in encounters between native and non-native speakers of English, often the "breakdown of communication is due not so much to accent as it is to negative social evaluation of the accent in question, and a rejection of the communicative burden" (2012: 73). Specifically, certain *types* of L2 speakers are identified as intruders whose duty it is to make themselves easily understood or else "they should go back to their country." Within this conceptual framework, white L2 speakers are given more leeway to sound non-native than Asian, Latino, or black speakers, whereas, as we saw above, simply seeing an Asian face can make an American listener believe that they hear a non-American accent. Native-speaking listeners, when confronted with a foreign accent that they do not wish to engage with, can choose to abdicate their share of responsibility for communicative success, although research shows that the latter is only possible as a collaborative effort between both parties (Schlegloff 1982; Clark and Wilkes-Gibbs 1986; Lindemann 2002). Even highly proficient L2 speakers may be assessed as unintelligible if listeners harbor prejudice against their accents or, indeed, against their particular racial or ethnic group (Lippi-Green 2012), and this prejudice may be amplified by cultural differences in discourse strategies (Gumperz 1982; Lindemann 2002).

Negative attitudes towards a specific accent have been shown to lead listeners to employ uncooperative conversational strategies such as avoidance or problematizing the speaker's utterances, which in turn leads to real or perceived communicative failure. For example, Lindemann (2002) demonstrates that in an experimental communicative task between native speakers and Korean L2 speakers of American English, the native speakers' attitude towards Korean accents predicted perceived communicative success in all cases: American English native speakers who harbored prejudice against Korean accents uniformly believed that the communicative task was not successful, as opposed to those with positive attitudes towards Korean accents, who felt that their communication went well. This was the case regardless of actual success of the communicative task assigned to the study's participants. In other words, native-speaking listeners who disliked Korean accents believed them to be incomprehensible despite evidence to the contrary.

Meanwhile, examples of unequal evaluation of accents depending on the speaker's race or ethnicity abound (e.g. Lippi-Green 2012; Cargile et al. 2010; Pantos and Perkins 2012; Shuck 2006; Lindemann 2005, 2003). According to Lippi-Green (2004), "none of the recent cases heard in US courts concerning alleged violations of Title VII of the Civil Rights Act . . . involve speakers with

French or Scottish or Norwegian accents" (29); rather, they involve speakers with Asian, Latin American, Middle Eastern, and African accents. Lindemann (2005), in a study of attitudes towards accents from various parts of the world, asked 213 undergraduate students to label the world map according to their ideas about English accents from different regions and to rate a set of countries based on the accents associated with them. The overall findings show that speakers from Western Europe and some Latin American countries (Costa Rica, Brazil, and Colombia) were rated highest with respect to correctness, pleasantness, and friendliness, followed by Central European, other Latin American (e.g. Mexico, Dominican Republic, Cuba), familiar Asian countries (China, India, Japan), and African countries. The lowest ratings were given to less familiar Asian countries (Korea, Taiwan, Thailand), Eastern Europe, and the Middle East. While these responses reveal the influence of the country's familiarity and political relationship with the United States on the respondents' attitudes (Lindemann 2005: 195), it is also clear that overall, non-white speakers' accents do not receive high evaluation. The qualitative descriptions provided in the map-labeling task reveal a similar pattern. Some examples include (adapted from Lindemann 2005):

- French accents: poetic, sweet, pretty, romantic (Lindemann 2005: 205)
- Italian accents: lots of emotion, "sing-song" melody (205)
- German accents: harsh, guttural, "close to normal" (204)
- Russian accents: "slurred," thick, harsh, broken English, guttural, "throat-like" (203)
- Mexican accents: "less Romantic than Spanish English" (presumably from Spain), sloppy (202)
- Indian accents: precise, enunciated, fast, "not enunciated clearly enough" (201)
- Chinese accents: quick, high toned, "leave out predicates in sentences," cut up, broken English, "hard time pronouncing many words w/r and l, many times forget to put plural '-s' on ends of words" (199–200).

Notably, although attitudes towards German and Indian accents seem conflicted, a closer look at the map-labeling task reveals that they are evaluated more positively or more negatively depending on whether respondents associate them with Western Europe or Eastern Europe (for Germany), and Great Britain or Asia (for India) (Lindemann 2005: 207). Unsurprisingly, it is the accents associated with whiteness, and with Western Europe in particular, that escape stigmatization – if not stereotyping.

Cargile et al. (2010) report findings similar to Lindemann's. Their verbal guise[4] study of sixty-five undergraduates at a large urban university shows that

[4] In a verbal guise study, participants hear different dialects or accents produced by multiple speakers. Speakers use their own native varieties. This differs from the matched guise technique,

when exposed to a variety of accents, respondents perceive speakers from Latin America and Asia as sounding more foreign than those from Western Europe. Within these large categories, Vietnamese speakers were rated as most foreign, followed by Mandarin, Spanish, Italian, and Hindi speakers. German speakers, however, were rated closest to MUSE speakers. Italian accents, meanwhile, tended to be identified as Spanish/Latin American, which may account for their evaluation. As Cargile et al. state in their summary, "it appears that the long-standing US American habit of attributing different degrees of belonging is still manifest in the guise of contemporary speaker evaluations" (71). Citing Sears and Henry's (2003) discussion of symbolic racism, they explain their findings as follows:

> Despite the fact that some citizens are considered more foreign than others, direct expression of this inegalitarian ideal is often frowned upon in today's post-civil rights society ... Thus, although US Americans may be reluctant to agree that persons of Chinese ancestry are any less "American" than those of German ancestry, the long-standing and shared prejudice against non-Europeans as full participants in US society may find expression in judgments that native speakers of Mandarin sound more "foreign" than native speakers of German (Cargile et al. 2010: 61).

This point echoes Lippi-Green's observation that linguistic discrimination is often perceived as justifiable because of the "common-sense" expectation that people should speak "correctly" and make themselves understood, yet it frequently masks racial and ethnic discrimination that would be deemed unacceptable if it were promoted overtly[5], as well as Phillipson's (1992) argument that "linguicism has taken over from racism as a more subtle way of hierarchizing social groups in the contemporary world" (241; cited in Shuck 2006: 260; see also Skutnabb-Kangas 1981).

Foreign accent ideology is an integral part of linguicism or linguistic discrimination directed at immigrants. Specifically, foreign accent ideology enacts racially and ethnically based barriers to being accepted as an American, under the guise of such ostensibly reasonable criteria as successful communication and comprehensibility. Like all language ideologies, foreign accent ideology operates through the naturalization of various discourses surrounding perceived language structure and use (Silverstein 1979). In this process, the "foreign accent" is constructed as a problem and an obstacle. On one hand, it is portrayed as incomprehensible and impeding successful communication. This idea is supported by the same naturalized assumptions as those motivating standard language ideology: that there exists a neutral,

in which the same speaker produces different language forms (accents, dialects, etc.) (Cargile et al. 2010).

[5] See Lippi-Green's (2004, 2012) discussion of the Civil Rights Act, Title VII, and its provisions regarding discrimination based on national origin. I will also return to this point in Section 4.2.

uniform, accent-less, "American" way to speak, and newcomers to the United States are responsible for learning it; and that we need a common, uniform way of speaking in order to understand each other. On the other hand, the foreign accent is assumed to mark one as born and raised outside of America, and thus one is also responsible for shedding the accent as part of proving one's loyalty to the United States. This reasoning is part of the same discourse on Americanness and immigration as the original concept of the melting pot, the pseudo-scientific hierarchies among immigrants, and the rejection of the hyphen, which I discussed in previous chapters. And it seems that the more suspect one's loyalty or capacity for assimilation – which is usually a factor of race and ethnicity – the more objectionable and "incomprehensible" one's accent is perceived to be.

In contrast to the studies I have discussed so far, which rely on matched guise or verbal guise techniques to elicit listeners' attitudes towards foreign accents, Shuck (2006) focuses on explicitly stated beliefs about foreign accents to explore the operation and circulation of language ideologies. Shuck draws on twenty-one interviews with pairs and three-person groups of first-year undergraduates, in which she asked open-ended questions about language in educational settings. As she correctly points out, "to become dominant in the collective consciousness, an ideology must be available for use in everyday talk among laypersons" (Shuck 2006: 260), and the discussions among her participants demonstrate how foreign accent ideology is constructed in local face-to-face interactions. Shuck argues that the students invoke "dominant ways of talking about race in the United States ... as templates for creating arguments about language" (259) and in doing so reproduce the iconic links (Irvine and Gal 2000) between nativeness in English on one hand, and whiteness and Americanness on the other. Some salient themes in the interviews include making explicit connections between accent and race, marking non-native speakers as Other, and invoking other racialized discourses "such as colonialism or the notion of reverse discrimination" (Shuck 2006: 263).

One example is Jen, who complains about the foreign accents of her two teaching assistants (TAs) and makes explicit her assumption that the Asian TA would have an accent and the white TA would not, in addition to emphasizing at length the incomprehensibility of the Asian TA's English (adapted from Shuck 2006: 265):

> I took – . . . what did I take. . . . MATH . . . 121 last semester. . . . and . . . my TA:, . . . was <[high pitch] very ni:ce, [high pitch]> . . . but she was fro:m – . . . I don't know where she was from. . . . an Asian-speaking country though. . . . because she was Asian.
> . . . I had no clue, . . . what she said, . . . the whole semester (. . .) couldn't..understand.. what she said (. . .)
> [*Moves on to talk about another TA*]

... who I assumed ... spoke ... um – ... or, wh- I s- I assumed he was from America. ... okay? 'cause he was like Caucasian, ... he (wa?)s from New Zealand. ... couldn't understand ... what ... HE said.

Another student, Joe, draws on colonialist discourses in his ostensibly sensible appeal to the need for comprehensibility (adapted from Shuck 2006: 269):

I'm I'm not saying he [an instructor] has to be a native English spea/ker./ = uh, ... he can be ... from – ... or she – ... /can be/ from ... I don't know, some little island somewhere. ... /they/ just have to have a certain level of ... uh proficiency.

Here, Joe envisions the non-native speaker who would typically be expected *not* to speak English proficiently as from "some little island somewhere," which, in Shuck's words, "subtly evokes an image of a primitive, brown-skinned island-dweller who speaks an exotic language" (269). Other participants complain that non-native-speaking students create problems in the classroom, because they receive "special help" and the instructors "cater" to their needs (270), while still others explicitly accuse foreign students of refusing to learn English – a common argument in the anti-immigration discourse. Thus, Cindy says, "They need to be able to function in society (...) if they want to speak Spanish (...) go back to Mexico, you know?"; Kelli wonders, "I can't imagine anyone living here, who would be intentionally trying NOT to learn the language"; and Laura comments, "Why didn't they stay where they were from, if they wanted to be isolated still" (272). Shuck identifies this "learn English or go back to your country" theme as "the canonical xenophobic argument" (272), which exhibits clear ties to the anti-immigrant rhetoric of the early twentieth century (Chapters 2 and 3).

A telling contrast to Shuck's data comes from Katharine W. Jones' (2001) book *Accent on Privilege*, which discusses the experiences, identities, and ideologies of British expatriates living in the United States in the context of American Anglophilia. Unlike immigrants from non-English-speaking, non-European countries, Jones' participants do not face stigmatization or an expectation that they change the way they speak to become more American. They are often otherized and reduced to their linguistic Britishness by comments such as "Oh, I could listen to you talking forever!" or "Oh, gee, I love your accent!" (Jones 2001: 135), but in this process they are not constructed as less-than-equal to US-born English speakers; to the contrary, they are able to maintain a sense of superiority when evaluating American English and American culture (cf. Hosoda and Stone-Romero 2010; Cargile and Bradac 2001). Their freedom to preserve and even emphasize their British origins stems from their position not as aspiring Americans, as is the case with most immigrants, but as representatives of the cultural and linguistic roots of America itself. And, as discussed in previous chapters, American roots have been consistently established in dominant discourses as deriving from the Anglo-Saxon, English-speaking tradition. Jones' participants are aware of their position of privilege and report frequently taking advantage of it, even though they also feel that living in America frees them from the rigid constraints of ideologies that tightly link specific accents to social class in Britain. Consequently, many of them focused on preserving their accents and expressed concern that their children "sound American." Jones also describes at length her participants' accent manipulation, emphasizing their linguistic skill and flexibility in "moving between shades of American English and English English" (115) to variously construct their identities, and to accomplish specific social goals.

Shuck's and Jones' work complements the numerous matched guise and verbal guise studies by offering a perspective on how US-born, native-speaking listeners come to respond most negatively to foreign accents of speakers who are not white. Matched guise and verbal guise studies have been criticized for their inability to explain what exactly their respondents are evaluating; in other words, what the accents they hear during the listening tasks mean to them and how they are categorized (Lindemann 2005). Some studies ask respondents to identify the accents, but misidentification is common. In Cargile et al.'s (2010) study, for example, Italian and Vietnamese speakers were identified correctly only 7 percent of the time. Similarly, Lindemann (2005) found that her respondents identified the speakers' accent correctly as Korean only 8 percent of the time, with other guesses being Japanese (13 percent), Chinese (18 percent), Asian (23 percent), Indian (16 percent), and Latino/a (12 percent) (Lindemann 2005: 354). Nonetheless, we see that the accent was identified as having some type of East Asian origin 62 percent of the time, and the other guesses also point to non-European, non-white regions. As Lindemann argues, "While the listeners identified speakers as widely disparate ethnicities, all of the commonly-named groups – East Asians, Indians, and Latinos/as – are stigmatized in the United States" (358). Cargile et al. also noted that most of their participants identified Vietnamese and Mandarin speakers simply as "Asian," but they still ranked Vietnamese accents as more foreign and as lower in status and attractiveness than Mandarin ones. This suggests that although the listeners grouped these accents together as Asian, they perceived them as different. It also means that they were evaluating at least partly how a particular accent sounds.

Crucially, responding to a Vietnamese accent more negatively than to a Mandarin one without being able to identify them does not mean that there is anything inherently less appealing about Vietnamese speakers' English. Rather, such results point to the successful operation of iconization, whereby linguistic features become so closely linked with the purported attributes of the groups they index that they evoke these attributes directly (Irvine and Gal 2000; Preston 2011). Listeners may not realize that they are listening to a Vietnamese accent, but the sounds they hear evoke attributes such as "unattractive," "working in a low-status job," or "difficult to understand." This process is accomplished in part through the representation of different accents in the media and popular culture, which I will discuss further in Section 4.2. At the same time, the listeners realize that the accent they hear is stigmatized (Lindemann 2005), and may be able to identify it generically as "Asian." Furthermore, we have seen that US-born American English speakers believe they hear a foreign accent when they see a non-white face, and they articulate beliefs that link foreign accents with non-white, non-European speaker backgrounds.

Linguistic Discrimination

Language ideologies surrounding foreign accents have powerful social and economic consequences for the immigrants perceived to speak with them. Accent-based discrimination at the workplace has been well documented (Lippi-Green 2012). Non-native accents or other features (e.g. syntax) can also be used as justification for unnecessarily placing students in ESL courses (an issue that I return to in Chapter 6), which impedes educational opportunities and professional success. Foreign accent ideology obscures any meaningful discussion of what language skills are in fact necessary to perform one's job adequately, in part because it absolves native speakers from responsibility for effective communication while also granting them the right to evaluate non-native speakers' English and to punish them for its perceived shortcomings. Moreover, poorly defined English proficiency is invoked as the gatekeeper in professional contexts, which in practice allows for racial and ethnic discrimination, and for achieving political goals.

This appears to have been the case for Alejandrina Cabrera, whose story was reported in a number of news outlets, including the *New York Times*.[6] Cabrera's name was removed from the ballot when she tried to run for city council in San Luis, Arizona. Although San Luis is a border city whose population is 90 percent Mexican American and whose dominant language is Spanish, Cabrera's political opponents filed a legal challenge against her because of her allegedly insufficient proficiency in English. They cited Arizona law that disqualifies persons unable to speak, read, and write English from holding office. Since the law does not specify how English proficiency is to be evaluated, judgments regarding Cabrera's English were left to interpretation. Cabrera herself described her English as limited, but fully sufficient for the needs of San Luis. She communicates with local residents in Spanish and insists her English is competent enough to conduct government business in this bilingual

[6] http://ideas.time.com/2012/02/13/do-elected-officials-have-to-speak-english/; www.nytimes.com/2012/01/26/us/arizona-candidates-english-under-challenge.html?_r=0; both accessed February 3, 2016. A video excerpt from Cabrera's court case can be viewed at www.youtube.com/watch?v=10Zg-T5m5pk, accessed February 4, 2016.

city. But the judge disagreed and struck her name from the ballot, influenced by the testimony of a language expert who had been tasked with evaluating Cabrera and found her English wanting. Crucially, the expert in question is Australian, which introduces several problems. First, he is an outsider whose evaluation of Cabrera's language skills is necessarily decontextualized and decoupled from the sociolinguistic realities and needs of San Luis. Second, his own Australian accent proved challenging to understand for Cabrera, which she claimed influenced her ability to perform on his tests. Finally, as an Australian college professor living and working in the United States, he is in a similarly privileged position as the English expatriates in Jones' (2001) study. His own "foreign accent" does not undermine his position as a native speaker and a language expert, and, paradoxically, he is able to exercise his authority to police the accent and grammar of someone born in the United States, but who is of a non-white, non-European, non-English-speaking background.

As can be gleaned from news media, Arizona, with its border with Mexico and a large Spanish-speaking population, frequently makes headlines because of its treatment of bilingualism and bilinguals. Arizona's 2000 passage of Proposition 203, English for the Children, which dismantled the state's bilingual education, left Spanish-speaking ESL teachers forced to teach in English. As L2 speakers, many have perceptible non-native accents. In 2002, the state began mandating that the evaluators dispatched by the education department to audit schools assess ESL teachers' English proficiency. Those found to speak "ungrammatically" or with a perceptible accent were removed from teaching ESL students and either fired or reassigned to mainstream classrooms.[7] In this case, the policy was halted in 2011 following a possible civil rights lawsuit. Nonetheless, we can see how foreign accent ideology allowed these teachers, many of whom have extensive experience and are also Latino immigrants, to have their qualifications evaluated primarily on how close their English resembled MUSE.

Employment discrimination on the basis of national origin violates Title VII of the Civil Rights Act. The directives on what constitutes discriminatory behavior, as stated by the Equal Employment Opportunity Commission (EEOC) in 2002, stipulate:

> Linguistic characteristics are closely related to national origin, and basing employment decisions on a qualified individual's foreign accent or limited ability to speak English may constitute national discrimination. Not all employment decisions based on linguistic characteristics will violate Title VII, however . . . For example, if effective communication in English is required to perform a job and an individual's accent materially

[7] http://archive.azcentral.com/arizonarepublic/news/articles/20110912arizona-teacher-accent-scrutiny-halted.html; www.wsj.com/articles/SB10001424052748703572504575213883276427528; accessed February 3, 2016.

interferes with the ability to communicate in English, rejecting the individual for the job because of the accent would not violate Title VII (EEOC 2002, cited in Lippi-Green 2012: 150).

The wording of these guidelines leaves crucial points open to interpretation, such as what constitutes "effective communication," what counts as an "accent," and when the accent may be said to "materially interfere" with performing a job (Lippi-Green 2012, Matsuda 1991). Lippi-Green (2012) points out that whereas judges and juries accept testimonies of specialists such as geneticists or biochemists, when it comes to language, laypersons often feel empowered to hold and express their own beliefs. Consequently, "a judge may choose to believe one expert over another simply because one of them provides an opinion that very closely matches his own personal opinions" (Lippi-Green 2012: 151). Lippi-Green supports her argument with examples of over a dozen legal cases that she cites and describes. In some of these cases, the judges relied on their own assessment of the plaintiff's accent, outright dismissing testimony by linguists. One judge even stated that the linguist "was not an expert in speech" (158). And since, as we have seen, judgments of accent are not objective and are frequently informed by racial prejudice, fair protection from accent-based discrimination in such cases is elusive at best. If listeners can perceive an accent as difficult to understand even as they demonstrate that they understand it in listening comprehension tasks, determining when an accent interferes with communication at work becomes an impossible goal. In cases of educational settings, several of which are described by Lippi-Green, it is also difficult to define what counts as job performance. Negative student evaluations of non-native-speaking professors' speech may reflect racial biases as well as other sentiments. In the case of Arizona's ESL teachers described above, bilingual teachers for whom English is L2 can be more effective in addressing Spanish-speaking children's educational needs than teachers monolingual in English, and this advantage may prove more significant than the exact modeling of MUSE pronunciation.

Having seen the above examples of how courts handle cases of linguistic discrimination, it is important to remember that the vast majority of instances of such discrimination never make it as far as the courts. Many immigrants are not in a position to file a lawsuit, and some may not even realize they have been discriminated against. Hosoda and Stone-Romero (2010) cite a 1990 US General Accounting Office survey which found that 10 percent of surveyed employers admitted to discriminating "on the basis of a person's foreign appearance or accent" (Hosoda and Stone-Romero 2010: 114). A telephone hiring audit, also conducted by the US General Accounting Office (1990), found that 41 percent of employers screened applicants based on the presence of a foreign accent, "telling accented callers that the jobs were filled, but telling unaccented callers that the same jobs were still open" (114). In the same paper, Hosoda and Stone-Romero report the results of their own study, in which 286 college students were asked to evaluate potential job applicants according to the criteria of job suitability and skills, and the likelihood of being hired by a potential employer. The types of jobs included high and low status, and those requiring high and low communication demands. The participants read each applicant's résumé and listened to a recording of a two-minute mock interview. Among the three sets of applicants – those speaking with MUSE, French, and Japanese accents – Japanese-accented applicants were evaluated more negatively than French-accented applicants and more negatively than MUSE-speaking applicants when applying for jobs that demanded a lot of communication, such as a customer service representative positions. French-accented applicants in this study were evaluated the most favorably. The authors conclude that for certain jobs, foreign accents linked to Asian countries seem to evoke more negative reactions than those linked to European countries. In a similar study, Hosoda et al. (2012) compared evaluations of applicants speaking with a MUSE accent and a Mexican-Spanish accent by 203 undergraduate students, who were told the applicants were seeking an entry-level software engineering job. In this case, the Mexican-Spanish-accented applicants were rated as less suitable for the job and "less likely to be promoted to a managerial position" (347).

Immigrants speaking with foreign accents are routinely stereotyped and reduced to the essentialized attributes that their accents evoke. This produces real-life challenges, both in the practical terms of job opportunities and in the more general sense of being positioned as outside "real" American society: the "accented speaker" is automatically framed as a foreigner. Gluszek and Dovidio (2010), for example, show that speaking with a non-native accent can correlate negatively with feelings of social belonging in American society. Furthermore, there is a hierarchy of accents in terms of the positive and negative characteristics that their speakers are assumed to possess. French accents may be seen as romantic, British accents as intelligent, and Chinese accents as incomprehensible or unfriendly. In every case, the accent becomes, in Irvine and Gal's (2000) terms, an iconic representation of the qualities that are associated with specific parts of the world, and with racial and ethnic groups.

4.2 Representing Foreign Accents in Popular Culture

California-born comedian Anjelah Johnson, whose own background is Mexican and Native American, is known in part for portraying the characters of a Vietnamese nail salon employee and a particularly rude fast food employee named Bon Qui Qui. The former, part of Johnson's early stand-up routines, became a YouTube success and helped her join the cast of the comedy show *MADtv* in 2007 and then get her own show on Comedy Central in 2009.

One video including the nail salon character available on YouTube[8] is an eight-minute stand-up routine that begins with Johnson talking about her Mexican family and Mexican Americans in general. This sets the stage for the second half of the routine, which opens with Johnson talking about getting manicures with her sister. She then enacts an encounter at a nail salon between herself and the employees. The employees – both the hostess and the manicurist – "speak" with what is meant to represent a Vietnamese accent, but in case the audience had any doubt, they are quickly framed as some type of Asian when the hostess tells Johnson that "Mai Ling" will take care of her. The stereotype is recognizable to the audience because the majority of nail salons in California, where Johnson is from, and half in the United States overall[9] are Vietnamese-owned. For those in whose area nail salons employ Koreans, Chinese, and Latinos, such as in New York, the name "Mai Ling" and the accent may evoke the image of someone of Asian background more generally. Very quickly, Johnson tells the audience that Mai Ling's "American name is Tammy," presumably to make this character more memorable to the English-speaking audience, which suggests that the Asian name was mentioned to construct the employee as unmistakably Asian.

In the routine, Johnson employs several distinct English accents representing different characters. She speaks Chicano English when portraying herself in interactions with her family and when addressing the audience directly, manifesting a number of Chicano English features described by Fought (2003). For example, she asks a man in the audience if he goes to get his nails done and jokingly admonishes him: "Don't lie. Sir, don't lie," pronouncing the diphthong in "lie" with a raised nucleus, a feature that Fought describes as /aj/ realized as [ɐj] (65), while also simplifying the cluster /nt/ to [n] (68–69) and lengthening the stressed syllables "don't" and "lie" (75). Johnson also loses the glide in the [ej] diphthong in "nail" so that it sounds more like [nel] (64), tenses the /ɪ/ in *-ing*, as in [glimiŋ] for "gleaming" (65), shows a lack of unstressed vowel reduction (64), employs TH-stopping (67–68), and speaks with Chicano English prosody (70–80). She then adopts a Mexican-Spanish accent and some English-Spanish code-switching while portraying her mother and father. She imitates a Vietnamese accent when speaking as the salon employees. And, crucially, she speaks MUSE when she portrays herself as the customer at the nail salon, which accomplishes two effects. First, it positions Johnson as someone who has access to MUSE and is able to switch

8 www.youtube.com/watch?v=t2xip4bH2fg, accessed February 8, 2016.

9 http://files.nailsmag.com/Market-Research/NABB2014-2015-Stats-2-1.pdf, accessed May 14, 2016, and www.nailsmag.com/article/113653/the-vietnamese-american-nail-industry-40-years-of-legacy, accessed May 14, 2016.

between it and Chicano English. This on one hand denaturalizes the image of Mexican Americans and Chicanos as foreigners (Bucholtz and Hall 2004; Chun 2009), but on the other underscores Johnson's privileged position as compared with first-generation immigrants or those monodialectal in Chicano English. Second, her use of MUSE while portraying herself as Tammy's customer emphasizes the foreignness of Tammy's accent, which is now heard against the unmarked "standard" English. Johnson the customer's accent achieves adequation with mainstream American society, while simultaneously emphasizing Tammy's distinction from it (Bucholtz and Hall 2004).

Johnson's enactment of accents that are clearly intended as not hers – the Mexican-Spanish and Vietnamese ones – reinforces the association between these accents and the stereotypes that the characters using them invoke. While portraying her Mexican-Spanish-accented relatives, who appear as loud, direct, somewhat overbearing, and very traditional in matters of family, Johnson is speaking as an in-group member, not a representative of the white public space that produces and sanctions racist uses of Mock Spanish (Hill 2001) – although of course her own ability to easily switch into MUSE positions her as someone with access to mainstream American identities. Tammy's character, meanwhile, is constructed from an outsider's perspective. Tammy is portrayed as very adept at coaxing her customers to spend much more money at the salon than they had intended. Throughout the scene, during which Johnson switches between the characters of herself and Tammy, the manicurist continually pushes various additional services on the somewhat confused and embarrassed Johnson. When Johnson finally complains that one of her nails turned out "crooked," Tammy gets angry, and although she fixes it, she speaks loudly to a coworker in a fake Vietnamese, presumably badmouthing Johnson before turning back to her to say, in Vietnamese-accented English, "She say you so pretty!," which additionally constructs her as rude and devious.

Tammy's character draws heavily on the representations of Asians or "Chinamen" as wily, greedy, untrustworthy, and manipulative that date back to the early nineteenth century (see Chapter 3). Her pseudo-Vietnamese accent frames these characteristics as Vietnamese or Asian, and not, for example, as attributes of nail technicians as a profession. This representation of the Vietnamese immigrant turned shrewd and manipulative businessperson stands in rather stark contrast to the grim reality of nail salon work faced by Asian and sometimes Latino immigrants across America, which made the news in the summer months of 2015, following an investigative report by *The New York Times*.[10] According to the journalists' research interviewing 150 nail salon

[10] www.nytimes.com/2015/05/10/nyregion/at-nail-salons-in-nyc-manicurists-are-underpaid-and-unprotected.html?_r=1 and www.nytimes.com/2015/05/11/nyregion/nail-salon-workers-in-nyc-face-hazardous-chemicals.html, accessed February 9, 2016.

workers and owners in the New York area, many workers are vastly mistreated, underpaid, intimidated, and abused. They work ten to twelve hours a day and are expected to survive mainly on tips. Some owners monitor the employees' every move by video camera and expect them to refrain from talking throughout their shifts. Employees face health hazards from the chemicals and acrylic dust that they work with, which have been linked to miscarriages and cancer. Some are victims of human trafficking.[11] Johnson's comedy routine contrasted with these investigative reports exemplifies the disparity between the image of the immigrant in dominant discourses, in which he/she is portrayed as alien and threatening, as well as comical, and the reality of immigrant American lives.

Crucially, also, Johnson's character Tammy speaks very proficient English. She skillfully argues with her customer, out-talking her and manipulating her into buying additional services, which also suggests advanced listening comprehension. Although the investigative report cited above describes nail salon employees as quiet, withdrawn, and frequently speaking minimal to no English, Tammy's vocabulary and linguistic creativity, her casual informality (e.g. addressing her customer as "honey"), and her awareness of American cultural phenomena such as cheerleading ("Oh honey, why you don't have [a boyfriend]? You so pretty! Like model, cheerleader, something pretty"), present someone who is confident and comfortable conversing with native speakers of MUSE.

At the same time, Tammy has a "Vietnamese" accent that veers between emphatically exaggerated and minimal. Johnson's rendition of the accent draws on the most salient features that her audience will recognize, and even these are employed inconsistently. In addition to an exaggerated intonation pattern with excessively long phrase-final syllables, which does not represent actual intonation patterns of Vietnamese speakers of English, Tammy deletes word-final consonants, pronouncing "make" as [meɪ], "like" as [laɪ], and "nice" as [naɪ]. It is true that since Vietnamese has a limited set of possible syllable codas – according to Thao (2007), they include [p, t, k, m, n, ŋ] – and no consonant clusters, as well as a consonant system that does not overlap with the English one, Vietnamese L2 speakers of English may find English syllable codas and consonant clusters challenging. In a study of five Vietnamese learners of English, Thao (2007) finds that syllable codas not permissible in Vietnamese are often deleted, for example "choose" is realized as [tʃu:], and "place" as [pleɪ] (Thao 2007: 19). Consonant clusters are simplified, modified, split with an epenthetic vowel, or deleted completely, for example: "round" pronounced as [raʊ], "told" as [ton] or [toʊ], "feels" as [fi:ʊ], and "lives" as [lɪvəz] (23). In addition, syllable-final diphthongs in Vietnamese cannot be followed by

11 www.huffingtonpost.com/phillip-martin/nail-salons-and-human-tra_b_669076.html, accessed February 8, 2016.

a consonant, resulting indeed in frequent pronunciations of "like" as [laɪ] or "side" as [saɪ] (26).

But whereas Johnson's Tammy very audibly deletes most syllable-final consonants and clusters, she consistently pronounces the final [l] in "nail," and her realization of "short" approaches MUSE, including the initial [ʃ]. She has no trouble with sibilants generally, including [s], [ʃ], [tʃ] (in "cheerleader"), and [dʒ] (in "gel"), despite these having been shown to be frequently confused by Vietnamese speakers (Thao 2007; L.T. Tuan 2011). Finally, as Tammy tries to convince Johnson to buy the "crystal gel" treatment (prounced as [kwɪtəl dʒɛl]), an emphatically stressed "nice" [naɪ] is embedded in a mostly MUSE-accented utterance: "It's the best thing you can have for your nail, make [mek] look nice [naɪ], it sparkle like diamond in the sky." Here, words that Tammy should have trouble with, but does not, include "the," "best," "thing," "sparkle," and "sky." Furthermore, "like" is pronounced as [laɪk], and we may also note Tammy's creative use of the simile "sparkle like diamond in the sky." The sentence sounds "foreign" mostly because of its exaggerated non-native-like intonation. The overall result is the production and reproduction of a stereotype of a "Vietnamese" accent, in which selected phonetic and grammatical features are mixed with exaggerated and inaccurate ones, such as the intonation pattern. The Tammy character enacts both a comedic caricature of a Vietnamese accent, juxtaposed with her customer's unmarked MUSE, and the undesirable personal attributes of a pushy salesperson that invoke historically established portrayals of Asians as alien, cunning, and untrustworthy.

Comedy routines such as Johnson's "Nail Salon" become sites where the iconic links between mock foreign accents and undesirable characteristics associated with non-white immigrants are established and reinforced. And when these shows and performances reach a wide audience, the foreign accent ideologies they (re)produce enter circulation in everyday talk among diverse groups of people, which in turn allows them to become dominant – a process described by Shuck (2006), as seen in the previous section. This process contributes to the type of situation witnessed in some studies, whereby native-speaking listeners hear features of an Asian accent, and, although they cannot correctly identify it, they evaluate its speaker as incomprehensible and as possessing negative traits that are, in fact, racial stereotypes.

From the Hilarity Songster *to Margaret Cho*

Perhaps a better known performer whose routines are built around the issue of Asian American identity and who regularly employs the "Asian foreign accent," is the Korean American comedian Margaret Cho. Cho uses the accent, which Chun (2009) calls Mock Asian, to portray speakers of Korean, Japanese, or Chinese ethnicities, but as Chun argues in her detailed analysis of Cho's performances, her use of it must be understood as a linguistic practice with multiple meanings, simultaneously racist and subversive. Chun writes:

> [W]hile Cho's use of Mock Asian may necessarily reproduce mainstream American racializing discourses about Asians, she is able to simultaneously decontextualize and deconstruct these very discourses. I suggest that it is her successful authentication as an Asian American comedian, particularly one who is critical of Asian marginalization in the United States, that legitimizes her use of Mock Asian and that yields an interpretation of her practices primarily as a critique of racist mainstream ideologies (Chun 2009: 262).

Indeed, Cho's use of accents is much more complex and deliberate than Johnson's. In one routine,[12] in which she directly addresses the topic of race, she says at one point (in MUSE), "Although it's difficult to be the only Asian person among a bunch of white people, it is way worse to be the only white person among a bunch of Asian people, because we will talk shit about you right to your face." In this statement, Cho refers to a specific stereotype of Asian culture as allowing for directness that may be judged as rude by Anglo-American standards. This stereotype, however, is not a widely circulating one, and may be accessible primarily to Asian Americans, in this way indexing the Asian American in-group. By using the pronoun *we* ("we will talk shit about you"), Cho positions herself as a member of this in-group. She then switches to Mock Asian to illustrate "talking shit" about someone right to their face (adapted from Chun 2009: 281; capitals indicate loud volume):

> YOUR EYE IS TOO BIG. [jo ai iz tʰu big] WHY IS YOUR EYE IS SO:: BIG. [wai iz jo ai iz so:: big] (*enlarges eyes unnaturally and points to them, speaking fast*) YOUR EYE LIKE THIS LIKE THIS YOUR EYE LIKE THIS LIKE THIS WHY YOUR EYE LIKE *THIS* [jo ai laik dɪs laik dɪs jo ai laik dɪs laik dɪs wai jo ai laik dɪ] YOUR EYE IS LIKE *THIS* [jo ai iz laik di] ARE YOU GONNA CATCH A FLY WITH YOUR EYE? [a ju gʌnə kɛtʃ ə flai wis jo ai]

Chun (2009: 280–282) presents a linguistic analysis of the passage in which she describes the features of Mock Asian that it uses, as well as Cho's nonverbal expressions, which together produce particular discursive effects. In the above passage, for example, Cho uses exaggerated features of Mock Asian – for example increased amplitude, syllable-timed rhythm, increased tempo, syllable coda deletion, and monothongization of [o] (Chun 2009: 281) – while performing a sort of "generic Asian person" making fun of a white person. By singling out the white person's "big eye," the Asian character inverts the dominant discourse that racializes "Asians" as a group based on supposedly clear physical traits (Lee 1999), one of which is narrow eyes, that diverge from the normative white phenotype. Chun (2009) argues that this inversion of

[12] www.youtube.com/watch?v=f9Ys4Xjndb4, accessed February 12, 2016.

reductionist stereotyping works to "decenter whiteness" (282). It destabilizes racial hierarchies that allow for the objectification of Asian bodies by casting the Other as the one who objectifies. This denaturalizes (Bucholtz and Hall 2004) the normative power dynamic between the dominant white group and subordinate racial minorities. In this context, the use of Mock Asian is an additional commentary on this point: it can be interpreted as mocking white imitations of actual Asian accents. It can also become a way for Asian Americans to claim ownership of Asian accents, as well as of their caricature – Mock Asian.

Chun's comprehensive tables (2009: 267–270) compare "prototypical features of Mock Asian" (267) with those used by Cho in her performances. Here, I would like to highlight four of them: confusion of [l]/[r]/[ɹ] (e.g. "flied lice" for "fried rice," or "herro" for "hello"), adding "ee" [i] to words ending in closed syllables (e.g. "likee" for "like"), nonsensical syllables (e.g. "ching-chong"), and the use of accusative "me" first-person singular pronoun for the nominative "I" (e.g. "me play joke"). These features are commonly used to index any type of "Asian person" in popular culture, who is usually also associated with undesirable or comical characteristics. These may be deviousness and untrustworthiness, as in the 1998 film *Lethal Weapon 4*, when the Chinese mafia boss corrects Mel Gibson's character's impersonation of him by saying, "It's fried rice, you plick!" Not only is the mafia boss the film's evil character who dabbles in human trafficking, but his failed attempt at producing "standard" English additionally paints him as ridiculous: he cannot even insult his opponent without slipping into his "Asian" accent. Or, the stereotype may be that of extreme foreignness and sexual deviance, as in the case of Long Duk Dong, the foreign exchange student from an unidentified Asian country in the 1984 high school comedy *Sixteen Candles*, who pronounces American [ɹ] as [r] (e.g. in words like "interesting" and "round") and drunkenly exclaims to his white host family following his night of partying and romance, "Oh, no more yankee my wankee, the donger needs food!" As NPR's journalist Kat Chow writes in her piece about the film, "Asian men have been fighting this on-screen stereotype for years: the socially inept mute; the lecherous but sexually inept loser; one part harmless Charlie Chan, one part mustachioed villain Fu Manchu."[13] Many more examples of the way Asian speakers' language is imagined, racialized, and used to represent disparaging and mocking stereotypes of Asian identities, are explored in detail by Lippi-Green (2012: 281–302) and by several authors in Reyes and Lo's (2009) edited volume *Beyond Yellow English*.

[13] www.npr.org/sections/codeswitch/2015/02/06/384307677/whats-so-cringe-worthy-about-long-duk-dong-in-sixteen-candles, accessed February 15, 2016. Kat Chow writes for NPR's team called Code Switch: Frontiers of Race, Culture and Ethnicity.

Many of Mock Asian features, including the four described above, reflect historically established stereotypes of how Asians are perceived to speak English. As soon as the first Asians arrived in California in the mid-nineteenth century, comical representations of their talk appeared in songsters and in minstrel performances, which also depicted Asians as a moral threat (see Chapters 2 and 3). Some of the features comprising the early stereotype were derived from Chinese Pidgin English spoken by traders in Chinese ports, in particular Canton. Lee (1999) writes, "On the minstrel stage, Canton English and nonsense words were often deployed together in the construction of John Chinaman. The collapsing of linguistic difference between pidgin and non-sense dislocated language and collapsed meaning . . . The conjoining of pidgin with nonsense simultaneously diminished the status of Canton English as an important commercial language and infantilized its speakers" (37). Thus, for example, in the 1885 publication *Chas A. Loder's Hilarity Songster*, the song titled "The Heathen Chinee" that was sung by the famous minstrel performer Luke Schoolcraft (Lee 1999: 37), includes the refrain:

> Hi! hi! hi! Ching! ching! ching!
> Chow, chow, wellie good, me likie him.
> Makie plentie sing song, savie by and bye.
> China man a willie man, laugh hi! hi! *(Loder 1885, cited in Lee 1999: 37).*

In another nineteenth-century song whose exact publication date is unknown, titled *Two Ring Circus Songster*, we read the following lines in the song "Hong Kong":

> Me likee bow wow, wellee goodee chow-chow,
> Me likee lillee gal, she likee me
> Me fetch Hong-Kong, whitee man come long,
> Takee lillee gal from a poor Chinee. *(Gardner, cited in Lee 1999: 37).*

Lee (1999) points out that "[m]instrel songs paid great attention to Chinese foodways; indeed it is uncommon not to find some reference to Chinese eating habits in a minstrel song" (38). We see this exemplified above in the verse, "me likee bow wow, wellee goodee chow-chow." The Chinese were portrayed as commonly eating dogs and cats, animals that Westerners consider pets, and mice and rats, which in turn are considered dirty and disease-carrying (Lee 1999: 38–39), resulting in the depiction of the Chinese as "barbarian," "heathen," and uncivilized, as well as dirty and contaminated. They are constructed as unclean in both the physical and moral senses. In minstrel performances, this image of the "Chinaman" is constructed through the use of stereotypical "Chinaman speech" that seems to draw on some features of Chinese Pidgin English mixed with nonsense words. In this way, this nine-teenth century "Mock Asian" becomes an iconic representation (Irvine and Gal

2000) of physical weakness and moral corruption. As we can see, the examples above include the four features cited by Chun (2009). American [ɹ] is rendered as [l] in "wellie" and "wellee" for "very," almost every word ending in a closed syllable acquires the "ee" [i] ending, nonsense words such as "ching" appear, and "me" is used in place of "I" in the song "Hong Kong."

It seems that the nineteenth-century minstrel songs about the Chinese were precursors of Mock Asian and the stereotypes it represents today in movies such as *Sixteen Candles* or *Lethal Weapon 4*. The "Asian accent" language ideologies circulate in current everyday discourse as well. For example, in February 2013, an American fraternity chapter made national news with an Asia-themed party, advertised in an email complete with racist images and renditions of Mock Asian accent, such as "herro" for "hello."[14] The use of "herro" in particular calls to mind a 2008 episode of *Comedy Central*'s popular and controversial animated sitcom *South Park*, titled "The China Probrem," in which the character Cartman, seeking to impersonate a Chinese person, adopts [ɹ] for [l] as the primary indicator that he is speaking "Chinese." Cartman's "herro prease" for "hello please" line became widely recognizable and even made it onto various memes, which can be located through any search engine, or on websites such as icanhas.cheezburger.com.[15]

The stereotype of the "Asian accent" in nineteenth-century America may have spread through trade with China, where Chinese Pidgin English (CPE) was used. It may also have been derived from the version of CPE spoken on the West coast of the United States, which Kim (2008) calls California Chinese Pidgin English, or CCPE. As Kim points out, not much is known about this variety and it seems research on the topic is lacking (Kim 2008; J. Li 2004). Kim's preliminary analysis of CCPE draws on three sources: a collection of telegrams sent among Chinese immigrants in 1874 in California's Sierra County; legal testimony from the 1874 trial of *The People of the State of California vs. Ah Jake, Defendant*, which records the speech of both Ah Jake and the interpreter for one of the witnesses; and the 1879 "yellow peril" drama titled *The Chinese Must Go: A Farce in Four Acts*, published in San Francisco. While the play is likely to contain stereotypes and parody of CCPE, the court records and the telegrams may in fact constitute a more accurate representation of the actual languages spoken by Chinese immigrants in California at the time. Kim (2008) identifies eleven features of CCPE, most of which are attested across Pacific Pidgin Englishes, and some have worldwide distribution (336). They include (adapted from Kim 2008: 333–335; the examples below are taken from the court records and telegrams, except for *by and by*):

[14] Reported for instance at www.huffingtonpost.com/2013/02/06/duke-kappa-sigma-party_n_2630598.html, accessed February 22, 2013.

[15] For example, http://cheezburger.com/2249155840, accessed March 15, 2017.

- *sabee, saby* "know": "I no **saby** you"
- *heap* + noun "lots of": "I will tell you **heap** lots"
- *what for* "why": "**What for** you want fifty dollars"
- *all same* "also, like": "**All same** place"
- *by and by* "soon" – attested in the play along with the stereotype of the Chinese taking white men's jobs: "**By and by** white man catchee no money"
- *get* + verb: "Afraid they **get** fighting"
- *one* as indefinite article: "he write **one** piece paper to Lew Barnhardt"
- *down* as a locative or directional preposition: "going **down** Downieville," "**down** Joss House"
- resumptive *he*: "Jake say no, then Wah Chuck **he** want take off pair boots"
- transitive verbal suffix *him, -um*: "Ah Jake use **him** pair boots," "Me ask**um** him."

Other features we see in these examples are the use of "me" for "I," and the addition of "ee" [i] to the verb "catch" to form "catchee." Crucially, the confusion of [l]/[r]/[ɹ] does not appear in Kim's sources, although it does in the minstrel songsters, raising the question of the status of this feature in actual CCPE and in its stereotyped version. Conversely, most of the features that Kim identifies do not occur in either the nineteenth century representations of Asian speech, or in present-day Mock Asian.

Kim concludes: "The picture of CCPE that emerges . . . is thus of a variety of CPE that had undergone some independent development in California . . . and/or been influenced by other Pacific Pidgin Englishes" (Kim 2008: 336). He suggests that the generalized preposition *down* may have been a local innovation, while some other features (*heap*, suffix *him*) may be borrowings from American Indian Pidgin English (337). Kim also points out the frequent migrations between California and Hawai'i, and the resulting contact between the developing Hawai'i Creole (HC) and CCPE. The circumstances in which Chinese immigrants learned English, and in which CCPE developed, were clearly as complex as any encountered today in multilingual communities, and characterized by a diversity of interactions and almost certainly by hybridization and translanguaging. At the same time, the speech of Asian immigrants was stereotyped and mocked by selectively exaggerating features of CCPE and Asian accents and combining these with nonsense words and expressions.

Foreign accent ideology, as we can see, has a long history in the United States, but as all ideologies, it is neither monolithic nor uncontested. The old stereotypes and the linguistic forms that are presented as embodying them continue to be reproduced, but they can also be questioned, countered, reclaimed, and critiqued. We saw a recent example of such reclaiming and critique in Margaret Cho's comedy. Similarly, Maxine Hong Kingston brought CCPE into her fiction writing in the last two decades of the twentieth century, using it to depict the rich fabric of immigrant life in Chinatown, giving her characters their own "real" voices, and casting CCPE as creative rather than deficient. I will return to Kingston's work below. And at least one nineteenth-century publication by a white author seems to treat the hybrid language of Chinese traders and immigrants as a serious subject.

Charles Godfrey Leland's *Pidgin English Sing-Song*, first published in 1876, is a collection of songs, poems, folk tales, and parables presented in what appears to be CPE. Leland himself refers to the language as Pidgin English or simply Pidgin, and does not distinguish between its varieties on different sides of the Pacific; he intends his book to be useful to "those who expect to meet with Chinese, either in the East or California" (Leland 1892: 8). At the same time, he recognizes its internal variation:

> I trust that the critical reader will make allowance for the difficulty of spelling a jargon for which no standard is established, and which varies with every speaker . . . If I have sometimes given one and sometimes the other pronunciation, it is not through carelessness; and I have done so in such a manner as to illustrate different phases of expression (7).

Kersten (2006) points out that while some texts in the collection refer to strange Chinese eating habits or calling Europeans "foreign devils," for the most part the songs and stories "may be generally categorized as popular narratives or folk tales of Chinese or Chinese American background. In form and content they resemble traditional Chinese muk-yu chantefables in that they are derived from the experiences of historical figures and popular legends" (81). Some of the themes we encounter in the collection are the importance of dignity, politeness, worldly wisdom, and respect for one's elders. There is also some reversal of the power dynamic between Chinese and Westerners, and between Chinese and English languages: in the story "Fire and River," an Englishman's inaccurate pronunciation of Chinese causes a Chinese boy to mock him in CPE, "Englishman no can talkee Chinee, he no plenty smart inside" (82). The collection's author, Charles Leland, was apparently passionate about folklore and non-Western cultures, as commented upon by the English historian Frederick York Powell: "He had something of Burton in his delight in human beings other than the ordinary frock-coated, tall-hatted, and tight waisted, high-heeled European types, and he had something of Schu[c]hardt's warm instinct for the 'tongues in transition' between indigenous and imported civilization" (cited in Kersten 2006: 85).

Kersten acknowledges that as a white American, Leland cannot represent the Chinese or Chinese American voice. And, to be sure, the stereotypically racialized image of a Chinese person on the book's front cover, complete with a Buddha-like chubby face, narrow slanted eyes, a queue, and a huge gong, frame the text as otherizing and exoticizing, and as such, racist. But

Leland's work has to be viewed differently from minstrel songs filled with nonsense words and aimed at mocking and dehumanizing Asian subjects. Kersten argues that Leland's collection represents "a genuine attempt to grasp and convey to an American audience pieces of a cultural reality that had entered America through its trade relations with China and the presence of Chinese immigrants in the American West and elsewhere" (85). He emphasizes Leland's belief, expressed elsewhere in his writings, that CPE would continue to spread and become "the language of the future" (86) and a worldwide lingua franca. In a way, *Pidgin English Sing-Song* may be an attempt at approaching CPE – and by extension, CCPE – as a legitimate speech variety used for communication and cultural expression. Nonetheless, it has to be remembered that this treatment of CPE/CCPE was not typical of Leland's time.

Nearly a century later, Chinese American writer Maxine Hong Kingston uses a variety of Chinese-English hybrid language – a descendant of CCPE, or what Juan Li (2004) terms "Chinese immigrants' pidgin English" or CIPE – in her 1990 novel *Tripmaster Monkey: His Fake Book*, set in 1960s San Francisco. Li argues that Kingston's incorporation of this Chinatown language accomplishes two main effects.

First, it allows Kingston "to present a truthful picture of the way her characters speak in daily life" (Li 2004: 270). In the process, she recreates "Chinese immigrants' distinctive ways of using English" (270) by rendering much of their speech in CCPE and other hybrid forms instead of in a MUSE translation. This both documents aspects of actual local talk, and "invent[s] a 'new American language' that would be appropriate for the use of Chinese immigrants in literary works" (270). Commenting on the success in the United States of literature incorporating the vernacular, whether a regional dialect or an immigrant one, Kersten (2006) concludes, "Ultimately, literary critics determined that it was exactly the deviation from the literary standard of the time that laid the groundwork for a truly 'American' literature" (77). Work such as Kingston's takes an active step towards including immigrant Englishes in the repertoire of American vernaculars, contributing to the production of this "truly 'American' literature." Li (2004) explains this point as follows: "Kingston's use of pidgin expressions in the characters' speech enables her to question the status of their language from the center of the discourse and aim toward an integration of Chinese Americans' language and culture into American society" (279).

Second, Li argues that the use of this CPE-influenced vernacular in *Tripmaster Monkey* is "an act of reclaiming Chinese immigrants' linguistic freedom and Chinese Americans' rights of using standard English" (279). At the same time, Chinese immigrants' English is presented as complex, useful, and important, and its speakers as "intelligent and quick-witted rather than

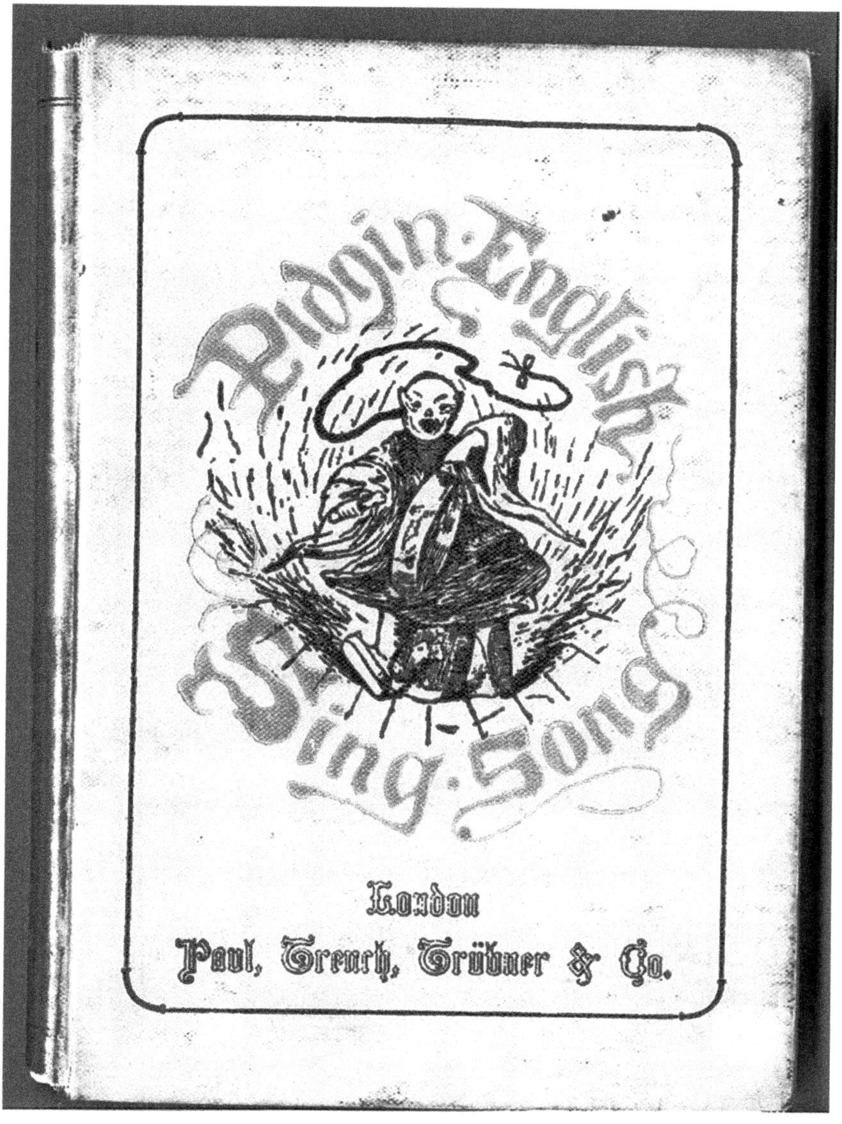

Figure 4.1 Cover of Charles Leland's 1896 book *Pidgin English Sing-Song*

thoughtless or inarticulate" (280). This, like later performances by Margaret Cho, redefines what it means to speak CPE, CCPE, and other Chinese-English hybrid forms, and in doing so, challenges mainstream white-centered ideologies. These mainstream ideologies, however, continue to circulate widely, as we saw on the example of Anjelah Johnson's "Nail Salon" routine that led to her success as a comedian, as well as in attitudes towards foreign accents that I discussed in the previous section.

A Note on Mock Spanish

The discussion in this section has centered specifically on Asian Americans and Asian American Englishes. This is partly because of how central these linguistic forms have been in American imaginings of "foreigner talk," from the mid-nineteenth century until today, and because of Asian Americans' persisting status as "perpetual foreigners." To be sure, European immigrants' Englishes have been stereotyped and mocked in popular culture, as documented by Lippi-Green (2012), but these immigrants' descendants can, by speaking MUSE or a "native" regional dialect, be accepted and read as Americans. Meanwhile, African or West Indian immigrants encounter the black-versus-white racial discourse in America and must position themselves and their language varieties with respect to it. I come back to this last topic in Section 5.1.

One major group whose language is constantly being policed by mainstream society is also the largest minority group in the United States, namely Latinos. Spanish-English bilingualism and Spanish-accented English are viewed with suspicion and evaluated negatively. But while many linguistic groups face having their languages imitated with nonsense words in racist jokes and mocking, as we saw above on the example of Vietnamese and Chinese, Latinos in particular experience their language being appropriated by white Americans in a variety of public contexts, without any negative repercussions. Using Spanish words and phrases (e.g. *amigo, hasta la vista, adios*) or expressions that draw on Latino linguistic and cultural items (e.g. "the whole *enchilada*") is rarely if ever identified as racist or in any way problematic. Jane Hill (2001, 2008) discusses this and other uses of what she terms Mock Spanish, arguing that in the white-dominated public space, white Americans are free to use Spanish without trying to master an authentic accent or correct grammar. We hear Mock Spanish expressions such as "correctomundo," "*el* cheapo," or "no problemo" (Hill 2004), which rely on the language ideology that sees Spanish as a simple language that can be spoken by anyone by simply adding an *-o* ending to an English word (Hill 2001; Zentella 2003). Not only does this contribute to a trivialization of Spanish as a language and to its portrayal as comical, but it also reproduces racist stereotypes of Latinos. The portrayal of Spanish as trivial and easy suggests that its speakers are simple, unintelligent, and lazy, all of which are common representations of Latinos in America. Many Mock Spanish expressions index Latinos as violent, as when "correctomundo" is used by Samuel L. Jackson's character in *Pulp Fiction* (Zentella 2003), or hypersexual, as in the expression "hot *tamale*" (cf. Chavez 2008). Hill (1999) argues that to use and understand Mock Spanish, interlocutors must have access to these negative representations: the Mock Spanish expressions would not be "funny" if they did not rely on the connection between Spanish speakers and the negative characteristics attributed to them.

As both Hill and Zentella point out, the uncensored freedom with which white Americans throw around Mock Spanish expressions contrasts sharply with the negative evaluation and policing of Spanish-accented English, and with the expectation that Latino immigrants should strive to speak English with a MUSE accent. As a result of the "elevation of whiteness" (Hill 1999: 684; Zentella 2003: 52) that the monitoring of Latinos' linguistic practices and the liberal use of Mock Spanish achieve, the racist implications of random Spanish words used by white Americans are all but erased. Spanish accents and Spanglish (see Section 5.3), meanwhile, continue to be critiqued, mocked, or linked with monolithic stereotypes, a recent example of which is the character of Gloria Pritchett, played by Sofia Vergara, in the popular and critically acclaimed sitcom *Modern Family*. Gloria as a character is constructed through a combination of a pronounced Colombian-Spanish accent and a hyper-feminine sexuality. Elsewhere, the license to use Spanish without repercussions takes on dangerously innocuous forms. For example, an otherwise educational children's chapter book, *Daisy Dawson* by Steve Voake (2011), whose main character is an independent and fun-loving little girl with the power to talk with animals, features crabs that for an unclear reason love dancing the *cha-cha* and occasionally shout "*Ay, caramba*!" The crabs speak English with Daisy and there is no indication anywhere in the book that they have any links with Latin America. The story takes place at a regular beach somewhere in the United States. Spanish stands out among immigrant languages in that its use by white Americans in its most stereotypical, often derogatory ways has been naturalized as completely acceptable.

4.3 Emerging Dialects: When the Native Speaker Has a Foreign Accent

So far in this chapter, I have discussed issues surrounding foreign accents – accents, that is, that mark those who speak with them as non-native speakers and, consequently, as outsiders, or Other. This section, however, challenges the very notion of a "native speaker" and a dichotomous classification of accents as either native or foreign.

The criteria for defining the native speaker, despite this designation being taken for granted within generative linguistics, have been shown in recent research to be far from clear, leading some to question the usefulness of the concept itself. As Andrews (2014) points out, "So-called native speakers of a particular language demonstrate a very broad range of differences at a variety of levels . . . How does one determine a common baseline for all 'native speakers'?" (Andrews 2014: 41). Consequently, and in light of recent evidence challenging the hypothesis of critical periods for language learning that I discussed earlier in this chapter, Andrews opts for the more flexible terms *nativelike, nativelikeness*, and *nativelike attainment* (162) instead of the problematic *native speaker*.

The distinction made by Andrews is between the idea of a fixed state – *being* a native speaker – and the idea of accomplishing, to various degrees and in flexible, dynamic ways, linguistic practices typical of L1 speakers. Significantly, not only is the state of being a native speaker not reflective of linguistic reality but rather a problematic social construct; it is also a construct that presupposes a binary distinction between the "native speaker" and the "foreigner" (Shuck 2006: 260). Even though all speakers, native-like or not, have an accent – that is, specific pronunciation that may be tied to one's regional, socio-economic, and cultural background – in mainstream discourse some accents are identified as "foreign" because they seem to index the speaker's birthplace as outside the country, which in our present context means outside the United States. In this mainstream discourse, the construct of the "native speaker" maps onto that of an "American," while that of the "foreign accent" maps onto that of "immigrant." This process is dialogic: as we saw above, when a person's physical features do not match the dominant image of Americanness, listeners may perceive a non-native accent even when there is none, or they may feel compelled to compliment the speaker's English. Similarly, when the accent a person speaks with indexes another language, even if that person was born and raised in the US and speaks English "natively," their accent is likely to be classified as foreign and the speaker as an immigrant. This is true even in cases of monolingual English speakers.

Language contact produces new language varieties: dialects, accents, and hybrid forms. The most dramatic example of new language forms emerging from language contact is, of course, creolization, which in the United States is perhaps best illustrated by present-day Hawai'i Creole. In addition, there are also numerous instances of newly or recently emergent dialects of American English whose characteristic features derive from their speech communities' bilingualism. Monolingual English speakers raised in these communities speak English with what may sound like a foreign accent. As a result, they may be classified as English-language learners at school, or discriminated against at the work place even if they are US-born American citizens. Their native-speaker English is not accepted as such; instead, it is reinterpreted as "foreign." Below, I will describe several examples of "foreign-accented" native-speaker English.

Chicano English

Chicano English is an ethnic dialect that is influenced by Spanish but also, crucially, separate from it. It is a dialect of native English speakers; those, that is, who grew up acquiring English since childhood. Some may be bilingual in Spanish and English, while others are monolingual English speakers. As Fought (2003) emphasizes, Chicano English is *not* the non-native phonology or grammatical interference found in the speech of immigrants for whom English is a second language, even though non-Latino Americans often assume it to be a Spanish accent. In fact, studies show that listeners cannot accurately distinguish between bilingual and monolingual Chicano English speakers (Fought 2003; Callahan-Price 2013). Fought explains the status of Chicano English very clearly: "These speakers have in reality learned English perfectly, like children of all ethnic backgrounds who grow up in English-speaking countries, but the local variety of English they've learned is a non-standard one, and one which happens to reflect the historical contact with Spanish" (Fought 2003: 3). Chicano English is spoken by hundreds of thousands of people in California and the Southwest. It exhibits local, socioeconomic, gender, and contextual variation like any other language or dialect. It can be spoken more or less formally, with MUSE syntax but nonstandard phonology or with Chicano English syntactic features; it can be manipulated to construct allegiances and identities. And crucially, it is a truly American variety of English. Not only has it developed in the United States like all immigrant Englishes, but its speakers are only partly descendants of immigrants. The region they live in had been controlled by Spain, and the history of Spanish-English language contact there dates back to American expansion and annexation of the Southwest. Fought writes that "before and since that time there has been significant population movement between southern California and all parts of Mexico" (11); indeed, we may add, between the Southwest and Mexico – a point also made by Farr (2006) and Dunbar-Ortíz (2014) (see Chapter 1).

Fought identifies a number of Chicano English features based on her field-work in California, emphasizing that these contrast both with what she calls California Anglo English, and with the Mexican Spanish accent of L2 speakers. She describes Chicano English prosody, specifically stress patterns, intonation, and syllable patterns. She also points to several vowel and consonant features specific to Chicano English. Some of these include:

- Less frequent vowel reduction in unstressed syllables than in Califronia Anglo English
- Frequent lack of glides in diphthongs [ej] and [ow]
- Frequent lack of glides in the pronunciation of the high vowels /i/ and /u/, in contrast to MUSE speakers' [ij] and [uw]
- Raising of the nucleus in the diphthong /aj/ so that it is realized as [ɐj]
- Tense realization of /ɪ/, especially in the *-ing* morpheme (see also Mendoza-Denton 2008)
- Fronting of the vowel in *mom* from [ɑ] to [a]
- TH-stopping whereby apico-dental stops replace interdental fricatives in words like *think* and *then*
- Consonant cluster simplification and loss of final consonants
- Glottalization of final stops.

Chicano English also exhibits syntactic and semantic features. Some of these are shared with AAVE or other non-standard dialects, such as alternation of *was/were* (e.g. "They was gonna win") or the AAVE habitual *be* (Fought 2003: 94–96). Others are particular to Chicano English, for example specific uses of modals and prepositions, such as "If *he'd* be here right now, he'd make me laugh" (99) or "We all make mistakes *along* life" (101). Fought also lists some Chicano-English-specific lexical items, for example "fool" meaning "guy" or "to talk to" meaning "to date" someone (103).

Despite the long history of the Mexican American community in the Southwest, speaking Chicano English continues to be associated with being an outsider. For example, Fought reports that in the high school where she did her fieldwork, students with Spanish-speaking parents who were themselves native speakers of English would be tested and classified as Limited English Proficient (LEP) because of their use of Chicano English features. Mendoza-Denton (1997, 2008) also discusses the problem of LEP classification of children speaking non-standard English natively in her fieldwork site in San Francisco.

Hispanic English in North Carolina

Unlike in the Southwest or in the Northeast, the formation of stable Latino communities in North Carolina is a new phenomenon. Accordingly, while both Chicano English (Mendoza-Denton 2008; Fought 2003; Santa Ana 1993; Ornstein-Galicia 1984; Peñalosa 1980) and the Latino Englishes of the Northeast (Newman 2010; Newman 2003; Zentella 1997; Poplack 1978; Wolfram 1974) have been subjects of study for some time, researchers have recently noticed the emergence of a new Hispanic English variety in the South. Since the early 2000s, this new dialect has been studied by Walt Wolfram and other researchers at the North Carolina Language and Life Project (e.g.

Callahan-Price 2013; Wolfram et al. 2011; Kohn and Franz 2009; Kohn 2008; Carter 2007; Wolfram et al. 2004).

The Latino population in North Carolina has experienced massive growth at the turn of the millennium. The increase in in-migration by Latino immigrants was 394 percent between 1990 and 2000, and 111 percent between 2000 and 2010 (Callahan-Price 2013). The rural area in Siler City, fifty miles west of Raleigh and one of the fieldwork sites of the North Carolina Language and Life Project, saw a growth in its Hispanic population from 3 percent to 50 percent between 1990 and 2004 (Wolfram et al. 2004). Studies have mostly focused on young participants who have mostly been acquiring English as children through a native-like process; not all of them, however, are equally proficient. Many of them – including those born in the US – are placed in various ESL classes because their home language is usually Spanish. Because of the recent establishment of these Hispanic communities and the resultant prevalence of Spanish as the dominant language of the home and other social interactions, Hispanic English (HE) speaking children are often – though not always – bilingual and exposed to Spanish as well as English in their daily lives. Whereas Chicano English is the product of language contact over many generations, in North Carolina we witness the birth of an immigrant variety – or what Chicano English may have been at the turn of the twentieth century. As Wolfram et al. (2004) explain, "the examination of the early stages of English usage in developing Hispanic communities offers a unique opportunity to observe some of the underlying dynamics of new dialect formation in the context of learning English as a second language" (353). Features observed in some less proficient English learners show up also in those more proficient or English-dominant, and are therefore likely to become part of a future Southern Hispanic English spoken by monolinguals.

In North Carolina, the emerging Hispanic English is characterized by contributions from interference in L2 learners, such as the unmarked past tense or Spanish-like realization of the /ai/ diphthong, as well as from local varieties of Southern English: North Carolina Piedmont white Southern English and local African American Vernacular English. The latter two might produce variations of monothongized /ai/ through accommodation to local speech, especially in certain lexemes such as "Carolina," or for speakers who identify more strongly with local culture (Wolfram et al. 2004; see also Carter 2007). Wolfram et al. observe, "Such variation suggests that there is not a simple, generalized transfer effect from Spanish in the production [of /ai/]. Instead, there appears to be variation between a more Spanish-like phonetic production of /ai/ and a more English-like production that includes a flatter, weakened glide trajectory" (Wolfram et al. 2004: 349). This suggests a new variety emerging through an interaction of transfer effects and accommodation to local non-standard norms. Sometimes, forms may emerge that are not found in either Spanish or local

English dialects; rather, they resemble in-between compromises described by Trudgill (1986) as "interdialectal forms" (Wolfram et al. 2004: 354; Trudgill 1986: 62). Another such form is timing, with speakers of Hispanic English falling somewhere between Spanish-like syllable-based timing and North Carolina English stressed-based timing (Wolfram et al. 2011). These novel forms stand a chance of being incorporated into a future stable dialect, as has happened with many forms in Chicano English (Wolfram et al. 2004: 354; Mendoza-Denton 2008; Fought 2003).

A detailed study by Callahan-Price (2013a and 2013b) of Hispanic English (HE) spoken by children in elementary and middle schools in Durham, North Carolina, focuses on past-tense unmarking, showing that it is a systematic process structured by both linguistic and social factors. Callahan-Price, in keeping with Andrews' (2014) argument regarding native-like proficiency mentioned at the start of this section, points out that the children in the Durham community defy easy classification as either "native speakers" of English or English language learners (ELLs). For example, some Mexican American children born in the US later spent significant time in Mexico, resulting in better Spanish proficiency than their Mexican-born peers who, despite being classified as ELLs, are nearly monolingual in English. Callahan-Price concludes from her findings:

> [T]he Durham [HE] speakers provide striking evidence for how ethnolect grammars develop by sourcing both idiosyncratic norms present in English interlanguage as well as the local grammars of a speech community of peers. They demonstrate that second language learning and second dialect configuration cannot be thought of as two separate processes. As an ethnolect stabilizes, its speakers incorporate both nonnative (aspectual marking) and native English rules (marking by phonological environment), and these rules continue to operate even for speakers who know very little Spanish (Callahan-Price 2013b: 128).

She also shows that while Durham HE speakers exhibit some forms similar to those of their Durham AAVE speaking peers, they also show some contrast with Latino speakers elsewhere; for example, Durham HE speakers' consonant cluster reduction (CCR) shows accommodation to local AAVE but contrasts with Philadelphia Latino English of speakers with similar backgrounds (Callahan-Price 2013b: 123; Labov 2010). Again, these findings suggest that North Carolina HE is emerging as the product not simply of Spanish interference or influence of local varieties, but of a locally specific combination of factors negotiated by this newly developing community. Callahan-Price writes: "In this way, the Durham HE community demonstrates it is sociolinguistically distinct from English language learner communities of speakers from both Chinese and Vietnamese backgrounds, as well as showing accommodation to local vernaculars in ways that other Latino communities do not" (2013b: 124).

And, crucially, speaking local HE has significant implications for Latino schoolchildren. Callahan-Price (2013b) demonstrates how using HE as well as mostly local non-standard English features can result in English-dominant or English monolingual students' classification as Limited English Speaking (LES) and placement in ESL training.

Polish-American English in New York City

In addition to varieties of English influenced by contact with Spanish in Latino communities, there are other ethnolects and ethnically marked immigrant Englishes spoken natively in the United States. One obvious example is Hawai'i Creole (HC) accent in the English of Hawai'i residents who may or may not be bilingual in HC. An HC accent is often viewed as nonstandard and possibly "foreign" because of the stereotype of HC as "broken English" spoken by descendants of plantation workers who were immigrants from all over the world, many of them from various parts of Asia. The discrimination faced by those who speak English with an HC accent is discussed in some detail by Lippi-Green (2012) and also in the 2009 PBS documentary *Pidgin: The Voice of Hawai'i*. Other examples include the nonstandard, often stigmatized, working-class dialects of East coast cities, such as New York and Boston, whose features have been traced to immigrant groups that contributed large numbers to their populations (Babbitt 1896). But while these dialects and accents may be identified with ethnic groups, such as Italian Americans, they are not typically perceived as non-native English; rather, they are non-standard, regional Englishes that have been accepted as American, in contrast to Chicano English or North Carolina Hispanic English. However, there are also more recent and newly emerging immigrant English varieties whose phonological markers are more likely to be perceived as non-native. One of these is the English of Polish Americans in New York City, analyzed in a variationist sociolinguistic study by Newlin-Łukowicz (2014, 2012).

Two related features that, according to Newlin-Łukowicz, mark Polish-American NYCE are TH-stopping and voice onset time (VOT) in /t/ and /d/ stops. TH-stopping, which is the pronunciation of the interdental fricatives [θ] and [ð] as stops [t] and [d], for example in "think" or "then," is a common feature of New York City English, attributed to the influence of Irish, Italian, and Polish speakers who settled there in large numbers during the early waves of immigration (Newlin-Łukowicz 2014, 2012; Labov 1966; Babbitt 1896). TH-stopping is also common in other dialects of English associated with immigrants, such as the Chicano English of female gang members researched by Mendoza-Denton (2008). Despite the suggestion implied in the term "TH-stopping," it turns out that speakers who engage in it preserve a distinction between the so-called underlying stops, in words such as "tin" or "den," and "derived stops" that are produced through TH-stopping. For example, whereas the place of articulation for the underlying stops is alveolar, for the derived stops it has been shown as dental, demonstrating "that stopped /ð/ and /θ/ retain the place of articulation of the original fricatives" (Newlin-Łukowicz 2014: 364). TH-stopping, therefore, is not a merger of interdental fricatives with alveolar stops but a separate process (377).

Newlin-Łukowicz (2012) examines TH-stopping in the speech of first- and second-generation Polish immigrants in New York City today. She argues that whereas first-generation speakers who learned English as a second language exhibit TH-stopping as a substrate effect or interference from Polish phonology, since Polish does not have interdental fricatives, for second-generation speakers TH-stopping becomes an ethnic marker. She finds that, contrary to the expected generational differences in substrate effects (Fishman 1985), TH-stopping does not decrease between the first and second generation.[16] However, in the second generation, TH-stopping seems to be more common for speakers who identify strongly with Polish ethnicity and culture. Newlin-Łukowicz writes:

> . . . high rates of stopping correlate robustly with a strong orientation toward the Polish culture. Frequent stoppers often engage in Polish cultural activities and have large numbers of Polish and Polish American friends in their social circles . . . . The emergence of this ethnic marker would reflect the changing position of Polish Americans in the host country, and would parallel the development of an "imagined" (Anderson 1983) unified Polish American community known in the US and abroad as *Polonia* (Newlin-Łukowicz 2012: 158).

The author suggests that prior to the 1970s, Polish immigrants focused their efforts on assimilation rather than community-building. As I described briefly in Section 1.2, this is not necessarily the case throughout the history of Polish immigration. Strong, enduring, and active Polish American communities have existed since the mid-nineteenth century, although perhaps the pressure to assimilate increased as nativist sentiments in America intensified (see Chapters 2 and 3). But the features described here as emerging in present-day speech of New York Polish Americans are, indeed, particular to this new community that grew out of the large wave of immigration in the 1980s, the last decade of Communist Poland.

In her subsequent (2014) study, Newlin-Łukowicz focuses on voice onset time (VOT) of the underlying and derived stops in the speech of Polish Americans. VOT is the amount of time between the release of a stop and the beginning of voicing (vocal chord vibration) of the vowel following it. VOT ranges differ among languages. English is classified as an "aspiration"

[16] Newlin-Łukowicz's precise findings are that the rates of TH-stopping decrease for second-generation men, but actually increase for second-generation women.

language, which means that it contrasts shorter VOT for unaspirated (voiced) stops /b d g/, with longer VOT for aspirated (voiceless) stops /p t k/. Polish, on the other hand, is a "voice" language, which means that it pre-voices voiced stops (i.e. the voicing begins before the stop is released) and employs short VOT for voiceless stops. When Polish speakers learn English, their pronunciation of the L2 stops is affected by their Polish phonology. While the produced sounds are accurate enough to cause no difficulty in communication, the Polish VOT pattern results in what may be perceived as a foreign/Polish accent (cf. Romaine 1995: 53).

Newlin-Łukowicz compares first-generation and second-generation Polish Americans with non-Polish New Yorkers to examine how the three groups voice underlying and derived /d t/ stops. She finds that non-Polish New Yorkers differentiate underlying /t/ from the other three stops (underlying /d/ and derived /t/ and /d/) with a longer VOT, which means that they treat the derived /t/ differently by de-aspirating it. First-generation Polish immigrants apply Polish-like voicing to underlying /d/ and derived /t/ and /d/, while pronouncing underlying /t/ with American-like VOT. However, second-generation Polish Americans make a clear distinction between underlying and derived stops, pronouncing only the latter with Polish-like voicing. These findings suggest that second-generation Polish Americans treat the stops the way native speakers do, preserving "slight phonetic differences between sounds that underlyingly represent different phonemes" (Newlin-Łukowicz 2014: 377), much like when the derived stops are pronounced as dentals rather than alveolars. These speakers, then, can be argued to have native-like awareness of American English, but at the same time their way of differentiating the two types of stops is influenced by Polish phonology. Newlin-Łukowicz summarizes her findings thus: "This selective presence of a non-native contrast suggests a degree of control that no longer resembles L1 interference. Rather, Polish-like VOTs in derived stops represent a case of transfer that is both linguistically and socially motivated" (2014: 377). She argues that those second-generation Polish Americans who identify more strongly with their Polish heritage are more likely to use both TH-stopping and Polish-like voicing in stops derived from this stopping as ethnic markers in their otherwise native-like English.

As the above examples of Chicano English, North Carolina Hispanic English, and NYC Polish-American English demonstrate, substrate features and transfer effects from immigrants' heritage languages continue to shape the subsequent native-speaker or native-like English of the US-born generations, including those who are monolingual. Meanwhile, the complexity of the communities in which many speakers of these immigrant Englishes live does not allow for an easy distinction between native-speakers and L2 learners. Rather, we see a range of proficiencies along the native-like to learner continuum. This fluidity contributes to the formation and stabilization of ethnolects, characterized by ethnic markers that may be perceived as foreign accents. In some cases, especially when the speakers are not of European descent, this may lead to discrimination or curtailing of educational opportunities. But in reality, these immigrants' unique ways of speaking contribute to the development and diversity of American English, while at the same time producing new, hybrid, immigrant-American identities.

5 Multilingual Practices

In his influential work *Languages in Contact* (1953), in a chapter section titled "Characteristics of the Bilingual Speaker," Uriel Weinreich describes bilingual individuals in the following often-quoted passage:

> The ideal bilingual switches from one language to the other according to appropriate changes in the speech situation (interlocutors, topics, etc.), but not in an unchanged speech situation, and certainly not within a single sentence . . . There is reason to suspect that considerable individual differences exist between those who have control of their switching, holding it close to this ideal pattern, and those who have difficulty in maintaining or switching codes as required (Weinreich 1953: 73).

From the perspective of current sociolinguistic research, Weinreich's assessment is wholly inaccurate, because it assumes that languages are fully discrete entities that a bilingual speaker will always wish to keep separate, and consequently does not consider that bilinguals may have reason to mix and blend languages in unconventional, creative ways. Any speaker who does so is judged as having failed at his or her bilingualism. But Weinreich was not alone in his views at the time of his work. Jespersen (1922) argued that learning two languages placed a child at a disadvantage, since he or she will learn neither as well as a monolingual child (cited in Romaine 1995: 107). Weisgerber (1966) believed that "bilingualism could impair intelligence of a whole ethnic group ... and lead to split personalities" (Romaine 1995: 108). These perspectives reflected the sociopolitical climate of the time (see Chapters 2 and 3), in whose light Weinreich's definition of the "ideal bilingual" may perhaps be seen as a defense of bilingualism constructed by demonstrating that bilingual speakers are capable of controlling their two languages according to monolingual patterns.

Nonetheless, Weinreich's conceptualization of bilingualism is built on monolingualist ideologies, in which monolingual speakers are seen as the norm, and their language use is understood according to the structuralist paradigm (Andresen 2014). Unfortunately, this perspective remains influential in educational policy-making, as well as in mainstream popular perception. Bailey (2007) argues, "Frequent switching as a discourse mode is always socially marked in a wider US society in which being a monolingual English speaker is an ideological default against which difference or distinctiveness is constructed" (268). As many themes discussed in this book illustrate, this observation indeed holds true.

Recent research, on the other hand, treats bi- and multilingualism as distinctive and valid in its own right. For example, Birdsong assesses differences between bilingual and monolingual competence in this way: "Rather than invoke deficiencies in learning . . . it is more reasonable to argue that minor quantitative departures from monolingual values are artifacts of the nature of bilingualism, wherein each language affects the other and neither is identical to that of a monolingual" (Birdsong 2006: 22). The nature of bilingualism also involves practices that are similar to the monolingual mixing and shifting of dialects, accents, registers, and styles, but encompass resources spanning two or more language varieties. The creative playing with these resources, which are tied in complex ways to sociocultural factors, is crucial in bi- and multilingual speakers' discursive construction of identities.

In this chapter, multilingual practices of immigrant Americans are examined from the perspective that sees bi- and multilingualism as fluid and flexible continua rather than accomplished states, and that recognizes the usefulness of thinking about language as a verb – rather than an object – *languaging* rather than *using a language*. While the chapter is divided into four sections, this is not intended to imply that the phenomena described in each of them are separate from each other. Rather, these multilingual practices – code-switching, translanguaging, creating hybrid varieties, and transforming heritage languages – are seen as performed in a fluid, continuous space. Each section below aims to bring into focus particular aspects of multilingualism, but the practices discussed in it overlap with those discussed in others.

5.1 Code-Switching as an Identity-Making Practice

Code-switching is perhaps the most frequently and extensively researched bilingual phenomenon. As Gardner-Chloros (2009) explains in the introduction to her book on code-switching, the term "refers to the use of several languages or dialects in the same conversation or sentence by bilingual people," which "affects practically everyone who is in contact with more than one language or dialect, to a greater or lesser extent" (4). Gardner-Chloros then lists various types of mixed talk that have come to be known by popular monikers: Tex-Mex, Franglais, Chinglish, Spanglish. She points out that code-switching itself is just one of the "possible outcomes of language contact," others including "borrowing, convergence, pidginization, language death, etc." (4). As I have stated above, drawing a distinct differentiating boundary between these phenomena is oftentimes impossible. Code-switching and borrowing, for example, despite extensive efforts at formulating distinguishing criteria between them (Haugen 1950; Poplack 1980; Poplack et al. 1988; Poplack et al. 1990; Sankoff et al. 1990, Myers-Scotton 1993, 1992; Baran 1999), appear to exist along a continuum of bilingual practices, prompting Gardner-Chloros (1987) to declare that "a loan is a code-switch with a full-time job" (102). The inclusion of Spanglish or Chinglish as examples of "mixed talk" (Gardner-Chloros 2009: 4) further underscores this point, since these hybrid varieties are characterized by creative use and mixing of multiple bilingual resources: code-switching, borrowing, translanguaging, and hybridization of lexical and grammatical forms – an issue that will be explored in Section 5.3.

In this section, I will focus on how conversational code-switching is employed as a resource for the construction of identities. Code-switching is viewed here as a social practice that both invokes and produces meaning in interaction. Code-switching relates to macroscopic external factors, drawing on language ideologies circulating in the wider society: the notions of dominant and official languages, the status of private or minority languages, language policy, the value of heritage languages, and discourses of linguistic pride or shame (Kyratzis 2010; Schieffelin 2003; Zentella 1998, 1997; Gal 1988); and, crucially, it also produces new meanings on the microscopic or local level (Kyratzis 2010: 559–560; Gardner-Chloros 2009: 72). These can only be interpreted by analyzing the effects of code-switching in interaction without relying on *a priori* assumptions. This approach, favored by researchers applying Conversation Analysis (CA) methods to the study of code-switching, allows for an examination of bilingual identity-making processes without falling back on essentialist notions of identity. Because language varieties brought together in code-switching tend to index ethnic or national groups, and often have unequal social status, it is all too easy to explain instances of code-switching by appealing to speakers' ethnic identity as perceived by the researcher, invoking motivations such as building ethnic solidarity or choosing *we-codes* or *they-codes* (Gardner-Chloros 2009; Cashman 2005; Myers-Scotton 1993; Gumperz 1982). While these interpretations may indeed be correct, such conclusions have to be arrived at in the process of examining a specific interaction. In other words, local meanings of code-switching cannot be assessed based on external factors, because they are negotiated and "talked into being" (Cashman 2005*a*) in interaction, just as social roles of the speakers – those of parent, child, spouse, teacher, employee – or aspects of their identities – gender or ethnicity – are made salient, asserted, and negotiated in interaction.

The CA approach calls for local, interaction-based evidence for any claims about the reasons for code-switching. In this way, it aligns with the approach to identity adopted in this book. Immigrant speakers who are multilingual have at their disposal the resources of multiple language varieties and the creative ways in which they can combine and mix them. These resources are drawn upon to accomplish various social goals, including the negotiation of social relationships and identities. However, just like anyone else, immigrants participate in a multiplicity of social networks, take on numerous social roles, and inhabit many different subject positions. Immigrant identities are fluid and complex. While ethnicity and nationality, as well as one's identity as an immigrant, may be important components of one's sense of self, they are not the default explanations for one's multilingual practices. Language ideologies that link the different codes, as well as the practice of code-switching itself (Bailey 2007), to external norms and values inform and are reproduced in the speakers' choices (Schieffelin 2003), but at the same time, code-switching needs to be viewed and examined as a local practice (Kyratzis 2010; Eckert and McConnell-Ginet 1992).

Peter Auer, the first researcher to seriously apply CA to code-switching, emphasizes that code-switching "has and creates communicative and social meaning, and is in need of an interpretation by co-participants as well as analysts" (Auer 1998: 1). This statement both highlights code-switching as a local social practice which *creates* meaning, and draws attention to speakers' agency. It is the participants in the code-switched interaction that produce the meaning of the switching. For the study of immigrant groups, such focus has two-fold implications. First, it helps to debunk the mainstream depictions of code-switching, adopted also by language purists, as stigmatized, "suspicious" foreign speech that betrays linguistic deficiency (see Section 5.3 on Spanglish; also Auer 2007). Second, it allows researchers to explore code-switching as more than simply "reflecting" (Cameron 1990; Cashman 2005a) or "signaling" ethnic and national belonging. Instead, code-switching is seen as a creative practice that draws on the participants' multilingual resources and produces new meanings through dialogic interaction (Bakhtin 1981; Kyratzis 2010; W. Li 2011). In the remainder of this section, I will discuss some examples of how code-switching is used for identity-making and for the negotiation of social roles and relationships by multilingual immigrants of different generations. A number of the studies cited adopt the CA methodology, and all look to locally produced meanings. Each example highlights the complexity and creativity of code-switching.

Locally Negotiated Meanings

De Fina (2007) adopts the premise that ethnic identity is a process: participants "align or distance themselves from social categories of belonging depending on the local context of interaction and its insertion in the wider social world" (372), and so ethnicity should be seen as "an interactional achievement grounded in concrete social contexts and evolving with them" (374). From this perspective, De Fina examines the construction and management of Italian ethnicity in Il Circolo della Briscola, an all-male card playing club in Washington, DC, focusing on linguistic strategies and in particular on code-switching. The club, started in 1991, meets once a month for dinner, after which members play a popular Italian card game called briscola. In 2003, the club had forty-eight members, of whom about thirty show up at any given meeting. Most of the members are between fifty-five and sixty-five years old, and belong to the middle and upper middle class. Roughly half the members are second- or third-generation immigrants who grew up in Northeastern cities and who do not speak Italian. The other half, meanwhile, are bilingual first-generation immigrants who came to the United States as children with families or adults in search of work. While the collective identity co-constructed by the club members is that of a card-playing community that emphasizes "competitive camaraderie," De Fina argues that the club's practices significantly center around the club's Italian identity as well: "The display of and emphasis on Italian identity is achieved officially and informally through the enactment of both linguistic and nonlinguistic symbolic strategies" (378). Practices related to the club's organization and activities are transformed into ones that "index Italianness" (378): the club meets at Italian restaurants or an Italian learning center, the food served at meetings and events is always Italian, and Italian is frequently used at the game table. Members code-switch during games when challenging each other's moves or responding to these challenges (381–382). Code-switching from Italian to English is employed in more formal contexts, such as the president's address to the members, in which names of dishes are first offered in Italian, in this way emphasizing their Italian origin and consequently the shared Italianness of the members, but then translated into English for the benefit of monolingual English speakers, which in turn constructs their collective identity as members of the club, rather than Italian speakers: "Next month if it's ok with you people it's gonna be *pasta con vongole* (. . .) Does anybody have a problem with clams or clam sauce?" (383–384). Furthermore, code-switching into Italian for terms associated with the card game (e.g. knight of clubs, jack of cups, trump, high trump, open hand) by even those members whose Italian proficiency is limited accomplishes the construction of the identity of a competent player and also indexes the game's Italian origin and enacts the players' shared Italian ethnicity. Code-switching into Italian plays an important role in the negotiation of ethnicity as a central component of the collective identity of the club.

Ethnicity is not always, however, the salient aspect of identities and social roles being negotiated and achieved in interaction. Williams (2005) analyzes a mother-daughter dispute in which Cantonese-English code-switching works to structure and restructure their family relationship throughout the interaction. But Williams argues that at no point can it be assumed *a priori* that code-switching invokes external associations such as Chinese cultural norms or specific social roles; instead, participants make these relevant turn by turn in their conversation. The two women are members of a small, generally highly educated and affluent Chinese American community in Detroit, Michigan, where both languages are spoken but older members generally prefer to speak Chinese, while younger members prefer English. In this family, the mother, May, now in her fifties, emigrated from Hong Kong at about age twenty, works several manual jobs (cook, salesperson), and speaks Cantonese, English, and Mandarin. Cantonese is her preferred language. Her daughter, Liz, is college-educated and in her mid-twenties. She speaks Cantonese but her preferred language in English. During the dispute, May and Liz argue about whether May should continue working at a Chinese restaurant. Liz tries to dissuade her mother from working there and in doing so tends to adopt a more authoritative role that contradicts her relationship status as "daughter." May reacts to this in various ways, for example by becoming defensive or rejecting Liz's claims to authority. This negotiation of roles is accomplished interactionally in part through code-switching, often away from their preferred patterns and into the dispreferred language. Williams sees May and Liz's code-switching as a method for preference marking (Pomerantz 1984; Li and Milroy 1995), used in conjunction with other methods such as silence, delay between turns or weak agreement to mark dispreference, or immediate response to mark preference (Williams 2005: 320). In one example, May explains that even though she does not make a lot of money at the restaurant, she does not have to pay taxes, a statement that is quickly challenged by her daughter (Williams 2005: 324):

87 May: =okay (.) *zau6 syun3 keoi5 hai6 bei2 heoi3 jat1 go3* quarter *dou1 hou2* (.)
<< Even f she gives me just a quarter >>
88 *gam2 ngo5 m4 sai2 naap6 seoi3 aa1*
<< I don't have to pay taxes >>
89 Liz: oh. (.) .hhh WE LIVE IN AMERICA (.) [IT'S A] LAND OF TAXES
90 May: [I don't care]
91 May: uh (.) I don't care (.) okay?
92 (5.0)
93 May: that's a two reasons and then then ah (0.7) but I hhh (.)

In line 89, Liz raises her voice (capital letters), and appears to adopt "the attitude of being knowledgeable about employment in the United States" (Williams 2005: 324) as she points out that taxes are part of life in America. But May promptly responds with "I don't care," twice, in English, ending with the tag question "okay?" which amplifies her statement and challenges Liz to accept it. As Williams argues, May's code-switch into her less preferred language – and thus away from the typical pattern of language choice between the two women – "overtly mark[s] her disagreement with Liz's statement and her loudness structurally, [and] also flags May's disapproval and rejection of Liz's attitude and role" (324). May's turn is then followed by Liz's giving up her next turn, as she remains silent during the five-second pause in line 92. The dispute is characterized by numerous code-switches that similarly work to negotiate the roles and positionings May and Liz take in their interaction. Williams further explains that while their everyday pattern is to alternate languages in every turn in a talk style that Zentella (1997: 86) describes as "non-reciprocal conversations," in arguments such as this one May and Liz sometimes switch away from their preferred languages (Williams 2005: 320).

Kyratzis (2010) presents an example where code-switching is also used to negotiate social roles and meanings in interaction, at the same time as it invokes and interprets larger social discourses. Kyratzis examines language choice and code-switching among Latina girls in a bilingual Spanish-English preschool in central California. The girls' bilingual practices respond to what Kyratzis defines as Bakhtin's (1981) heteroglossia – the multiple and conflicting socio-ideological meanings and values associated with various language varieties (Kyratzis 2010: 558; see also Bailey 2007). Specifically, during dramatic play involving preparations for a make-believe birthday party, the girls invoke the association of Spanish with the domains of food and family, and those of English with "US consumer culture" (Kyratzis 2010: 557, 564). Kyratzis argues that the preschoolers code-switch in ways that respond to what Bailey (2007: 268) calls "the larger sociopolitical field" in which the dominant discourses are those of English-only monolingualism within educational contexts in the US. The girls "draw upon these discourses to organize their local social order" (Kyratzis 2010: 560), at times reproducing dominant ideologies, and at other times challenging or subverting them through "hybrid utterances" (565). Kyratzis writes, "Although their language practices in certain ways reinforce boundaries between language varieties and social groups, the girls also at moments use hybrid utterances and cut across the frames to forge alliances, thereby blurring the boundaries and affirming heteroglossia and linguistic hybridity within the peer group" (Kyratzis 2010: 565).

Kyratzis argues that the preschoolers orient to different events within the make-believe birthday party. Two of the girls who are also each other's best friends, Gaby and Tracy, orient to events in the play that seem to invoke aspects of US consumer culture: they enact going shopping for dresses using credit cards, writing party invitations, dancing to music and watching a popular American children's film. Norma, Carmen, and Erika, on the other hand, enact birthday party activities such as cooking food for the party. The former set of activities is performed by the girls using English, while the latter involves the other group of girls speaking Spanish. There is, therefore, a correlation between activities associated with each language in the mainstream culture, and the girls' local use of language. This fits with Kyratzis' more general observation that the Spanish-dominant girls in the group tended to engage in play involving traditional activities such as caring for babies, conducted in Spanish; on the other hand, the monolingual English speaker, Gaby, initiated play having to do with topics such as grocery shopping or birthday party play, conducted in English (564). Sometimes, however, these boundaries are broken down. For example, at one point Gaby, Tracy, Norma, and Gloria come together at a table and engage in a renegotiation of the ongoing play. Gaby, who typically speaks only in English, says "*Sí pero* she's- she's mine," using the Spanish discourse marker *sí pero* "yes but" in an apparent effort to orient towards the Spanish-dominant pair, Norma and Gloria, and to her bilingual friend Tracy, at the same time. In Kyratzis' view, "the insertion of Spanish words into her utterance breaks down any associations between codes and groups of players, or between codes and frames" (572). A few turns later, Norma announces "Okay! I'm gonna part the *comida* and start," mostly in English with the switch into Spanish for *comida* "food," and a hybrid expression "part" which Kyratzis interprets as "referring to the Spanish verb 'repartir' (meaning 'distribute,' as in distributing or passing around)" (572). Norma is talking about her own activity – food preparation – but the use of English makes the announcement relevant to Gaby and Tracy, including them in the play. Kyratzis again argues that "[t]he hybrid utterance and insertion of Spanish or Spanish-derived words . . . into the otherwise English utterance and birthday party play challenge regimented patterns of codes and frames, thereby celebrating the heteroglossic nature of the play" (572). Code-switching such as that exemplified by the girls at this bilingual preschool engages with language ideologies that link English with "public" activities such as shopping and with US consumer culture which the participants encounter outside their homes, and Spanish with family-centered activities such as cooking and childcare. The girls invoke these ideologies to structure their play, both in terms of play activities, where different types of activities are conducted in a specific language, and in terms of social groups, where Spanish-dominant children focus on Spanish-linked activities, while English-dominant children organize English-linked play. The girls also subvert these associations by mixing and blending activities and languages, as well as breaking down boundaries between social groups. Their bilingual practices most often enact and reproduce social inequalities experienced by immigrant groups in mainstream US society, but they also at times challenge them. These practices also construct and rearrange the girls' local relationships as playmates, and negotiate the organization of their play.

Writing from a similar perspective of identity and group membership as interactional achievements (Antaki and Widdicombe 1998) and not static attributes, Cashman (2005b) analyzes a bilingual dispute in a second-grade dual-language classroom in Phoenix, Arizona, in which bilingual proficiency constitutes social capital, in contrast to the dominant US norms that value English (37). During her six-month study, Cashman observed that code-switching is an important resource for the bilingual students in distancing themselves from both Spanish and English monolinguals. In this case, the practice of code-switching allows the students to enact a challenge to dominant ideologies of monolingualism, and specifically to English-only movements that produce legislation such as Arizona's Proposition 203 (Cashman 2005b: 36). At the same time, code-switching allows them to claim desirable social status within their local peer group by demonstrating their bilingual skills. While, as in Kyratzis' (2010) study, Spanish-English code-switching engages with and responds to language ideologies in "the larger sociopolitical field" (Bailey 2007: 268), it is also a crucial resource in negotiating locally relevant identities and roles. The Mexican-American students in this classroom do not simply switch to Spanish to "signal" their ethnicity, and while code-switching may be important in producing their identity as Mexican-American bilinguals, it can also be drawn upon to achieve other conversational aims. In the speech event analyzed in the article, code-switching among three bilingual children serves to construct and manage disagreement. The children, Arturo, Jessica, and Julia, are collaborating on a class activity involving basic engineering: they are meant to use sand and stiff paper to construct an arch bridge. At one point Arturo begins to direct the others in English, but while Jessica follows his lead, Julia disaligns herself from the other two, insisting that she knows what to do and intends to do it by herself. The disaligning move is accompanied by a switch to Spanish (line 8), and followed by Arturo's protest in English (line 10) (Cashman 2005b: 39):

6 Arturo: put sand in there and make it sa- it's [water
7 Julia: [cómo:
[H:OW]
8 Julia: yeah yo sé cómo hacer la water
I KNOW HOW TO MAKE THE water
(0.5 second)
9 Julia: yo sé- yo la hago solamente
I KNOW- I'LL DO IT ALONE
10 Arturo: NO porque YO porque THAT WAS MY ide- [IDEA
NO BECAUSE I BECAUSE THAT WAS MY ide- [IDEA

In Cashman's example, code-switching is an interactional resource available to the bilingual children for expressing and responding to opposition and disagreement, and for claiming and rejecting social roles in the course of their collaborative activity. In this case, it would be unhelpful to look for any ethnic associations with particular languages, since it is not the language being switched into but the switching itself that is significant. It is an example of "exploit[ing] the *contrast* which the two varieties provide, regardless of their connotations" (Gardner-Chloros 2009: 66; emphasis original).

In her extensive ethnographic study of a Puerto Rican community in New York City, Zentella (1997) describes similarly diverse and localized uses of code-switching, connected in specific ways to the local linguistic (bilingual and multidialectal) repertoire. While bilingualism is common on *el bloque*, there is a tendency for children and young speakers to be English monolinguals, or English-dominant, and for older speakers to be Spanish-dominant or Spanish monolinguals. In addition, the characterization of the community's linguistic repertoire as bilingual is misleading, because, as Zentella shows, there are a number of ethnically and socially significant varieties spoken on *el bloque*. These include Standard Puerto Rican Spanish, Popular (non-standard) Puerto Rican Spanish, English-dominant Spanish, Puerto Rican English, African American Vernacular English (AAVE), Hispanized English (HE), and Standard NYC English (Zentella 1997: 39–48). Speakers control a varying number of these codes to different degrees, relating to factors such as age, gender, immigrant status (whether first or second generation), and social networks both within *el bloque* and outside of it. Identities are therefore constructed in ways that do not follow what may seem to be a predictable pattern whereby Spanish equals Puerto Ricanness. As Zentella explains:

> Bilingualism and multidialectalism flourished, but a generation that could not speak or understand Spanish was beginning to appear. In response, Puerto Rican identity was being re-defined without a Spanish requirement in order to accommodate monolingual English youngsters instead of relegating them to a separate US American category. Also undergoing change was the socialization of children into stereotyped male and female roles that should have predicted female superiority in Spanish proficiency over males in every case ... In language proficiency, cultural identity, or gender roles, extensive participation in the life of *el bloque* revealed the multiplicity of variables that worked together in unpredictable ways and defied neat classifications (Zentella 1997: 55).

In this context, code-switching on *el bloque* is a common practice. Zentella describes it as an aspect of Spanglish, which in turn represents a way of producing a Nuyorican identity (Zentella 1997: 81–82; see also Section 5.3). Crucially, the linguistic complexity of the community offers numerous and multifaceted resources for code-switching. Some instances of switching follow established community norms. For example, children typically address siblings and peers in English, and caretakers and elders in Spanish (Zentella 1997: 84). Code-switching sometimes follows norms such as repetition and translation for clarification and emphasis (85–86, 95–96) or "following the leader," where the switch, initiated by one speaker, is then followed by the others (86–87). Another possibility are non-reciprocal conversations, in which each participant speaks their dominant language. This pattern is adopted when the participants understand both languages, but are not "proficient enough to be able to favor the dominant language of their addressee" (89). Code-switching is also frequently an interactional device, in the same way as described by Kyratzis (2010) and Cashman (2005b) above. Zentella demonstrates how code-switches serve to mark a change in footing (Goffman 1979), including realignment, mitigating or aggregating requests, and attracting attention (Appeal and Control switches) (95). For example, the switches may highlight a shift in topic (*Vamo/h/ a preguntarle.* It's raining! "Let's go ask her. It's raining!"), direct and indirect quotations, referent check (*Le dió con irse pa(-ra)* – you know Lucy? – *pa(-ra) la casa del papá de Lucy* "She up and decided to go to- you know Lucy? – to Lucy's father's house"), or a role shift (My-*mi nombre es Lourdes.* Now we're going to my sister. "My name is Lourdes. Now we're going to my sister.") (93–94). The *el bloque* community studied by Zentella is one in which bilingual and multidialectal practices work to construct locally relevant identities and locally functioning social relationships. They produce ethnic identity (Puerto Rican, Nuyorican, immigrant), but also serve as resources for negotiating gender, or the social roles of sibling, child and caretaker, and as conversational devices. Crucially, all the different, innovative and complex ways in which code-switching is used on *el bloque* are possible specifically in this local context, in relation to the different layers of locally relevant identities, including Puerto Rican and Nuyorican, but also those produced by participation in this specific community (cf. Kyratzis 2010: 558).

Bailey (2000b) challenges Zentella's (1997) use of the term "conversational strategies" (Zentella 1997: 92) as applied to code-switching, arguing that while it "captures the notion of skilled performance in code switching, it can also imply a fixedness, intentionality, and prior planning" (Bailey 2000b: 166). He points out that code-switching does not reflect strategies that "pre-exist actual interactions," and that such an interpretation "is fostered by typologies and taxonomies of code switching that decontextualize and reify functions of code switching," while simultaneously assuming "Western theories of mind, intentionality, and meaning" (166) that have been criticized by anthropologists (166; Stroud 1998). Accordingly, Bailey emphasizes the sequential aspect of the way the meaning of code-switching is produced. He revisits some of Zentella's (1997) examples, pointing out ways in which the code-switching she describes emerges interactionally. For example, the "referent check" cited above (*Le dió con irse pa(-ra)* – you know Lucy? – *pa(-ra) la casa del papá de Lucy*) works the way it does not just because the speaker is switching to English for the "referent check," but also because the switch back to Spanish "is likely triggered by a nod or other acknowledgment from the interlocutor that he/she does, in fact, know Lucy" (Bailey 2000b: 169).

In his own work with Dominican American teenagers in Providence, Rhode Island, Bailey (2001) demonstrates how identity categories are invoked through claiming the knowledge of, and active use of, multilingual and multidialectal resources, in response to what he later calls "the larger sociopolitical field" (Bailey 2007: 268), but also while constructing locally relevant categories and variously aligning oneself with or against them. Second-generation Dominican Americans use syntactic features of AAVE – ones that, unlike hip-hop vocabulary, are not typically used in crossing (Rampton 1995), for example the habitual *be* and the stressed *bin* (Bailey 2001: 201–203; Rickford and Rickford 2000) – as a default and unmarked variety of English, but this does not translate to a self-identification as African American or black. The teenagers are aware of phenotypically based racial categories, but differentiate themselves from the black-white dichotomy dominant in the US by describing themselves as "Spanish," which "in local terms" means "that one is Spanish-speaking and ethnically/culturally/racially Hispanic" (205). Crucially, this includes those Dominican American teenagers who could be and frequently are classified as black based on their phenotype and its cultural meanings in the United States. Their self-expressed allegiance to their Spanish identity, their claim to speak Spanish, and their everyday use of Spanish underscore both their resistance to dominant racial categories, and a challenge to the historical perception of people of African descent as ethnically undifferentiated (208). The use of AAVE, meanwhile, aligns second-generation Dominican Americans with African Americans in terms of sociopolitical and socioeconomic experience. Bailey shows that in conversation, code-switching between the several language forms – Standard Providence English, Non-Standard Providence English, AAVE, Standard Dominican Spanish, and Regional Non-Standard Dominican Spanish (195) – accomplishes aligning oneself with and against different locally and situationally relevant identity categories sequentially in an ongoing interaction (Bailey 2000a, 2000b). Bailey points out that "success in enacting Dominican American ethnolinguistic identities is heavily dependent on opportunities to display Spanish speaking" (Bailey 2001: 208). At the same time, some Dominican Spanish forms that are used by recent, first generation immigrants index "a lack of urban US sophistication" (209) in the eyes of their second generation peers, demonstrating how diversity in the multilingual repertoire serves to produce and interpret a variety of identities within the Dominican American community. Ethnicity is thus revealed as an important component of these teenagers' identity work, but it is locally and situationally defined, multilayered, and linguistically enacted.

Code-switching can be, however, also used in crossing (Rampton 1995): the adoption of linguistic forms typically associated with identities that are not "one's own" (cf. Section 3.3). This is the case with Chazz, a Chinese American man in his early twenties, who code-switches into Korean in conversations with his Korean American friend Ken, thereby claiming for himself membership in the Korean American speech community, which is then variously accepted or rejected by Ken (Lo 1999). Ken is observed as complimenting Chazz's knowledge of Korean, thus "ratifying his competence as an outgroup speaker" (Lo 1999: 472). Elsewhere, however, Ken responds to Chazz's Korean switches in English, even when Chazz explicitly demands, in Korean, that Ken "speak Korean" (466–467). In addition, the turn-by-turn code choices work to realign the relationship between the two men in this interaction. In a discussion centered on a particular woman that Chazz finds attractive, the woman's ethnicity becomes the focus as Ken tries to guess what it is. Chazz explains that she is not Chinese, which is presented as a problem: "That's the only one point of- of question. She's not Chinese" (465). Ken subsequently asks if she is Vietnamese, which, as Lo explains, is not a highly regarded ethnicity in either Chinese or Korean communities, and thus "an undesirable ethnicity in a girlfriend" (467). Ken's question, "What is she Vietnamese?" (466) could thus reflect his own viewpoint, or his attempt to demonstrate his understanding of Chazz's perspective. In response, Chazz responds by recoiling his head and first frowning, then smiling, and finally responding in Korean: *Ttangkhong anya!* "She's not a peanut" (466). "Peanut" is a highly derogatory term for Vietnamese used by second-generation Korean Americans in Los Angeles. By using it here, Chazz is positioning himself as "higher" than Southeast Asians within the "stratified cultural Asian hierarchy" (Lo 1997: 52) that he subscribes to, and at the same time on the same level as other East Asians including Ken, who is Korean. But, as Lo explains, "Because it is produced in Korean, this derogatory attitude towards Vietnamese is marked specifically as a Korean one" (Lo 1999: 468). In this way, Chazz is also reinterpreting Ken's question "What is she Vietnamese?" as a reflection of Ken's own Korean perspective, and claiming a shared understanding of this perspective between himself and Ken. This latter move is reinforced by Chazz's use of plain register in Korean, which presumes intimacy with Ken (469). Ken's reaction, however, appears to reject Chazz's moves (Lo 1999: 466):

34	Chazz:	***Ttangkhong anya!*** *((smile voice))*
35		"She's not a peanut!"
36	Ken:	hh(h)O(h)o(h)::::: *((Ken recoils back sharply, smiling))*
37		(.4)
38	Ken:	What is she then.

It turns out that while Chazz believes *ttangkhong* "peanut" to be an expression used in Korea that is "bordering on rude," in fact it is used only by second-generation Korean Americans in the United States, and in Los Angeles specifically. Moreover, it is perceived by in-group members as extremely vulgar and derogatory in its affective force (Lo 1999: 469). From Ken's perspective, then,

Chazz's use of this term reifies linguistic and cultural divisions between the two men, since Ken belongs to "1.5 generation," having been raised in Korea until adolescence (469). Furthermore, Ken, having been socialized in Korea and not among Korean Americans, expects for example the use of proper terms of respect when talking to him, which Chazz fails to do when using the plain register (Lo 1997: 55). Ken's exclamation in line 36 demonstrates his strong reaction to Chazz's use of the term *ttangkhong*. His continuation in English in line 38, not following Chazz's lead into Korean, disaligns Ken from the shared identity and cultural perspective that Chazz's statement in line 34 invokes. This local, sequential negotiation of meanings relates to the broader context, in which Ken admits to his feelings of discomfort when interacting with second-generation Korean Americans (Lo 1997: 54), while Chazz feels a sense of affinity with this group. Chazz was born in the United States and grew up on the East Coast, where he felt a dissociation from the Chinese American community. He admires the vibrant Korean American community that he encountered upon moving to Los Angeles, and what he perceives as Korean Americans' dedication to Korean culture and values. He established an extensive network of friends in this community, and learned Korean, even studying it for a year in college (Lo 1999: 463).

In this way the two men's code-switching works locally to construct and reconstruct their relationship as they align and distance themselves to and from each other, while on another level it relates to their broader positioning within the Asian American sociocultural and linguistic landscape – the positioning that informs the linguistic moves they make in their conversation. For example, it highlights intergroup differences based on one's generational affiliation, whereby first- and 1.5-generation immigrants perceive their Asian Americanness differently from Asians born and raised in the United States. Additionally, Chazz's and Ken's code-switching invokes and reproduces various larger social discourses, such as the ethnic and cultural Asian hierarchy as perceived by East Asians. And in this specific case, it allows for crossing and claiming identities that one is not typically associated with, as is the case with Chazz.

Code-switching is a powerful resource available to multilingual immigrants for the negotiation of their locally relevant relationships, whether it be friendship alliances or family roles, while at the same time it highlights the interconnectedness of these various roles and aspects of ethnicity and race. But, as the next section will demonstrate, code-switching can also transform into a creative practice through which speakers claim an agentive role with respect to both their identity and language.

5.2 Translanguaging

Translanguaging refers to the process and practice of "both going between different linguistic structures and systems and going beyond them" (W. Li 2011: 1222). More than just code-switching, translanguaging involves creative recombination and reinterpretation of linguistic forms and modalities to construct new identities, values, relationships, and social spaces (W. Li 2011; García and Li 2014). This conceptualization of translanguaging focuses on "language" as a verb, as an evolving process rather than a static entity. In applied linguistics, the notion of translanguaging has been used to describe pedagogical approaches that allow bilingual students to engage with and develop both of their languages, as well as the practices through which speakers make sense of their multilingual lives (Bartlett and García 2011; Canagarajah 2011a and 2011b). Translanguaging is also a fundamental component of an immigrant's multilingual experience. Examining it focuses our attention on the immigrant speaker's agentive and creative engagement with English and other languages regardless of his or her competence (Canagarajah 2011a). In other words, it allows us to acknowledge and analyze the bilingual or multilingual experience without the need to define when a speaker can be considered a bilingual: the translanguaging speaker is defined by what he or she is engaging in, not what state he or she has achieved. Since immigrants vary greatly in their language competence yet they all experience more than one language, focusing on translanguaging makes it possible to account for these diverse experiences without the need to classify them. The translanguaging approach rejects the dichotomy between monolinguals and multilinguals, and dispenses with evaluating multilingual repertoires through terms such as "native speaker," "mother tongue," "fluent bilingual," or "interference." Instead, translanguaging "helps us adopt orientations specific to multilinguals and appreciate their competence in their own terms" (Canagarajah 2011a: 3).

Translanguaging is a relatively new and contested concept. García and Li (2014) trace the term itself to the Welsh *trawsieithu*, coined by the Welsh educator Cen Williams in the mid-1990s to refer to the pedagogical practice of asking students to alternate between languages in their various tasks (reading, writing, etc.) (20). However, they see the concept as more akin to the Cuban anthropologist Fernando Ortiz's notion of *transculturación*, which is a process producing a new reality. They write: " . . . translanguaging refers to *new* language practices that make visible the complexity of language exchanges among people with different histories, and releases histories and understandings that had been buried within fixed language identities constrained by nation-states" (García and Li 2014: 21). Crucially, for García and Li, translanguaging rejects the idea that languages are discrete and separate systems, and consequently explicitly denies the idea that multilingual speakers negotiate between these different systems. Rather, in translanguaging speakers draw on resources that form an integrated system, but that have been socially constructed as belonging to different entities through ideologies of nationality, ethnicity, race, and culture (cf. Arnaut and Spotti 2014). On this basis, the authors posit an epistemological difference between the concepts of code-switching and translanguaging, arguing that the former invokes a monoligualist perspective because it relies on the idea that speakers "switch" between separate languages, while the latter focuses attention on multilingual speakers' practices as processes through which these speakers make sense of their world, drawing on a variety of integrated resources. Nonetheless, since languages do exist as sociocultural constructs that are assigned names (Makoni 2012), and as such evoke strong emotional responses and meanings for their speakers, it is still useful to discuss code-switching, as I have in the previous section, as a means for speakers to draw simultaneously on ways of speaking that are, for them, tied to different and sometimes separate aspects of their identities.

Some other concepts related to the idea of translanguaging that have emerged in the last two decades are crossing (Rampton 1995), transidiomatic practice (Jacquemet 2005), polylingualism (Jørgensen 2008) and poly-languaging (Jørgensen 2012), metrolingualism (Otsuji and Pennycook 2010; Pennycook 2010), multivocality (Higgins 2009), and codemeshing (Canagarajah 2011b). I will not discuss the distinctions among these concepts here, as such a discussion would take us on an extended tangent beyond the scope of this book; however, they are discussed at some length by García and Li (2014). What is important to recognize here is that all these approaches emphasize the agentive, creative, and critical role of speakers as they engage with multilingual resources, as well as the resulting production of new linguistic and social realities.

In this section, I focus on translanguaging as a practice that goes beyond code-switching to construct and negotiate new sociocultural meanings. Below, I will briefly discuss languaging: the conceptual move from "language" as a noun to "language" as a verb, or from "language" as a thing to "language" as activity. Then I will discuss an example of translanguaging in a language exchange context that emerged spontaneously among Mexican migrants and native-born locals in the city of Cobden in southern Illinois, leading to the production of hybrid alphabets. Finally, I will turn to examples of translanguaging in the education of immigrant students.

"Language" as a Verb

At the heart of the shift from "language" as a noun to "language" as a verb is the critique of structuralist linguistics rooted in the work of Saussure and Chomsky (e.g. Becker 1991, 1995). Andresen (2014) points out that as the discipline developed in the twentieth century, its practitioners – Saussure in particular – sought to establish it as an independent science, which in their view required that linguistics have a concrete, well-defined object of study. The result was the reification of language as an independent, discrete, decontextualized system that "exists" in the minds of speakers and is "used" by them to communicate ideas (cf. Vološinov 1973). Andresen draws particular attention to this reification of language, or to turning it into and thinking about it as a "thing," because it leads to a study of linguistics that is speaker-biased and in which "the so-called native speaker produces living monuments, severed from contexts, to be recorded and analyzed by the linguist" (Andresen 2014: 28). But, as she points out, language is never a "finished fact" and thus "structural descriptions are idealizations and distortions of always-moving targets" (31). Andresen then argues in favor of shifting the focus of linguistic study to *languaging*, and of replacing the concept of the Saussurian and Chomskyan "speaker-listener" with that of *languaging living beings*. She writes: "The term *languaging living being* is maximally flexible in that it does not specify a particular role, disposition or activity of the languaging living being at any given time" (36). A similar effect is achieved through the term *languager* as used by Jørgensen (2008). These shifts in terminology, and the crucial emphasis on the verb *to language*, are ways of emphasizing that language does not in fact exist as an independent object, but rather emerges as a set of continuously changing human behaviors and practices. By shifting from talking about *a language* or *the language* to talking about the verb *to language*, we focus our attention on the doing of language, on language as a social, interactive, experienced activity. This activity cannot exist independently of human beings (Jørgensen 2008) and outside of their engagement with each other, and it includes, among other behaviors, speaking, listening, understanding, and thinking.

Languaging as a term in the literature has been traced back to the work of John Dewey (Becker 1991: 35; Pennycook 2010: 125) and of Chilean biologists Humberto Maturana and Francesco Valera (Becker 1991: 35; Andresen 2014). It was reintroduced more recently by Alton Becker (1991, 1995), who writes: "Try to think of it this way: assume that there is no such thing as language, only continual languaging, an activity of human beings in the world. Children hear particular bits of languaging. Having robust (if as yet unplanted) memories, they mimic and repeat the particular bits, and they gradually learn to reshape these particular little texts into new contexts" (Becker 1991: 34).[1] In Pennycook's (2010) words, Becker's notion of languaging allows us to think "in terms of time and memory rather than system and structure" (125). Similarly, Hopper (1998) focuses on grammar as emergent:

[1] Becker's idea of child language acquisition stands in stark opposition to the Chomskyan one. The discussion of these differences, however, is outside the scope and theme of this book.

"structure, or regularity, comes out of discourse and is shaped by discourse in an ongoing process. Grammar is, in this view, simply the name for certain categories of observed repetitions in discourse [and language is] a confederation of available and overlapping social experiences" (Hopper 1998: 156–171, cited in Pennycook 2010: 125). Pennycook cites other scholars who examine language as an activity and a practice, not an object, including Thorne and Lantolf (2007), and Lave and Wenger (1991).

Other significant aspects of linguistic behaviors that the term *languaging* highlights are intentionality and creativity. Thus, Debes writes:

> Languaging is the intentional, creative use of biologically, culturally, and technologically favored signs, including aspects-of-self-and-environment, arranged in culturally favored linear (sequential) patterns so as to make a part of something someone has thought available in a culturally favored manner to himself or some other; it is also the intentional perception and creative interpretation ("reading") of such sequential patterns. Languages are the perceptible products of the various kinds of languaging (Debes 1981: 188).

Debes, crucially, emphasizes that languaging is multimodal: it can encompass oral/aural and visual behaviors (speaking/listening, writing/reading, signing/perceiving), and it can be limited by either time or space (e.g. speaking *versus* recording speech). This multimodal, temporal, and spatial flexibility and variety of languaging can be imagined more readily when "language" is a verb. The intentionality of languaging is also central to the recent definition provided by Jørgensen (2008): "We use the term *languaging* for this behavior: language users employ whatever linguistics features are at their disposal with the intention of achieving their communicative aims" (169). For Jørgensen, polylingual languaging occurs when languagers – as he calls them – use any features they are familiar with, which may be associated with different groups of features culturally described as "languages" (i.e. English, Spanish, Chinese), to achieve a communicative aim. Such aims may include being understood, establishing solidarity, or distancing and showing off. The intentional activity of languaging contributes to the production of identities.

Translanguaging, to which we will now turn in more detail, is languaging that draws on resources or features of multiple sociopolitical and cultural constructs that we commonly refer to as "languages," but whose meanings and definitions are open to negotiation and reinterpretations. Below, I will discuss two case studies of translanguaging in action, of languaging across and through two sets of resources: Spanish and English; but also across different modalities: speaking/listening/understanding, metalinguistic discussion, writing/reading quietly/reading out loud, translating. These translanguaging activities are situated in specific local contexts and embedded in them together with other sociocultural activities.

The Cobden Glossaries

The story of the Cobden glossaries – or, as their creators dubbed them, *diccionario mojado*, a "wetback dictionary" – contains all the elements that have been posited as defining translanguaging and transculturation: the speakers' agentive, creative, and critical engagement with multiple languages, and the creation of a new social reality. Furthermore, it is a story that is deeply enmeshed with the hopes, fears, and losses of migrant life in the United States, which makes it especially relevant to consider here.

In the summer of 1980, Tomás Mario Kalmar, author of the 2001 book *Illegal Alphabets and Adult Biliteracy: Latino Migrants Crossing the Linguistic Border*, worked as the Education Coordinator for the regional branch of the Illinois Migrant Council (IMC) in the Cobden and Carbondale area of southern Illinois. For the past ten years, the IMC had organized adult education classes geared at migrants who came to work in the area's peach, apple, and other farms. The classes, funded by the US Department of Labor, were open to documented immigrants only, and ranged from basic ESL to GED and Pre-Vocational Education classes. But in 1980, the funds were cut and the classes were cancelled (Kalmar 2001: 15–16).

In the absence of formal instruction, local migrant farmworkers, Mexicans as well as Tarascans bilingual in Tarascan and Spanish and many of them undocumented, began to spend time at the Su Casa Grocery Store in the town of Cobden, which also attracted a number of local Anglo-Americans interested in a language exchange. Some of them worked as pickers alongside the Mexicans. These cross-cultural meetings took place in the store, or in its basement which housed some tables, chairs, and a white board, and sometimes spilled onto the street or the local park. Kalmar, who took part in these weeknight meetings as a private participant rather than IMC representative, describes one evening during which as many as eighty people converged in the park, about half of them migrants and half of them locals:

> Little kids were on the swings, teenagers on the basketball court, and more mature adults on the bench or in the shade of the tree .... On the basketball court two teams had formed. It was not Mexicans *versus* Anglos. Each team was mixed .... Players and spectators kept up a supportive banter of phrases in English and Spanish. From time to time, to comment on a good or bad shot, players or spectators tried out some rather mild cusswords in each other's language. Much laughter (Kalmar 2001: 5).

The vignette quoted above matters because it was followed by two significant events just a few days later. First, on July 11, 1980, the chief of police convened a meeting with several representatives of local organizations servicing migrants as well as some members of the local Latino community, during which he urged the attendees to keep an eye on the Mexican farmworkers who appeared to be "taking over the town" (Kalmar 2001: 11). Then, that same night, an undocumented Tarascan-Mexican laborer, Leonardo Valdez, was found dead by the side of a highway following an apparent altercation at a bar. The bartender, who had been witnessed attacking Leonardo and his two seventeen-year-old friends with a baseball bat, was not charged with any crime, not even with selling alcohol to minors. The chief of police's apparent concern with the open, friendly integration between the farmworkers and the locals that was taking place in the Cobden park, and the unsolved killing of an undocumented migrant, highlighted the uneasiness that surrounded Mexican presence in the area and resulted in an abrupt halt to the spontaneous formation of a multicultural community in Cobden.

Mexicans and Anglo-Americans started to come together again in the basement of Su Casa Grocery Store following Leonardo Valdez's funeral a few weeks later. On this occasion, however, the migrants seemed to agree that their primary goal should not be language exchange, but mastering English: *tenemos que dominar el inglés* (Kalmar 2001: 19). This, they argued, could only be accomplished by discarding formal dictionaries and books, and working together to write down English *como de veras se oye* "the way it really sounds." And so they began with the simple question, "Where do you live?" – four words which one of them had rendered as JUELLULIB. Written this way, the English phrase appeared unintelligible to the two English-speaking women present that day, Bridget and Danon. "I don't know Spanish – that's why I can't read it!," explained Danon (Kalmar 2001: 20). Spanish-speaking Cipriano, meanwhile, also claimed he could not read it because it was English. When he finally tried to read it out loud using Spanish pronunciation of the letters, the sounds made sense. Cipriano's friend Alfonso then directed JUELLULIB to Bridget, who responded "In Carbondale. Where do *you* live?" (21). Kalmar comments: "It was the first face-to-face gringo-mojado exchange of the evening, unmediated by an interpreter. It broke the ice" (21). In this way, the English phrase written down in Spanish, a translanguaged phrase pronounced with the best Mexican-Spanish approximation of the Southern Illinoisan American English sound, created a new reality: direct communication between speakers of different languages, and thus beginning of a new relationship between them.

The translanguaging taking place at Su Casa Grocery Store in Cobden, Illinois, exemplifies what Heath (1983) defines as "literacy events," or as Alvarez (2014: 329) describes them, events in which participants pool their bilingual resources together and "in which writing, reading, or speaking mediate participants' agencies and relationships" (329). It also exemplifies what Hornberger calls continua of biliteracy (Hornberger 1989, 2003; Hornberger and Skilton-Sylvester 2000; Hornberger and Link 2012). The continua of biliteracy model is grounded in the concept of translanguaging: it rejects binary notions such as bilingual/monolingual or literate/oral, focusing instead on the intersections of the continua between these (Hornberger and Link 2012). I will return to Hornberger's model in Section 6.1 in reference to bilingual education. Here, at Su Casa Grocery Store, we observe the emergence of a translanguaged literacy; the participants themselves are aware of this when they describe JUELLULIB as a *rompecabezas* "mind-bender" (Kalmar 2001: 20). Being literate in Spanish allows the migrants to dismantle the barrier between themselves and the locals because it allows them to write down American sounds in a way that makes sense to them. This process is empowering: unlike the study of conventional English orthography, the new written rendition makes speaking and communicating possible right away. Crucially, however, texts such as JUELLULIB are not just English sounds written in Spanish. Spanish orthography is the basis of the pronunciation – *j* is pronounced as [h] in Spanish, and *ll* is read as [dʒ], as in "Where d'you live?" – but the writing is also completely new: for example, the Spanish version of this question, *donde vives*, is orthographically composed of two words, "where" and "live (second-person singular)," rather than written as one word. The one-word spelling of this phrase as JUELLULIB is a unique, local creation.

The death and funeral of Leonardo Valdez influenced the moods and concerns felt by those who came to this particular meeting. Soon, the appropriate written rendition of a new phrase was being discussed: *La ley no nos ampara* "The law doesn't protect us." Various suggestions appeared on the board, as follows, with the ones voted the best in bold and underlined (adapted from Kalmar 2001: 26):

The law	*doesn't*	*protect*	*us*
DOLOR	DATSUN	PORTEX	**AS**
DOLOD	DASUNT	PORTEEX	
DOLOC	DATSNT	PROTKT	
DOLÓ	DANTS	PROTEKT	
TOLOON	**DASN'T**	PROTEEKT	
	DSNT	**PROTECT**	

This powerful statement describing their own sense of their migrant status within American society is spoken in Southern Illinoisan American English, and learned with the help of a translanguaged orthography that blends Spanish and English conventions, producing entirely new written/oral forms.

Eventually, the frequent meetings resulted in a dictionary – *diccionario mojado* – that was printed out, photocopied, and distributed to newly arrived migrants to help them "master English the way it really sounds." The Cobden glossaries represent translanguaging in action: spontaneous, both oral and written, invoking numerous ways of speaking, creating new shared meanings between migrants and locals, and revealing speakers as agents.

Translanguaging in Pedagogy

If we recognize that literacy is a set of continua as described by Nancy Hornberger, and that literary practices are socially, culturally, and politically contextualized and therefore greatly varied (Bartlett and García 2011), then we can appreciate the challenging school experiences of immigrant students whose first language is not English. As Bartlett and García (2011) demonstrate in their study of Gregorio Luperón High School in New York's Washington Heights, learning to speak English does not automatically translate to culturally appropriate and academically successful English language literacy. Due to the differences between the norms and expectations in Dominican and American educational systems, the Dominican immigrant adolescents who constitute Luperón's student body are "unable to apply what they know about reading, writing, and testing in Spanish to tasks in English" (Bartlett and García 2011: 121). For example, in the Dominican Republic they were expected to copy from the board and memorize, or associate good reading with elegant oral performance in church or in school plays (Rubinstein-Ávila 2007), but in the United States they are asked to do internet research and formulate opinions (Bartlett and García 2011). The authors argue that "to educate these students appropriately, and for any transfer of literacy practices to occur, they have to *develop academic literacy practices in Spanish* that are similar to academic English literacy practices in US schools, or they need to receive explicit instruction in different writing conventions and opportunities to practice them" (Bartlett and García 2011: 122, emphasis original).

At Luperón, translanguaging is an accepted classroom practice because the school's pedagogy is rooted in the belief that bilingual students' languages and language practices are interdependent and are best developed simultaneously. This applies especially to adolescents who face culturally-specific yet very consequential tasks such as standardized exams required for high school graduation (e.g. Regents exams in New York), college-entrance prerequisites (e.g. SATs and ACTs), and advanced academic reading and writing expected at high school level. As shown in the literature, it can take from five to seven years for English language learners to develop academic English skills (Bartlett and García 2011; Cummins 1991), which is too long for a newly arrived high school student who hopes to succeed academically. Immigrant high school students placed in typical ESL programs or in English immersion have the odds stacked against them when it comes to culturally specific advanced academic performance. They are at a disadvantage when compared with American-born peers who have been educated, both linguistically and culturally, in English. At the same time, if they stop developing their academic Spanish skills, they compromise their ability to perform well on Spanish-language exams that may be available to them. Students at Luperón can take New York's Regents exams in math, science, US history and government, and global history in Spanish, but this requires advanced Spanish literacy. And even then, passing the English Language Arts Regents demands academic English skills. Luperón addresses this challenge by constructing an educational space in which teachers' language practices "adapt to those of the emergent bilinguals who are moving along a developmental continuum that is not solely about one language or the other, but simultaneously about both" (Bartlett and García 2011: 142). The school adopts the perspective of dynamic bilingualism (Bartlett and García 2011; García and Kleifgen 2010; García 2009), which recognizes that far from being two separate and autonomous systems, the emergent bilingual's language practices and skills function in an ongoing interrelationship. I will discuss dynamic bilingualism further in Section 6.1, where I turn specifically to the schooling of immigrant children.

Students at Luperón take classes conducted in both Spanish and English. Spanish is used to teach content in math, science, and social studies, with the express goal of developing Spanish literacy and appropriate Spanish academic discourse, as well as establishing Spanish as equally valuable and prestigious as English. However, as Bartlett and García point out, Luperón's students develop their Spanish in ways different from what they would experience in Latin America, because the teaching practices they encounter are rooted in norms, expectations, and pedagogical ideologies specific to the United States. The authors explain, "Unlike in the Dominican Republic where copying from the book was a prevalent practice, students are now expected to use Spanish to discuss ideas, engage with historical and scientific concepts, and to imagine a new world" (129). Such blending of Spanish and American English sociocultural and linguistic practices, where Spanish literacy is developed while engaging in American-style learning processes, is one aspect of the translanguaging that occurs at Luperón. In addition, code-switching and other multilingual practices are used in both Spanish and English classes. Teachers do not try to conduct any classes exclusively in one language. This not only facilitates comprehension and learning, but also reflects and validates the students' real-life linguistic experience.

For example, in Spanish-language math classes, teachers translate key concepts into English and explain them to make sure that the students know how to discuss them in both languages. Sometimes the only textbooks available are in English, even though the students are preparing for a Spanish-language Regents. In these cases, teachers work with students to translate textbook material into Spanish, which extends both Spanish and English academic vocabulary and discourse skills. Teachers in English language arts classes discuss parallels between Spanish and English grammar structures and draw attention to cognates, which helps to reinforce academic knowledge of both languages. Bartlett and García describe also how a social studies teacher discussed the structure of the US government with his level 2 ESL students through code-switching and building on the students' knowledge of each language to develop the other. When a student mistakenly identified Condoleezza Rice as the secretary of state, the teacher gave a translanguaged response (adapted from Bartlett and García 2011: 140; Spanish in italics and translated in brackets):

Condoleezza Rice is *Asesora de Seguridad Nacional* – National Security Advisor, not secretary of state. *Ella no es miembra del gabinete del presidente.* [She's not a member of the president's cabinet.] El National Security Council is like an independent board, *no responde a nadie* [it doesn't answer to anyone].

The authors point out that, rather than directly translating the term "independent board" as *junta independiente*, the teacher used Spanish to explain the concept (*no responde a nadie*). Examples such as this demonstrate how translanguaging is used at Luperón to expand and extend bilingual literacy skills as well as bilingual practices that facilitate learning and that help students construct bilingual US Latino identities. Often, translanguaging is accompanied by making connections between class material and the students' cultural background and experiences, for example by including Latin American writers in language arts classes, or comparing historical and political events in Europe and the United States to those in the Dominican Republic. The effects of translanguaging pedagogy employed at Luperón are impressive: " ... Luperón has managed to achieve much higher graduation rates for Latino foreign-born youth than citywide averages. In addition, the school manages to place a high percentage of graduates in postsecondary schooling" (Bartlett and García 2011: 230). Unfortunately, once they leave Luperón, these Dominican American youth encounter sociocultural and economic structures that reflect monolingual ideologies and racial stratification prevalent in the United States (230). But the example of Luperón demonstrates that the acceptance and encouragement of dynamic bilingualism and of translanguaging are more successful in educating immigrant children and helping them adapt to life in the United States than traditional ESL programs informed by the ideology of assimilation.

5.3. Hybrid Varieties

For all the scholarly focus on languaging as an activity, the reified notions of language and of *a* language constitute a commonsense reality (Fairclough 2001). The purist ideas evident in Weinreich's (1953) definition of the "ideal bilingual" may not be acceptable to linguists today – at least not to descriptive linguists who do not see their job as that of language arbiters – but they are alive and well among educators, politicians, and in popular discourses (see also Zentella 1997: 80; Bailey 2000b: 170). Language mixing and blending of all sorts – code-switching, loanwords, and linguistic hybrids – generate passionate and often extreme feelings among speakers. Hybrid varieties – Spanglish, *polsko-amerykański* (Polish-American), *italoamericano*, or Chinglish – are targets of conflicting judgments that demonstrate a clash of perspectives, and a complexity of experiences. For some, bilinguals and monolinguals alike, they are hodgepodges born of educational deprivation or failure, posing a threat to the wellbeing and integrity of the contributing languages, or at best convenient shortcuts, street jargons helpful in bridging language barriers, but also obstacles to successful assimilation. For others, however, they are embodiments of the lived experience of the immigrant. They give faithful expression to the duality and hybridity of identities, to the ambiguity of ethnic and national affiliation, to the multiplicities of understanding. And of the many hybrids that exist in immigrant America, Spanglish is probably the best known and, due to its visibility, the most controversial. It is also the most theorized as a site for the negotiation of language, nationality (or transnationality) and race (Morales 2002). This section will thus begin with a discussion of Spanglish, starting with the Spanglish-skeptic perspective and moving on to a broader understanding of Spanglish as a creative process, following which we will turn in some detail to a less known example: *polsko-amerykański* or Polish-American – what I prefer to call Polamerican.

Spanglish

In a rather critical assessment of the notion of Spanglish, Lipski (2014) notes that "more than anything else, 'Spanglish' has become a deeply-rooted cultural construct highly charged with emotion while eluding a widely accepted definition" (Lipski 2014: 658). Based on his extensive literature review, Lipski concludes that Spanglish is essentially a term subsuming a number of "unremarkable language contact phenomena, found in virtually every bilingual society, past and present," which "cluster" around borrowings and calques on one hand, and fluent code-switching on the other (669). Lipski argues that from a linguist's point of view, Spanglish does not constitute a new and separate language: "Knowing how to switch languages does not constitute knowing a third language, any more than being ambidextrous when playing, e.g. tennis constitutes playing a new sport" (669–670).

A similarly skeptical evaluation is offered by Montes-Alcalá (2009), who questions the existence of Spanglish because of the apparent lack of distinction between phenomena such as code-switching and Spanglish in the literature (103), as well as the multiplicity of perspectives on Spanglish that she describes as "the chaos of definitions and mayhem that surround this mode of speaking" (102). According to this view, what is described as Spanglish is in fact a collection of previously documented bilingual practices, and the term

"Spanglish" is misleading, because it suggests a clearly definable language variety. In addition, some references to Spanglish portray it as an exaggerated parody, akin to "junk Spanish" (Hill 1993a) or Mock Spanish (Hill 2001; Potowski 2011; Zentella 2003; Lipski 2014; Montes-Alcalá 2009). It might be argued that the association of the term with well-documented and rule-governed language contact phenomena like code-switching, borrowing and calques perpetuates stereotypes that see the latter as "a haphazard jumble of two languages" (Zentella 1997: 116). Indeed, Montes-Alcalá (2009) claims that the confusion around Spanglish is "the likely cause of the negative stereotypes ascribed to the Spanish spoken in the US" (109). Similarly, Lipski (2014) states: "Because of the presence of junk Spanish in American popular culture and the elevation of some apocryphal specimens to iconic status, humorous pseudo-Spanish constitutes an impediment to the serious study of Spanish dialect in the United States and to the determination of what – if anything – 'Spanglish' might actually be" (668; see also Lipski 2008: 38–74).

The harmful effects of language ideologies that produce Mock Spanish certainly need to be recognized, and have been discussed elsewhere in this book. However, for supporters of the idea of Spanglish as a linguistic entity, it is clear that Spanglish is not synonymous with Mock Spanish even if it is sometimes represented this way. Meanwhile, statements such as "Hispanic bilinguals can and do speak beyond the alleged *Spanglish*" (Montes-Alcalá 2009: 98) reproduce this limiting association.

The backlash among some educators, writers and literary critics against the notion of Spanglish as a legitimate linguistic practice has its roots in prescriptivist ideas about language on one hand, and the concern for the advancement of Latinos in the United States on the other. Montes-Alcalá (2009) cites a *Miami Herald* columnist stating that Spanglish is tantamount to settling "for substandard English and menial jobs," and a writer for the *Houston Chronicle* opining that "*Spanglish* users are condemned to a 'lifelong state of limbo'" (100). Yale professor of Hispanic and comparative literatures, Roberto González Echevarría, known for his anti-Spanglish stance, writes in a 1997 *New York Times* article, "Spanglish, the composite language of Spanish and English that has crossed over from the street to Hispanic talk shows and advertising campaigns, poses a grave danger to Hispanic culture and to the advancement of Hispanics in mainstream America."[2] He defines Spanglish as "an invasion of Spanish by English" that is spoken primarily by "poor Hispanics, many barely literate in either language." Similarly, the Mexican Nobel-Prize winning writer Octavio Paz famously declared Spanglish "neither good nor bad, but abominable" (Rell 2004: 143).

[2] www.ampersandcom.com/GeorgeLeposky/spanglish.htm, accessed May 14, 2016.

These perspectives are not surprising and exemplify beliefs and sentiments typically voiced by language purists. Significantly, however, they stem from similar language ideologies that can be seen as underlying Lipski's (2014) and Montes-Alcalá's (2009) argument that Spanglish is not a real entity because it does not seem to correspond to a distinct language variety. The structuralist assumption about the concept of "language" implicit in these ideologies is that languages are discrete, bounded entities that can be defined by sets of characteristics such as a sound system and a set of morphological and syntactic rules. But as has been often pointed out, and as I discussed in the previous section on translanguaging, this structuralist view of language is limited at best, for languages are anything but clearly definable and contained entities. There are sociopolitical and historical factors implicated in how a language and its borders are defined by those having a stake in this definition: linguists, speakers, politicians, and writers (Romaine 1995). The different challenges to a clear-cut concept of "language" suggest the possibility that seeing language as a contested concept, or as a verb and a process, more accurately captures the everyday sociolinguistic reality than seeing it as an object. In this perspective, Spanglish is both the product and reflection of the linguistic and sociopolitical reality of Latino Americans, as well as an everyday lived practice (Andresen and Carter 2015), and as such it does not need to be clearly defined as an entity. Zentella (2003) hits this nail on the head: "Spanglish alternation of several dialects of Spanish and English challenges the notion of bounded languages and identities so successfully that any effort to halt the crossing of linguistic boundaries seems as foolhardy as the proverbial finger in the dike" (61).

Some linguists and many non-linguists have adopted this perspective. Ilan Stavans, known for advocating Spanglish as a bona fide language variety, defines it as "the verbal encounter between Anglo and Hispano civilizations" (Stavans 2003: 5), with the concept of "encounter" invoking an activity or a process. As a scholar of literature, he is interested in the creative and expressive power of Spanglish, and in its unique capacity to be "used by Latinos [in the United States] to define their own turf" (45). Stavans tries to situate Spanglish in a historical perspective, as a reflection of ongoing ethnic and linguistic contact in the Americas, at the same time seeing it as ever-changing, vibrant and diverse. Based on his experience with discussing Spanglish in the classroom, he argues that "there is really not one Spanglish but many" (13). Stavans points out language forms that are regional, both in terms of where they are spoken and where their speakers' heritage hails from – for example Tex-Mex (in Texas) or Cubonics (in Miami) – and which differ in vocabulary and style. Thus, for example, Stavans' student from San Antonio, Texas, referred to a laundry store as "washatería," whereas in Zentella's (1997) ethnography of a New York Puerto Rican community the corresponding term is "londri" (81).

Stavans' enthusiastic approach to Spanglish, including the creation of a Spanglish dictionary and a translation into Spanglish of the first chapter of Miguel de Cervantes' *Don Quijote*, has encountered skepticism. Critics include most notably Zentella (2008: Preface), who describes his dictionary as "an overzealous attempt to stop Spanglish-bashing" which "distorts the practice and the principles of Spanglish" (7). But, even if Stavans' work employs distortions and exaggerations of actual Spanish-English bilingual practices, he is trying to participate actively in what might be deemed Spanglish languaging. Connected with this is Stavans' commitment to Spanglish as a cultural phenomenon, a manifestation of *mestizaje*: the racial and cultural mixing that characterizes Latin America and sets it apart from the Anglo-dominated North America. In *mestizaje*, the mixing of Spanish, African and indigenous peoples produced a multiracial and multicultural population whose hybridity finds reflection in aesthetic, cultural and linguistic beliefs and practices.

Mestizaje as a concept became, in Martínez-Echazábal's (1998) words, "a trope for the nation" (33) in Latin America, especially thanks to the Mexican writer, ideologue and secretary of public education (1921–1924) José Vasconcelos' influential book *The Cosmic Race* (1979 [1925]), and subsequent work by authors such as Nicolás Guillén (1972 [1931]), Gilberto Freyere (1946 [1933], 1986 [1936], 1963 [1959]), and Fernando Ortiz (1947). Their theorization of *mestizaje* as blending and transculturation (Martínez-Echazábal 1998) allowed it to become a key symbol of national identity, and a discourse that served to legitimize Latin America's distinctiveness and independence from Europe, and thus ultimately the basis of an assimilationist and monoculturalist nation-building ideology (Martínez-Echazábal 1998: 38). In this sense, *mestizaje* represents a homogenizing and idealized process whose product is a uniform and inclusive mestizo culture (Wade 2005: 240). Critiquing this understanding of *mestizaje* in anthropological literature, Wade (2005) proposes a shift of focus whereby *mestizaje* is viewed as a lived process. This approach renders *mestizaje* as "multiple and with many meanings, among them the image of a mosaic, made up of different elements and processes, which can be manifest within the body and the family, as well as the nation" (Wade 2005: 254). The mosaic as Wade envisions it is not static or fixed in mortar, as it were, but rather "allows for the permanent re-combination of elements in persons and practices" (252).

It is this dynamic view of *mestizaje* as hybridization and constant recombination that is invoked by Stavans (2003) and Rell (2004) with reference to Spanglish. Spanglish is thus a continuation of the processes begun with the Spanish colonization of the New World. Spanish-speaking Latin America does not retain linguistic loyalty to Spain, nor does it look to

Spain for its language norms, because it is linguistically and culturally distinct from it, incorporating African and indigenous elements in an ongoing process of mixing. Spanglish continues this *mestizaje* where Latin America interacts with North America, and more specifically, with the growing power of the United States from the mid-nineteenth century onwards. While to critics Spanglish represents "Spanish under siege," a victim of an English incursion that enacts linguistically the United States' neocolonial presence South of its borders, the *mestizaje* perspective sees it instead as enacting Latin America's agency in its interaction with the United States, allowing Latinos to participate in the "world of English" and blend it with "the multicultural content of Latin America" (Morales 2002: 6). Spanglish is seen as creative, malleable, and diverse, a hybrid that is constantly being produced, incorporating English as another linguistic element contributing to the continually created American identity that spans both continents.

Morales' (2002) extensive discussion of Spanglish from a literary, cultural, and sociopolitical perspectives brings into focus the contextualization of language. Morales presents Spanglish as a complex set of practices spanning multiple domains of life. He talks about the Spanglish work and lives of the Nuyorican Poets Caffe artists, of the Spanglishness of the 1940s zoot suit and mambo craze, of Chicano artists blending rock and Afro-Cuban music, such as Santana, as well as of Latin influence on the music of non-Latin artists, such as the Doors. For Morales, Spanglishness characterizes both the themes and the bilingual practices in the work of the Nuyorican poets and writers such as Oscar Hijuelos and Junot Diaz. It is intricately bound up with issues of race, miscegenation, and cultural hybridity. Morales writes, "Spanglish is the ultimate space where the in-betweennness of being neither Latin American nor North American is negotiated. When we speak in Spanglish we are expressing not ambivalence, but a new region of discourse that has the possibility of redefining ourselves and the mainstream, as well as negating the conventional wisdom of assimilation and American-ness" (Morales 2002: 95).

In a similar vein, Alvarez (1998) paints the following picture of Spanglish:

> The headlines of a glossy new magazine aimed at young Hispanic women spout a hip, irreverent Spanglish. Young Hispanic rappers use the dialect in recordings, and poets and novelists are adapting it to serious literary endeavors. Spanglish has few rules and many variations, but at its most vivid and exuberant, it is an effortless dance between English and Spanish, with the two languages clutched so closely together that at times they actually converge. Phrases and sentences veer back and forth almost unconsciously, as the speaker's intuition grabs the best expressions from either language to sum up a thought. Sometimes, words are coined (Alvarez 1998: 484).

Such descriptions may be unsettling and uncomfortable for linguists, because they rely on metaphors such as the "dance" between two languages, while failing to describe specific linguistic phenomena. But they do present Spanglish as a lived process/experience (Andresen and Carter 2015). This is not to say that one cannot describe its features, but rather that these are multiple and dynamic, characterized by creativity and translanguaging, rather than forming a bounded whole. This view of Spanglish contextualizes it historically and locally, focuses on its dynamism, and incorporates conscious efforts by writers described by Morales (2002) or Zapf (2006), the bilingual production of popular culture through magazines such as *Latina* (Alvarez 1998), the musical fusion and bilingual lyrics of Latino artists, as well as the everyday linguistic practices of the children of New York City's *el bloque* (Zentella 1997). It even includes the subversion of English in a superficially monolingual text, the novel *Raining Backwards* by Roberto G. Fernández (1988), in which the author "hispanizes" English so that "its full meaning becomes lost to the monolingual reader" (Alvarez 2013: 446). Alvarez points to calques, semantic transfers and idiomatic expressions that only make sense to a Spanish speaker, and which abound in the novel, such as "seafood sprinkle" (seafood stew), "material for conversation" (something to talk about), "arms" (branches), or "It smells bad to me" (something's fishy) (450–451). The text is Spanglish in the sense that its language represents not just the infusion of English with Spanish, but also the experience of Latino, and in particular Cuban, immigrants.

Having established Spanglish as more than just a mixture of Spanish and English, and as a sociocultural as well as a linguistic phenomenon, I will now turn to an overview of some Spanglish features as discussed by a number of authors.

Zentella's analysis of Spanglish in her ethnographic study of New York Puerto Ricans on *el bloque* centers mainly on code-switching. This is not, however, simple switching between English and Spanish, but rather among the various dialects of each that are current in the *el bloque* community, and which include Popular (non-standard) Puerto Rican (PR) Spanish, Standard PR Spanish, English-dominant Spanish, PR English, AAVE, Hispanized English, and Standard NYC English (Zentella 1997: 41). Zentella's analysis reveals code-switching as complex, fluid, and fluent, as well as fulfilling a multiplicity of social and interactive goals, and both reflecting and developing local linguistic and cultural norms (as discussed in Section 5.1). Zentella also describes a grammar of Spanglish, which highlights the point that proficient Spanglish speakers "demonstrate a shared knowledge of rules about appropriate boundary sites for Spanish-English linkages" (116), including preferences for switching at some constituent boundaries over others, avoiding switches that would violate grammatical rules of either language, or switching between a lexical form and a bound morpheme if the former has not been phonologically and morphologically assimilated to the language of the latter, which supports Sankoff and Poplack's (1981) equivalence constraint and free morpheme constraint (122).

Nash (1970) writes about Spanglish in Puerto Rico: "In the metropolitan areas of Puerto Rico, where Newyoricans play an influential role in the economic life of the island, there has arisen a hybrid variety of language, often given the slightly derogatory label of Spanglish, which coexists with less mixed forms of standard English and standard Spanish and has at least one of the characteristics of an autonomous language: a substantial number of native speakers" (223). The language Nash describes is typified by large-scale, ongoing borrowing: it "retains the phonological, morphological, and syntactic structure of Puerto Rican Spanish" but "much of its vocabulary is English-derived" (223). The English loans are assimilated into Puerto Rican Spanish phonology, so that "street" becomes [ehtri], "stuff" becomes [ehtofa], "overtime" becomes [obeltajŋ], and "nurse" becomes [nolsa] (227). Verbs are borrowed and integrated into Spanish morphology. Nash gives examples of sentences such as:

> No jangues por aquí. "Don't hang around here." (janguear "hang")
> El rufo liquea "The roof leaks" (liquiar "leak")
> Sabes taipir? "Do you know how to type?"
> (228)

Nash also gives examples of calques (229). Nash's contribution is significant because it is an early analysis of Spanglish as spoken not in the continental United States, but rather in its Spanish-dominant Caribbean colony. Continental Spanglish, then, especially when spoken by Nuyoricans, becomes a continuation of a phenomenon present in the colonial context and remains in dialogue with it.

De Jongh (1990) distinguishes between code-switching and "the variety commonly known as Spanglish" which she presents as characterized by assimilated borrowings. Her examples come from Miami federal court proceedings, and include English loans that are unique to the US – or perhaps even Miami – context, and are so integrated as to be unintelligible as English lexical forms. This leads De Jongh to argue that courtroom interpreters need to be able to understand and interpret Spanglish as much as Spanish and English. Table 5.1 presents six examples adapted from De Jongh (1990: 276).

Sayer (2008) sees Spanglish as "a *social language*, one that reflects and projects Latino borderland identity" (95, emphasis original). His paper focuses on the border states – specifically Texas. His concern is educational, and he argues in favor of treating Spanglish like a real language variety, and, instead of demonizing it, embracing it and including it in the languages and dialects used in schools. He poses this question: "Do we encourage kids who have been

Table 5.1 *Spanglish examples in De Jongh (1990)*

Spanglish example	English translation	English loanword
Yo era el **bajonista**. Yo era el que manejaba el **bajó**	I was the "**backhoe-er**." I was the one that drove the **backhoe**	**bajó** < a backhoe; "retroexcavadora" in Spanish
Estoy en **estanbai**	I am in **stand-by**	**estanbai** < stand-by
El estaba ahí de **guachimán**	He was a **watchman** there	**guachimán** < watchman
El avión está **lisiado**	The plane is **leased**	**lisiado** < leased
El chofer del **forlif**	The driver of the **forklift**	**forlif** < forklift
Tengo **esteimens**	I have the **statements**	**esteimens** < [bank] statements

socialized in Spanglish to maintain and develop it and look for innovative ways to use Spanglish as a linguistic and pedagogical resource, or is this doing kids a disservice by denying them access to standard forms and effectively relegating these students to the 'linguistic ghetto'?" (96).

Sayer sees Spanglish as comprising loanwords, calques, and code-switching. The loanwords are, crucially, *particular* to Spanglish (97). They are phonologically integrated, as discussed above, and do not occur in Spanish spoken outside the United States. His examples are *troca* "truck" for Spanish *camioneta*, and *parquear* "to park." Sayer ultimately believes that there is a place for Spanglish in schools, because it is, in the US Southwest, "a linguistic borderland that serves to express Mexican Americans' borderland identity" (109), and as such should not be discouraged or derided. He points out that dual-language programs appear to focus not on the students' actual home language, but rather on its standard variety (109). The schools tend to adopt a system whereby both languages are used in equal amount, but with strict separation. This "artificial separation," Sayer argues, does not reflect the students' sociolinguistic reality (108). To this argument we might add that such a separation does not reflect the sociolinguistic reality of any bilingual person or community.

Ardila (2005) presents Spanglish as "an Anglicized Spanish dialect" characterized by borrowing and code-switching, as well as "lexical-semantic, grammatical, and the 'equalization to English'" phenomena (60). He points out that Spanglish is "barely recognized in the Spanish-speaking world" (62), at the same time as its forms are observed in use by immigrants who have little or no knowledge of English, but have resided in the United States for an extended time (65). At the same time, Ardila, like many others, stresses that Spanglish in not homogeneous but rather characterized by variation, and that it "involves not only a merging of Spanish and English but also a reflection of the unique Latin American way of life" (66). Thinking back to our discussion of *mestizaje*, we might rephrase that as the blending and mixing of Latin American and North American ways of life. Table 5.2 shows examples of calques and semantic shifts and extensions offered by Ardila.

Table 5.2 *Semantic shifts and extensions in Ardila (2005)*

Calques	**Spanglish:** Cómo le gusto la película? **Spanish:** Cómo le pareció la película? **English:** How did you like the movie?
Semantic shifts	**Spanglish:** Actualmente —> "in reality" **Spanish:** Actualmente —> "currently" **English:** Actually —> "in reality"
Word hybrids	**Spanglish:** Escortar —> "to accompany" **Spanish:** Escoltar / acompañar **English:** To escort

To summarize, the various perspectives on Spanglish from linguists as well as writers, poets, cultural theorists, and everyday speakers, emphasize the point that Spanglish is more than the sum of its parts. It is not just a collection of features, a bundle of loanwords and code-switches. Rather, through the dynamic use of the various "unremarkable," as Lipski (2014) argues, bilingual phenomena, Spanglish emerges as something new, and Spanglish languaging allows for the expression and production of new and unique identities.

Polsko-amerykański *or "Polamerican"*

While Spanglish is the most famous – and infamous – of hybrid varieties born in immigrant communities in the United States, it is by no means the only one. Other immigrant languages have also interacted with English over the past several centuries, and produced, through code-switching, borrowing, calques, word hybrids and neologisms, local ways of speaking that are clearly distinct from any dialect form spoken in the immigrants' countries of origin. Crucially, in each case these new language varieties express – like Spanglish – more than the sum of their parts; rather, they reflect the immigrant experience and enact their speakers' immigrant, hybrid identities. The Polish-American dialect, or as I call it, Polamerican, has a 150-year history in the United States, with its first examples documented by the immigrant priest Wacław Kruszka (1905) in his extensive history of Polish-American communities (Kruszka 1905; Doroszewski 1938; Olesch 1970; Dubisz 1981; Gruchmanowa 1979, 1984; Miodunka 1990).

Like Spanglish, the language of Polish-Americans has been the target of jokes and denigration. A humorous take on it is expressed in the following excerpt from a poem circulating among the Chicago Polish community (cited in

Gruchmanowa 1984: 202). Below, I include a verse-by-verse English translation, with the English loanwords marked in bold.

Z boku **hauzu** był **garden**	At the side of the **house** was a **garden**
na **tomejty** i **kabydź**	for **tomatoes** and **cabbage**
Choć w **markecie** u **Dziona**	Although at **John**'s **market**
Mery mogła je nabyć.	**Mary** could buy them.
Czasem **ciery** i **plumsy**	Sometimes **cherries** and **plums**
bananusy, orendzie	**bananas, oranges**
wyjeżdżała, by kupić	she went out to buy
przy **hajweju** na **stendzie**.	near the **highway** at a **stand**.
Miała **Mery dziob** ciężki	**Mary** had a hard **job**
pejda też niezbyt szczodra	the **pay** was also not so generous
klinowała ofisy	she **cleaned offices**
za dwa **baki** i **kwodra**	for two **bucks** and a **quarter**
Dzian był różnie:	**John** was variously:
waćmanem, helprem u **karpentera**	a **watchman**, a **carpenter**'s **helper**
robił w **majnach**, na **farmie**	he worked in the **mines**, on a **farm**
w **szopie** i u **plombera**.	in a **shop** and for a **plumber**.

As a comedic poem, this text certainly represents a stereotype. Its intended audience are Polish-Americans who are either relatively fluent in English, or are themselves speakers of Polamerican. They are the only group who is able to not only make sense of the poem, but also understand the humor that the use of Polamerican here produces, and the immigrant experience that it invokes. While the poem may be intended as a parody, the words represented in it as features of Polamerican are either actual examples of real speech, or close approximations that could in fact occur. As will be discussed below, recordings and notes taken among the Polish-American community show many of the words included in this poem, or those similar to them. And the poem itself is both a product of and a commentary on the Polish-American lived experience and language, especially in the urban communities and among those with limited access to better employment opportunities. The content of the poem describes rather accurately the daily realities of life for Polish immigrants, and the extensive use of English loanwords and English-Polish hybrid words (e.g. *ciery* "cherries," *pejda* "pay, wage"), despite the existence of commonly known Polish equivalents (see Table 5.3), amplifies the sense that the subject here is not Polish life, but Polish-American life.

Consequently, it may be worth it to take a closer look at the English-derived vocabulary that characterizes the poem, making it incomprehensible not only to a non-English-speaking Pole, but also to anyone who has not shared in the immigrant experience even if they have a knowledge of English. Table 5.3 lists these lexical items, including the original English words, the form in which they occur in Polamerican, and their Polish equivalents where they exist. Much

Table 5.3 *Polamerican words in the poem in Gruchmanowa (1984)*

English	Polish-American – spelling, IPA and grammatical form (case, tense, person, number etc.)	Polish equivalent
house	hauzu [hawzu] Genetive, singular, masc. inanimate	domu
garden	garden [gardɛn] Nominative, singular, masc. inanimate	ogród
tomatoes	tomejty [tɔmɛjtɨ] Accusative, plural, gender unclear	pomidory
cabbage	kabydź [kabɨdʝ] Accusative, singular, gender unclear	kapustę
market	markecie [markɛtɕɛ] Locative, singular, masc. inanimate	sklepie
John	(1) Dziona [dʝɔna] Genetive, singular, masc. virile (2) Dzian [dʝan] Nominative, singular, masc. virile	Jana
Mary	Mery [mɛrɨ] Nominative, singular, fem.	Maria
cherry	ciery [tɕɛrɨ] Accusative, plural, gender unclear > the English "y" ending seems to be reinterpreted as the Polish plural ending	wiśnie
plums	plumsy [plumsɨ] Accusative, plural, gender unclear > English and Polish plural endings	śliwki
bananas	bananusy [bananusɨ] Accusative, plural, gender unclear > English and Polish pl. endings	banany
oranges	orendzie [orɛndʝɛ] Accusative, plural, gender unclear	pomarańcze
highway	hajweju [hajwɛju] or possibly [hajvɛju] Locative, singular, masc. inanimate	autostradzie
stand	stendzie [stɛndʝɛ] Locative, singular, masc. inanimate	straganie
job	dziob [dʝɔb] or possibly [dʝɔp] Accusative, singular, masc. inanimate	pracę (fem.)
pay	pejda [pɛjda] Nominative, singular, fem. > Polish-American adaptation of "paid" > "to get paid" is interpreted as "to get a wage," "paid" becomes a noun (Kruszka 1905)	płaca
clean	klinowała [klinɔvawa] Past, imperfective, sing., fem.	sprzątała
office	ofisy [ɔfisɨ] Accusative, singular, masc. inanimate	biura
buck	baki [baki] Accusative, plural, masc. inanimate	—
quarter	kwodra [kfɔdra] Accusative, singular, masc. inanimate < Nom. "kwoder" [kfɔdɛr]	—
watchman	waćmanem [watçmanɛm] or possibly [vatçmanɛm] Instrumental, singular, masc. virile	stróżem
helper	helprem [hɛlprɛm] Instrumental, singular, masc. virile < Nom. "helper" [hɛlpɛr]	pomocnikiem
carpenter	karpentera [karpɛntɛra] Genetive, singular, masc. virile	stolarza
mine	majnach [majnah] Locative, plural, fem.	kopalniach
farm	farmie [farm'ɛ] Locative, singular, fem.	gospodars-twie
shop	szopie [ʃɔp'ɛ] Locative, singular, fem. or masc.	sklepie/warsz-tacie
plumber	plombera [plɔmbɛra] Genetive, singular, masc. virile	hydraulika

like the Spanglish examples, these borrowings are fully phonologically and morphologically integrated.

It is clear from looking at Table 5.3 that nearly all of the borrowings have Polish equivalents. Some refer to items that speakers would definitely know from Poland, such as cherries, plums, house, or garden. In other words, these are not cultural but rather core borrowings (Baran 1999), whose presence in the speech of Polish Americans is not a product of exposure to new ideas or inventions. Rather, they represent, much like the parallel borrowings in Spanglish, the Polish American encounter that is more than bilingualism and biculturalism, but the site of the emergence of a new, hybrid identity. Thus the purchasing of *ciery* "cherries" instead of *wiśnie* – a quintessentially Polish fruit used, among other things, to make the traditional cherry liqueur called *wiśniówka* – emphasizes that these cherries are being bought in the immigrant context, in the United States, at a stand near an American highway (*hajwej*), which is larger, faster, and far more ubiquitous in daily life than the Polish *autostrada*. The term *hajwej* is in fact widely used in the Polish-American community. These borrowings emphasize the encounter and blending between the familiar and the foreign: the cherries are not from Poland, despite looking the same and tasting similar, and the entire event of buying American cherries at a local stand by the highway is part of the larger fabric of immigrant life. Finally, the hybridizing process is embodied in the borrowing *ciery* itself. The syntax of the Polish sentence, with the verb phrase "to buy cherries," makes it clear that *ciery* is the accusative plural form. Theoretically, *ciery* could also be the singular "cherry," following the rules for feminine nouns that have atypical endings and look the same in the nominative and accusative. However, this would be first, surprising given that the other objects of "to buy" in this sentence – *plumsy, bananusy, orendzie* – all appear in the plural, and second, pragmatically unlikely since Mary is probably not buying just one cherry. Rather, it makes sense to interpret *ciery* as a fully integrated plural form. Interestingly, *ciery* does sound almost exactly like the English *cherry*, but it has been reinterpreted as the plural rather than singular form, most likely because the *-y* [ɨ] ending is the Polish nominative and accusative plural ending for feminine, masculine inanimate, and masculine animate (but not virile) nouns. Since "cherry" is feminine in Polish, most likely *ciery* here is the feminine plural. We can contrast that with a different type of hybrid, *plumsy* "plums," where the Polish plural ending is added to the English one. Like the Spanglish forms cited by De Jongh (1990) and listed in Table 5.1 above, borrowings such as *ciery*, *orendzie*, *pejda*, or *waćman* are not intelligible as English lexical forms, while at the same time remaining unrecognizable as Polish words to speakers outside of the American context.

As for the names of the poem's two protagonists, they are polonized English versions of Polish names Jan and Maria. Presumably, they are used here to stand in for any average Polish immigrant, the way Americans used "Bridget" to refer to – in a pejorative sense – any female Irish immigrant at the turn of the twentieth century. But while Bridget is an actual Irish name, John and Mary are clearly English, not Polish, and yet the characters in the poem are obviously Polish Americans. The rendition of these names as Dzion or Dzian and Mery – a kind of polonization of the anglicized name of the immigrant – underscores the blending of the two languages to produce a Polish-American experience and identity.

Borrowings and hybrids such as those in the poem are similar to the ones documented by Wacław Kruszka (1905) in his book, in a chapter titled *Gwara amerykańsko-polska* "The Polish-American Dialect." Kruszka offers the following assessment (I have highlighted the English-derived forms in bold in the original passage, and followed it with an English translation in which they appear in italics):

Wkrótce atoli ten sam "**grynhorn**," który jeszcze niedawno tak się gorszył amerykańsko-polską gwarą, zaczyna pomału sam się wyrażać, że dziś pojedzie "**karą**" ("car" – wagon kolejowy) do miasta za "**biznesem**" ("business" – interes, sprawunek) ... Wnet nauczy się inne angielskie słowa polszczyć i mówi, że był w "**salunie**" ("saloon" – karczma), gdzie przy "**barze**" stał **barkiper** (barkeeper – szynkarz) i podał **wiski** ("whisky" – gorzałki), następnie wzięli **luncz** ("lunch" – przekąska), **potrytowali się** ("treat" – częstować) nawzajem piwem. I wtedy to już nowy przybysz, po takim egzaminie, przestaje być "**grynhornem**," przestaje być "zielonym," a staje się dojrzałym "Amerykaninem," który przy następnym "**elekszen**" ("election" – wybory) będzie **wotował** ("vote" – głosować) (112).

Soon it so happens that the same "greenhorn" who not so long ago was appalled at the American-Polish dialect, slowly begins to express himself so, that today he will ride in *kara* (car – train car; Inst. Sg. Fem.) into town on *biznes* (business; Inst. Masc. Inan.) . . . Soon he will learn to polonize other English words and say that he was in a *salun* (saloon; Loc. Sg. Masc. Inan.), where at the *bar* (bar; Loc. Sg. Gender unclear) stood *barkiper* [barkipɛr] (barkeeper; Nom. Sg. Masc. Virile) and served *wiski* (whisky), then they took *luncz* [luntʃ] (lunch; Accus. Sg. Masc. Inan.), *potrytowali się* [pɔtrɨtɔvali ɕɛ] (treated; past tense, perfective, reflexive, plural masc.) each other to beer. And at this point this new arrival, after such an examination, ceases to be a "greenhorn," ceases to be "green," and becomes a mature "American," who, during the next *elekszen* [ɛlɛkʃɛn] (election; no case marking, masc. Inan.) will *wotował* [vɔtɔvaw] (vote; past tense, imperfective, sg. Masc.; *będzie wotował* means "will vote").

The English words cited by Kruszka, like the ones in the poem about Dzian and Mery, for the most part have Polish equivalents, and are fully integrated phonologically and morphologically: the Polish spelling represents a polonized pronunciation, and the words have the required Polish inflections. Similarly to Spanglish words such as *janguear* "to hang out" from *hang* (Eng) + *-ar* (Sp. Infinitive ending), Polamerican verbs are formed by adding the infinitive ending *-ować* or, less commonly, the perfective ending *-nąć* (Dubisz 1981).

For example, Kruszka cites *potrytowali się* from *po-* (Polish prefix, in this case marks the verb as perfective, a one-time event) + *treat* (Eng) + *owali* (Polish third-person plural form of *-ować*). Writing eighty years after Kruszka, Dubisz (1981) notices similar word formations in his study of the spoken language of Polish-Americans in New England. Dubisz claims that the imperfective ending *-ować* is the most productive, and does not necessarily have an iterative (imperfective) function when applied to English borrowings. However, when verbs formed in this way are meant to refer to a one-time or completed action, they are often given a prefix that indicates this. Such prefixes, plentiful and very productive in the making of complex verbs in Polish, include *za-, z-, po-, prze-, pod-, od-, do-, na-, nad-*, and others, and they are frequently prefixed to English-origin verbs in Polamerican. For example:

(1) *redżistr**ować*** "to register" (imperfective, iterative) > *Wczoraj redżistr**owali** (3rd person, pl, past imperfective) nowych studentów* "Yesterday they were registering new students."
Versus
za**redżistr**ować "to register" (perfective, one-time or completed action) > ***Za**redżistr**owałeś** (2nd person, sg, masc, past perfective) się już?* "Have you registered already?"

(2) *indżoj**ować*** "to enjoy" (imperfective) > *Czy indżoj**ujesz** (2nd person, sg, present) wakacje?* "Are you enjoying your vacation?"
Versus
po**indżoj**ować "to enjoy" (perfective, one-time or completed action) > ***Po**indżoj**owaliśmy** (1st person, pl, masc, past perfective) spacer po mieście* > "We enjoyed a walk around town."

Dubisz (1981: 57–58) presents a large number of examples of integrated verbs, including:

With the *-ować* ending, sometimes with a prefix (prefixes in bold)

badrować [badrɔvatɕ] "to worry" (*bother)*
blejmować [blɛjmɔvatɕ] "to blame" (*blame*)
drajwować [drajvɔvatɕ] "to drive (a car)" (*drive*)
fajtować [fajtɔvatɕ] "to fight, to beat" (*fight*)
fiksować [fiksɔvatɕ] "to fix, to repair" (*fix*)
finiszować [finiʃɔvatɕ] "to finish" (*finish*)
***z**finiszować* [sfiniʃɔvatɕ] "to have finished" (completed action)
gemblować [gɛmblɔvatɕ] "to gamble" (*gamble*)
grajnować [grajnɔvatɕ] "to grind" (*grind*)
juzować [juzɔvatɕ] "to use" (*use*)
klinować [klinɔvatɕ] "to clean" (*clean*)
krosować [krɔsɔvatɕ] "to cross (the street)" (*cross*)
***prze**krosować* [pʃɛkrɔsɔvatɕ] "to cross the street" (one-time or completed action)
orderować [ɔrdɛrɔvatɕ] "to order (a purchase)" (*order*)

***za**orderować* [zaɔrdɛrɔvatɕ] "to order" (one-time or completed action)
kulować [kulɔvatɕ] "to cool" (*cool*)
łacziować [watʃjɔvatɕ] "to watch out, be careful" (*watch*)
mufować [mufɔvatɕ] "to move" (*move*)
pańtować [pan"tɔvatɕ] "to paint" (*paint*)
slajsować [slajsɔvatɕ] "to slice" (*slice*)
***po**slajsować* [pɔslajsɔvatɕ] "to slice" (one-time or completed action)
sprejować [sprejɔvatɕ] "to spray" (*spray*)
rentować [rɛntɔvatɕ] "to rent" (*rent*)
***wy**rentować* [vɨrɛntɔvatɕ] "to rent" (completed action)
szopować [ʃɔpɔvatɕ] "to shop" (*shop*)
***z**bastować* [zbastɔvatɕ] "to break, bust" (*bust*) (one-time or completed action)

With the perfective *-nąć* ending, sometimes with a prefix
dżiampnąć [dʒjampnɔ̃tɕ] "to jump" (*jump*)
grebnąć [grɛbnɔ̃tɕ] "to grab" (*grab*)
kolnąć [kɔlnɔ̃tɕ] "to call on the phone" (*call*)
zypnąć [zɨpnɔ̃tɕ] "to close/open a zipper" (*zip*)
odzypnąć [ɔdzɨpnɔ̃tɕ] "to unzip" (one-time or completed action)

Both Kruszka (1905) and Dubisz (1981) describe the same phenomena forming Polish-English blends, and often refer to the same borrowed words. The same is true of Doroszewski's (1938) study of Polamerican words used by Polish writers in memoirs and letters from travels to the United States, or novels about Polish Americans. Meanwhile, young Polish-Americans that I have interviewed recently claim to speak and hear the Polamerican hybrid described here in their communities. One twenty-one-year-old who grew up in Chicago's Polish neighborhood identified fourteen out of the thirty-one verbs adapted above from Dubisz (1981) as ones she uses herself on a regular basis. What emerges, therefore, is a blended Polish-American (*polsko-amerykański*) or, as others call it, American-Polish (*amerykańsko-polski*) language with deep historical roots. An illustrative example of this is the word *kara*. Derived from the English *car*, over time it has referred to different objects. Kruszka (1905) lists it as meaning "train car." Doroszewski (1938) has it as *kar* (masc.) meaning "carriage," but then adds "today its only form is the feminine *kara*, mostly referring to automobiles" (22). And indeed, Dubisz's (1981) list of Polamerican nouns has *kara* (fem.) meaning "car, automobile." Thus the word *kara* has a long history, but also has undergone semantic shift. Examples like these help us to think about Polamerican as a separate hybrid language variety, or at least a dialect of Polish.

Table 5.4 below lists some of the Polamerican nouns that appear in the three texts from 1905 to 1981, and shows how they have been assigned to Polish grammatical gender categories. Because Polish has both grammatical gender and seven-case declension with inflectional endings that depend on the noun's

Table 5.4 *Comparison of Polamerican hybrid words over eighty years*

Gender	Kruszka (1905)	Doroszewski (1938)	Dubisz (1981)
Masculine inanimate	bas "boss" blok "city block" buczer "butcher" kiesz "cash" korner "corner" morgecz "mortgage" ofis "office" owerkot "overcoat" paj "pie" salun "bar" sztor "store"	bedrum "bedroom" bortnik "boarder who rents a room" buczer "butcher" hauz "house" korner "corner" kostumer "customer" market "market" morgecz "mortgage" ofis "office" rent "rent" sztor "store" sztornik "storekeeper"	batrum "bathroom" gan "gun" garden "garden" hajłej "highway" hauz "house" jard "yard, garden" kliner "cleaner" klozet "closet" kol "cold" (as in, catching a cold) kostumer "customer" moskit "mosquito" połder "powder" prajs "price" rent "rent" slajs "slice" trok "truck"
Feminine	grosernia "grocery" kara "train car" korna "corn" kryka "creek" pejda "pay, wage"	baksa "box" ewnia "avenue" grosernia "grocery" kara "car" majna "mine" mećka "match" (as in matchbox) morgeca "mortgage" pejda "pay, wage" susajta "society, association" sztryta "street"	baksa "box" broszka "brush" kara "car" moda "mother" nerska "nurse" pejda "pay, wage" pikcza "picture" pikczera "picture" picziesa "peach"
Neuter	bebi "baby"	bejbi "baby" dypo "depot, train station"	dżielo "jello" pary "party"

gender, for a borrowed noun to be fully integrated into Polish morphosyntax, it has to be assigned to a gender category. There are five genders: masculine virile (human males), masculine animate (male animals), masculine inanimate, feminine, and neuter. As I discuss in my study of Polish-Americans in the Boston and New York area (Baran 2001), gender is assigned to borrowed nouns based on the negotiation of three factors: the gender of the Polish equivalent, the phonological appearance of the English word (i.e. whether it "looks like" a Polish masculine, feminine or neuter noun), and whether Polish phonological rules allow for the adding of a particular gender-specific case ending. The latter consideration sometimes leads to a borrowed word's gender changing from one case to another to comply with Polish phonology (Baran 2001). Dubisz (1981: 65) also reports some nouns with shifting grammatical gender, including *mesydż* [mɛsɨdʒ] "message," *stejszyn* [stɛjʃɨn] "station," and *cziendź* [tʃjɛndʝ] "change, coins" (which can also be pronounced [tʃɛjndʒ]). An example from Table 5.4. is "mortgage," which shows up in Kruszka and Doroszewski as *morgecz* (masc.inan.) and in Doroszewski as *morgeca* (fem.). Overall, however, we witness the same ongoing patterns through which gender is assigned to English-origin nouns, and some nouns that have been established in the Polish-American dialect for decades, including their phonological adaptation and gender (e.g. *buczer, kostumer, sztor, grosernia, paj, kara, pejda, baksa*, and *pary*). The gender-assignment process in Polamerican loanwords is another example of variation and continuity, both of which characterize Polish-American speech.

At the same time, the process of gender assignment to loans becomes a site for the negotiation of Polish-American identity. In addition to the internal factors described above, speakers' gender-assignment choices are also affected by their language ideologies: their individual attitudes towards language mixing, their views on the relative value of Polish and English, and their sense of ethnic and national identity (Baran 2001). Miodunka (1990) describes the Polish American experience in a similar way: "The construction of ethnic and cultural identity is a long and complex process, made up of many choices, rather than a state imposed on an individual by someone and remaining unchanged for years" (10). For this reason, he believes that "it is the individual him/herself who makes the bulk of the decisions regarding his/her Polishness," and he proposes "to locate all speakers of Polish outside Poland along a continuum between two points: a foreigner of non-Polish descent – a Pole living in Poland. Between these points one finds successively, for example, foreigners (Americans) of Polish descent, Polish-Americans, and Poles living in America" (10). Miodunka sees a connection between one's place on this spectrum and one's language, suggesting that perhaps each of these groups may have its own dialect or sociolect (11).

Miodunka's point is illustrated in an excerpt from Gruchmanowa's (1984) study of speakers in the Northeast. The speaker in the excerpt is a sixty-seven-year-old woman from a village in Southeastern Poland, who had lived in a Polish community in Plainfield, NJ, for nearly thirty years. Her English proficiency is judged as limited. The excerpt below is adapted into IPA from Gruchmanowa's Polish phonetic transcription, and followed by an English translation (loanwords underlined and in bold):

f kraju pʃɛd vɔjnom bɨwɔ pʃɛzrɔbɔtɕɛ / mɨ tu sɔ pʃɨjɛzdnɛ / tʃɨ razɨ ɕɛ mufɔvalɨm / tsorka tu ɕɛ ʷurɔdjɨwa / kolɛktujɛ pɔlsk'ɛ p'in'ɨdzɛ / muj hazbɨnd zabraw jɔm dɔ ɕtɔru / karom pɔ djus sɔdɛ i kuk'is / n'ɛ htɕawa ɕɛdjitɕ v domu / lub'ʲɔ razɨm kupuvatɕ / ʷona skuʲntɕɨwa ajskul / jeʃtʃɛ n'ɛ zatʃɛwa pratsuvatɕ / mõʃ kupʲɨw jɛj uʒɨvanom karɛ / stɔji tamoj na dvoʒu na drɛvʲɛ / ɕɛ bɔjɛ ʒɛbɨ n'ɛ mʲawa aksɨdɛnt / jeʃtʃɛ dɔbʒɛ n'ɛ drajvujɛ / n'ɛh ɕɛ pan'i potʃẽstujɛ pajem / lub'ʲɛ pajɛ alɛ n'ɛ mɔgɛ spotkatɕ paja s p'itʃɛsuf / tɛra jɛzdɨm na dajɛt / ʒɔwondɛg mn'ɛ badruje / jɛʃtʃɛ mɔgɛ pratsuvatɕ / tɕasɨm zwapɛ jakõɕ rɔbɔtɛ / zgan'am dɔlarɨ dla hʃeɕn'aka

In homeland before the war there was unemployment / here we are outsiders / we **moved** three times / my daughter was born here / she **collects** Polish money / my **husband** took her to the **store** (masc. inane.)/ in the **car** (fem.) to get **juice soda** and **cookies** / she didn't want to sit at home / they like to go shopping together / she finished **high school** / she hasn't started working yet / my husband bought her a used **car** (fem.) / it's standing there outside on the **driveway** / I am afraid that she may have an **accident** / she doesn't **drive** well yet / please have some **pie** (masc. inane.) / I like **pies** but I can't find **peach pie** / now I am on a **diet** / my stomach **bothers** me / I can still work / sometimes I catch some work / I save money for my godson

This transcript of a casual monologue by a first-generation immigrant with limited English proficiency demonstrates how Polamerican functions in everyday life, and it includes a number of loanwords found in lists presented above, including *to move, to collect, store, car, to drive, pie*, and *to bother*, phonologically and morphologically integrated in similar or identical ways as shown in previous research. This speaker, however, maintains features of her regional Polish dialect, such as the labial off-glide and the raising of the first vowel in [ʷona] "she," which in General Polish (*ogólopolski*, Miodunka 1990) would be pronounced as [ɔna]. The raising of the [ɔ] vowel, common in this dialect, applies also to the loanwords, where we get [karom] "car" (fem., Inst. Sg.) as opposed to the General Polish [karõ] or [karɔm]. This variety of Polamerican combines features shared by most Polamerican speakers (e.g. specific lexical items and the way they are assimilated) with those specific to a regional dialect in Poland, contributing to the evolution of a speech variety that is common to all Polish-Americans yet not uniform across Polish-American communities. As Gruchmanowa (1979: 101) observes, English-origin words are frequently assimilated into the phonology of the speakers' specific regional dialect, and Olesch (1970) reports similar examples among speakers in the oldest Polish communities in Texas.

It is notable that Polish scholars from Kruszka in 1905, through those writing in the interwar period (Doroszewski 1938), to later Communist-era researchers (Dubisz 1981; Gruchmanowa 1984), treat the speech of Polish-Americans as a separate, independent, and legitimate dialect of Polish. They do not deride it, do not take a Poland-centric prescriptivist approach, and eagerly cite Kruszka's (1905) pronouncement: "To an immense upset and scorn of our 'purists,' or cleaners of language, the Pole in America – like the Pole in Silesia or Kashubia – created for himself his own dialect, that is American-Polish speech, which he employs in everyday life" (Kruszka 1905: 111). To be sure, there are derisive, purist, critical voices, such as those cited at some length in Doroszewski (1938) and ones easily encountered in the Polish American community today, but the attitude of Polish researchers is fully accepting of, and fascinated by, Polish-American speech as one of the dialects or forms of Polish spoken around the world. Their attitude is expressed in explicitly rejecting purists who despise the speech of Polonia, and further confirmed in the names they give to the language spoken by Polish-Americans. It is referred to as the Polish-American dialect (*gwara polsko-amerykańska*, Doroszewski 1938), the American-Polish dialect (*gwara amerykańsko-polska*, Kruszka 1905), "American-style Polish language" (*polszczyzna amerykańska*, Doroszewski 1938), and as a variety of the Polonia dialect (*dialekt polonijny*, Gruchmanowa 1984). My own term Polamerican is thus an English-language synthesis of the names given to the variety by Polish researchers.

One could argue, of course, that all we see in Polish-American speech is a case of massive borrowing, which is hardly unique among immigrant communities, as emphasized by Lipski (2014) in his argument against the concept of Spanglish. However, crucially, Polamerican – like Spanglish – is more than the sum of its parts. Hybrid varieties that emerge in the American immigrant communities – Spanglish, Polamerican, Italoamericano (Prifti 2014), Romglish (Andersen, personal communication), and others – are formed through "typical" language-contact processes (Lipski 2014), but speakers clearly employ these processes to produce new, hybrid ways of speaking, and with them, distinct hybrid identities. If we think in terms of Miodunka's (1990) spectrum of ethnic identity discussed above, encompassing various configurations of allegiance to and identifications with one's heritage country and with America, then hybrid languages truly become enactments of the dynamic and ever-shifting negotiations surrounding immigrant identity.

5.4 Variation and Change in Heritage Languages

The distinction between hybrid varieties and heritage languages undergoing change is not a clear one. Certainly, one could argue that the lexical, semantic, and syntactic innovations that characterize the hybrid could just as easily be described as innovations in the heritage language. This seems to be the interpretation of those Polish researchers of Polamerican who describe it as a *dialect* of Polish. I begin this section with the understanding that hybrid languages and new heritage languages are fluid categories located along a spectrum of bilingual or multilingual phenomena. Accordingly, the previous section focused on hybrid identity as expressed in language, with an emphasis on code-switching and large-scale borrowing and assimilation of words. In this section, I shift the focus from immigrant multilingualism *with* English, to the implications of immigration for the heritage languages spoken in the United States, with an emphasis on phonological and morphosyntactic developments. These are influenced by the separation of the heritage language in a diaspora context from the home country, as well as by contact with English and with other immigrant languages. Also, in the United States, speakers of immigrant languages interact with speakers of other regional dialects of their language in ways that would not have been possible in their countries of origin, leading to localized dialect mixing and leveling. And, although languages of the place of origin are typically lost by immigrants by the third generation (Fishman 2004), in communities with a constant in-flow of newcomers from the home country, and where the value placed on speaking the heritage language is high (e.g. Puerto Rican community in New York), the heritage language continues to be used (cf. Potowski 2010). The same may be true of some isolated ethnic communities, such as Swedish, Norwegian, German, or Polish towns in the Midwest or in Texas.

The Polish community in and around Panna Maria in Texas, introduced in Section 1.2, remained in relative isolation for over a century after its foundation in 1854. Local life centered around farming, the Polish church, and Polish cultural life. As a result of these conditions, the inhabitants of Panna Maria continued to speak Polish until very recently. Writing in 1970, Olesch states that "Polish . . . is still spoken by the older and middle generations at home. It is spoken in a dialectal form which has been preserved astonishingly well and whose linguistic features allow a fairly easy determination of the exact origin of the settlers" (1970: 154). Similarly, Franciszek Niklewicz, a first-generation immigrant living in Wisconsin and a historian of Polish America, writes in 1938: "After the service, in front of the church you hear everywhere Polish spoken with a Silesian accent. I even heard children speaking with each other in Polish, which is a very rare phenomenon in our Northern states, because where we are, young people usually speak English with each other" (Niklewicz 1938, cited in Brożek 1972: 63).

Reinhold Olesch, who studied the Polish communities in Texas in 1963–1964, observed the preservation of Silesian Polish in the local speech, as well as of traditional Silesian religious hymns, over 100 years after the establishment of Panna Maria. Olesch reports some borrowing of English words as discussed in Section 5.3 above – most notably, the word *kara* (fem.) "car." He also notices features such as the adaptation of Silesian dialectal forms to the new Texan environment. For example, the Polish settlers would have encountered rattlesnakes, and may not have known the general Polish term *grzechotnik*, from *grzechotać* "to rattle." Instead, they adapted the Silesian verb *szczyrkać* "to rattle" to form the new word *szczyrkowa* "rattlesnake" (Olesch 1970: 156). The Silesian phonological rules are also applied to English borrowings. Thus, the English word *tank* (i.e. cistern), pronounced [tæŋk] in Texas American English, emerges in Texas Polish not as [tank] or [tɛnk] but as [tɨŋk], following the Silesian rendition of General Polish [ɛ] + nasal as [ɨ + N] (Olesch 1970: 157). The Texan Polish-Americans thus preserved Silesian Polish for over a century, and continued to productively apply its phonological rules to new vocabulary.

This unusual longevity of the heritage language was made possible by the relative isolation of the Texas communities. Brożek (1972: 74) writes:

> Silesians in Texas were for many decades secluded in their micro-society; they were – in comparison with other Polish immigrants, flowing into large urban and industrial conglomerations in Chicago or Pennsylvania – largely isolated from the English, German or Mexican surroundings of their New World. Thus they did not feel the need to alienate themselves from their ties to the Old Country. In this way, they persisted in their Polishness, as it were through the forces of inertia . . .

Interestingly, Brożek points out the *need* for alienation among those who experience linguistic and cultural contact with the dominant society, as contrasted with the "inertia" of those who remain isolated. According to this viewpoint, the continued use of Polish in villages like Panna Maria is not so much an accomplishment achieved through effort as a product of relative ethnic homogeneity.

Brożek also emphasizes that a heritage language is influenced not just by English, but also by other immigrant languages dominant in a particular area. In Texas, these included Spanish and German. German settlements abounded in Texas, and indeed numerous studies have been devoted to their history and development (e.g. Boas 2009; Eikel 1966a, 1966b, 1967; Gilbert 1970; Pulte 1970). Thus, Olesch, who also studied the Czech and Sorbian communities in Texas, observes changes in Sorbian spoken there that are due to German influence. The Sorbs are a Slavic minority in Germany, and already in the nineteenth century they were under considerable pressure to assimilate to the dominant culture and language. In Texas, Sorbian settlers established the village of Serbin, where they shared a Lutheran church and an elementary school with German immigrants. The dominant language in these institutions soon became German, and thus, as Olesch comments, "The enforced Prussification or Germanization which the Sorbs had sought to avoid by emigrating caught up with them in their new home" (Olesch 1970: 160). On one hand, many Sorbian Texans experienced language shift to German. On the other hand, their Sorbian shows influences of both Texas American English and Upper Saxon Texas German, including lexical loans and calques (162). But these influences are not unidirectional. Thus, Texas American English has caused changes in both Sorbian and German, while Sorbian bears German influences and vice-versa. Olesch writes:

> On the phonetic level, one immediately notes the (Texas) English retroflex [ɹ] and diphthongized [ɪ] [ɪɪ̯̃] (as in Texas English [ɪ̃ɪ̯̃ɫ] "ill" or [mɪ̃ɪ̯̃s] "miss") which appear in

both German and Sorbian, the bilabial articulation [w] of the labio-dental spirant [v], the loss of palatalization of the Sorbian front palatal phonemes . . . and the voicing of German /b/, /d/, /g/. The latter phenomenon is very striking since in the Upper Saxon German dialect, voicing is phonemically irrelevant. This is undoubtedly an influence of Sorbian on German and suggests the existence of other such "substratum" influences in the phonemic system of local German (Olesch 1970: 162).

Wilson (1970), on the other hand, presents a five-page list of "unusual vocabulary" found in the German spoken in Texas Sorbian communities, which in his study includes an area spanning Lee and Fayette Counties.

Meanwhile, since German was for a time a major regional language in Texas that was spoken in an area – the "German Belt" – of similarly isolated and homogeneous communities (Boas 2009; see Section 1.2), it also evolved into a separate variety. Boas (2009) describes Texas German as having developed through "new-dialect formation that took as its input various donor dialects brought to Texas by German immigrants beginning in the 1840s," resulting in a variety that "is (virtually) mutually unintelligible with standard German" (Boas 2009: 2). And, according to Boas, as of 2009, there were between 8,000 and 10,000 German speakers left in Texas, most of them elderly since intergenerational transmission of Texas German stopped after World War II, mainly due to the anti-German sentiment caused by the two world wars, as well as demographic changes that followed. This, however, means that Texas German has been a viable, dynamic, evolving language with its own particular history and features, spoken by large numbers of people for over 150 years, which represents a very substantial part of American history.

Pioneering extensive research on Texas German was conducted by Glenn Gilbert in the 1960s (Gilbert 1963, 1970, 1972; Salmons and Lucht 2006), including his *Linguistic Atlas of Texas German* (Gilbert 1972). In Gilbert (1970), he analyzes a text written, and subsequently read and recorded, in 1964 by William David Walter, a college-educated native of Fredericksburg, Gillespie County, Texas. According to Gilbert, "The informant calls the type of language he spoke (and speaks) at home the 'Fredericksburg Dialect'" (Gilbert 1970: 63). The text, titled "A Tale from Fredericksburg," is a story of the origin of the local Easter tradition of having bonfires lit on the hills surrounding the town. In this story, the fires commemorate a night one Easter when the women stayed alone at home at night, while their husbands were away negotiating a peace treaty with the Comanche Indians. The Indians lit fires around the town, and one Fredericksburg mother found herself explaining to her terrified children that it was the Easter bunny and his helpers building fires to boil and dye Easter eggs.

The recording of Mr. Walter's reading of his story reveals numerous differences between the grammar of Fredericksburg German (FG) and Standard German (SG). Some of the phonological differences include: /b/ can appear as a bilabial fricative intervocalically; in clusters /pt/, /kt/, /nt/, /ft/, often /t/ appears as a glottal stop; /v/ has a "bilabial fricative allophone which sometimes appears initially, or medially after /ts/ before vowel" (Gilbert 1970: 95); initial /s/ can appear as [s], [z] or [z̥]; /ʒ/ is very rare in comparison with SG; /r/ has only two allophones as contrasted with SG four; many vowels are affected by merging, for example the SG /i:/ and /y:/ correspond to the FG /i:/, SG /e:/ and /ø:/ correspond to FG /e:/, and SG /œ/ and /ɛ/ correspond to FG /e/; and finally, [e] and back vowels have an off-glide, [j] and [w], respectively (92–97). Morphosyntax is also affected: in Fredericksburg German, Accusative forms "have replaced the dative almost everywhere" (97). The Fredericksburg tale that celebrates the shared hardships, history and traditions of the local German-speaking inhabitants enregisters their identification with and allegiance to place – Fredericksburg – through the use of local phonological and morpho-syntactic features. To what extent these features are used consciously is unclear: Gilbert describes Mr. Walter as having "much greater than average education and extensive training in SG" (Gilbert 1970: 68). Regardless of whether the speaker was speaking naturally or performing the dialect, the features he employs are in fact those listed for the area in the *Linguistic Atlas of Texas German* (Gilbert 1972). And here, Mr. Walter is using these very features in a story – chosen and told by him – that centers around local shared history and tradition. Together, these produce a local identity, which is uniquely American and, crucially, expressed in local – Texan and American – German.

German speakers have a long-established presence in Texas and other parts of the United States, as discussed in Chapter 1 (Section 1.2), and as described in detail by Boas (2009), Gilbert et al. (2006), and Gilbert (1963, 1970, 1972), among others. Potowski (2010) describes the historical development and present sociolinguistic situation of many other heritage languages in the United States, which it is impossible to include in the limited space of this section. Among those, however, Spanish may be argued to have as much of a claim to be an American language as English, given the historical relationship of Spanish speakers to the United States (see Chapter 1; Hill 2008). New dialect formation and variation within Spanish spoken in the United States have long been the subject of extensive research, including Otheguy and Zentella (2012), Lamanna (2012), Lipski (2008), Otheguy et al. (2007), Zentella (2004), Roca and Lipski (1993), Gutiérrez (1994), Gutiérrez González (1993), Elías-Olivares (1983), Phillips (1967), Porges (1949), and Espinosa (1911), among many others,[3] and I wish to direct interested readers to these sources. For the purposes of the present discussion, I will summarize just a few examples of features that distinguish US Spanish from varieties spoken in Latin America or Spain.

[3] For a comprehensive overview, see Lipski (2008).

Most US Spanish varieties are products of dialect contact and leveling between groups of speakers from across the Spanish-speaking world. Lipski (2008), for instance, includes chapters on Mexican, Cuban, Puerto Rican, Dominican, Central American, Salvadoran, Nicaraguan, Guatemalan, and Honduran Spanish in his book on Spanish in the United States. In addition, there is Spanish spoken by immigrants from elsewhere in South America, for example, Columbia, Chile, and Peru. Lipski (2008) emphasizes that varieties of American Spanish should not necessarily be treated as entirely separate entities, and points out, for example, the ongoing contact between Mexican American Spanish and Mexican Spanish that "replenishes" the former with characteristics from the latter (Lipski 2008: 83). Similar contact exists between New York Puerto Rican and Puerto Rican Spanish (Zentella 1997), as well as other Central and South American varieties, which come in contact with each other in ways that do not take place in Central or South America (Otheguy and Zentella 2012).

In a few cases, however, a US dialect of Spanish has developed separately due to the relative isolation of its speakers. One such example is what Lipski (2008) refers to as the "traditional Spanish of New Mexico and Southern Colorado" (Lipski 2008: 192). New Mexico was settled as early as the sixteenth century by Spanish colonizers, who established missions and settlements mainly in the northern mountainous areas (Lipski 2008: 195). The original settlers came from a variety of sociolinguistic backgrounds traceable to many different regions of Spain. Subsequently, the region had limited contact with other Spanish-speaking areas. It was difficult to reach, relatively unattractive as a colony due to its harsh climate, few resources, and a persistent threat of conflict with local Native Americans, and as a result saw virtually no immigration from Mexico. On the other hand, established northern New Mexicans developed a strong sense of local identity that centered on the qualities of resilience and independence. Furthermore, partly due to its remoteness, the region lacked public education until well into the nineteenth century, had little contact with the prestige urban Spanish of Spain or Mexico, and was marked by widespread illiteracy, which led to "the gradual fading from collective memory of literary language" (Lipski 2008: 201). All these factors contributed to the development of a distinct local variety of Spanish, characterized by clear differences from other Mexican American varieties or from northern Mexican Spanish. Some of its features include the weakening or elision of intervocalic /j/ and /d/ (e.g. *colorao* for *colorado*), a uniformly alveolar final /n/, the pronunciation of /r/ resembling the English [ɹ], the frequent realization of /b/ as labiodental [v], the aspiration of /s/ to [h], the presence of syllabic consonants (e.g. *un beso* "a kiss" realized as [Mbeso]), and the frequent pronunciation of /tʃ/ as [ʃ] (Lipski 2008: 204–206).

An example of dialect contact and leveling, on the other hand, is the Spanish spoken in New York City. As Otheguy and Zentella (2012) explain, "Anyone familiar with the life of the city's Latino communities knows of the daily interaction of Spanish speakers from different countries and regions and of many cross-national and cross-regional friendships and work teams" and even marriages (Otheguy and Zentella 2012: 18). The authors document effects of dialect contact in the city by analyzing rates of pronoun presence with finite verbs among New York-raised (NYR) as compared with Latin American-raised (LAR) Spanish speakers. In Latin America, as among newcomers or LAR speakers, Mainlanders (from Colombia, Ecuador, and Mexico) tend to use pronouns more frequently than Caribbeans (from Puerto Rico, Cuba, and the Dominican Republic). But the differences in pronoun rates narrow among Mainland and Caribbean NYR speakers. That this change is due to dialect leveling is supported by the fact that speakers who associate mostly with others from their own region maintain greater regional differences in pronoun rates than speakers with a more out-group orientation (Otheguy and Zentella 2012: 123).

Finally, Lamanna (2012) analyzes a case of more recent dialect contact between speakers of Colombian and Mexican Spanish in North Carolina's Piedmont Triad area, as well as of the effects of English on North Carolina Colombian Spanish. His study demonstrates that Colombian Spanish speakers in North Carolina use a significantly higher percentage of imperfect progressive (IP) constructions (e.g. *estates hablando*) than speakers in Bogotá when compared with imperfect (IM) constructions (e.g. *hablabas*). He notes that both of these correspond semantically to the English past progressive "you were speaking," but only the former corresponds to it structurally. Furthermore, Colombian and Mexican Spanish speakers in North Carolina appear to be converging in the relative importance that they assign to factors such as status, age, and degree of familiarity when selecting pronouns with which to address interlocutors. Based on these findings, Lamanna argues that a new US Spanish variety is being formed in North Carolina, a state that has seen an unprecedented growth in the immigrant Latino community in recent years, and an emergence of a new Hispanic English variety as well (Section 4.3, Callahan-Price 2013a, 2013b; Wolfram et al. 2004).

The examples of variation and change in heritage languages discussed in this section serve to highlight the fact that by no means have English speakers been the only stakeholders in the linguistic development of America over the past several centuries. The multilingual practices that have always been a feature of American sociolinguistic life include localized, American developments in languages other than English, many of which are dynamic and ongoing. Crucially, an American variety of a heritage language is not foreign, but rather it is as integral to the picture of a multilingual United States as Boston, Pittsburgh, or Appalachian English dialects, or as Hawai'i Creole or Gullah.

6 Immigrant Children and Language

In this chapter I turn to the effects of immigration on children and, concomitantly, on their families, with a specific focus on language. Since the issue of education has emerged several times in Chapters 4 and 5 – we saw how speakers of emerging dialects such as Hispanic English may suffer by being placed in ESL classrooms, or how encouraging translanguaging practices in schools can benefit bilingual students – we will open this chapter with a focused look at the schooling of immigrant children. Subsequently, we will shift the discussion to children as language brokers between their families and the English-speaking outside world, and finally to the impact of immigration on family life and dynamics. My aim is to draw attention to the complex role of language in the lives of immigrant children, calling for the recognition and examination of these issues not just by academics, but by educators and policymakers.

6.1 Education and the Immigrant Child

Little Manuel, so nicknamed to distinguish him from his classmate, Big Manuel, is a seventh grader at a predominantly Latino middle school in Southwestern United States. Despite his recent arrival from Mexico and unfamiliarity with English, Little Manuel was placed in all-English classes. He is not alone: many of his classmates are also new to English, or are still learning it. The science teacher, however, is a monolingual English speaker. While she is known as one of the best science teachers in the district, Ms. Jackson has difficulty conveying the scientific concepts to her Spanish-speaking immigrant students. This situation, described in detail in a study by Bayley et al. (2005), results in confusion such as, for example, in the following classroom interaction, recorded by the researchers in October 2001 (Bayley et al. 2005: 223):

MS. J:	Now, to get milligrams, you multiply by a thousand, so seventy-five times a thousand is . . .
PEDRO:	One seventy-five.

MS. J: Seventy-five times one thousand, how much, very good, seventy-five thousand, okay, you done now, you done?
BIG MANUEL: *Qué?* [What?], oh.
PEDRO: A thousand, *cómo se escribe* [how do you write] a thousand?
LITTLE MANUEL: *No me entiendo nada.* [I don't understand anything.]

Throughout Bayley et al.'s article, we see Little Manuel struggling to follow the lessons, constantly asking his classmates for help and translation, and becoming frustrated and confused. Bilingual students who understand English well try to help, but, as the authors observe, their translations almost always focus on the teacher's procedural directions while leaving out the scientific content. Bayley et al. conclude that what routinely does not get translated "is distressingly simple: science" (230). They argue that this fact is not surprising, given that the teacher's procedural directions – what to copy from the textbook or which picture to draw – "generally employ relatively familiar language," in contrast to "teacher explanations of new academic content [which] involve complex concepts that are unfamiliar both to the translator and to the beneficiary of the translation" (230). One can imagine that, under the circumstances, an immigrant student like Little Manuel would make little progress in learning either English or science. Falling behind academically will be an unfortunate outcome for Little Manuel, who, according to his Mexican school records, "had been quite a successful student before moving to the United States," but never studied English (226).

Falling behind due to lack of understanding not only prevents students from achieving their academic potential, but can lead to frustration and boredom, resulting in behavioral difficulties. This is very problematic in light of the many voices that oppose any kind of bilingual education for immigrant children, even as it has been shown time and again that immersion is not conducive to immigrant children's success in school, and that children do not necessarily learn a second language fast, despite popular belief (Cummins 1979; Valdés 2001; Suárez-Orozco and Suárez-Orozco 2001; Combs et al. 2005; Bartlett and García 2011). Although typically immigrant children do acquire English faster than their parents, the process is not easy or effortless (see Section 5.2). Furthermore, while seemingly fluent children may have acquired conversational English, their academic literacy lags behind. Children who learn English under English-only curricula on the whole fare worse in school than those taught in bilingual programs that valorize and support the home language (Combs et al. 2005; Valdés 2001; Bartlett and García 2011). The many state and local policies that reject bilingual education and opt for various types of immersion programs are at direct odds with current research, which clearly shows the overall benefits of developing both of the child's languages and literacies. Meanwhile, most bilingual and English as a second language (ESL) programs are beleaguered by problems such as test-driven education and its impact on immigrant students, inaccurate and arbitrary classification of students as English language learners (ELL), and misguided bilingual education methodology that is out of touch with current research in education and bilingualism. These problems are often also bound up with institutionalized discrimination, and specifically, the unequally distributed access to resources, including educational resources, available to students of minority racial and ethnic backgrounds.

In the rest of this section, I will discuss these points in reference to the impact of testing under No Child Left Behind (NCLB) and Every Child Achieves on ELLs, as well as other damaging policies for ELLs stipulated in educational legislation. Then I will turn to the paradoxical classifications of children as LEPs or FEPs – English learners or fluent speakers. Finally, I will close with a discussion of the conflict between the ideas driving language and educational policy in general, and towards immigrant children in particular, and the increasingly robust current research findings as regards optimal learning conditions for bilingual children.

No Child Left Behind and ELL students

The No Child Left Behind (NCLB) Act of 2001 officially expired in September 2007, but continued to stay in effect for eight more years. By spring of 2015, there was renewed pressure on Congress to revise the law from major education groups including the National PTA, the National Education Association (NEA), the National Federation of Teachers, the Council of Chief State School Officers, and "organizations representing principals, superintendents and school boards."[1] The NCLB was replaced by the Every Child Achieves Act of 2015,[2] which became law on December 10, 2015.[3]

During the fourteen years of its existence, the NCLB legislation came under severe attack by many educators for punishing struggling schools and undermining public education (Ravitch 2010), despite its ostensibly positive goals of assuring opportunity for academic achievement to disadvantaged students partly by requiring states to report progress for specific disadvantaged groups (economically disadvantaged students, racial and ethnic groups, students with

[1] www.washingtonpost.com/local/education/education-groups-to-congress-please-get-rid-of-no-child-left-behind-already/2015/06/22/3c3b094e-18ff-11e5-93b7-5eddc056ad8a_story.html, accessed July 2, 2015.

[2] www.natlawreview.com/article/senate-passes-every-child-achieves-act-to-replace-no-child-left-behind, accessed July 22, 2015.

[3] www.congress.gov/bill/114th-congress/senate-bill/1177/all-actions?overview=closed, accessed May 24, 2016.

disabilities, and ELLs). Researchers have also been documenting the harmful effects of test-driven schooling that NCLB produced (Wright and Li 2008).

For the ELL student population, NCLB presented an additional set of problems (Abedi 2004; Wright and Li 2008; see also Crawford 2004, 2007; Wiley 2005). For one, while leaving states the flexibility to define the category of English language learner (ELL) or Limited English Proficient (LEP) students, NCLB nonetheless required all states to identify ELLs through state-selected testing methods, to assess these students English proficiency annually in grades K–12, and to demonstrate LEP students' progress in English proficiency, as well as attainment of high level of academic achievement in core content areas.[4] Abedi (2004) identifies a number of problems that the law generated or did not account for, including the following:

- the inconsistency of the ELL/LEP definition, which affects accuracy of progress (adequate yearly progress or AYP) reporting;
- the cultural, ethnic, educational, religious, and linguistic diversity within the ELL/LEP population, which is not reflected in Home Language Surveys or English proficiency assessments but which has an impact on different ELL students' educational outcomes;
- the uneven distribution of the ELL/LEP population across states, which skews the analysis of AYP reports;
- the instability of the LEP subgroup, given that unlike students in the other disadvantaged subgroups, LEP students move out of the group upon reaching proficiency while new LEP students move in, leading to a situation where the LEP subgroup never shows marked progress and schools with large numbers of LEP students continue to remain in the "in need of improvement" category;
- the measurement of ELLs' AYP via assessment tools designed for native English speaking students, which means that core content knowledge of ELLs is not measured accurately;
- low baseline scores in schools with high numbers of ELL/LEP students, which places the pressure on these schools to improve their students' English as well as content area test performance or risk losing federal resources; and
- the requirement, introduced by NCLB, that students' higher scores in areas that rely less on language skills cannot compensate for lower scores in those that do, posing an additional challenge for schools with high numbers of ELL/LEP students.

As this extensive list suggests, NCLB placed unrealistic demands on schools with large ELL populations, while ignoring very real needs of specific ELL students. When immigrant children have to be drilled to improve their

[4] See, for example, www.asha.org/uploadedFiles/advocacy/federal/nclb/NCLBELLAssess.pdf, accessed July 1, 2015; www.learningpt.org/pdfs/qkey5.pdf, accessed July 1, 2015.

performance on standardized tests that may be, due to the language used, difficult for them to understand, an accurate assessment of their content learning in their second language is compromised. A number of studies show that LEP students perform better on math tests whose linguistic structures have been modified to account for non-native English proficiency (Abedi 2004: 7). Linguistic features reported as difficult and confusing for ELLs include, for example, passive voice constructions, subordinate and conditional clauses, past participial clauses, long sentences, abstract and impersonal presentations, comparatives and superlatives, negation in questions (as in, "which is NOT the answer?"), and math-specific vocabulary such as *digit, congruent, diagram, parallel*, or *denominator* (Abedi 2004; Wright and Li 2008. See also Abedi and Lord 2001; Brown 2005; Dale and Cuevas 1992). Meanwhile, NCLB requires LEP students to take their state's math test, and for their scores to be included in their school's AYP report, regardless of the amount of time that they have been in the United States, which for some might mean as little as a few months (Wright and Li 2008). At this point, they are likely to speak little to no English.

Wright and Li's (2008, 2006) case study of two sisters from Cambodia attending a Texas middle school illustrates this problem. Although NCLB allowed for offering ELLs math and science tests in their native languages, few states implemented such accommodations. Texas offers its standardized tests in English and Spanish, but non-Spanish speaking ELLs have to take the same test as native English speakers. The Cambodian girls, Nitha and Bora, took the Texas Assessment of Knowledge and Skills (TAKS) Math test in English in the 2004–2005 academic year, the same year they arrived in the United States. Despite the school's best efforts at helping them catch up to grade level, including classroom instruction using materials geared at their language and academic level, pull-out ESL instruction with an experienced teacher, and regular tutoring in Khmer by the study's first author, Wayne Wright,[5] the girls failed the test, each getting only 15 percent of the questions right (Wright and Li 2008: 243). By the time they took the test, six months since their arrival, Nitha and Bora had learned enough English to function at school at a basic level. The authors demonstrate that even when the mathematical operations being tested were within the girls' competence, the language proficiency required to comprehend the questions was far beyond their level of English at both the lexical and syntactic level. Furthermore, the authors argue, the disparity in the areas and skills of mathematics between what Nitha and Bora would have learned in Cambodia and what American children in Texas

[5] Wright reports being proficient in Khmer and states that he volunteered as the girls' tutor throughout the course of his research, from November 2004 to May 2005 (Wright and Li 2008: 242).

learn by the fifth grade means that to pass the TAKS Math test, the girls needed to acquire additional content knowledge at the same time as learning English. The authors conclude, "As the above analyses of the linguistic demands of the TAKS test and the students' opportunity to learn the content before taking the test reveal, NCLB's mandated expectations for newly arrived ELLs to pass their state's math test in English are unreasonable. The real failure here is on the part of US federal policy" (Wright and Li 2008: 262).

Nitha and Bora were fortunate to have "dedicated teachers and support staff doing everything possible to meet their unique language and educational needs" (262), but this was not enough to get them to pass the TAKS test. And one could argue that because of the pressure to prepare them for the NCLB-mandated test, the school was not free to address the girls' needs appropriately. Nitha and Bora's case shows how difficult it is for schools to develop the best environment for their ELL students to learn both English and academic content while they face the demands of standardized testing. This is especially true for struggling schools with large ELL populations, which, as Abedi (2004) points out, may be very heterogeneous. Immigrant students of different linguistic backgrounds and national origins who go to the same school do not necessarily face the same challenges just because they are all English language learners.

An example of the latter point is an elementary (PK–5) school in Durham, North Carolina, which I will refer to as Maple Elementary. Maple has a very high number of minority students (96 percent), including African American and Hispanic students. Hispanic students account for 47 percent of the student body, compared to 11.02 percent of the North Carolina state average. Many of these are also ELLs who participate in the school's ESL program. The ESL coordinator and teachers are deeply committed to their students: they know them each by name, they know their family circumstances very well, and they work very hard to ensure that every student's needs are met. This is apparent to me every year when they discuss assigning their ESL students to tutors from my service-learning course. Still, Maple Elementary is a low-performing school according to state standardized test scores: in the 2012–2013 academic year, only 16.3 percent of tested students scored at or above grade level in reading. Like all schools with large numbers of disadvantaged students, Maple has to grapple with balancing the pressure to improve test performance with the genuine needs of its students. As the tutors from my course have observed during their service involvement at Maple, it is not always clear from tests and homework whether Latino children's difficulties stem from content-related or language-related problems. Children who are sent to the ESL program may be communicating fluently in English with their peers, but struggle with literacy skills. There is a YMCA-run after-school tutoring program at Maple, but eligibility for it depends on the student's English proficiency.

In addition to Latino children, Maple has recently been receiving Southeast Asian refugee children. They are typically members of the Karen minority in Burma (Myanmar) and constitute less than 1 percent of the student body. Crucially, however, these children do not speak English *or* Spanish when they arrive, so, like Nitha and Bora in Wright and Li's study, they become a linguistic minority within the ELL minority at the school.[6] In terms of its infrastructure, Maple is effectively a bilingual school: all brochures, notices, and signs are in English and Spanish, and many teachers, including ESL teachers, speak Spanish. But there is no parallel accommodation for Karen language speakers. Upon arrival, Karen-speaking children are a tiny ethnic minority at Maple, do not have an established cultural and linguistic community – there is no one to translate for them the way classmates do for Little Manuel discussed at the start of this section – and their parents have no effective way of communicating with school authorities. Their personal stories are different also: as refugees from life-threatening situations, they may suffer from psychological trauma that is not addressed in any language proficiency evaluation or subsequent ESL placement. Finally, there are also a few Arabic-speaking refugee children at Maple Elementary. The ESL coordinator described how one of these children, already having emergent literacy in Arabic, struggled with writing the unfamiliar Roman alphabet. Again, this is reminiscent of Nitha and Bora, who Wright and Li describe as "educated, literate, bright and highly motivated" (Wright and Li 2008: 262), but who had to learn a new alphabet to become literate in English. All of these different children face unique challenges that cannot be effectively addressed with a one-size-fits-all ELL/LEP policy geared at raising test scores.

Immigrant children in schools with large ELL and large minority populations are at significant risk of having the challenges they face overlooked. These are the schools where multiple disadvantaged categories specified by NCLB co-occur and overlap. García and Kleifgen (2010) point out that the majority of ELL students live in urban, high-poverty school districts; for example, in schools classified as "high LEP schools," as many as 72 percent of children qualify for free or reduced-price school lunches, and the 2000 census shows that about half of all immigrant children and children of immigrants come from low-income families (García and Kleifgen 2010: 16). Under NCLB, these schools would have lower base scores and be under greater pressure to improve. However, improvement might mean overlooking their students' individual needs, while on the other hand focusing on those needs

[6] Nitha and Bora's school's student population was 58 percent Caucasian, 29 percent Hispanic, 10 percent African American, and only 2 percent Asian and Pacific Islander (Wright and Li 2008: 241).

instead may mean low scores and ensuing loss of funding and other repercussions.

The new Every Child Achieves Act that replaced NCLB in 2015 scales back on federal control over education, returning decision-making in numerous areas to the states, and ostensibly recognizing the importance of education responding to local, district-specific needs. However, the law retains the principle of accountability through testing. Title III, which deals with instruction of ELL and immigrant students, repeatedly emphasizes students' achievement of English proficiency as the main objective, to be assessed via "standardized statewide entrance and exit procedures"[7] for the ELL category. The law provides "recognition" for educational agencies "that have significantly improved the achievement and progress of English learners in meeting . . . annual timelines and goals for progress . . . based on the State's English language proficiency assessment."[8] Every Child Achieves continues to set uniform and unrealistic goals for ELLs' progress; for example, states are expected to "describe how the [state educational] agency will assist eligible entities in decreasing the number of English learners who have not yet acquired English proficiency within 5 years of their initial classification as an English Learner."[9] Here, English learners who are not "proficient" after five years are framed as a problem or a failure, even though research shows that it takes five to seven years for children to develop abstract language abilities to a level proficient enough for successful learning in a second language (García and Kleifgen 2010: 40); furthermore, as I mentioned above, children are not better or faster at learning a second language than adults, except possibly in the area of phonology (Valdés 2001: 20; Suárez-Orozco and Suárez-Orozco 2001: 137–138; Wiley 2004), and success in learning a second language depends on a host of social and educational contexts and opportunities for learning (Wiley 2004: 332). The reality seems to be that even with its improvements over NCLB, the new legislation makes inaccurate and generalizing assumptions about immigrant children's language situations and needs.

Who Counts as an English Language Learner?

Title VII of the 1968 Elementary and Secondary Education Act (ESEA), also known as the Bilingual Education Act, established as federal law the goal of helping ELL students learn English and function well in the American

[7] www.help.senate.gov/imo/media/S_EveryChildAchievesActof2015.pdf, p. 318, accessed July 21, 2015.

[8] www.help.senate.gov/imo/media/S_EveryChildAchievesActof2015.pdf, p. 319–320, accessed July 21, 2015.

[9] www.help.senate.gov/imo/media/S_EveryChildAchievesActof2015.pdf, p. 326, accessed July 21, 2015.

education system (García and Kleifgen 2010s: 29). As discussed above, NCLB, which was a new incarnation of ESEA, reinforced this goal while establishing ELLs as one of several disadvantaged subcategories of students whose progress was to be measured regularly via standardized tests. Accordingly, school districts have over time established screening policies for identifying LEP/ ELL children. These typically combine surveys and tests. For example, as explained in the FAQ document regarding the IDEA English Language Proficiency Test or IPT, North Carolina Public Schools use the Home Language Survey, distributed to families upon student registration. The survey "determines if the student is a language minority student/National Origin Minority (NOM) student. If the answer to any question on the home language survey is 'a language other than English,' the student must take the IPT at initial enrollment."[10] The IPT must be administered to all language minority or NOM students at first enrollment, as well as every year thereafter, as long as the particular student remains classified as Limited English Proficient (LEP) based on his or her IPT scores. The student is moved out of LEP classification upon scoring "Superior" on all four sections (listening, speaking, reading, and writing) of the IPT[11] during a single administration of the test. The reading and writing sections are administered to all students in second through twelfth grades.

However, the IPT is a problematic assessment tool for various reasons. One of these is that it is based on a particular interpretation of Mainstream US English, thus excluding many fluent, as well as native and monolingual, speakers of English from the Fluent English Proficient (FEP) category. Callahan-Price (2013) points out that "an appreciable number of monolingual speakers of local and regional dialects would be scored by the IPT Oral test as English language learners" (Callahan-Price 2013: 105). She shows that a monolingual speaker of North Carolina Hispanic English (HE), which was discussed in Section 4.3, could conceivably score as low as 33 percent on the IPT Oral test, simply by producing answers consistent with his or her dialect of English, which in turn calls for the classification as non-English speaking (NES) (106). Furthermore, many of the HE features – such as copula deletion, multiple negation, habitual present *be*, or irregular past tense (105–106) – are shared with Southern English and African American Vernacular English (AAVE), underscoring the ethnic and socioeconomic dimensions of the exclusionary effects of English proficiency screening.

LEP/ELL educational policies in other states suffer from similar problems: inadequate or inappropriate testing, one-size-fits-all standardized approaches

[10] Available at www.ncpublicschools.org/docs/accountability/policyoperations/faqiptjanuary2005.pdf, accessed June 30, 2015.

[11] See also the slide presentation by the NC State Board of Education, available at http://slideplayer.com/slide/711603/, accessed June 30, 2015.

that do not focus on individual students or accommodate heterogeneous ELL populations, and the reproduction of socioeconomic and racial inequalities. Mendoza-Denton (1997, 2008) describes the strict English proficiency classifications at Sor Juana High School, the site of her research in the San Francisco Bay area. During the time of her research (early 1990s), potential ELL students were identified via the Home Language Survey consisting of four questions about the home language environment to be answered by parents. If the answer to any of the four questions was a language other than English, the student would subsequently be evaluated and assigned either to the LEP or FEP category. To qualify for reassignment as FEP, an LEP student had to pass several standardized tests, have passing grades, and be "functioning" in school (Mendoza-Denton 2008: 33). Reclassification as FEP was impossible if any of these criteria were not met. However, in addition to the challenges of standardized exams discussed by Mendoza-Denton (2008: 33–34), students could be prevented from advancing to FEP status if they were judged as "not functioning" at school, which included "disruptive behavior" (34). Unfortunately, "disruptive behavior" was sometimes a response to being bored, unchallenged, and undervalued (cf. Eckert 2000) in the ESL system. An example of this was Armando, who immigrated from Mexico at age five, and by the time he was in high school did not speak Spanish to his family, but was instead a fluent Chicano English speaker. Armando remained classified as LEP because, according to the teachers, he was "too rowdy." But Armando was bored in his ESL classes that were far below his now fluent level of English: "*What is this? This is a dog. This is a cat.* Give me a break! I'd rather get kicked out of class" (Mendoza-Denton 2008: 35). Students like Armando were punished for "bad behavior" by being denied access to an appropriate level of education, and remaining in unchallenging classes led to more bad behavior.

The repercussions of continued LEP classification went beyond being bored in class. As Mendoza-Denton (2008: 34–35) explains, LEP students could not enroll in college-preparatory courses because until being reclassified as FEP, they had to take only ESL courses. Of those, only the four most advanced courses counted towards basic four-year college entrance requirements, including at the University of California (UC) and the California State University (CSU). This situation is not unique: at many American high schools, enrollment in college-preparatory courses is not open to students in the ESL program, who are placed instead in "sheltered" ESL courses or in vocational courses (Valdés 2001: 6–7). As a result of these restrictions, most of the Sor Juana High School students who entered the ninth grade as LEP did not have the opportunity to apply to four-year colleges. They were limited to community colleges, where they still had to catch up if they were to transfer to a four-year college later, setting them back "at least one full year" (Mendoza-Denton 2008: 35). This extended higher education timeline was not economically viable for "poor families who relied on their children for increasing financial contributions to the household" (35).

Situations such as those described by Callahan-Price (2013) and Mendoza-Denton (1997, 2008) are examples of how ineffective policies and programs geared at immigrant students end up reproducing social inequalities. Students classified as LEP may not, in fact, be speakers of a language other than English, but speakers of local dialects, such as Chicano English, North Carolina Hispanic English, Puerto Rican New York English (Zentella 1997), or English with AAVE features. They learn these varieties of English because they grow up among their speakers and identify with them ethnically, culturally, and socioeconomically. Educational policy, however, expects these children to be not only speakers of English, but of the prescriptive Standard English, or MUSE (Lippi-Green 2012). The consequences of failing to do so lead to exclusion from educational opportunities. At the same time, the various school practices reflect and reproduce racially based stereotypes: non-standard English spoken by a child that fits a certain profile – non-white with a Spanish last name, for example – is assumed to be "limited" English in the process of being acquired as a second language.

Educating Immigrant Children: From Learners of English to Emergent Bilinguals

Title III: Language Instruction for English Learners and Immigrant Students of the Every Child Achieves Act of 2015 appears to do away with the term Limited English Proficient (LEP), replacing it everywhere with "English learners."[12] However, while not specifically referring to one's "limitations" in English proficiency, the phrase "English learners" continues to position immigrant children's education as centered around learning English. In other words, immigrant children are constructed as English learners first, and only second as students, children, and individuals with valid existing knowledge and complex developmental needs.

Educational policies and practices rooted in the assumption that immigrant children who are new to English are primarily English language *learners*, and that they need to be classified according to how limited their English is, produce what researchers have called *subtractive schooling* (Valenzuela 1999; Bartlett and García 2011; García and Kleifgen 2010). Subtractive schooling emphasizes students' perceived deficiencies and lacks, thereby negating and erasing the knowledge these children already have instead of nurturing and developing it. When immigrant children are defined first and foremost as "learners of English" (García and Kleifgen 2010: 3), educating

[12] www.help.senate.gov/imo/media/S_EveryChildAchievesActof2015.pdf, accessed July 21, 2015.

them ends up centering around improving their English proficiency. For this reason, authors such as García and Kleifgen opt for the term *emergent bilinguals*, which recognizes and values the children's existing linguistic and cultural knowledge, emphasizes their potential to become bilingual, and reframes bilingualism as "a cognitive, social, and educational resource" (2010: 3; see also García et al. 2008). In practice, this approach allows teachers to see the children's home languages and bilingual practices as strengths to be built on, rather than obstacles to suppress or overcome. This alternative approach, described as *additive schooling* (Bartlett and García 2011), seeks to move away from the ideology of English monolingualism in both schools and society, as well as from the assumption that languages are discrete entities and that in teaching English, the home language is at best irrelevant. Instead, this approach "builds on and extends the social, cultural, and linguistic assets brought by multilingual, diverse student populations" (Bartlett and García 2011: 22). It treats English language learners as "emergent bilinguals, whose language development exists within a bilingual continuum" (García and Kleifgen 2010: 3), and demands a sound bilingual pedagogy complete with rigorous and challenging curricula and teaching materials. García and Kleifgen explain, "By focusing on the students' emergent bilingualism and making bilingualism the norm, the field of language education is able to move to the center of educational endeavors for *all* US children" (2010: 4; emphasis original). It seems to make sense that as soon as bilingualism and bilingual development are normalized, and immigrant children's learning of English stops being seen as a problem, educators will be able to refocus their attention on children's real educational needs. Unfortunately, however, educational policy in the United States continues to view immigrant children in terms of English language deficit, while many states move away from any form of bilingual education and towards a speedy placement of immigrant children in English-only classrooms (García and Kleifgen 2010: 4; Linton 2009; Schmid 2001). Such policies have detrimental effects on the education, lives, and family dynamics of immigrant children.

The English-centered approach to educating immigrant children needs to be located within the larger discourses of English as the American language, and of English monolingualism as evidence of successful assimilation, which were also discussed in earlier chapters. Any serious attempt at actually educating immigrant children instead of just teaching them English has to acknowledge and encourage their bilingual development, and thus challenges the ideology of the US as an English-speaking country. For those who believe that using a language other than English in public spaces such as schools is un-American, the idea of not just tolerating but developing schoolchildren's bilingualism poses a threat to America's national identity, just like it did for the early critics of hyphenated identities (see Chapter 3; Portes and Rumbaut 2006; Schmid 2001; Pavlenko 2002).

The use of immigrant languages as the medium of instruction in schools was not unusual in the early days of American education until the late 1800s, even if it was controversial, "with alternating cycles of acceptance and rejection depending on the relationship of the United States with the countries from which immigrants came and their levels of immigration" (Gándara et al. 2010: 23). According to Wiese and Garcia (2001), during the seventeenth and eighteenth centuries, because "educational policy was fundamentally in the hands of towns and districts, the language of instruction was frequently the language of the community" (231). German-language schools operated in German-speaking communities in Pennsylvania, Maryland, Virginia, and the Carolinas (Pavlenko 2002: 170). In the nineteenth century, state language policies were often supportive of multilingualism and recognized the language rights of non-English speakers (Linton 2009: 13). Pennsylvania legislature authorized state support for private German schools, and allowed the University of Pennsylvania to teach courses in German (12). The vibrant German-language schooling at this time is also discussed in Salmons and Lucht (2006) and Pavlenko (2002). Some states passed laws requiring that German-language instruction be offered in public schools if demanded by a sufficient number of parents (Pavlenko 2002: 170). In the 1860s, California had public "cosmopolitan schools" which "promoted fluency and literacy in French and German as well as English" (13). During the same time, Iowa, Kansas, Nebraska, Wisconsin, and Illinois all passed laws providing for instruction in non-English languages in public schools. For example, in Illinois, an 1869 law allowed French and German to be "the primary means of communication in schools" (14). Other states where bilingual or non-English language instruction was provided at this time included Maryland, Ohio, Indiana, Missouri, Colorado, Oregon, Minnesota, North and South Dakota, Washington, Michigan, Texas, and Louisiana. Common languages of instruction were German, French, Swedish, Norwegian, Danish, Dutch, Polish, Italian, Czech, and Spanish (Gándara et al. 2010: 23; cf. Pavlenko 2002; Crawford 1999; Kloss 1977). Educators in areas with thriving German-English school programs – such as Cincinnati, Indianapolis, St. Louis, or Milwaukee – openly praised the political, economic, and intellectual value of bilingual skills and learning (Pavlenko 2002).

Certainly in some cases, these policies were not reflected in local practices. Stasiewicz-Bieńkowska (2011), for instance, cites Swedish-American memoirs whose authors recall their language banned and their ethnic heritage mocked in public schools in late nineteenth century. But since official policy largely supported multilingualism, ethnic communities frequently established their own schools, often tied to ethnic churches, where the medium of instruction was the heritage language. Swedish children who lived in larger Swedish American communities could attend daily Swedish parish schools, while between 1860 and 1914, as many as thirty Swedish institutions of higher education were established by Swedish-American churches (Stasiewicz-Bieńkowska 2011: 52). Likewise, new Polish settlements typically established their own Polish parishes and schools. In these communities, Polish children were expected to attend the parish schools as opposed to public ones. According to Panek (1898), who spent five years among Polish-American communities before writing about them in Poland, the parish schools were often understaffed, with as many as eighty to one hundred children per teacher, and consequently did not teach much in terms of content. Nonetheless, they contributed to the maintenance of the Polish language since they used it as the medium of instruction for subjects such as math, reading and writing, calligraphy, Polish history, singing, and also English. The often-cited historian of Polish American communities, Father Wacław Kruszka, describes the schools as "cornerstones" of Polish culture and religion in America: "Polish schools are the best sources for sowing the seeds of Polishness and patriotism in this foreign American soil" (Kruszka 1905, volume 6: 84). In addition to the roughly 400 parish schools (Kruszka 1905), which typically included first through sixth grades, there were also a few advanced schools, including a Polish seminary and a parallel bilingual high school in Detroit (Panek 1898), and the College of the Polish National Alliance that was opened in 1912 in Cambridge Springs, Pennsylvania (Dziembowska 1977a: 235).

But the mood was changing. At the same time as ethnic schools teaching in heritage languages thrived, anti-immigrant voices such as the nativist Know-Nothings were gaining strength. English was increasingly being linked with Americanness, and with an American education (Pavlenko 2002; Schmid 2001; Gándara et al. 2010). The 1906 legislation standardizing the naturalization process (the Naturalization Act) acknowledged nativist concerns by requiring candidates to demonstrate knowledge of spoken English (Linton 2009: 15). World War I brought an increase in anti-immigrant sentiment and a focus on English monolingualism, and by the 1920s, "the laws of twenty-two states prohibited non-English language instruction in elementary education" (Myhill 2004: 400, cited in Gándara et al. 2010: 24). In addition, teaching German in elementary school became illegal in Louisiana, Indiana, and Ohio, while all foreign language instruction in grades I through VIII was outlawed in Alabama, Colorado, Delaware, Iowa, Nebraska, Oklahoma, and South Dakota (Pavlenko 2002: 179). German-English, Spanish-English, and Japanese-English programs were dismantled (Pavlenko 2002).

As Pavlenko points out, now "it was no longer enough to learn English and assimilate: the political climate of the era required that immigrants discard all other allegiances but to America" (Pavlenko 2002: 178). Immigrant children were expected to receive their education in English, which lay the foundation for subtractive schooling and, in Portes and Rumbaut's (2006) terms, "subtractive acculturation": "Immigrants were not only compelled to speak English, but to speak English *only* as the prerequisite of social acceptance and integration" (209, emphasis original). To help them assimilate into English-medium mainstream schools, teachers encouraged families to adopt English as a home language as well. In his memoir *Hunger of Memory*, Rodriguez (1982) recalls the day when nuns from his 1950s English-medium, Catholic school in Sacramento, California, came to his home and instructed his parents to only speak English to their son. This, they insisted, would aid his school performance. Rodriguez's parents complied, and from this point on the boy mourned the loss of their intimate Spanish conversations that he had come to look forward to. The nuns' thinking was common at the time, yet misguided, as demonstrated by later research. For example, a study by Ramirez and Politzer (1976), cited in Cummins (1979), showed that "use of Spanish at home resulted in higher levels of Spanish skills at no cost to English achievement, while the use of English at home resulted in a deterioration of Spanish skills but no improvement in English" (Cummins 1979: 236).

As the status of English as the medium of instruction in American schools became the accepted norm, immigrant children were easily problematized as lacking in English language proficiency. Meanwhile, the Civil Rights movement also drew attention to immigrant children's right to education. This resulted in the passing of the Bilingual Education Act (BEA) as Title VII of the 1968 ESEA. The BEA recognized the unique educational needs of students classified as Limited English Proficient, as well as their right to the same education as English-speaking children, even as it described their education as "one of the most acute educational *problems* in the United States" (cited in Wiese and Garcia 2001: 229; emphasis mine). Acknowledging that ELLs cannot learn effectively in a language they do not understand, the BEA called for federal financial assistance to schools for the development, implementation, staffing, staff training, and long-term maintenance of innovative bilingual programs.[13] The passing of the BEA was followed in 1974 by *Lau* v. *Nichols*, in which the Supreme Court affirmed the right of non-English-speaking students to the same curriculum as English speakers "and made it incumbent on the schools to facilitate that access through whatever effective means they chose, including bilingual education" (Gándara et al. 2010: 25). *Lau* v. *Nichols* helped to strengthen the BEA (Gándara et al. 2010: 25; Ancheta 2006). The decision did not specify how non-English speakers are to be accommodated, leaving school districts considerable leeway in designing and

[13] http://education.uslegal.com/bilingualism/landmark-legislation/bilingual-education-act-1968/, accessed August 6, 2015.

implementing their programs. For example, Smith (2002) reports that Tucson, Arizona – the state that later banned bilingual programs – is known as "'the cradle of bilingual education' due to the pioneering work of local Mexican-American educators such as Roxita Cota, Maria Urquides, Hank Oyama, and Adalberto Guerrero" (167). Smith describes a thriving, as of 2002, dual-language program that started in 1994, at a Tucson school that had previously been a K–5 bilingual magnet school since 1980.

In recent decades, however, the dominant political tide has been shifting more and more away from support for bilingual education, despite growing evidence that immersion is at best a more difficult, and at worst a traumatizing and destructive, method of educating non-English-speaking children (Cummins 1979; Combs et al. 2005; Gándara and Hopkins 2010; Skilton-Sylvester 2003; Hornberger and Link 2012). To emphasize this, Cummins (1979) refers to the placement of minority-language children in English-only classrooms as "submersion" rather than immersion. Nonetheless, subsequent versions of the BEA increasingly cut funding for bilingual education, and limited federal assistance to transitional bilingual programs (Gándara et al. 2010). These moves were closely linked to the growth of the US English, formerly English Only, movement, that began in 1981 (Gándara et al. 2010: 26). The anti-bilingual education trend continued to intensify, and several anti-bilingual education referenda succeeded in passing English-only legislation for schools. In 1998, California voters passed Proposition 227, which would "bar the use of primary languages for the interaction of English learners . . . [and allow] citizens to sue teachers if they were found not to be in compliance with the barring of primary-language instruction" (27). In 2000, Arizona followed suit by passing Proposition 203, as did Massachusetts in 2002, both of which were modeled closely on the California Proposition 227. Crucially, Californians have since repealed the ban on bilingual education, passing Proposition 58 that restores it in November 2016 by a significant margin of 73 to 27 percent. Positive developments such as this one offer some hope that policymakers and voters will begin to take education research findings into greater consideration.

The former and existing anti-bilingual education laws stipulate that ELL children be placed in a program known as Structured (or Sheltered) English Immersion (SEI), unless the child's parents apply for a waiver. SEI classrooms are English-only, but instruction is somewhat modified to account for the students' developing English proficiency (Combs et al. 2005: 702; Gándara and Hopkins 2010). Ignoring robust research evidence, all three laws adopt the erroneous view that "young immigrant children can easily acquire full fluency in a new language, such as English, if they are heavily exposed to that language in the classroom at an early age" (cited in Combs et al. 2005: 702; and in Gándara et al. 2010: 28). Not only is this view unsupported by research, as discussed above in this section, but in practice, many ELL students do not experience anything approaching "heavy exposure" to English. Instead, they end up in classrooms filled with non-English-speaking students like themselves, where the only English input comes from the teacher (Combs et al. 2005). Gándara et al. (2010) report that "EL students in Arizona are segregated into classrooms with no exposure to English-dominant peers for 80 percent of the schoolday" (27). Waivers exempting a child from placement in SEI classes, meanwhile, are available based on specific conditions, such as that the child is already proficient in English or has special needs, and are handled very inconsistently by different school districts. In California, districts with strong bilingual education programs responded to Proposition 227 by proactively encouraging parents to request waivers and were, as a result, able to keep many of their programs in place while the law was active (Uriarte et al. 2010). Similarly, the Massachusetts legislation, Chapter 386 of the Acts of 2002, commonly known as Referendum Question 2, is applied more or less strictly depending on the particular district's approach to waiver provisions. By encouraging waiver applications, some districts have variously implemented "two-way bilingual programs, English as a Second Language, transitional bilingual education, world language, and general and modified bilingual education programs in addition to Structured English Immersion" (Uriarte et al. 2010: 71). In Arizona, on the other hand, the enforcement of waiver provisions was made less flexible in 2003, resulting in fewer options available to schools. Paradoxically, once Arizona's ELL students demonstrate through testing – typically the Language Assessment Scales (LAS) – "a good working knowledge of English" (cited in Combs et al. 2005: 703), they are allowed to petition for transfer to a dual-language classroom. In all three states, test scores have fallen and achievement gains have diminished following the implementation of English-only education laws (Gándara and Hopkins 2010).

In one Arizona school, described in detail by Combs et al. (2005), 92 percent of the students are of Mexican origin, and almost everyone comes from low-income backgrounds, including 6 percent who are homeless. In the 2003–2004 school year, 70 percent of the students were designated as ELLs (Combs et al. 2005: 706). Responding to evidence from current research, the school had begun a dual-language program in 1998, but with the passing of Proposition 203 just two years later, the students most in need of bilingual support were forced by law into English-only classrooms. Combs et al. (2005) report that schoolteachers, administrators, and staff described children "traumatized by being instructed exclusively in a language they did not understand" (710):

> Some children had to be peeled, crying, off of relatives or out of cars, every morning. A few children vomited on a daily basis. The prevention specialist, who speaks Spanish, was often dispatched to sit and calm children . . . Parents were shaken by the effect of the

> SEI experience on their children . . . Some children who had happily attended a bilingual education classroom the previous year now pleaded for their parents to let them stay home. Twelve of the 15 parents having children in SEI classes either in the current or previous school year described their children's despondency, self-loathing, and bursts of anger (Combs et al. 2005: 711).

In addition, parents felt upset by their own inability, due to language limitations, to help their children at home. The homework, whose content should have been well within the children's abilities, became impossible because neither the students nor the parents understood the instructions. Parents witnessed their children's self-esteem plummet and excitement about school dwindle. One mother reported that her son, who had previously been depressed, began to talk frequently about wanting to die since his placement in the SEI program (712). Meanwhile, teachers were barred from using Spanish in their SEI classes even if they were themselves bilingual and could have easily assuaged the pain their students went through. In a rather self-evident pronouncement, "teachers stated often that children need to understand instruction to learn" (715).

In addition to emotional trauma, the anti-bilingual education legislation denies the value of immigrant children's existing linguistic knowledge, instilling in them instead feelings of guilt and shame for speaking their home language, and constructing their home language as something transgressive. At Nopal Elementary in Combs et al.'s study, the library placed limits on how many Spanish books children from the SEI program could check out (716). Skilton-Sylvester (2003) quotes an ESL teacher from Philadelphia as describing his classroom language policy this way: "Using the native language is forbidden. Forbidden. When they talk to each other, I say, 'Don't speak that kind of language' . . . Everyone must speak English. This is America after all, the land of the free and the home of English" (9). Not only is this teacher equating America with English and declaring languages other than English "forbidden," but he positions them as inappropriate or even vulgar by referring to them as "that kind of language" – an expression typically used in reference to disrespectful expressions or swearing.

It is indeed unfortunate that such suppression of immigrant children's home languages continues to be standard practice in American education, especially given evidence that the support and development of bilingualism and biliteracy produce better educational and social outcomes. Even most dual-language programs, although they establish a space that legitimizes and valorizes the home language of immigrant children, work to undermine these children's bilingual practices and developing hybrid identities. Dual-language or two-way programs typically espouse the practice of strict separation of the two languages (Palmer 2009; Palmer et al. 2014). Dual-language classroom literature and professional development programs for teachers are opposed to bilingual practices such as code-switching in the classroom and "admonish teachers to separate languages deliberately and systematically, by time of day, or day of the week, or subject area, or teacher" (Palmer 2009: 43). In an urban elementary school in Northern California, in research conducted in the 2002–2003 school year, Palmer (2009) observed teachers instituting a motivation system for students not only to avoid code-switching or slipping into the "wrong" language, but also to monitor the linguistic behavior of others. While conceding that the policy of the separation of languages is intended in part as protection of the minority language space, given the tendency of bilingual classrooms to move towards English, Palmer describes how the policy becomes a resource for students to assert and negotiate power relationships. Thus, code-switching may be tolerated among students within a group that is smoothly working together on a project, but when the collaboration falters and conflicts emerge, policing the linguistic "transgressions" of other students can be used to alienate and socially punish them. Clearly, this is not the intended outcome of the dual-language classroom. Moreover, under the separation methodology, teachers are "encouraged to build students' bilingualism through separately focusing on the so-called standard registers of each language" (Palmer et al. 2014: 98). This raises the question of how the particular standard form chosen relates to that spoken natively by children in the classroom. Rubinstein-Avila (2002) describes how, in an otherwise successful two-way English/Portuguese immersion program in New England, heated debates surround the use of Iberian, Cape Verdean, Azorean, and Brazilian Portuguese, all of which, as well as Cape Verdean Creole, are spoken by both students and teachers. In this case, productive discussions ensued, and teachers were also willing to educate themselves on the Portuguese varieties other than their own and act as cultural and linguistic brokers in their classrooms (Rubinstein-Avila 2002: 82). It is possible, however, that under a strict implementation of recommendations for the separation of languages and setting one standard as a target, speakers of other dialects may end up feeling stigmatized rather than empowered in the two-way classroom.

Moreover, strict separation of languages contradicts recent literature on bilingual and biliterate development, which builds on ideas such as the developmental interdependence of L1 and L2 (Cummins 1979), and emphasizes the dynamic, complex, and interrelated nature of bilingualism and biliteracy (Reyes and Vallone 2007; Hornberger and Link 2012; Palmer et al. 2014). Cummins (1979) argues that scholars of bilingual education, in addition to analyzing linguistic, sociocultural, child input, and school program factors that impact on children's learning of L1 and L2, need to focus on the interaction among these factors on various planes. He proposes two concepts with reference to which we may examine this interaction. One, the threshold hypothesis, states that children do benefit from bilingualism cognitively and academically, but only once they have attained a certain threshold of competence in L2. The second, the developmental interdependence hypothesis, "proposes that the level of L2 competence which a bilingual child attains is partially a function of the type of competence the child has developed in L1 at the time when intensive exposure to L2 begins" (Cummins 1979: 233). This may explain, Cummins argues, why children who continue to develop their literacy in L1 as they begin to acquire literacy in L2 perform better on reading tests than children whose learning of L1 was stopped as L2 was introduced.

Along the same lines, Grosjean (1989) famously pointed out that a bilingual is not two monolinguals in one person. Rather, Grosjean argues, "the coexistence of two languages in the bilingual has produced a unique and specific speaker-hearer" (1989: 3). Building on this observation, Hornberger and Link (2012) invoke García's (2009) comprehensive work on bilingual education in the twenty-first century, which argues that bilingualism is "not like a bicycle with two balanced wheels," but "more like an all-terrain vehicle," whose wheels "extend and contract, flex and stretch, making possible, over highly uneven ground, movement forward that is bumpy and irregular but also sustained and effective" (Hornberger and Link 2012: 268; García 2009: 71). García focuses on translanguaging as a concept that allows us to understand the fluidity, complexity and irregularity of bilingual processes, and to construct sound and effective methodologies in bilingual education. Hornberger and Link (2012) subsequently discuss the continua of biliteracy model, proposed in Hornberger (1989, 2003) and Hornberger and Skilton-Sylvester (2000). They examine translanguaging and transnational literacies as tools that can help teachers to understand and utilize the resources that bilingual students bring to the classroom.

The continua of biliteracy model is proposed as an alternative to binary categorizations such as first language versus second language, monolingual versus bilingual, or oral versus literate (Hornberger and Link 2012: 264). Instead, these labels are seen as applying to "theoretical endpoints of what is in reality a continuum of features" (264). Hornberger and Link explain:

> The continua model posits that the development of biliteracy may start at any point on any of three intersecting continua of first language-to-second language (L1-L2), oral-to-written, and receptive-to-productive language and literacy skills, uses, and practices; and that individuals' biliteracy learning may proceed steadily – or just as easily backtrack, spurt, or criss-cross – in any direction along those intersecting continua, usually in direct response to the contextual demands placed on them (Hornberger and Link 2012: 267).

For classroom practice, this implies that not just what, but also how, when, and where children read and write is crucial for their biliteracy learning (270). Translanguaging, discussed in detail in Chapter 5, if accepted as a natural and positive bilingual practice, can become a productive tool in developing children's bilingual and biliterate competencies. Rather than insisting on the artificial separation of languages in dual-language classrooms, teachers can choose to treat both languages as interrelated resources, and translanguaging as a facilitator of learning. Palmer et al. (2014), for example, describe the practices of two dual-language elementary school teachers in central Texas, who recognize their students as coming from various points on the bilingual/biliterate continuum, and strive to position them as bilingual from the start. By doing this, the teachers hope to encourage bilingual practices by all students, and to promote bilingual identities. They also actively model dynamic bilingualism by drawing attention to, encouraging, and engaging in code-switching, hybrid practices, and metalinguistic commentary. The authors conclude that the teachers' translanguaging pedagogies "open up spaces for students to engage in sensitive and important topics (e.g., immigration, identity) and take risks to express themselves in developing languages (e.g., attempting to translate)" (769). Examples such as this one and others (Campano 2007; Bartlett and García 2011), demonstrate that it is indeed possible to implement pedagogies that seek to nourish and develop, rather than overcome, immigrant children's home language, not just alongside, but simultaneously, with English.

Translanguaging pedagogies, modeling of dynamic bilingualism, and a focus on the continua of biliteracy allow for a repositioning of immigrant children who speak languages other than English from "learners of English" to emergent bilinguals, as advocated by García and Kleifgen (2010). They allow for additive schooling within which children can construct bi- and multilingual, and bi- and multicultural identities. Furthermore, these approaches allow for shifting the pedagogical focus away from teaching immigrant children English, and towards educating them. As this section demonstrates, there is an abundance of research supporting the benefits and feasibility of translanguaging pedagogies and additive schooling for bilingual children. The obstacle is, as is often the case, political and ideological, and it lies in the enduring notions of America as the "home of English" (Skilton-Sylvester 2003: 9). In the next section, we will explore how immigrant children navigate the English-speaking American reality within which their families find themselves by acting as language brokers for their relatives and other adults.

6.2 Language Brokers

Every day, immigrant children and children of immigrants engage in translanguaging practices such as those described in the previous section and in Section 5.2; practices that are argued to be key to successful bilingual education: code-switching, translating, metalinguistic awareness and commentary, collaborative interpretation and negotiation of meaning, hybridization of language forms, and construction of identities through bilingual performance. Children who act as language brokers may attend English-only schools where they are pressured to demonstrate that they have acquired English language and literacy proficiently enough to engage in schoolwork meaningfully. Or, they may be placed in ESL or SEI classes despite their biliteracy, because they speak English with regional features or refuse to conform in some way. Or, in fewer cases, they may be enrolled in a research-informed two-way classroom that implements translanguaging pedagogy. All these children, however, in their actual day-to-day lives as members of families and social networks, perform tasks testifying to the ingenuity, dynamism, complexity and fluidity of a bilingual mind.

Language brokering refers to the various activities that mediate and negotiate interactions between monolingual speakers, or between minority language speakers and mainstream, majority-language speaking society (Orellana 2009). Crucially, child language brokers – sometimes abbreviated as CLBs (Reynolds and Orellana 2015) – do not simply translate one speaker's words into the language of the other, so they cannot be described adequately as child translators or child interpreters. Rather, they advocate on behalf of their families; they are linguistic and cultural mediators who represent their families to the outside, English-speaking world. In this role, they also "influence the contents and nature of the messages they convey, and ultimately affect the perceptions and decisions of the agents for whom they act" (Tse 1995: 180; see also Tse 1996a; Tse 1996b; De Ment et al. 2005). In addition, as they convey to their parents complex cultural knowledge about their new environment, such as the way schools, businesses, and public services operate, or the meaning of American holidays such as Halloween and Thanksgiving, CLBs become "socializing agents" for their parents (Tse 1995: 182; De Ment et al. 2005: 257). Language brokering involves both orality and literacy, crossing from one to the other through continua of biliteracy (Hornberger and Link 2012; see previous section). Children accompany adults to meetings and to public offices, make phone calls in which they speak on behalf of a relative or the family, and translate documents, often in collaboration with adults, by bringing together everyone's linguistic and cultural resources to make sense of and interpret the text (Orellana 2009; Reynolds and Orellana 2015; Granillo 2011). Documents that CLBs translate may include notes from school, phone conversations, job applications, bank statements, credit card statements, medical prescriptions, and government forms (Granillo 2011: 4).

Language brokering is a common practice in immigrant families. For example, one set of early survey studies finds that 100 percent of surveyed Latino high school students reported brokering (Tse 1995), as did 90 percent of Chinese and Vietnamese-American students (Tse 1996b). Among the latter, most of those who had not served as brokers reported having an older sibling who did (Tse 1996b: 489). People that Tse's participants reported brokering for include parents (92 percent), friends (62 percent), other relatives (56 percent), neighbors (37 percent), and teachers (34 percent), while locations where brokering took place include home, school, stores, and offices, among others (Tse 1996b: 490). Language brokering is also a daily practice that can be called upon spontaneously whenever the need arises, for example, when the doctor's office telephones to reschedule an appointment in the middle of a family meal. As such, it is embedded within a larger web of bilingual and biliterate practices of the brokering child's family and community. It is difficult to separate language brokering from other aspects of ongoing bilingual interactions, such as the negotiation of identities and of sociocultural meanings. Reynolds and Orellana (2015) argue that "brokering practices are fundamentally *socio*linguistic practices related to other bilingual forms of communication that surely take place in these encounters as youths negotiate meaning with their interlocutors" (317, emphasis original). They go on to say that for this reason, language brokering should not be analyzed in isolation "from other forms of bilingual communication that can co-occur within multilingual contact zones" (329). Such isolating analyses presume "that languages as codes are strictly autonomous, bounded systems that a speaker either does or does not command," and tend to prioritize concerns for the developmental impact of language brokering on CLBs (329). As a result, language brokering is sometimes constructed by researchers as a problem that uniquely weighs on bilingual children, and potentially interferes with their development according to Western and American notions of what childhood should be (Orellana 2009; Valdés 2003: 64–66). And indeed, there is a large body of work centered around research questions that frame language brokering as a factor impacting CLBs' development, self-concept, academic performance, acculturation, and family functioning (e.g. Niehaus and Kumpiene 2014; Granillo 2011; Love and Buriel 2007; Trickett and Jones 2007; Jones and Trickett 2005; Weisskirch 2006; Weisskirch and Alva 2002; Buriel et al. 1998; Baptiste 1993). In the rest of this section, I will first discuss the complexity of the language brokering experience for immigrant children and their families, and then turn to language brokering as a sociolinguistic skill and an important community resource in need of recognition and support.

The Conflicted and Multilayered Experience of CLBs

To be sure, language brokering encroaches on children's free time as they accompany family members to run errands from doctor's appointments to shopping trips (De Ment et al. 2005; Tse 1995; McQuillan and Tse 1995). As one participant in Love's (2007) study explains:

> My older sister Araceli, she's sixteen, and she's the one they pick first. Like she's always with my mom and stuff. If they [the parents] have important stuff to do, she's usually with them. Sometimes I go too, so I'm definitely number two. Like last week my dad had to meet with the teacher, but Araceli had to stay with my other sister, so I went with my dad (Love 2007: 96).

Children like Araceli and her brother are constantly called upon to invest their time in accompanying and assisting their parents whenever the need arises. Sometimes, more than the children's free time may be affected: Díaz-Lázaro (2002) cites a study by Delgado-Gaitán and Trueba (1991), in which teachers expressed concern "about the frequency with which some children were asked to leave school to help the family" (Delgado-Gaitán and Trueba 1991: 83; cited in Díaz-Lázaro 2002: 43). Children often broker not just for immediate family members, but for the larger community, including relatives and neighbors (Orellana 2009; Valdés 2003).

Researchers have also noted the challenges to family structure and relationships in families where children act as language brokers (De Ment et al. 2005; Suárez-Orozco and Suárez-Orozco 2001; Baptiste 1993). Baptiste (1993), writing from the perspective of a family therapy practitioner, discusses problems facing immigrant families in which children acculturate faster than the parents. Based on specific examples from his own experience with counseling immigrant families, Baptiste argues that child language brokering can challenge the traditional structure of generational boundaries, especially for immigrants coming from societies with rigid family hierarchies. As children are recruited to interpret for the parents, they are "frequently exposed to information usually reserved for adults and thus cross the generational line between adults and children" (Baptiste 1993: 347). Some parents, while forced to accept this arrangement due to practical reasons, resent their own position of helplessness and reliance on their children. Baptiste notes that these parents "oftentimes tend to treat the child-interpreter much more harshly and criticize such children's behaviors more frequently compared to other children in the family," while the children "often complain of feeling like yo-yo's because parents tend to abruptly change them from an adult role to a child's role and back" (347; see also De Ment et al. 2005: 266–267). Baptiste gives the example of a child who is expected to interpret for a parent during a doctor's visit, but is later reprimanded for asking the parent about his or her health outcome because the parent feels that such questioning is disrespectful. And in some cases, Baptiste has seen children who use the information they are privy to because of their brokering activities in order to gain the upper hand in intrafamilial conflicts (348). We must remember, of course, that as a family therapist, Baptiste encounters cases in which child language brokering is implicated in family difficulties, not ones in which it benefits the family. Some researchers point out that when negative experiences with language brokering are reported, this could be due to already strained parent-child relationships (Granillo 2011: 11; Weisskirch 2007). Meanwhile, as Orellana (2009) shows, many families strengthen their mutual ties and grow closer thanks to language brokering, which can become more of a joint family enterprise, a point that I will return to below. Nonetheless, examples such as those discussed by Baptiste are real, and testify to the potential challenges child language brokering can bring (see also Díaz-Lázaro 2002 for a discussion of child language brokering in family therapy contexts).

Such challenges, however, should not be seen as an indictment of the practice; rather, they exemplify one aspect of the complex experience lived by immigrant children and children of immigrants. CLBs have to negotiate multiple, complex, and often conflicting roles within their own families; roles that vastly complicate the meaning of their status as children. Unsurprisingly, their reactions to this situation vary, and are often multiple and contradictory. As a number of studies have found, CLBs feel proud that they are able to contribute to their family's acculturation in the United States, and to act both as the family's advocates, and as responsible, socially mature individuals (Orellana 2009; Weisskirch 2006; Tse 1996a). On the other hand, however, they also feel frustration, confusion, and resentment at having to learn English and acculturate themselves, and simultaneously to function as linguistic and cultural brokers for their parents (De Ment et al. 2005; Tse 1995; McQuillan and Tse 1995). De Ment et al. (2005) report findings from focus groups made up of 13 college students who acted as CLBs, including Mexican, Central American, Vietnamese, and Chinese Americans. The participants discussed feeling appreciation for their parents' sacrifices, and a resultant obligation to do their part to help them by brokering. On the other hand, they also spoke of feeling embarrassed, traumatized, and overwhelmed. For example, they felt embarrassed when their parents demanded that they convey messages that the CLBs found culturally inappropriate, such as getting angry at someone in a position of authority who is trying to help them. They also felt uncomfortable when English-speaking adults did not take them seriously, or refused to interact with them altogether. One student described an instance when a cardiologist insisted that her father describe his pain in his own words, without his daughter's translation, even though the father spoke no English. The daughter ended up arguing with the doctor, an experience that she said "was kind of traumatizing" (266). The complexity of emotions and resultant reactions that surrounds such experiences is also shown by Cindy, a fourteen-year-old Chinese American language broker in Orellana's (2009) study, who listed many reasons why she likes her role: it made her feel smart, she improved her knowledge of both languages, it helped her bond with her mother, and it even "cheered her up when she was in a bad mood or felt bad about herself" (Orellana 2009: 9). At the same time, Cindy's role made her feel grown up in comparison to other children; for example, she said that unlike her peers, she does not pester her parents to buy her things, because she knows and respects her family's financial situation: "[Other kids] don't know exactly how much is in their bank deposits, the bills and stuff. But *I* know personally because I write the bills. I write the checks" (cited in Orellana 2009: 9; emphasis original). Significantly, this sense of personal maturity and responsibility that made Cindy feel special, also led her to feel upset when adults she brokered for treated her "like a kid" (9).

CLBs in De Ment et al.'s study also reported feeling overwhelmed because, despite their apparent fluency in English, they felt inadequate to perform the brokering task competently. This in turn led to feelings of frustration and anger. In addition to these experiences, as the CLBs assume "adult worries and responsibilities" (De Ment et al. 2005: 260), such as bill paying and managing the family's health issues, they "sense the frustration that their parents feel because they cannot understand and negotiate the English-speaking world" (260). This awareness of their parents' helplessness and frustration may variously cause CLBs' to feel uncomfortable and confused by their new role, or empowered and committed as a family caretaker. In some cases, they may manipulate their family's internal power dynamics as we saw in Baptiste (1993) above, or capitalize on their linguistic advantage by "censoring and modifying the information that was exchanged by the two parties" in contexts such as parent-teacher conferences (De Ment et al. 2005: 264). De Ment et al.'s participants recalled omitting negative reports about their siblings' behavior in their translation, or signing permission slips and other school documents for themselves and their siblings (264).

Even when their intentions are purely to be helpful, some CLBs end up making educational decisions for themselves and their younger siblings. McQuillan and Tse's (1995) in-depth interviews with nine language brokers showed that young children handled communication with the school with minimal parental involvement, sometimes deciding which messages needed to be relayed and which did not, and bypassing the parents when writing notes to teachers and signing report cards and permission slips for their siblings (McQuillan and Tse 1995; Tse 1996a). At the same time as Tse's work highlights the mediating role of immigrant children in the relationship between home and school, which could be implicated in immigrant parents' involvement in the schools (Tse 1995, 1996a), she also reports that the majority of her research participants have positive attitudes towards language brokering. For example, 53 percent say that they like to broker, 63 percent are proud to be brokers, and 41 percent report feeling more independent and mature due to brokering, while only 14 percent see brokering as a burden and 10 percent are embarrassed by it (Tse 1996a: 229). Additionally, 46 percent of Tse's participants felt that brokering helped them learn English, which is an important educational goal for immigrant children. Therefore, while CLBs may be taking on unconventional roles in the school-parent relationship, they are also benefiting from this role in their development of English skills, maturity, independence, and interpersonal communication. I will return to this point below in discussing language brokering as a skill and asset.

Children's relationships with teachers and peers may also be affected by their brokering activities. CLBs may find themselves helping teachers communicate with their non-English speaking classmates. We saw an example of this at the start of the previous section, where Little Manuel, newly arrived from Mexico to an English-only classroom in the Southwest, struggles to comprehend the lesson and turns to his classmates for help (Bayley et al. 2005). In this case, the authors find that, in the language brokering process, children typically translate the teacher's instructions but not the lesson's content, most likely because the content is new to them and they do not have the vocabulary in either language to express it. In another study, Niehaus and Kumpiene (2014) use survey data to measure the relationship between frequency and context of language brokering, and CLBs' self-beliefs such as academic self-concept and popularity with peers. Their findings suggest "that students who broker more frequently for peers feel like they are less accepted by peers, have a harder time making friends, and have fewer friends at school" (137). The authors suggest that being asked to broker for teachers and peers may be problematic for the CLBs' positioning in the social structure of the classroom because it disrupts the typical teacher-student and peer relationships (137). Another problematic situation arises when children's language brokering interferes with their academic progress, which can happen when schools adopt English immersion/submersion methods in teaching immigrant students (see Section 6.1). Valdés (2001) describes a situation in which some students who were advanced in English were retained in beginning-level ESL classes so that they could serve as translators and interpreters for newly arrived classmates. This way, teachers were able to conduct ESL classes entirely in English. As I discussed in the previous section, remaining in classes that are below their level of ability is detrimental to immigrant students' academic performance.

As we have seen so far, language brokering positions young immigrants and children of immigrants in roles that challenge and complicate conventional relationships between adults and children, and among the children themselves. However, as Orellana (2009) cautions, we must remember that what is perceived as "conventional" in terms of family relationships and obligations, and in terms of the meaning of childhood, is culturally contextualized. Immigrant families' experiences can easily become objects of otherization when viewed from the perspective of mainstream American society. For this reason, below I will turn to a discussion of language brokering as a sociolinguistic skill, and of the CLBs as important resources both for their families and for the communities they live in, including mainstream institutions such as schools.

Language Brokering as a Skill and Asset

A crucial aspect of language brokering that often gets lost in discussions of the practice's positive or negative impact is the extraordinary sociolinguistic skill that it involves. The sophisticated work that goes into language brokering is overlooked by both researchers and the adults that the children broker for. Reynolds and Orellana (2015) point out that in their research, "children and youths clearly shouldered a heavy burden, as both their parents and institutions assumed that interpretation and translation must be easy for bilinguals" (320; cf. Jones and Trickett 2005). De Ment et al.'s (2005) focus group participants recalled feeling frustrated at being unable to fulfill certain translation tasks because of the complexity of the English involved – for example, filling out insurance forms – but their parents in turn "were upset because they expected their children to be able to do these tasks, as they were studying English in school" (De Ment et al. 2005: 266). In this scenario, children may appear willful and uncooperative to their parents, while in fact they are feeling frustrated and out of their depth.

Not only is interpreting and translating work not automatically "easy" for a bilingual speaker, but language brokering involves much more than just interpreting and translating. Rather, unlike formal translators or interpreters, CLBs mediate communication, typically not translating literally what is being said, but "modify[ing] the literal meaning of the message . . . to fit the appropriate cultural and social context as well as incrementing the chances of a successful outcome" (Díaz-Lázaro 2002: 4; see also McQuillan and Tse 1995; Tse 1995). For example, Orellana (2009) describes how María, a ten-year-old US-born Mexican American, reinterprets her teacher's comments during a parent-teacher conference with María's mother. The teacher, Ms. Salinger, praised María at length and in glowing terms, saying things like: " . . . she's always consistently very, very good. She uses her time constructively, she's very cooperative with other students. Um, always does her homework and her classwork. Um, practicing self-control. She's been very good . . . She does a really great job. Her, uh, she completes her homework with quality and her, uh, her classwork with quality" (Orellana 2009: 81). María, however, downplayed and diminished these praises, summing them up in Spanish with "She says that, um, everything like is very good in everything? Like, (I do) well on my homework or like all my work in school in class I do well" (82). She also took personal responsibility for improvement, stating for example that she needed "to practice more" for her tests, although Ms. Salinger only said that María's test scores were not always consistent with the rest of her school performance (81–82).

Although María's mother ends up missing out on hearing the teacher's praises of her daughter, Orellana nevertheless assesses this interaction as successful transculturation on María's part: "In glossing all the positive detail into a simple 'She says I do well,' María took up a socially appropriate position as a child speaking to adult authority figures: she diminished her ego and assumed a self-effacing stance" (Orellana 2009: 82). María was negotiating culturally specific expectations on part of different adults – her teacher and her mother – of what learning and schoolwork is about, and how a child like herself should behave. Orellana makes similar observations with regards to other children in her study. When twelve-year-old Briana came along to a doctor's appointment to help her mother discuss her younger siblings' health issues, she was speaking on behalf of her family, positioning herself as a caretaker, and mediating "potentially variant perspectives on how to promote children's health and well-being" (20; also 74–77). Shannon (1990) describes the Mexican American family of Adán and Leti, in which Adán, as the eldest, acted as the language broker until he entered middle school and became less available, transferring his brokering duties to his younger sister Leti. Adán's job was very important because his immediate family anchored the extended family for whom he also brokered. Despite being only between eleven and thirteen during Shannon's fieldwork, Adán demonstrated confidence and socio-linguistic maturity. According to Shannon, "[h]is behavior demonstrated that he not only knew what to say in both English and Spanish, but also that he understood how to speak in each situation" (Shannon 1990: 264). These situations were many, including interactions with doctors, lawyers, school administrators, law enforcement officers, landlords, banks, and so on.

Subtle transculturating moves such as shown by María and Briana, and the sociolinguistic maturity exhibited by children like Adán, testify to CLBs' "linguistic virtuosity and versatility" (Reynolds and Orellana 2015: 318), which has prompted scholars to call for better support for language-brokering children in schools and communities. Accordingly, in her book *Expanding Definitions of Giftedness*, Guadalupe Valdés (2003) argues that "when children serve as young interpreters for their families for whatever reasons and in whatever settings, they develop a set of abilities that are unique and complex. These abilities are a special form of giftedness that must be taken seriously by both practitioners and researchers as they learn to work with immigrant children" (Valdés 2003: 66; see also Alvarez 2014).

As an education researcher, Valdés (2003) presents the same perspective on bilingual children as Valdés (2001), García and Kleifgen (2010), and Bartlett and García (2011), which I discussed in the previous section. She points out the problems with assessing bilingual children's abilities through a monolingual lens, which prevents one from appreciating the intellectual dexterity and bicultural communicative competence involved in bilingual practices, especially when dealing with "minority children schooled in a majority language," as opposed to "privileged child bilinguals" whom Valdés describes as "middle-class or upper-middle-class children who are raised by their parents as bilinguals from birth or from infancy," in contexts such as families of diplomats, foreign students, or political exiles (Valdés 2003: 39). This, according to Valdés, finds expression in the process of identifying "gifted children." Programs for the gifted tend to favor those exhibiting traditional types of "intelligences." Assessments assume a native-like knowledge of English, and focus on linguistic and mathematical skills. The linguistic skills tested, however, do not incorporate immigrant children's bilingual and bicultural skills as language brokers. This in turn means a lack of support for child language brokers, and a lack of understanding of the complex and important job that they perform. Valdés argues, "As long as definitions of giftedness do not incorporate bilingual performance such as that manifested by the young interpreters that we studied, the special kinds of potential giftedness exhibited by such youngsters will not be valued, fostered in instruction, or positively evaluated in formal education" (Valdés 2003: 5). Valdés is not, however, a proponent of programs for the gifted. Rather, she emphasizes that her and her colleagues' research demonstrates another dimension in which such programs are inadequate, and tend to exclude children from minority or working class backgrounds, including children of many immigrants. She concludes that "even if researchers and practitioners were willing to consider the performance of young interpreters as manifestations of gifted behaviors, they would still face enormous challenges in convincing the general public that these children should be identified as gifted" (Valdés 2003: 182).

Child language brokering, if it is discussed by institutions, is viewed as a problem, even though institutions such as schools or hospitals clearly benefit from it. Valdés comments on her team's experiences during their research on child language brokering:

> Interestingly, as we began our observations in public settings, for example, in lobbies of welfare offices, immigration offices, the office of the California Department of Motor Vehicles, and hospital emergency rooms, we soon discovered that there were strong feelings surrounding the use of young people as interpreters for their families . . . . inquiries about young interpreters were frequently met with some hostility and suspicion. Public service workers, for the most part, denied ever having seen young interpreters at work . . . . A few individuals . . . . described the use of youngsters as family interpreters as a particularly cruel form of child abuse (Valdés 2003: 64).

Valdés and her colleagues concluded that the antagonism they encountered was because according to various regulations, most of these institutions were supposed to provide interpreters or locate bilingual employees to help immigrant clients. Not surprisingly, their representatives resented any mention of their relying on child language brokers. Orellana (2009), however, additionally points out that immigrant children are evaluated not just according to monolingual norms of childhood development, but also according to Western or Anglo-American assumptions about what children should do and be. Citing research in the history of the social construction of childhood, Orellana notes that in the twentieth century, there was a "shift from viewing children as 'useful' – active contributors to household economies – to economically 'useless' but sentimentally 'priceless'" (Orellana 2009: 17). Children in America are thus viewed as precious, but also as passive and helpless; they are not expected to take on adult responsibilities or be trusted with them. An example of this attitude is when certain institutions refuse to speak with the child interpreters because of their young age, even though their parents cannot communicate in English, and even though the children themselves are capable of handling the interaction or they would not have been chosen by their parents to do so (Valdés 2003: 75–76). The view of children as "persons-in-the-making" (Orellana 2009: 15) is apparent also in social science research, where they were for a long time treated as passive objects of adult actions and decisionmaking. Even access to children for research purposes is typically obtained via consent forms signed by the parents. Only recently have researchers begun to acknowledge children as subjects by seeking their own consent to participate in research in addition to parental consent (Baran 2013). More generally, recent decades have seen the emergence of the critical social science of childhoods, a perspective that gives importance to what children experience as active participants in social processes, and that highlights "childhood" as a socially constructed, and thus culturally contextualized, category (Orellana 2009: 16).

However, as of now this theoretical framework does not find reflection in mainstream discourses, which is in part why the arrival of large numbers of unaccompanied child migrants from Central America caused an outcry in American media and in everyday discussions of the topic in 2014. Among the myths surrounding this crisis was the idea that these children are alone and thus in danger, and need to be apprehended for their own protection. However, in addition to the dangers faced by child migrants in shelters and facilities, some of them are misidentified as "unaccompanied," whereas in fact they are traveling to join family in the US or live with relatives and do not know that they are undocumented (Terrio 2015). Paradoxically, another myth surrounding unaccompanied Central American children was that they pose a national security threat. Susan Terrio argues that such fears reflect mainstream Americans' discomfort with children who exercise agency by leaving home, traveling alone, working, and lying about their background and age when necessary, because such behavior contradicts the Western normative view of children as vulnerable and developmentally "unfinished"; unaccompanied child migrants who exercise adult-like agency thus become "matter out of place" (Terrio 2015). In a similar way, child language brokers present a problematic phenomenon for Americans who are uncomfortable with children demonstrating their capacity for acting as agents and decision-makers.

Child language brokers, as Orellana points out, "make things happen for themselves and their families; they forge connections and open up lines of communication. They make it possible for adults to do things that they could not otherwise accomplish" (2009: 21). CLBs enter public spaces from which children in American society are typically absent: banks, real estate agencies, legal offices, insurance companies. They also, as I discussed above, make decisions on behalf of their families, both by modifying the messages conveyed according to their own judgment, and by directly making decisions such as signing siblings' permission slips. For this reason, Tse (1995) argues that "the role students play as transmitters of information [between home and school] is a critical factor in understanding interactions between these two institutions" (189). For example, elsewhere (Tse 1996) she notes the correlation between children acting as language brokers and low levels of parental involvement in school activities, suggesting that the children's brokering role may help researchers and educators gain a deeper understanding of the parent-school relationship than simple assumptions about parental lack of interest (Tse 1996: 230). Recognizing CLBs' role and taking it seriously may be a prerequisite for developing productive relationships between immigrant families and school.

Children who broker provide crucial services to their communities (Tse 1995; Orellana 2009). By helping siblings with homework or speeding up the process of bill paying by translating documents, children free up parents to engage in other activities, such as housework or employment. They spare institutions the need to provide interpreters. They also provide their families and communities with access to economic opportunities by translating and helping fill out job applications (Tse 1995), which serves wider society by connecting job applicants with employers. Orellana argues that the work these children perform "is especially important for considerations of immigrants' contributions to society," but, much like the labor of homemakers, it remains largely invisible (Orellana 2009: 21).

Language brokering, far from being merely a "problem" that detracts from immigrant children's experience of childhood, is an important part of a child's identity and family role. Like other researchers, Orellana reports some mixed feelings regarding brokering among the children she studied over the course of a decade. Some reported feeling annoyed when their brokering responsibilities interfered with other activities, and uncomfortable when forced to interact with strangers or on the phone. However, most often children saw language brokering as "normal and not a big deal" (Orellana 2009: 62). They also viewed it positively, as a source of pride: "Ten-year-old Jenna spoke proudly: 'I feel that I am a big girl now and I could help the family a little bit'" (63). Children enjoyed being able to participate in the adult world, being respected for their linguistic skills, and being able to contribute. Some felt a sense of accomplishment, which, we might surmise, they may not have experienced at school, where their abilities would typically be evaluated from the perspective of monolingualism, and of English fluency – rather than bilingual development – as the ultimate goal (see Section 6.1). For some children, language brokering was part of a reciprocal relationship that tied their family together: twelve-year-old Randy explained that "They [his parents] take care of me, like they help me to grow up and stuff. They just gave me life" (Orellana 2009: 64).

Family bonding is enhanced through language brokering in other ways, too. Children may be helping parents with *their* English homework if the parents attend ESL classes. In these cases, mutual learning takes place as the children help parents make sense of unfamiliar English vocabulary, while also spending time together. Although, as Orellana notes, this may appear "as a clear case of role reversal" (57), in her research such activities did not cause the parents to feel a loss of parental authority. One might expect, in fact, that they fostered a sense of family togetherness as parents and children sit down together to read stories and write assignments. In fact, Orellana reports that children often carried out translation tasks with the help of adults, so that language brokering became a collaborative task:

> Even when parents did not speak much English, they supported children in translation tasks. They did this by supplying background information and Spanish vocabulary and negotiating meaning with them. Briana explained how she and her family would "figure things out together;" she said that she attempted "different ways" and that "they figured it out too." María's mother put it simply: "Nosotros nos ayudamos" [We help each other]. Ashley told of working in collaboration with her brother and parents … (Orellana 2009: 55).

Such collaborative activities fulfill a number of important functions. They encourage family bonding through the sense that everyone is "helping each other." They also allow children to feel that they have a stake in family life because the family's success is experienced as a joint enterprise. Finally, collaborative language brokering contributes to everyone's learning of English, which is on one hand expected of immigrants, and on the other, not adequately provided for by government and social institutions. Thus, while perhaps some traditional concepts of family relations may be challenged by child language brokering as we saw above, the practice can also work to strengthen immigrant families and help them adjust together to their new life.

Overall, it is clear that language brokering is not a homogenous experience for immigrant children and their families. It is not easily evaluated, especially when viewed from the Anglo-American perspective that sees children as passive and vulnerable, and monolingualism as the norm. Trickett and Jones (2007) present CLB research as belonging to two camps: either viewing child language brokering as a "necessary evil," a practice that seems inevitable and pragmatically necessary but leads to an undesirable "adultification" of immigrant youngsters and a problematic role reversal between parents and children, or conceptualizing CLB practices as an equivalent of other family chores that children may be responsible for as contributing members of their families (Trickett and Jones 2007: 143). While different researchers may focus on opposite sides of the child language brokering "coin," the picture that emerges is a complex one. Almost all researchers, regardless of their focus, recognize that the practice has positive and negative effects; it can be simultaneously enriching and stressful, empowering and frustrating, a source of pride and a source of embarrassment. Also, as argued by scholars such as Orellana and Valdés, child language brokering is better viewed as a resource, asset, and skill, than as an impediment or problem.

Child language brokering has a profound impact on individuals and communities, as well as on the society at large. It contributes to how children make sense of their immigrant experience; it structures family dynamics, power relationships, and roles; it binds immigrant communities by being one of their key sociocultural practices; and it mediates between immigrant communities and social institutions. It also brings into question our assumptions about the sociocultural meanings of concepts such as "childhood" and "family." Finally, child language brokers are an example of the inadequacy of the monolingual perspective when thinking about immigrant families, about the education of immigrant children, and about these children's intellectual potential.

6.3 Language and the Family

As much of the discussion of child language brokers in the previous section demonstrates, language plays an important role in the negotiation of power dynamics and relationships in immigrant families. Bilingual families may face challenges such as disparate proficiencies in English and in the heritage language (HL)[14] on part of members of different generations. Research

[14] Researchers have variously referred to the language of the immigrants' place of origin as "ethnic language" (Medvedeva 2012), L1 (De Fina 2012), "immigrant family's native language" (Seals 2013), and heritage language or HL (Oh and Fuligni 2010; De Fina 2012). Ultimately, none of these terms are fully satisfactory. "Ethnic language" implies a one-to-one relationship between language and ethnic group, potentially erasing other important meanings languages hold for immigrants. The term "L1" suggests that English is L2 for everyone in the family, whereas for the younger members, it may be an L1. The family's "native language" likewise implies that all the family members are not native speakers of English, since here "native language" is used as a contrast with English. Finally, "heritage language" or HL suggests the opposite: that the family members are descendants of this language's speakers, not dominant in the language themselves. Given these imperfect choices, I have decided to use the term heritage language/HL, because it seems to me the most inclusive of all the possible linguistic repertoires of the family, and it

shows that while first-generation immigrants may retain their L1 in most of their daily interactions, second-generation immigrants tend to shift into the language of the country of immigration, while by the third generation HL is typically lost (De Fina 2012; Fishman 1991; Portes and Rumbaut 2006). In families, older members may also feel greater emotional attachment to HL, while younger members tend to shift away from it more readily as they develop relationships with peers in the dominant/majority language (De Fina 2012: 349–350). For the young generation, HL becomes mainly a family language, or the language of their ethnic community if the family participates in one. The dominant/majority language, on the other hand, is used in multiple social domains, including ones that facilitate forming strong emotional connections with and through the dominant language, such as intimate friendships, dating, prayer, or writing in a diary. As a result, for young immigrants or children of immigrants, the dominant language may evoke equally strong emotional responses as HL, which is unlikely to be the case for older and first-generation immigrants (see also Section 7.1 in the next chapter). Such different sociocultural and emotional ties to English versus to HL among immigrants in America are bound to have as much of an impact on intergenerational communication as divergent levels of proficiency.

Multiple languages can also become a resource for establishing authority or negotiating emotional involvement among family members. We might recall from Section 5.1 the Chinese American mother-daughter dyad, May and Liz, who negotiate their way through an argument by code-switching between Cantonese and English (Williams 2005). When Liz, the daughter, oversteps her role by lecturing her mother in a raised voice about the nature of employment in America, May responds in her less preferred language, English ("I don't care"), thus flagging her disapproval of Liz's attitude and assumed role. She succeeds in silencing her daughter for an entire five seconds, thus reasserting her status as the dominant family member. The two women's family roles are negotiated throughout their interaction, and code-switching is an important resource for this process.

At other times, multilingualism may come to define an immigrant family, with practices such as code-switching, translanguaging, and intra-family language brokering seen by family members as inextricable components of the family's identity. In this sense, the immigrant family's multilingualism not only positions it as belonging to a specific ethnic or cultural group – Italian Americans, Chinese Americans, and so on – but also defines its inner workings as a kinship group whose mutual bonds are reinforced by shared norms and practices, including particular language use. An example of this is the Italian

establishes a contrast between the dominant language in the US (English), and the language of the land of one's heritage.

American family described by De Fina (2012), whose members, in metalinguistic commentary, recognize family identity as defined by multilingualism, and see multilingual practices as an essential "survival strategy" (268) for the family.

In this section, I examine the impact of language-related issues on family life in immigrant contexts. First, I take a look at language choices and language socialization in immigrant families, and the different decisions family members make to function in their new homeland, finding a balance between acculturation and maintaining their heritage language and traditions. Then I turn to the way that multilingual practices structure and enact family relationships, for example by defining the family's identity as in De Fina (2012), or serving as resources for the negotiation of power dynamics and family roles, as in Williams (2005).

Language Choices

For many immigrant families, whether newly arrived or second and third generation, decisions about whether and how to maintain HL become, at some point, an important aspect of family life. In some families, they may result in an explicit family "language policy" (Tannenbaum 2012), while others have implicit norms and expectations as to who speaks which language and when. Adhering to such overt or assumed language policies is not easily accomplished, since daily language use is subject to multiple and conflicting influences: family members' motivations, practical matters such as tasks that need accomplishing, and the quality of familial relationships. In the conclusion to her study of Mandarin-English bilingual families with young children, Pan (1995) observes, "Even if parents are committed to maintaining the home language, strategies that might be helpful in achieving this goal run counter to the natural tendency of parents to accommodate their speech to their younger, less competent interlocutors" (326). If anyone in the family is monolingual in HL, for example a parent or a grandparent, encouraging children to speak HL at home is important for family cohesion, but can prove ineffective in a society where English is the dominant and the more valued language.

Seals (2013) examines daily bilingual interactions in five Mexican immigrant families living in Northern California, and notices that the youngest children in the family tend to be proficient in English, but they have much more difficulty functioning in Spanish than their older siblings. They cannot participate as effectively in the family's bilingual practices, so they adopt the strategy of HL avoidance in family interaction. Their direct conversations with monolingual relatives, which may include their parents, become impossible. Instead, they are brokered by an older sibling.

Each family that Seals studies has a somewhat different experience with bilingualism. Jasmine and her siblings are able to accommodate their mother's preference for Spanish, and switch out of English when she becomes part of the conversation. The mother strictly enforces the use of Spanish in this family, which helps with the maintenance of HL, but also leads the children to exclude the mother when speaking English with each other. The Spanish-only policy also creates a barrier between the mother and one of her grandchildren, who has very limited Spanish proficiency. In another family, the mother is unable to have any direct interaction with her youngest daughter, who avoids speaking Spanish because of her limited abilities, and speaks only English at home. The only possible mother-daughter communication is that mediated by the older siblings, which, according to Seals, "creates a completely divided family" (Seals 2013: 139). By contrast, the family in which everyone is bilingual to some extent, and in which bilingual practices are accepted and there are no HL-only rules appears to act the most "like a solid family unit" (139).

Schecter and Bayley's (1997) study also documents language norms and policies in Mexican immigrant families, two in California and two in Texas. The parents in the California families are newly arrived immigrants, while the Texas families are more established, with the parents being second-generation immigrants. The frequently reported process of language shift from HL to English within three generations is witnessed in this study up close, when second-generation immigrant mother, Elena, who learned to speak Spanish at home, makes the following comment: "I think it [loss of culture] is already in process and I think that my mother's generation knew lots of Spanish – her kids did not get to learn how – or I did not get to learn to read and write it and I think that's a shame. Because now I can't teach my children that" (quoted in Schecter and Bayley 1997: 528). Elena evaluates her Spanish proficiency as below that of her mother's. She also notes her lack of Spanish literacy. This, she believes, will cause her to fail to pass Spanish on to her own daughter, a third generation immigrant.

Elena makes a connection between heritage language and heritage culture, as do other immigrant families. What is noteworthy in this study is the diversity of approaches to preserving heritage culture and of factors that motivate them. The Texas families tended to be more open to code-switching, translanguaging, and Spanglish. The California families, and the Villegases from the San Francisco area in particular, had very high standards for "pure" Spanish. Coming from the professional middle class in Mexico, both with higher education, the Villegases were not impressed by the working-class Mexican American community they encountered in California, nor by the Spanglish heard on local Spanish-language TV. They also did not relate to Chicano identities: "I'm Mexican, but to me the Chicano movement is unfamiliar . . . I can't understand it," said the mother (quoted in Schecter and Bayley 1997:

519). The Villegases were willing to speak English at home when urged to do so by their daughter's kindergarten teacher, who espoused the misguided notion that being raised bilingually would cause the child problems in school (518). Eventually, the parents rejected this idea, and shifted back to using only Spanish at home, except when discussing specific school-related topics. But they continued to draw a distinction between "standard" Spanish linked with "high" culture, such as Mexican literature and arts, and working-class Spanish and Spanglish that they heard around them, and which they associated with "lower class Mexican values and mores" (519). And, while insisting on Spanish-only at home, the Villegases did not wish for their children to attend bilingual programs at school. When their son was placed in one, his mother complained and he was successfully transferred to the monolingual classroom. It is worth noting that the mother, Mariana Villegas, with her background as a member of Mexican elite, had the necessary social capital, including language skills and assertiveness, to be able both to educate her children in Spanish at home, and to intervene with the school on behalf of her son. Immigrants who do not speak English and have little education are much worse positioned to advocate for their children in the American education system.

Other families in Schecter and Bayley's study instituted "Spanish days" to encourage their children's Spanish skills, and relied on the grandparents to provide Spanish input, especially if the grandparents were the children's caretakers when the parents were at work. The Baez family in Texas, in which the second-generation parents were English-dominant, did not attempt to enforce Spanish as the family language. Instead, they focused on maintaining cultural practices such as cooking Mexican food together, listening to Mexican and Tejano music, and talking about Mexican history and heritage. Spanish was encouraged, but it was never the family's main language. As a result, the youngest children had no way of communicating effectively with their grandmother. The grandmother's comments on this fact describe very poignantly the emotional experience of language – an issue that I will focus on in the next chapter, but which also brings us to the question of how intrafamilial language repertoires influence family relationships:

> It would be beautiful for . . . my granddaughters to truly understand what I wanted to say because it was a way of, getting closer to them and knowing them, or for them to know me . . . because I could express my feelings, my dreams with them, to advise them, and they could understand me . . . And it seems to me that it's sweeter in Spanish, more emotional: the conversation of a grandmother with her granddaughter. And in English well I couldn't . . . speak to them from the heart . . . in Spanish I could speak to them . . . tell them the dreams that I have for them. But, well, they don't understand me in, in Spanish, well, how am I going to say these things? (Quoted in Schecter and Bayley 1997: 534).

Acculturations and Transculturations

Joshua Fishman wrote in 1966 that the immigrant family is "a meeting ground for two competing languages" (181). As such, it is also the site of negotiation between ethnic identity associated with HL, and Americanization that accompanies the shift to English. Fishman described the immigrant family as on one hand a "bulwark of ethnicity," and on the other "an agency of Americanization for the immigrant parents and children alike" (181), noting that the two roles are not easy to reconcile, resulting in an ongoing competition between cultural influences that tends to characterize immigrant family life.

In the first decades of the twentieth century, as discussed in Chapters 2 and 3, immigrant children and children of immigrants were encouraged to abandon their HL in favor of complete linguistic and cultural assimilation, in keeping with prevailing popular and scholarly views that bilingualism is a liability. Subsequent research demonstrated the cognitive advantages of bilingualism, and, as I have discussed in this chapter, both the intellectual agility of children who grow up moving between two languages, and the clear benefits of additive schooling in bilingual education that incorporates and builds on children's existing linguistic competencies. And, as it turns out, complete assimilation whereby children in the 1.5 and second generations reject the HL and their parents' culture is associated with less positive educational outcomes and downward socioeconomic trajectories. In their comprehensive study of immigration in America, Portes and Rumbaut (2006) present ample data to support what they call "selective acculturation." They summarize their findings in this area as follows:

> When second-generation children acculturate to American ways without abandoning their parents' language and key elements of their culture, it is easier for parents to guide and support the children's quest for achievement and success. This pattern ... is labeled *selective acculturation*. It is associated with strong parental social capital in the form of stable families and cohesive communities and commonly, but not always, with fluent bilingualism (English plus the parental language) in the second generation. The opposite pattern is labeled *dissonant acculturation* because children's learning of English and American ways is accompanied by the abandonment of their parents' language and culture. If the latter remain foreign monolinguals, the stage is set for the breakdown of intrafamily communication and the loss of parents' control over their children (Portes and Rumbaut 2006: 267; emphasis original).

The authors support their claims with data showing, among other correlations, a positive association between immigrant adolescent bilingualism and better family relations. Adolescent bilingualism is also strongly associated with successful academic performance in high school. Similarly, Portes and Hao (2002) argue that children's fluent bilingualism, defined as "*simultaneous* mastery of two languages and associated cultural repertoires" (Portes and Hao 2002: 907;

emphasis original), on one hand enhances self-esteem and ambition because it represents achievement, and on the other "helps to anchor youthful identities by facilitating knowledge and understanding of parental cultures" (907).

Crucially, Portes and Rumbaut (2006) point out that selective acculturation is also associated with "strong parental social capital," which, in addition to "stable families" and "cohesive communities," also includes higher parental educational levels and socioeconomic status (267–271). Thus, for example, among Latino immigrants, Cubans tend to have high levels of education in the first generation, and corresponding better educational and socioeconomic outcomes in the second generation, in contrast to Mexicans, who have both the lowest levels of education among the parents and the highest high school dropout rates among the children. As political refugees, many Cubans are highly educated intellectuals and professionals who fled communism, and who received asylum upon reaching the United States. They were able to settle in communities of similarly advantaged Cuban Americans, as was the case with the Entenza family described by the authors, whose son Ariel "attended Belén Prep, a Jesuit school transplanted from Havana into Miami" (Portes and Rumbaut 2006: 264). Cuban Americans' legally recognized status allows them to participate in the American economy in ways that are unavailable to undocumented immigrants. Meanwhile, Mexicans and Central Americans, who are often driven to immigrate by extreme poverty or by social instability and violence in their home countries, do not have the advantages of automatic asylum. As we can see, selective acculturation may be a desirable option for immigrant families, but it is not always a realistic choice.

As described by Portes and Rumbaut (2006), selective acculturation and dissonant acculturation appear in a dichotomy. In reality, however, these should be viewed as variable tendencies that exist on a spectrum of possible responses of families to the immigrant experience. It is also important to recognize the complexity of factors that contribute to a particular family's trajectory of acculturation. Portes and Rumbaut point out, for example, that Chinese immigrants tend to have more positive outcomes than Cambodian and Laotian immigrants, which seems to correspond to the racial and ethnic hierarchies among Asian Americans, such as we observed in Chapters 2 and 3. These, in turn, are related to numerous factors, including the history of different groups' immigration, and ideologies rooted in interethnic relations in the immigrants' countries of origin in Asia. In Section 2.3, I discussed how different immigrant groups are positioned within the American racial landscape. The fact that Chinese Americans are viewed as exemplifying the "model minority," but Cambodian and Laotian Americans are not, is just one of the factors that structure these groups' immigrant experience.

Similarly, phenotypically black immigrants may not have perceived their race as salient prior to immigration, and may not identify with African

Americans once in the United States, but they are positioned as such by mainstream society, and treated accordingly. Portes and Rumbaut's example of Ariel Entenza, who acculturated successfully to mainstream, white, middle-class American norms, is contrasted with that of Danny González, who, while also Cuban, did not have the advantages of private Jesuit education, attending instead troubled public schools in Hialeah, a working class, gang-ridden suburb of Miami. The authors explain, "For older, well-established Cuban families, Hialeah is the place that gives Cubans a bad name because of the diffusion of voodoo-like Afro-Cuban religious practices and the concentration of newly arrived refugees from the island" (Portes and Rumbaut 2006: 272). Although we never find out how Ariel Entenza and Danny González identify in terms of race, the reference to "voodoo-like Afro-Cuban religious practices" in the context of a working-class part of town that is "held in contempt by middle-class Americans and Cubans alike" (272) suggests that race is not inconsequential in Cuban immigrants' acculturation trajectories. Crucially, Cuba is a multiracial society: according to a 2002 population census, 65 percent are white, while 35 percent are registered as black, mulattoes, or mestizos (Fulger 2012). These numbers are not straightforward, however, because race in Latin America including Cuba is not conceptualized in the same way as in the United States – a point I made several times throughout this book, for example in Sections 2.3, 2.4, and 5.3. While race may have different sociocultural meanings in Cuba, it is still a basis for discrimination. This discrimination is strongly reflected in the Cuban diaspora in the United States, which has been described as highly inflexible on racial acceptance and socioeconomic mobility (Fulger 2012). It is therefore not coincidental that the older and well-established Cubans in Miami who regard the Afro-Cuban-influenced Hialeah suburb with contempt, also happen to be part of the first waves of Cuban refugees from the 1950s and late 1960s/early 1970s, which were composed of white, highly educated, economic elite. By contrast, the "newly arrived refugees" settling in areas like Hialeah tend to be more racially and socioeconomically diverse (Fulger 2012). It seems that the middle-class Americans' *and* Cubans' contempt for Hialeah is partly a symptom of racism.

Growing up in Hialeah, Danny González becomes interested in hip-hop and graffiti art, which Portes and Rumbaut, quite problematically, describe as a "peculiar direction" leading to a "semideviant lifestyle" (Portes and Rumbaut 2006: 273). It does not appear, however, that Danny engages in any illegal activity. Quite the opposite: he goes to school and holds a day job, but in addition he is passionate about hip hop, and, much like Eddie Huang in Section 3.3, he does not identify with the mainstream definitions of success or of Americanness. Even if Danny himself is not phenotypically black, it is clear that he has first-hand experience with the discrimination and disadvantages faced by young Americans of color, and identifies with them on some level. Significantly, he witnesses racism experienced by non-white Cubans on part of both mainstream American society, and white Cuban American elites. This likely contributes to his rejection of acculturation trajectories espoused by these elites, and his affiliation with Afro-Cuban cultural forms like hip-hop and graffiti art.

Challenges facing Afro-Cuban youth may be illuminated by the example of Haitians, who are the largest black immigrant group in Miami and in Southern Florida more generally (Stepick et al. 2001: 235). Haitian students in the Miami area tend to have low rates of academic achievement, and difficult relationships with their parents. Their experience is that of "triple minorities": foreigners in America; speakers of Haitian Creole, a language that no other group speaks; and blacks (Stepick et al. 2001; Bryce-LaPorte 1993). At the time when Cubans were automatically granted asylum and residency in the United States, efforts were being made to deport Haitian "illegal immigrants" (Stepick et al. 2001: 236). Haitians were stigmatized as a health threat when, in the 1970s, it was claimed they had high rates of tuberculosis, and again in the 1980s, when they were for a time listed by the Centers for Disease Control and Prevention (CDC) as a group at high risk for AIDS.[15] One effect of this was loss of employment opportunities: in the early 1980s, unemployment was at 80 percent for women and 50 percent for men among Haitian Americans in Southern Florida (237).

In a paper that is one of the outputs from their fifteen-year longitudinal, ethnographic project in Miami's Haitian community, Stepick et al. (2001) report recurring instances of racism directed at Haitian youth by other students as well as by adults and institutions. In one case, a vice principal interrupted and shut down a previously approved Haitian Flag Day celebration in a Miami high school without much explanation, giving the impression that a large gathering of Haitian adolescents celebrating their heritage by singing and shouting in Creole, dancing, and having fun is cause for distress (230). The entirely Haitian soccer team from another high school repeatedly encountered jeering and racial slurs during games against Anglo-American or Cuban-American teams from the other teams' players, coaches, and supporters (240). One of Stepick et al.'s research participants stated that Americans use the term "Haitian" like "some type of curse word" (239). In the 1980s, a school with a large Haitian population had to be closed on several occasions due to violence, as "[s]tudents severely ridiculed and beat up anyone Haitian looking or who spoke Creole or accented English" (240). And although one of the ways Haitians are minoritized in America is because they are black, they do not simply integrate with African Americans. In fact, as Stepick et al. (2001) find in their research,

[15] This example brings up, again, the discourse representing "undesirable" immigrants as carriers of disease, both physical and moral. The same discourse surrounded Chinese immigrants in California in the nineteenth century, as discussed in Section 2.2.

Haitian youth tend to experience a lot of discrimination from their African American peers as well. The authors argue "that in response to prejudice, many Haitian students develop an ambivalence about their cultural roots, including both an alienation from their parents' native language and conflict with and frequently alienation from their parents" (234). For example, although all the Haitian children in the study appear to understand Creole, they tend to deny their knowledge of it. In families where the parents claimed to speak Creole at home, as many as 39.8 percent of the children claimed that English was spoken instead. This disparity in self-reported language use at home suggests that a lot of Haitian children do not identify with Creole or harbor feelings of shame associated with it. Haitians were also found to be "statistically more embarrassed by their parents than other [immigrant] students," and they also had higher rates of parent-child conflict (245). Stepick et al. (2001) suggest that, upon encountering intense discrimination because of their background, Haitian American youth react by trying to hide or distance themselves from their roots, which is seen by the parents as challenging their authority. The parents, accustomed to strict control over their children's lives that is expected in Haiti, disapprove of American child-rearing norms and of the freedoms enjoyed by American youth, but their attempts to enforce control sometimes result in conflict and alienation from their children.

In the context of the experience of black immigrants in the United States, and in Southern Florida specifically, it makes sense that Cuban-American Danny González would distrust the promise of the American dream while growing up in Hialeah. And while I disagree with Portes and Rumbaut's assessment of Danny's lifestyle and artistic interests as "semideviant" and suggestive of failure, it is true that, like Haitian American parents in Stepick et al.'s (2001) work, Danny's parents are likely to experience greater cultural distance from their son than is the case for parents whose children acculturate to mainstream, middle-class norms that appear synonymous with success to immigrant parents. Consequently, Danny's family dynamic may suffer. Portes and Rumbaut also correctly point out that one cannot speak of "assimilation" or "acculturation" as a uniform process, because there are multiple segments of American society that young immigrants can assimilate to. There are multiple acculturations. And white, mainstream, middle class norms are not equally available or desirable to all immigrants.

Zentella's (1997) linguistic ethnography of *el bloque*, a Puerto Rican immigrant community in New York City (Sections 2.4, 5.1), demonstrates both this multiplicity of acculturations, and the fact that they can coexist and overlap in the same community. She shows that multilingual competencies, code-switching, translanguaging, and hybrid language forms are all resources through which young speakers – immigrant children and children of immigrants – negotiate their acculturation processes, and position themselves in various ways with respect to their HL and English, as well as to Puerto Rican and American cultural influences. Through these resources, the community also creates new ways of relating, and new identities, which I discussed in Section 5.1, and in the detailed discussion of Spanglish and Polamerican in Section 5.3.

The children of *el bloque* have several target choices when it comes to acquiring English: Puerto Rican English, African American Vernacular English, Hispanized English, and Standard NYC English (Zentella 1997: 41). Many of them control several of these codes, which also represent different sociocultural meanings that the children can identify with. Moreover, in order to function successfully in American society in ways that are relevant to their lives, multilingualism may be more appropriate as the goal than shifting to English for the children of *el bloque*. Their socialization in several varieties of English as well as Spanish produces a community that is defined by transculturations rather than acculturation. The ability to transculturate is more relevant in many immigrant contexts than the kind of assimilation or acculturation to the dominant culture that is posited in mainstream discourses, as I have sought to demonstrate throughout this book. Families that engage in translanguaging and transculturation produce their own, locally relevant sets of norms and identities. As a result, a speech community such as *el bloque* can maintain its cohesiveness even though not everyone can speak directly to each other in the same language, and it can adjust to accommodate to language shift among the young generation of New York Puerto Ricans who may, in time, follow their own diverse trajectories of positioning themselves in the wider American society.

All this is not to say, certainly, that tensions and rifts do not occur between parents and children when HLs and English, and the corresponding cultural meanings and norms, come into contact within the immigrant family. We saw this above on the example of Haitian Americans. Burck (2005), writing about immigrant families in Britain, describes both children and parents sensing a problematic role reversal. Children reported feeling embarrassment and even contempt for their parents when the latter could not function competently in English. These feelings conflicted with a sense of sympathy for their parents' struggles, and of protectiveness when the parents made mistakes in public or were treated badly because of their English. For their part, the parents were acutely aware of their children's ambivalent feelings, as described by a French father: "What I have noticed is both my son and daughter if I make a mistake in English they look at me and they say 'Daddy, how long have you been in this country?' and it means, speaking English better" (cited in Burck 2005: 125).

Writing about the American context, Suárez-Orozco and Suárez-Orozco (2001) make similar observations. As co-directors of the Harvard Immigration Project between 1997 and 2003, Suárez-Orozco and Suárez-

Orozco led the Longitudinal Immigrant Student Adaptation Study (LISA), gathering data from over 400 newly arrived immigrant children from Central America, China, the Dominican Republic, Haiti, and Mexico, settled in the Boston and San Francisco areas (Suárez-Orozco and Suárez-Orozco 2001: 9). They observe that the unequal language abilities within the family often contribute to alienation and conflict. Children's English improves faster than their parents', and their HL competence may dwindle, thus limiting the range of topics that can be discussed with their parents in depth, or missing subtleties of meaning that lead to misunderstandings. Coupled with their lack of cultural knowledge relevant in America as compared with their children, the parents experience a "demotion" in status (76). Attempts at disciplining their children in ways approved of in their home countries may sometimes lead to deeper rifts as some children threaten to – or do – report their parents to US Child Protective Services. This extreme situation was also observed in Stepick et al.'s research in the Miami Haitian community (Stepick et al. 2001).

Throughout their book, Suárez-Orozco and Suárez-Orozco emphasize the diversity of immigrant experience, and the resulting complexity of outcomes for immigrant families. Smoother resolution of intrafamilial problems through transculturations, hybrid language forms, and creation of hybrid identities, may be easier to achieve in established immigrant communities which already have a shared set of norms and practices, such as Puerto Ricans in New York City or Poles in Chicago, than it is for newly arrived immigrants or refugees that have been torn from their home countries and placed in an unfamiliar setting without a sense of community. It is also not unusual for families to be separated for long periods of time during the migration process. After a long time apart, parents and children have to get to know each other again, and in these conditions, reassertion of parental control can be difficult (Suárez-Orozco and Suárez-Orozco 2001).

The experience of forced migrants such as political refugees and exiles differs from that of voluntary immigrants who primarily seek more livable economic conditions. Refugees from war zones may be grieving for relatives or suffer from post-traumatic stress disorder (PTSD). Political exiles, such as Chileans who either left or were expelled from their country after the 1973 military coup, may have feelings of loss and guilt, and respond by viewing their exile as temporary, as a "parenthesis in their lives," which is "emotionally incompatible with becoming invested in learning the new language and adapting to the new culture" (Roizblatt and Pilowsky 1996: 516). The exiles' children, however, often do not share this perspective, which prevents the family from collaboratively constructing their immigration experience or working out a new family identity. In fact, disagreement regarding the appropriate way for the family to adapt to life in the United States, including family rules governing the children's language use, dress style, friendships, and pastimes, is a common reason for immigrants to seek family therapy (Baptiste 1987). Furthermore, depending on the parents' country and region of origin, cultural norms that children learn at home may clash directly with those expected of them at school. For example, Suárez-Orozco and Suárez-Orozco (2001) note that Haitian children are taught to show respect by averting their eyes while being scolded by an adult, which American teachers interpret as rudeness, expecting the child to look at them instead (73). Such conflicts in socialization are difficult to resolve without a community support network that many recent immigrants do not have.

To summarize, we can see that working out language and cultural dynamics within the family is an ongoing process that can have a number of different outcomes. Immigrant families negotiate their multilingual and multicultural dynamics in a multiplicity of ways. Studies such as Medvedeva (2012) support the argument that the use of HL or English by immigrant children tends to reflect a particular family's ways to negotiate the parents' and children's linguistic repertoires and their emotional relationships, and cannot be uniformly designated as positive or negative. On the other hand, research also suggests that immigrant children's maintenance of HL leads to higher quality of parent-child relationships (Oh and Fuligni 2010; Tseng and Fuligni 2000). Crucially, since families function in wider society, an immigrant family's choices and practices will depend to a significant extent on family-external factors, such as its interactions with the public domain: schools, doctors, employers, immigration officials, landlords, churches, neighbors. Many of the challenges affecting the functioning of immigrant families are rooted in the normative expectations of mainstream American society, including discursive frames such as "immigrants as a problem" and "English as the American language." Immigrant families must find ways to work out these challenges and negotiate their roles and relationships, which they accomplish to vairous degrees of success. Below, I turn to specific ways in which families enact their roles and construct family identities through multilingual practices.

Enacting Family Roles in Multiple Languages

In Section 6.2, I discussed how language brokering often becomes a joint family enterprise, with children and adults each contributing their expertise – linguistic and cultural knowledge on the children's part, and "real-world" financial and institutional experience on the parents' part – to navigate their communication with the English-speaking outside world. Such collaborative activity can reinforce the sense of belonging and closeness for the family. Language brokering then becomes part of what they do, one of the practices defining family membership.

The same can be true of intrafamily brokering, which takes place when members of different generations are dominant in different languages and thus have difficulty communicating with each other directly. Such brokering takes place in the tri-generational Italian American family whose interaction during an annual daylong get-together is examined by De Fina (2012). The family, consisting of two sisters, their parents, spouses, in-laws, and children, maintains a tradition of an annual gathering to make and bottle all the tomato sauce they will use that year. Marina, the twenty-three-year-old member of the youngest generation and De Fina's researcher, explains the significance of Sauce Day: "It is an important family tradition to us at this point and one of the traditions is that we have cold-cut sandwiches for lunch after a morning of making sauce and then the fresh sauce for dinner after we are all done" (cited in De Fina 2012: 361). Marina's family's Sauce Day is a great example of how community membership is reinforced through engagement in a shared practice (Lave and Wenger 1991; Holmes and Meyerhoff 1999; Meyerhoff 1999; Eckert and McConnell-Ginet 1992; Baran 2014): everyone participates in cooking and bottling the sauce, partakes in the traditional lunch and dinner, and discusses the merits of the finished product. Although De Fina does not mention this, we can imagine this family using a special family recipe from the old country. And just as the sauce-making tradition contributes to this particular family's construction of identity and of a sense of belonging, so do their multilingual practices.

Marina's mother's side of the family consists of relatively recent immigrants: her grandmother, mother, and maternal uncle were all born in Italy, and they as well as her maternal aunt – born in the US – can speak Sicilian and Italian. The grandmother claims not to know English, and she never speaks it, although, as the interaction unfolds, she appears to understand more than she admits. Marina's father and his relatives, on the other hand, are all US-born and only speak English. His parents have minimal passive knowledge of Italian and Sicilian. Marina herself understands Sicilian well, and is also fluent in Italian, having studied it extensively at the university. Marina's little cousins, eight-year-old Charlie and eleven-year-old Judy, children of her maternal aunt, speak and understand a little Italian and Sicilian. Judy, however, insists that she has no knowledge of the heritage languages. Aside from the maternal grandmother, Milena, the family's preferred language is English. Since Milena does not speak English, however, her children and her granddaughter, Marina, act as language brokers between her and English-monolingual members of the family. But, as De Fina points out, almost everyone in the family maintains "a certain degree of ... *engagement* with the heritage languages" (De Fina 2012: 360; emphasis original), demonstrating, both through their multilingual practices and metalinguistic comments about them, that "Italian and Sicilian are regarded as part of the family's repertoire and as markers of their collective identity" (360). De Fina's choice of the term "engagement" with the heritage languages reflects the fact that even English-monolingual family members sometimes try to use words and phrases that they hear from others, try to participate in translation, and comment on each other's proficiency in the two HLs. De Fina also observes: "A common linguistic pattern in the family's multiparty interaction is parallel use of different languages with separate conversations going on at the same time in different languages" (361).

Some of the ways in which members of Marina's family engage with the HLs include language accommodation, displays of metalinguistic awareness, and linguistic performances (360). For example, Milena, the maternal grandmother, almost always speaks Sicilian, which is her preferred language. In conversing with Marina, she occasionally switches to Italian, which is Marina's preferred HL. Marina also uses Sicilian words while addressing her grandmother in Italian. An example is the following exchange, adapted from De Fina (2012: 364):

1. Grandmother:	Pe' to nonno fu una vacanza l'America! [laughter] "For your grandpa America was a holiday!"	—>	Sicilian
2. Marina:	Ma anche ha *travagghiato*! "But he also has worked!"	—>	Italian and Sicilian
3. Grandmother:	**Yeah**, ha *travagghiato*= "Yeah, he has worked"	—>	English, Italian, Sicilian

De Fina points out that the grandmother and granddaughter are accommodating each other's linguistic preferences. The grandmother speaks in Sicilian in (1), followed by Marina's response that starts off in Italian, her preferred language, with *ma anche ha* "but he also has" in (2). Marina then switches to Sicilian for the second part of the past perfect construction *travagghiato* "worked." Marina's past perfect construction is a transfer from Italian, where it is used frequently; in Sicilian, the preferred tense is the remote past tense. The grandmother follows in (3) with her own accommodation to Marina's choice of tense and vocabulary. De Fina explains: "We see that in her next turn grandma repeats the same construction accommodating as well since in Sicilian she would have used the remote past tense *travagghiau* (as she does [later] in line 5) or at least she would have used the auxiliary *havi* [in place of Italian *ha*]" (365). De Fina argues that this language accommodation and code-switching allows speakers to align themselves with or against different people in the family as the interaction proceeds. For example, we read that "Marina's language use seems to be in accordance with the attitude of pride and identification that she shows towards the Italian language and her family's origins in her research notes" and in other interactions (366). This mutually accommodating pattern of multilingual interaction is also a process of negotiation that can help to define and reinforce the grandmother-granddaughter relationship.

De Fina observes that although the grandmother claims not to know any English, she not only shows herself to understand parts of English conversations, but uses English borrowings in ways similar to hybridizing practices that we saw in Section 5.3 with Spanglish and Polamerican. For example, the grandmother suggests to her eight-year-old grandson Charlie that he make himself a big cheese sandwich, but her Sicilian sentence ends with the noun phrase *un sanguiccio* ***bigge*** "a **big** sandwich," which is an example of translanguaging, with English lexicon adapted to Italian morphosyntax and phonology (370). Milena's daughter, Roberta, repeats the phrase and laughs, resulting in grandmother Milena's defensive inquiry whether she said something wrong. De Fina argues that "By laughing at her mother Roberta is in some sense distancing herself from her and indexing her own identity as a competent bilingual as opposed to her mother's incompetence" (370). But, given the prevalence of hybrid forms in immigrant linguistic repertoires, Roberta's reaction may be a comment on the translanguaging and language mixing speech styles characteristic of multilingual immigrant families, rather than an evaluation of Milena as a less competent bilingual. In this case, Roberta's laughter may be directed not personally at her mother, but as a mark of recognition that the family engages in unusual – from the mainstream, monolingual perspective – linguistic practices.

Another family member who insists that she does not have a multilingual repertoire is eleven-year-old Judy, Charlie's big sister. Judy claims not to understand any Italian or Sicilian, and very vocally rejects any suggestions to the contrary. When Judy appears to have understood an exchange in the HLs, Marina and Judy's mother, Lea, point this out to her, and Lea makes a more general comment that everyone in the family is multilingual to some extent because they need to interact with each other. De Fina writes, "Both Marina and her aunt here describe the family identity as fundamentally defined by multilingualism and therefore posit the need for mutual understanding as a survival strategy" (268). Judy, however, rejects this proposition, insisting instead that she does not identify with the family's multilingualism. Even so, Judy is aware of the importance of language for family identity, and of her own "need to define her role in relation to it" (369). Furthermore, both grandmother Milena's and young Judy's insistence on certain linguistic roles – as the fluent, native speaker of the heritage languages but not of English in Milena's case, and as the monolingual speaker of English in Judy's case – reinforces generational roles in the family. Even though in practice both Milena and Judy engage – in De Fina's words – with the family's multilingualism, outwardly they position themselves as inhabiting relatively fixed generational roles. As in most immigrant families, it is the grandmother's role to speak the heritage language, as well as to tell family anecdotes as Milena does on Sauce Day, while it is the members of the youngest generation who represent acculturation and fluency in English. The middle generations, meanwhile, function as language brokers. This arrangement, although not nearly as clear-cut and static in practice, frames the mutual roles that family members take up in relation to each other.

Similarly, in another analysis of cross-generational language brokering in Italian American families, Del Torto (2008) argues that brokering practices contribute to the production and reaffirmation of generational identity categories in the family. Del Torto draws on Bucholtz and Hall's (2004, 2005) work which sees identities as relational and emergent in interaction through tactics of intersubjectivity, as well as on the idea that "social actors bring expectations of their own and others' roles, responsibilities, and identities to every interaction, allowing them to make sense of the dynamic and intersubjective nature of identity" (Del Torto 2008: 94). These "brought-along" identities (Williams 2008) encompass the expectation that generations are socially relevant categories, that the family is composed of several generations which are linguistically and culturally distinct, and that the middle-generation language brokers are best positioned to bridge the flanking generations' differences, thus facilitating communication and maintaining family cohesion. One of the participants, middle-generation Ida, explains her brokering role in the family in the following way:

> the children and the grandparents have worked it out pretty good / I translate sometimes but not that often / we translate for you [3rd gen.] and we translate for them [1st gen.] so if it's not in English we translate for you and if it's not in Italian we translate for them / I don't know why because you understand and they do too / most of it anyway / but we do / I don't know we try to help it along maybe (cited in Del Torto 2008: 82).

Del Torto argues that Ida employs the tactics of distinction and adequation (Bucholtz and Hall 2004) to group individuals into categories that are different from each other, as accomplished in Ida's use of the pronouns *we, you*, and *they*, and to construct similarity "based on language use, relative generation, and kinship terminology" such as *the children* and *the grandparents* (83). Ida also recognizes that the different generations are actually able to engage in successful mutual interaction, but that she still feels compelled to "help it along" by translating. Unlike in De Fina's case study, where family members in the oldest and youngest generations refused to admit that they understood each other while the language brokers tried to convince them that they did, in this example it is the middle-generation language broker who on some level rejects or discounts the flanking generations' capacity for mutual understanding. Del

Torto writes, "Second-generation participants position themselves as a group that shares aspects of identity with the 1st and 3rd gens., more than those flanking generations share with one another" (83). Rather than encouraging the children's and grandparents' bilingual efforts, language brokers like Ida reinforce the idea that the two need help in order to maintain smoothly flowing relations. In one conversational example, another middle-generation participant, Nina, appears to assume that a pause in the conversation indicates a linguistic problem, and steps in to translate. In the excerpt below, adapted from Del Torto (2008: 88–89), the number in parentheses following the speaker's name refers to their generation, where 1 = grandparents, 2 = middle generation, 3 = children.

1	Ada (1)	and this guy you know he married Carlo's daughter he was uh
2		come from America he didn't grow to uh
3	Lisa (3)	which who did he marry? which daughter?
4		(1)
5	Nina (2)	**quale delle figlie?** *which of the daughters?*
6	Ada (1)	I don't remember the whole thing you know

The one-second pause in line 4 seems to occur because Ada stops to think, trying to remember which of Carlo's daughters is the one who got married, so that she can answer Lisa's question. Ada's statement in line 6 corroborates this interpretation. But Nina interjects with an Italian translation of the question (line 5), apparently interpreting the pause as "trouble in the sequential organization of the interaction" (Del Torto 2008: 89) caused by Ada's difficulty in understanding. Nina does this even though Ada is clearly more than capable of functioning in English, as demonstrated by her utterances in lines 1–2 and 6. Del Torto interprets this as Nina's move to "bridge a perceived gap between family members" (89). However, we could also see this as a recognition of Ada's status as the most proficient speaker of the heritage language, which – as in the case of grandmother Milena above – complements her role as the family storyteller, since here Ada seems to be telling a family anecdote. Nina may be translating Lisa's question not because she perceives Ada as lacking in English competence, but rather to show respect for and to recognize the value of Ada's dominant language. In either case, the one-second pause in line 4 gives Nina an opportunity to assert her own family role as the bilingual and bicultural language broker. Nina's interactional move in line 5 invokes Ada's status as the member of the Italian-speaking generation and Lisa's status as the member of the English-speaking, acculturated generation, and reinforces her own family role as she demonstrates her bilingual competence. The interaction is complex in the various ways in which it structures the three participants' mutual relations. And, although in Ida's and Nina's families the middle-generation members tend to emphasize linguistic differences between grandparents and children, as opposed to De Fina's case study in which language brokers highlighted the flanking generations' bilingual competence, in both studies we see generational roles as a salient feature of family structure, defined in part in terms of language knowledge and use.

Not only do multilingual repertoires and practices factor powerfully into how immigrant families make sense of their family identities and of their sense of belonging, but different languages can also invoke different expectations of what various family roles entail. As I discuss at length in Section 7.1, many bi- and multilinguals experience emotions and social roles differently in their different languages. Certain culturally contextualized meanings become untranslatable, because the closest translation is incomprehensible without adequate cultural knowledge. Accordingly, for a bilingual, words become connected with untranslatable emotions and ways of being. A mother-daughter interaction in the heritage language invokes different interactional norms, different concepts of family roles, and different ideological constructs of "motherhood," and negotiates mother-daughter roles differently, from an English interaction between the two. Code-switching and use of hybrid forms can serve as bridges between the two family ideologies, and help to construct new, alternative and hybrid forms of relating. But such negotiation will not necessarily produce complete mutual understanding and agreement. The process may be fraught with conflict, as we saw on the example of Liz and May in Williams (2005) that I discussed at the beginning of this section, and at greater length in Section 5.1. Liz and May variously invoke Chinese and English to pose or answer a challenge, or to create or diminish distance, as they negotiate conflicting meanings of their roles as mother and daughter.

Anna Wierzbicka (2007), in her reflections on the emotional meanings of Polish and English that I discuss in the next chapter, describes an argument with her daughter Clare, born and raised bilingually in Australia, which became especially painful because it moved from Polish to English. She writes:

> The matter was personal, and the disagreement . . . was painful . . . I was keenly aware that we had both shifted from Polish into English. Usually, if at some point during our conversations Clare shifts unconsciously into English, I ask her to move back to Polish, and she does. This time, however, I made no attempt to revert to Polish, and I heard myself pressing on in English. The longer this went on, the greater (I felt) the emotional distance between us. It seemed the chasm had opened: this was not our usual, close, Polish-based relationship (Wierzbicka 2007: 106).

The closeness between mother and daughter that is created and articulated in Polish, cannot be experienced by the mother in English. When Anglo-Australian norms of family interaction are invoked by switching into English, the closeness, achieved through Polish words and norms, is lost. Polish is the language through which this mother-daughter relationship is most powerfully constituted. This, of course, opens up the possibility for either party to challenge the existing relationship by switching into English, thus disrupting the accepted pattern of interaction, just as we saw between Liz and May in Williams (2005). There, Liz moves between different, culturally contextualized roles as "daughter," and May variously accepts or challenges Liz's identity claims through her own linguistic choices. For example, May's use of English challenges Liz's claim to being an authority on American sociocultural practices (see Section 5.1). Family relations are experienced differently in different languages, and, depending on their own experience of immigration, members of different generations may not feel equally comfortable in speaking and enacting their mutual relations in a particular language. Children, for example, may not know how to perform their role as "child" in the heritage language, because they are unfamiliar with and distanced from the meanings of being a "child" in their parents' home country. English terms take on real meaning because they connect with present-day, ongoing experience in the English-dominant immigrant country. But for the parents, switching to English represents distancing and a lack of directness, or a certain betrayal of the parent-child relationship. Aware of this, the children may stick to HL, but, finding its resources irrelevant, they refrain from engaging emotionally. Alternately, the parents may switch to English in order to accommodate the children's preferences and emotional needs, even though this may be emotionally difficult for the parents.

Burck (2005) engages with this idea extensively in her work with multilingual families in Great Britain. Burck interviews immigrants from countries including Italy, France, Belgium, Denmark, Poland, Hungary, Argentina, China, Iran, Iraq, South Africa, Kenya, and Zimbabwe. Most of her participants are in cross-linguistic relationships, meaning that their partners do not share their first language. Typically, the partners are English speakers. Burck examines the participants' experience living a multilingual life, including constructions of self, identities and power dynamics, relationships with partners, and parenting. In a chapter on language use and family relationships, Burck shows that her interviewees "experienced parenting in each of their languages as being a different kind of parent, embodying different values encoded in the language, including different conceptualizations of 'parenting' and 'children'" (Burck 2005: 143). The participants made different choices, some trying to parent in their first languages, while others settling on English. They also had different and sometimes conflicting feelings about their choices. A consistent theme, however, was the sense that parenting in each language is different. For example, a Shona speaker says this about parenting in English: "The children can identify with my values because they don't see them as alien. Whereas if I had parented as an African father, certainly there would have been a lot of clashes . . . So parenting in English has helped me to be aware of that, to be very respectful of where they're coming from" (cited in Burck 2005: 142–143). Similarly, a Danish speaker comments on how parenting in English helps her cultivate a different mothering style from that of her own mother: " . . . in my very down moments, I actually, when I spoke Danish, I heard myself as my mother. I thought God, and so I think yes, it was always a relief to get out of that mood, so, it allowed me to distance myself from myself, I suppose" (cited in Burck 2005: 146). Some mothers emphasized the "naturalness" of addressing their children in their first language, and the possibility for intimacy that it affords: "With my children there was a kind of intimate vocabulary and that's probably why with my daughter I spoke a lot of German because that kind of tender playfulness came much more naturally in German" (cited in Burck 2005: 132). Yet others reported using code-switching to achieve specific goals, such as a Mandarin-speaking mother who disciplines her daughter in English as a way of "performing authority" (Burck 2005: 140).

While focusing on British examples, the insights gained from Burck's research are certainly relevant for other immigrant contexts. One case study example in the United States shows how sometimes both parents and children may employ code-switching strategies to bridge the cultural differences between expectations of family roles and ways of relating that each language invokes and enacts. Chung (2006) describes a bilingual interaction in her own family, which consists of first-generation Korean immigrant parents who are highly educated and middle class, and who are Korean-dominant but fluent in English, and of two young children whose preferred language is English. The father, more than the mother, tries to enforce a Korean-only language policy at home (cf. Tannenbaum 2012), but he ends up switching to English to accommodate his children's preferences. For example, when the daughter is upset – as when her brother breaks her Chapstick – she expresses her anger in English, and the father switches to English to calm her down. More importantly, this family bridges expectations of culturally specific family roles by mixing the use of Korean and English for terms referring to family relationships and terms expressing affection.

Whereas in the case of the Italian American families in De Fina's (2012) and Del Torto's (2008) work we saw similarities constructed and reinforced within generational categories, in this case emphasis is placed on the Korean cultural expectation that individuals are situated along age-based hierarchies across generations as well as within the same generation. Thus, although the young children are English-dominant and routinely speak English with each other, the little boy does not call his sister by her first name when addressing her or referring to her, which is the typical American cultural norm. Instead, he refers to her as *Nuna*, or "older sister," which follows Korean cultural practice. While most of the time the siblings enact and negotiate their relationship in English, by maintaining the use of deferential address forms that give salience to their respective ages and mark their status as unequal, they are able to preserve this aspect of their sibling relationship and their roles within the family. On the other hand, the father is observed switching to English to express his affection. At one point, as he sends the children to bed, he says to his son: "I love you, *Midum*. Hug-*do haeyaji*" (Give me a hug) (Chung 2006: 301). Chung points out that neither overtly saying "I love you" to one's family members, nor hugging them, exist as practices in Korean cultural contexts. As in many other cultural settings, love for one's parents or children is assumed and expressing it with words is rarely done. It is unclear from the exchange alone whether the father is switching to English to say "I love you" and ask for a hug from his son because he recognizes and wishes to accommodate the son's greater rootedness in American culture, or if he is adopting the American practice because he also now identifies with it. In any case, the switch to English allows the father to engage with the American cultural practice, and to experience its meanings without disrupting them by translating them into Korean, which may end up feeling awkward and inappropriate.

In the next and final chapter, I will turn my attention specifically to the emotional and psychological aspects of multilingualism in the immigrant experience.

7 American Becomings

Pavlenko and Lantolf (2000) argue that personal motivation is a crucial component of an individual's process of learning a second language, and that this motivation is closely bound up with one's identity. The learning process is profoundly affected by the extent to which the learner is able to forge a coherent identity that incorporates elements associated with the second language. In situations where immigration is in some way traumatic, the new language may represent a potentially unwelcome identity, and learning it may take on a symbolic meaning of reinforcing one's perception of experiencing identity loss. The trauma may be extreme and physical, such as escape from violent persecution, but it may also be psychological, centered on the grief of being torn from one's homeland, for example by one's parents or by economic circumstances. The trauma then irreversibly complicates one's relationship to one's second and first languages.

In this final chapter, I will focus on how immigrants themselves experience their journey through language, and how they invoke language to enact their new identities. I will examine immigrants' representations of language, language learning, and language loss in memoirs, diaries, letters, autobiographies, and in recorded narratives. I will attempt to illuminate what it means for an immigrant to become re-socialized in the new language and culture (Weldeyesus 2007), and to live as "translated selves" (Wierzbicka 2007; Besemeres 2007, 2006).

Alvarez (1998), in discussing Spanish-English bilingualism, quotes the Cuban American poet and professor of comparative literature Gustavo Perez Firmat as saying that "English is very concise and efficient . . . Spanish has sabrosura, flavor" (Alvarez 1998: 486). Indeed, multilingual speakers often have very intense feelings about what their various languages represent, how they seem to sound, and in what ways they are untranslatable. They are familiar with the sense that not everything can be said in the exact same way in different languages. And if expressions or idioms cannot be translated, neither can the emotions and moods that they enact. The experience of being unable to translate one's attitude and personality may therefore be a common one for immigrants, who, used to performing a certain social role in their home country or in their L1 community, are at a loss when attempting to construct the same persona in L2. Because one's experience of language is so closely bound up with emotions, the negotiation of language in the process of becoming American can be particularly complicated and painful.

7.1 Embodied Words: Language, Emotion, and the Immigrant Self

Eva Hoffman, author of the autobiography *Lost in Translation* (1989), immigrated with her family to Vancouver in 1959, leaving behind her beloved hometown of Kraków, Poland. She was thirteen years old. She moved to the United States for college and eventually settled in New York City. Recording her memories thirty years later, Hoffman writes in the present tense, bringing the reader fully into the world of the adolescent girl who is mourning her past and struggling to situate herself in her new reality. She learns English fast, but the new language seems cerebral, removed from immediate experience and devoid of intuitive sensation. In a frequently quoted passage, Hoffman describes her feelings of disconnect from English words as compared with their Polish counterparts:

> . . . The signifier has become severed from the signified. The words I learn now don't stand for things in the same unquestioned way they did in my native tongue. "River" in Polish was a vital sound, energized with the essence of riverhood, of my rivers, of being immersed in rivers. "River" in English is cold – a word without an aura. It has no accumulated associations for me, and it does not give off the radiating haze of connotation. It does not evoke (Hoffman 1989: 106).

She continues:

> When my friend Penny tells me that she's envious, or happy, or disappointed, I try laboriously to translate not from English to Polish but from the word back to its source, to the feeling from which it springs. Already, in that moment of strain, spontaneity of response is lost. And anyway, the translation doesn't work. I don't know how Penny feels when she talks about envy. The word hangs in a Platonic stratosphere, a vague prototype of all envy, so large, so all-encompassing that it might crush me – as might disappointment or happiness (107).

Hoffman expresses what many late bilinguals (Pavlenko 2005) observe: that while they may know their L2 very well, they do not "feel" it in the same way as their L1. The language first heard from infancy tends to be perceived as more imbued with emotion. Richard Rodriguez writes about the intimacy shared by his family in Spanish, in their private world, closed off from English-speaking America: " . . . a word like *sí* would become, in several notes, able to convey added measures of feeling" (Rodriguez 1982: 17). As Pavlenko (2005) explains, similar sentiments about first and second languages and emotion are shared by other translingual authors who choose to write in their L2 despite, or sometimes because of, feeling less closeness to it than to their L1. In fact, it seems that some bilinguals experience the sense of intimacy evoked by L1 as beautiful, and others as overwhelming or unpleasant. In other words, while the "perception of *language embodiment*" (Pavlenko 2005: 155; emphasis original) is typically associated with the first language, the effects of this perception differ.

Jerzy Kosinski, the Polish American writer, author of *The Painted Bird* (1965), who as a six-year-old Jewish boy journeyed on his own through war-torn Poland having been separated from his family, speaks of the freedom afforded to him through English. In English, he is able to write about his childhood experience more easily: " ... as English was still new to me, I could write dispassionately, free from the emotional connotations one's native language always contains" (Kosinski 1976: xii; cited in Pavlenko 2005: 152). It could be that Kosinski's traumatic childhood is too painful to write about in the language in which it happened, although Kosinski argues that childhood itself is the trauma that leads to the pain invoked by L1, "not this or that war" (cited in Pavlenko 2005: 152). He writes, "One is traumatized by the language when one is growing up . . . I think had I come to the United States at the age of nine I would have become affected by this traumatizing power of language . . . When I came to the United States I was twenty-four. Hence, I am not traumatized by English . . ." (cited in Pavlenko 2005: 152). Kosinski finds English liberating because it does not evoke a conditioned response (Pavlenko 2005: 155) or "involuntary associations" (cited in Pavlenko 2005: 152) with childhood experiences; it thus opens up possibilities for exploration.

By contrast, Eva Hoffman is upset and confused by the disembodied words of English, at least initially. Upon receiving a diary as a birthday gift from her friend Penny, she struggles to decide in which language to write. Polish seems to her a dead language, "the language of the untranslatable past" (Hoffman 1989: 120), while English is not "the language of the self" (121). During her early immigrant days, Hoffman finds a silence in her mind when she would have previously heard inner language, because Polish seems to have atrophied, and "[i]n English, words have not penetrated to those layers of my psyche from which a private conversation could proceed" (107). Hoffman sees her distance from English as frustrating, not liberating. Consequently, she mourns the intensely emotional Polish words that are now eluding her because they cannot apply to her new reality (121). This is not a pleasant or freeing experience for her. She believes that all people have a need "to give voice accurately and fully to ourselves and our sense of the world" (124). While Kosinski talks about being traumatized by language, Hoffman feels traumatized by its absence:

> Linguistic dispossession is a sufficient motive for violence, for it is close to the dispossessions of one's self. Blind rage, helpless rage is rage that has no words – rage

that overwhelms one with darkness. And if one is perpetually without words, if one exists in the entropy of inarticulateness, that condition itself is bound to be an enraging frustration (Hoffman 1989: 124).

Kosinski experiences English as freeing him to tell his childhood story, while Hoffman simultaneously resents it for rendering her voiceless and struggles to master it so that she can speak about her new life in the relevant language. Her memoir describes her journey towards the gradual resolution of this conflict. In the end, Hoffman finds her English voice, becomes a successful writer, and receives a doctoral degree in English and American literature.

For other authors writing in a "stepmother tongue" (Pavlenko 2005: 181), their choice is motivated by a variety of reasons: the new language requires of the writer a specific kind of discipline, or it allows for greater creativity and playfulness because words and idioms are not taken for granted (181). As Pavlenko (2005) explains, the emotional embodiment of L1 as opposed to L2 elicits "responses [that] will vary from individual to individual, depending on personal experiences" (155). But the emotional intensity of L1 resurfaces time and again. Author Mingfong Ho writes, "Chinese is the language with the deepest emotional resonance for me . . . I think of it as the language of my heart. Perhaps that's why, even now, when I cry, I cry in Chinese" (Ho, in Pavlenko 2005: 180). Luc Sante identifies French as the language of the *coeur*, which is also the dwelling place of emotions – as opposed to the heart (180). Julia Alvarez describes her feelings when someone addresses her in Spanish: "Spanish certainly was the language of storytelling, the language of the body and of the senses, and of the emotional wiring of the child, so that still, when someones addresses me as 'Hoolia' (Spanish pronunciation of Julia), I feel my emotional self come to the fore" (cited in Pavlenko 2005: 152).

Pavlenko (2005) discusses a number of studies aimed at measuring affective linguistic conditioning in L1 and L2. One of these is Javier and Marcos' (1989) study measuring bilinguals' skin conductance response (SCR), which is one of the physiological responses present in autonomic arousal that words can activate. Pavlenko explains:

The results demonstrated that the mean SCR response to semantically or phonologically related words of the same language was always greater than to unrelated words. This response was not generalized to the words of the other language, however, explaining why translation equivalents of taboo words remain affectively neutral, unless learned and used in context (Pavlenko 2005: 157).

Indeed, similar research focusing specifically on responses to taboo words in bilinguals shows that L1 taboo words elicit higher anxiety responses than L2 taboo words or L1 neutral words (Gonzalez-Reigosa 1976, cited in Pavlenko 2005: 170). Bilinguals have stronger SCRs to L1 than to L2 emotional expressions, including taboo words, reprimands, and expressions of aversion or joy

(Harris et al. 2003, cited in Pavlenko 2005: 173). At the same time, speakers tend to rate L1 taboo words and swearwords as more emotional and forceful (Dewaele 2006; Dewaele 2004a, 2004b, and 2004c, cited in Pavlenko 2005: 170–172). Much as the authors discussed above have divergent responses to their emotional bond with L1 – some prefer to seek it out and others to avoid it – so the participants in Dewaele's studies sometimes prefer to swear in L1 because it is more intense, and other times favor L2 swearwords because of their relative emotional distance (Pavlenko 2005: 172). The emotional embodiment of L1 relative to L2 is perceived by most bilinguals, but its effects on linguistic and cultural practices are complex and diverse.

Pavlenko writes, "Taboo words are not an eccentric and quirky way to look at the interaction between language and emotions – rather, these words represent a unique intersection between the two realms, evoking a complex chain of feelings, affective associations, autobiographic memories, vivid imagery, and olfactory sensations" (Pavlenko 2005: 169). This complex web of human responses contributes to what Pavlenko describes as "the embodied and emotional nature of language that is taken for granted by monolingual speakers and continues to puzzle and delight bi- and multilinguals" (158). At the same time, Pavlenko warns against reading these findings as supporting a binary opposition between L1 and L2, or between primary and secondary language acquisition:

> Rather, [the framework] posits a language learning continuum where on the one end we have primary language acquisition – always an emotional and contextualized process – and on the other FL learning, typically a decontextualized process. In the middle, there is a grey area of L2 learning in a natural environment, where L2 users experience different levels of socialization and degrees of affective linguistic conditioning at different points in life (Pavlenko 2005: 156).

It seems that bilinguals can find themselves not only at various points on this continuum, but the continuum itself is also a dynamic process, a lived experience that does not remain in a balance throughout a bi- or multilingual's life. One's sense of language embodiment in L1 and L2 can shift and restructure, sometimes inadvertently, and sometimes in response to conscious effort. As their circumstances and practices change, people experience both L1 and L2 in new ways. Experiences that were first lived in L2 can become emotionally linked to L2, and not easily translated into L1.

Wierzbicka, who has written extensively about the bilingual's emotional experience (e.g. Wierzbicka 1998, 1999, 2004, 2007, 2008; Besemeres and Wierzbicka 2007; Harkins and Wierzbicka 1997), argues that in different languages, different emotions are being expressed by terms that, although they figure as each other's translations in dictionaries, are in fact untranslatable (Wierzbicka 2007). This is not just a lexical but a conceptual issue (Wierzbicka

2008): in different languages people categorize emotional experience according to different cultural scripts, "including different 'emotional scripts'" (Wierzbicka 2004: 98), and as a result, what one experiences in one language is not the same as in the other. Thus, the same event can be categorized according to different emotional scripts by speakers who do not share an L1. People may try to convey the emotional world they are experiencing through translating into their L2, but ultimately, Wierzbicka argues, such self-translation (Besemeres 2002) is never truly possible. She writes: "For bilingual people, living with two languages can mean indeed living in two different emotional worlds and also traveling back and forth between those two worlds. It can also mean living suspended between two worlds, frequently misinterpreting other people's feelings and intentions, and being misinterpreted oneself" (Wierzbicka 2004: 102).

Wierzbicka offers numerous examples of this experience from her own bilingual life. One is the Polish expression *gniewać się na kogoś*, which may be approximately translated as "to be angry at someone." Appealing to a close friend or family member *nie gniewaj się na mnie* "conveys something like 'I don't want you to feel bad feelings towards me' and it implies an underlying close relationship" (Wierzbicka 2004: 96). Wierzbicka stresses that the pragmatic meaning of this expression in Polish is that of a warm and affectionate move to restore mutual good feelings, which contrasts sharply with the potentially critical or accusatory English phrase *don't be angry.* In Wierzbicka's interpretation, the difference is linked to corresponding cultural scripts: the Polish one values strong feelings as revealing one's most authentic self (Besemeres 2006: 41), while the English/Anglo one emphasizes "cool reason" and self-control (Wierzbicka 2004: 97). Indeed, while the English word "cool" suggests admirable composure and a rational mind unclouded by emotionality, the Polish equivalent *chłodny* is pejorative, implying emotional distance and an "unpleasant lack of interpersonal warmth" (Wierzbicka 2004: 97). Another example is Wierzbicka's inability to talk emotionally about her baby granddaughter in English, because English lacks the diminutive forms such as Polish *rączka* "little hand," *nóżka* "little leg," *główka* "little head," and so on, which to her seem as the only natural way to refer to a little baby, conveying not just the sense of the baby's smallness, but also the speaker's gentle love and affection (Wierzbicka 2004, 2007). To Wierzbicka, English, her L2, does not express the feelings she experiences when she thinks about her granddaughter.

Other bi- and multilinguals also describe numerous untranslatable words and expressions that relate to emotion. Hoffman (1989) finds the Polish word *przyjaciółka* as not equivalent to its English translation "friend" (Hoffman 1989; Besemeres 2006: 38). Hoffman explains that the Polish word "has connotations of strong loyalty and attachment bordering on love" (Hoffman 1989: 148), whereas "friend" is used more liberally to describe those whom

Hoffman, thinking in Polish, would rather classify as "acquaintances." But in this case, the two languages prove for Hoffman to be non-equivalent, but both are valuable in their own ways, reflecting perhaps different cultural scripts surrounding friendship. She writes, "'Friend,' in English, is such a good-natured, easygoing sort of term, covering all kinds of territory" (148). It seems that the words *przyjaźń* and "friendship" emphasize different facets and intensities of human relationships, and invoke different kinds of emotional experience. Similarly, Besemeres (2006: 41–44) discusses poet Peter Skrzynecki's reflections on the Polish word *żal*, which stands for a culturally-specific feeling that could be variously translated as "grief," "sadness," "sorrow," or "regret," but does not correspond to any one of these words individually. *Żal* can involve a longing, as in for something from one's past or for a long-lost friend; it can also suggest a certain sadness at parting with something one is emotionally attached to, like a beloved place or a cherished object. It encompasses a range of intensities of feeling. Besemeres argues that for Skrzynecki, "*żal*'s untranslatability appears intuitive rather than analytical" and that "*żal* is not simply an emotion concept that is expressed somewhat differently in English" but rather "a category of emotion not recognized in English" (44). Elsewhere, she also discusses the notion of feeling *żal* towards another person: "the feeling that someone has towards a person they love, who they think has wronged them" (Besemeres 2006: 135). Such intuitive, almost physical sense of an emotion word's meaning and of its untranslatability resurfaces again and again in bilingual speakers' accounts.

This sense of untranslatability and the resulting frustration sometimes lead speakers to feel that they must choose between the two languages as if they were separate entities. For some, this choice feels very real and completely binary: accepting one language for certain situations implies either shutting off the other, or never quite feeling comfortable in the accepted language. Thus, Witcomb (2007) describes her experience of losing Portuguese following her family's move from Portugal, where her English-Australian parents had chosen to settle and start a family, to Australia. As a child, Witcomb lived in Portuguese: her father spoke only Portuguese to her, her mother spoke both Portuguese and English, but Portuguese was the dominant language of the home. All of Witcomb's friends were Portuguese, as was her school. However, the move to Australia signified a complete break with both Portugal and the Portuguese language. The Witcombs left Portugal due to political and economic instability, forced to give up a place that they had strongly identified with for years. This was particularly difficult for Witcomb's father, who responded by never again speaking Portuguese to his children. With the language, the family lost many of its intimate rituals, such as singing Portuguese songs together or the emotional expression the children had shared with their father (Witcomb 2007: 93–94). Witcomb switched entirely to English in all areas of her life, but the sense of loss that accompanied this switch persisted: "The emotional landscape I lost was also the ability to remember Portugal by talking about it in Portuguese. The place and the language used to discuss it or to be in it have now been broken apart" (94). At the same time, Witcomb cannot use Portuguese to express her adult self: "There is no getting away from the fact that I have been robbed of growing up in my first language. I think that the effect of that is a feeling of being territorially lost" (94).

Ye (2007) and Wong (2007) report similar feelings about the Chinese languages of their childhood, youth, and early adulthood (Shanghainese and Mandarin for Ye, Siyi and Cantonese for Wong) and English. In particular, they both describe Anglo-Australian cultural politeness norms expressed in English as incompatible with Chinese ones. For example, the Chinese distinction between *wairen* ("outsiders") and *zijiren* ("insiders" in the sense of family members) dictates that one should avoid formal expressions of politeness with *zijiren* because they create distance. Instead, family members and close friends are regarded as an extension of oneself (Wong 2007: 75) and it is expected that one will treat them with unmitigated directness. Similarly, it is not seen as necessary to overtly state one's feelings towards one another. Thus, Chinese families do not say "I love you" or "thank you" in the same way as English-speaking Anglo families do (Ye 2007: 60–65; Wong 2007: 74). On the other hand, Anglo values emphasize personal autonomy, and norms for politeness and respect require that family members use "please" and "thank you" with each other. Respect expressed in this way implies caring rather than distance.

As a result of these differences in cultural meaning, some bilinguals feel stuck or torn between two worlds that appear mutually exclusive. Wong complains: "I often find myself handicapped when it comes to the expression of my culture-specific emotions" (Wong 2007: 73), while Ye asserts: "Emotionally, I remain Chinese" and "English, though it has become my main language for communication, is just a shadow of my self" (Ye 2007: 59). Ye further describes Chinese emotion words as physically fused with herself: "simply part of my experience that is impossible to sever from 'me'" (64) and poignantly expresses her own take on L1 embodiment:

> The sounds of our mother tongue are like no other sounds. They are the first sounds coming from within ourselves, giving tangible forms to our thoughts and feelings, which put us in touch with the outside world and with the people around us. They are the sounds that are most dear to us. Of all the sounds that we can hear, they are the most meaningful to us. They are in fact internal to ourselves (Ye 2007: 66).

Wierzbicka's (2007, 2004) own account of her bilingual experience suggests an ongoing nostalgia for Polish and all the emotional meanings bound up with it, and its juxtaposition with English, which is often presented as its foil. Wierzbicka repeatedly invokes a Polish/English dichotomy, and presents it as parallel to a Polish/Anglo cultural one. She talks about the nonequivalence of Polish and English words, and links it to the incompatibility of Polish and English cultural scripts. In her reflections, the Polish language and script often appears romanticized, especially when Wierzbicka writes as a bilingual speaker rather than analyst. For example, she writes passionately about listening to Polish music, and focuses on religious and patriotic songs that invoke language as an iconic representation of nationality (Wierzbicka 2007: 109). She discusses the Polish word for "betray[ing] one's nation by ceasing to be, emotionally and linguistically, a part of it": *wynarodowić się* (110). At times, she even slips into essentializing Polish culture by treating it like an autonomous and coherent entity that "does" things (Holliday et al. 2004), for example: "Polish culture places a greater value on truth and sincerity in relations to others than on those other people's feelings" (Wierzbicka 2007: 105). This statement also suggests a belief in a greater objective sincerity of Polish speakers and culture: an essentialist sentiment to be sure, but one that may very well feel true to bilingual speakers of Polish as L1. Wierzbicka repeatedly refers to the contrast between the Anglo emphasis on one's interlocutors' negative face needs (Brown and Levinson 1987), such as validating their opinion and mitigating one's own, or acknowledging the advantages of something one dislikes in case the other person likes it, and "the emphasis in Polish culture . . . on an outpouring of *serdeczność*; that is, roughly, 'heartfelt warmth towards others'" (Wierzbicka 2007: 105). Especially throughout her personal account, Wierzbicka (2007) writes about Polish language, and by extension Polish culture and people, as warm, direct, and loving, in contrast to the cooler and more contrived English/Anglo language and norms. It has to be stressed that these are Wierzbicka's feelings and experiences, however, and as such they cannot be argued with. They are what many bilinguals feel and experience.[1]

Aside from the writers (e.g. Hoffman, Rodriguez, Kosinski, Ho, Sante, Alvarez) and linguists (e.g. Wierzbicka, Besemeres, Witcomb, Ye, and Wong) discussed above, the dichotomous experience of L1 and L2 surfaces among patients in psychotherapy, numerous studies of whom are reported by Pavlenko (2005). Most often, L1 has been found to bring up affect-laden memories, to trigger feelings and memories, and to raise anxiety and arousal, while L2 has been linked with emotional detachment (Pavlenko 2005: 160–161). Frequently, bilinguals exhibit emotional restraint in L2, while showing much more spontaneity in L1. They "performed distinct affective personae in their respective languages" (165). In some cases, therapists found a greater presentation of psychotic symptoms in bilingual psychiatric patients in one of

[1] Wierzbicka carries out a robust semantic analysis of the concept of *serdeczność*, which she argues is central to Polish culture, in Wierzbicka (1999).

their languages than in the other (Del Castillo 1970, cited in Pavlenko 2005: 166; Marcos 1973, cited in Pavlenko 2005: 165; Burck 2004: 316).

But, as I mentioned earlier, Pavlenko makes it very clear that much of the psychoanalytic and psychotherapeutic work suffers from "an essentialist view of a bilingual person with two languages, 'insulated from each other' . . . and maintained as two separate codes, each with its own lexical, syntactic, phonological and conceptual components" (Pavlenko 2005: 189). Pavlenko points out that such an approach does not recognize "the dynamic nature of the mental lexicon" or "the contextual nature of language learning," and overlooks the fact that L2 can be acquired through complex means at various points in one's life (189). Thus, bi- and multilinguals may experience their languages as more or less embodied and disembodied, but this does not mean that the languages are distinct entities or that intense emotional connections with L2 cannot be developed.

Rather, as demonstrated in previous chapters and in Chapter 5 in particular, multilinguals develop complex webs of attachments to the different components of their linguistic repertoires, which often come to form a fluid spectrum rather than a set of categories. The untranslatability of cultural meanings finds expression in code-switching and in hybrid varieties, which also become vehicles for multilingual speakers to explore a range of linguistic and cultural affiliations, and to construct and negotiate new identities and meanings.

The experience of embodied and disembodied words, of languages charged emotionally in different ways, and of emotion "feeling" different in each of them, has significant implications for an immigrant's project of reconstructing the self in the new environment, the host country. The dominant discourse in the United States demands assimilation which is to be proven by one's native-like proficiency in English, but how can one achieve such proficiency when English is felt as not belonging to oneself? How does one recognize and accept the English-speaking immigrant who is expressing emotion and thinking in unfamiliar, American ways – as one's own self? As Wierzbicka (2004, 2007, and 2008) and Besemeres (2002, 2006, and 2007) argue in their work, one is not necessarily the same person in each language. For many immigrants, moving into a life in L2 delivers a sense of frustration, loss, inadequate self-expression, of untranslatability of self, and thus of never being the same person in L2 as in L1. These feelings require negotiation and some type of resolution. The resolution requires giving oneself permission to own L2: Eva Hoffman's confusion in her new surroundings and her difficulty identifying with them, as well as her profound sense of loss and mourning for Poland and her former life in Polish seem to underlie her initial emotional rejection of English. Subsequently studying English literature up to graduate level and becoming an author writing in English in America allows her to accept

English as one of her languages, as well as to recognize herself as having a complex identity:

> When I think of myself in cultural categories – which I do perhaps too often – I know that I am a recognizable example of a species: a professional New York woman, and a member of a postwar interactional new class; somebody who feels at ease in the world, and is getting on with her career relatively well, and who is as fey and brave and capable and unsettled as many of the women here – one of a new breed, born of the jet age and the counterculture, and middle class ambitions and American grit (Hoffman 1989: 170).

Resolutions to the immigrant's emotional alienation from L2 necessitate a construction of a hybrid identity that not only brings together but combines and restructures two or more languages, and two or more sets of sociocultural and emotional meanings. Multilingual practices such as code-switching, hybrid languages, or crossing into and appropriating language varieties of other groups, emerge as creative responses to what may feel to speakers like an L1/L2 conflict. And there are, of course, those who never reach a resolution. For them, the sense of loss becomes permanent and the distinction between the meanings of L1 and those of L2 feels definite and profound (Pavlenko and Lantolf 2000).

The experience of loss and emotional alienation that comes with entering the domain of L2 is a painful one, and for most, the need to start living in L2 creates the need to reconstruct one's identity, not just socially but internally. In the next section, I will thus turn to the topic of identity: the challenges and the experience of locating, accepting, and presenting oneself in L2.

7.2 Identities in Flux

As we saw in the previous section, bilinguals typically report their experiences in L1 and L2 as not equivalent. Words appear untranslatable: although they may be listed as each other's glosses in a dictionary, they rarely overlap completely, especially if they are abstract or emotion words. Kayyal and Russell (2013) demonstrate in a study using translation and back translation as well as evaluation of facial expressions that out of twelve emotion words and their commonly used equivalents in English and Arabic, only one pair – *happiness/farah* – was judged as fully equivalent by English-Arabic bilinguals (the others were *sadness, anger, fear, interest, relaxation, embarrassment, disgust, contempt, surprise, perplexity*, and *hesitancy*, and their Arabic glosses). They conclude: "Evidence continues to mount that when we translate a word, we risk changing its meaning" (Kayyal and Russell 2013: 269).

The nonequivalence of emotion words across cultures has been argued for by many. According to psychologist William James, feelings are categorized based on "the introspective vocabulary of the seeker" – that is, one seeking to name an emotion – which depends on his or her language and culture (James 1890: 485; cited in Wierzbicka 1999: 31). Panayiotou (2004), in a study demonstrating bilinguals' different emotional reactions to the same story presented in either English or Greek, cites Searle (1995) to point out that "emotions are language dependent . . . as the raw or bodily experience of an emotion must be filtered through a cultural meaning-making system" (Panayiotou 2004: 125). Wierzbicka (1999) argues that interpretations of facial expressions are culture-specific and that terms used to describe these expressions in different languages do not in fact mean the same thing. She offers convincing evidence that the modern English word/concept *anger* cannot be expressed with a single equivalent term in many other languages, including Polish and early modern English (32). These arguments are supported by personal accounts given by bilingual writers, linguists and participants in various ethnographic studies, such as those cited in Section 7.1. In them, untranslatability extends beyond emotion words into a wider communicative territory. Words are imbued with complex meanings that often do not make sense outside their cultural context. When translated, swearwords lose their force (Dewaele 2007), idiomatic expressions become obscured, and jokes are no longer funny (Burck 2004, Hoffman 1989). Translations are only approximations, which is why in some cases we borrow the word along with the concept, as is the case with the German word/concept *angst* (Wierzbicka 1998, 1999).[2]

Taken together, this nonequivalence of language forms presents a challenge for the bilingual speaker. Unless a word, such as *angst*, has gained wide cultural currency as a borrowing, it cannot simply be used in its L1 form with monolingual speakers of L2. This is especially true in situations where L2 is the language of the culturally dominant majority. For immigrants to the United States, English is this L2 – they are expected to express themselves in it when interacting with English-speaking Americans, and attempts at explaining an untranslatable L1 concept may be met with awkward embarrassment, confusion, or even derision. For example, Eva Hoffman describes with poignant words her humiliation when she fails to translate an off-color Polish joke to her new teenage friends: " . . . as I hear my choked-up voice straining to assert itself, as I hear myself missing every beat and rhythm that would say 'funny' and 'punch line,' I feel a hot flush of embarrassment. I come to a lame ending. There's a silence. 'I suppose that's supposed to be funny,' somebody says. I recede into the car seat. Ah, the humiliation, the misery of failing to amuse!" (Hoffman 1989: 118). Hoffman's pain is inescapable: it will not disappear at the

[2] Even when borrowed, words denoting "foreign" concepts may be used differently in the host language, modified as it were by the cultural scripts current among the host language's speakers (Wierzbicka 1999: 123).

end of a foreign vacation or a university year abroad, as may be the case for tourists and exchange students. Immigrants are forced to express themselves and present their social selves in their L2 for the rest of their lives, as long as they choose to remain in their adopted country – and for most, especially refugees, that is not really a choice. Faced with the untranslatability of their L1, and the concurrent untranslatability of their L1 self – the self they have up until now come to know – as well as with the emotional distance from L2, the inability to "feel" it in the same visceral way as their L1, immigrants experience a traumatic rift and a sense of loss. The narrative of the loss of self is repeated time and again in immigrant accounts.

One aspect of this loss comes from being perceived in ways that do not match one's image of oneself, and the identity one is working to construct. Without fluency in L2, without access to its cultural meanings and ability to manipulate its nuances, one's success at constructing a social identity that others will understand and accept is compromised. Social construction of identity is by definition a *social* process: it is interactive and dialogic, with identities being continually negotiated between the subject performing them, and those that he or she interacts with (Baran 2013: 159). Identities emerge in and through interaction; they are continually produced through sociocultural practices, a central one of which is language (Bucholtz and Hall 2004; Burck 2004). The social situatedness of identities means that their definition depends on both the subject and his or her interactants; one's positioning with respect to others is achieved through an interactive process that depends on all the participants' actions, which is partly why identities are dynamic and not stable. Social identity requires validation from others, and language is a key resource for self-presentation. And thus, when their performance of self is misread or rejected, or cannot even be attempted because of limitations posed by their L2, immigrants may experience feelings of frustration, alienation, self-doubt, and loss. They may feel that they are forced into a "fake" role, or begin to question their own sense of self. This in turn may cause resentment towards the new surroundings, and towards the new language, which itself comes to be seen as fake, cold and constricting. Hoffman hints at these feelings as she describes watching herself morph from a witty, eloquent and light-hearted girl that she was in Poland, into a serious and demure Polish Canadian:

> I've never been prim before, but that's how I am seen by my new peers. I don't try to tell jokes too often, I don't know the slang, I have no cool repartee. I love language too much to maul its beats, and my pride is too quick to risk the incomprehension that greets such forays. I become a very serious young person, missing the registers of wit and irony in my speech, though my mind sees ironies everywhere . . .
>
> Perhaps the extra knot that strangles my voice is rage. I am enraged at the false persona I'm being stuffed into, as into some clumsy and overblown astronaut suit. I'm

enraged at my adolescent friends because they can't see through the guise, can't recognize the light-footed dancer I really am . . .

It will take years before I pick and choose, from the Babel of American language, the style of wit that fits. It will take years of practice before its nuances and patterns snap smartly into the synapses of my brain so they can generate verbal electricity (Hoffman 1989: 118–119).

The psychological trauma experienced by Hoffman because of her failure at self-translation produces shame and rage. Eventually, Hoffman is able to claim the English language and to use it to construct her social self in a way that works for her, but the process takes years. In the meantime, she feels that she is being "stuffed" into a "false persona." She does not recognize herself in others' perception of her.

Similar themes appear in Burck's (2004) interviews with people "living in more than one language" (314). Burck writes:

Experiences of inarticulacy in a second language also impacted profoundly on some individuals' constructions of themselves as speakers. Many individuals spoke of the difficulties they experienced with humour in their second languages, with the result that they became known and thought of themselves as lacking a sense of humour altogether, rather than being seen as an effect of being a second language speaker. Individuals mainly used metaphors of utilitarian articles for their second/subsequent language, in contrast with the notion of being inside one's first language. Images such as "ill-fitting shoes" and "pianos with keys missing" conjured up the insufficiencies of second languages (Burck 2004: 322).

Burck's interviewees include individuals living in Britain for whom English is not a first language, aged nineteen to fifty-eight, who had grown up in a range of countries in Europe, Africa, and Asia. Although their specific stories and experiences differ, most of them report a sense of greater intimacy linked with their L1, or different senses of subjectivity experienced in different languages, as in the following example: "You're, what you are, doesn't entirely overlap. When I was speaking German I was a slightly different person than when I was speaking English" (320). Another interviewee describes the difficulty with expressing emotion in L1 for the same reasons as discussed in the previous section: "I might be more intimate in certain things in English, because they would feel so uncomfortable. It's a foreign language . . . it's kind of artificial. In Polish it would be very disclosing . . . in English, it is this artificialness that the, the, the, that I've learned the meaning of the word, that gives me, you know, more of eh, um, gives me more courage to use it" (321). Burck suggests that because constructs of personhood and emotion are encoded differently in different languages, speakers are able to construct themselves in new ways when speaking and thinking in their L2, which explains why some bilinguals find that they can "express themselves more fully when released from constraints embedded in their first languages" (325). Such is the experience described by Kyoko Mori in her memoir *Polite Lies: On Being a Woman Caught between Two Cultures* (1997). Having moved to the United States as a young adult and settled in Green Bay, Wisconsin, Mori finds that in English she can construct and express herself as a confident and independent woman, without being bound by the traditional, submissive definitions of femininity that she feels are embedded in the Japanese language. She describes feeling confined and trapped in the complex system of deference and implicature that governs Japanese interactions:

> I don't like to go to Japan because I find it exhausting to speak Japanese all day, every day. What I am afraid of is the language, not the place. Even in Green Bay, when someone insists on speaking to me in Japanese, I clam up after a few words of general greetings, unable to go on . . . In Japanese conversations, the two speakers are almost never on equal footing: one is senior to the other in age, experience, or rank. Various levels of politeness and formality are required according to these differences: it is rude to be too familiar, but people are equally offended if you are too formal, sounding snobbish and untrusting. Gender is as important as rank. Men and women practically speak different languages . . . Until you can find the correct level of politeness, you can't go on with the conversation: you won't even be able to address the other person properly . . .
>
> Talking seems especially futile when I have to address a man in Japanese. Every word I say forces me to be elaborately polite, indirect, submissive, and unassertive. There is no way I can sound intelligent, clearheaded, or decisive. But if I did not speak a "proper" feminine language, I would sound stupid in another way – like someone who is uneducated, insensitive, and rude, and therefore cannot be taken seriously. I never speak Japanese with the Japanese man who teaches physics at the college where I teach English. We are colleagues, meant to be equals. The language I use should not automatically define me as second best (Mori 1997: 10–12).

Mori's feelings about the Japanese language do not mean that she is rejecting her connection to Japan. Her relationship with Japan and America is complex and bound up with her family relationships, her childhood memories, her marriage and divorce in America, as well as with her intellectual interests and her work as a writer and educator. Describing her plane coming in for landing in Japan, Mori is overcome with nostalgia when she sees the familiar landscape and muses, "*How could I have spent my adult life away from here? This is where I should have been all along,*" but quickly hears her "adult voice": "*Remember who you were*, it warns, *but don't forget who you are now*" (19; italics original). Mori's construction of self is an ongoing process of negotiation between her Japaneseness and her Americanness, and her two languages offer different possibilities for this negotiation because of the cultural scripts they encode (Wierzbicka 2004).

Mori, who is fluent in English, finds that English allows her more freedom than Japanese to construct her femininity on her own terms. In other cases, bilinguals find that presenting themselves as intelligent and capable is undermined by their L2, especially when their proficiency is limited or is perceived to be so due to their accents. Maulucci (2008) focuses on the experiences of a trainee science teacher, Elena, who immigrated to the US from the Dominican Republic at five years old, and is bilingual in Spanish and English. In her observations during her teaching practicum, Elena notes that students are *de facto* grouped in science classes according to their English proficiency, and those with lower proficiency struggle with expressing their ideas: "There were some students who would raise their hands and were eager to answer questions, but had trouble verbalizing the answer. They seemed to be rattling their brains for the right words" (Maulucci 2008: 32). Teachers, meanwhile, tended to underestimate the time and effort it takes to master not just English, but specifically *academic* English (32–33). In her own experience, Elena struggled with reading and writing in English throughout her school years, finding it difficult to prove her intelligence: "Being a smart person was a good thing in that class, so not knowing how to read well was a big issue for me in elementary school. I was always in the lowest reading group and I used to hate . . . reading out loud" (Maulucci 2008: 25). As a native speaker of Spanish, however, Elena expected herself to easily excel in a Spanish composition course she took in college. Instead, since her Spanish fluency was colloquial and not academic, she found herself working exceptionally hard to perform as well on compositions as her classmates who had been studying it formally as a foreign language. For Elena, validation of her intelligence comes when she is able to understand and write poetry better than anyone in her class, which also confirms her almost visceral sense of her L1: "Because poetry is sort of very unstructured, very much like, it's very idiomatic . . . And a lot of them were just like, 'I don't. I don't get this.' And I mean you don't, because there's a cultural aspect attached to it" (30).

Following Turner (2002) and Gee (1999), Maulucci argues for several "layers" of (psychological) identity: more stable or "core" aspects, and more fluid and contextually bounded ones (Maulucci 2008: 20). "Core identity" in this framework corresponds to "transsituational cognitions and feelings about who a person is" (Turner 2002: 101), for example such beliefs about the self as whether one is smart, competent, considerate, funny, or eloquent. As Turner explains, people have an emotional need for the recognition and validation of their core self by others, and "incongruence between presentations of self and the reactions of others" (Turner 2002: 103) can cause emotional distress. This theory of core identity contrasts with the poststructuralist view of identities as multiple, fluid, and emergent in social interaction. But, as Bucholtz and Hall (2004) persuasively argue, essentialist beliefs about identity do not disappear because scholars deconstruct them, and consequently such beliefs often inform individuals' own understandings of their subjectivities.[3] As we have seen, bilinguals sometimes acknowledge performing different selves in different languages, and other times express a loss of the "authentic" self when forced to live in L2. Thus, Elena in Maulucci's (2008) study believes herself to be smart and experiences distress when this self-assessment is not acknowledged by her teachers. She also believes herself to be a fluent Spanish speaker, so having to work very hard in her Spanish composition course upsets her. Similarly, Eva Hoffman believes herself to be witty and fun-loving, but instead sees herself as forced to appear prim and serious in English – an image she describes as a "false persona" (Hoffman 1989: 119). The sense of loss of identity that many immigrants report as they transition to their L2 life can be seen as distress over the inapplicability of hitherto constructed "core selves" to the new sociocultural and linguistic context. For many, this concept of the self is tightly bound up with language and culture. Thus, Wierzbicka (2007) takes issue with the idea, implied in Stuart Hall's influential discussion of identity (Hall 1992), that "there is, in [her] case too, no 'inherited identity,' no 'stable core of self'" (108). She recognizes that she makes choices and acts of identification in her daily life and that she has become culturally "partly 'Anglo,'" but adds: "At the same time, I believe that there is also in me, by necessity and by choice, a stable core of Polishness" (109).

Whether due to limited proficiency in L2, or to incongruent cultural scripts embedded in L2, the failure to effectively communicate one's own self-image to others is a painful experience for an immigrant struggling to acclimatize to an unfamiliar environment. For children and teenagers such as Eva Hoffman or Elena the crisis resulting from not having one's self-image validated magnifies the stresses of establishing one's sense of self already experienced in adolescence (Díaz-Lázaro 2002; Erikson 1968). For adults, meanwhile, it may be combined with a very real loss of their former social or professional role, as many face a demotion in social status post-migration. Tollefson (1991) describes the processing centers in the Philippines and Thailand, where refugees from Vietnam, Laos, and Cambodia are prepared for transfer to the United States. In 1989, these centers sent as many as 3000 refugees per month on to the US (Tollefson 1991: 108). Tollefson points out that the ESL classes at the processing centers, as well as those funded by the federal government once the refugees arrive in the US, focus on preparation for the most entry-level jobs,

[3] Crucially, describing individuals as believing themselves to have certain traits that together constitute a "core identity," and arguing that these beliefs have emotional consequences, does not presuppose the Cartesian concept of an innate identity that inheres in the individual and unfolds throughout his or her life without change. Indeed, it does not even presuppose that the individuals who see themselves as having a core identity assume it to be unchanging. Conversely, adopting the post-structuralist perspective whereby identities are fluid and emergent in social interaction does not require one to disqualify individuals' own beliefs about their identities as very real *for them*.

regardless of the refugee's qualifications. Doctors, teachers, and engineers are expected to, and do, work as cleaners, cooks, or factory workers. The United States does not recognize many foreign degrees, and the exams required to obtain an American license in one's field demand both time to study, and a high proficiency in English. While Tollefson's work describes the situation in the 1980s, not much has changed in subsequent decades. Currently, refugee assistance agencies and non-profits also emphasize the refugees' self-sufficiency as the most immediate goal, even though this typically means low-skill jobs with low pay and long hours, and a near impossibility of achieving the goal of working in one's learned profession. In my collaboration with one of these agencies, Church World Service (CWS), in the service-learning course I teach every year, I have found that newly arrived refugees are consistently reminded that they must immediately accept any available work. My students who have visited and tutored refugee families in Durham, North Carolina, have described the distress and disillusionment of educated professionals who realize that life in America will not offer them the opportunity to continue their studies or advance in their careers. Crucially, organizations such as CWS are funded by the federal government and are therefore constrained in what they can offer refugees by federal immigration policy.

The loss of professional identity and concomitant fall in prestige of one's social status is often accepted as a sacrifice for one's children's future, or as a price paid for refuge from oppression or war, but it is inevitably painful and traumatizing. For some, such as teachers or newscasters, speaking English as L2 is an explicit obstacle to continuing or advancing in their profession. A Filipina immigrant, born in Manila in 1940, who became a mathematics teacher in an American high school near San Diego after working in Peace Corps, has this to say about Asian teachers in America:

> For the Asians, here is where they have difficulty getting a job: their accent . . . I think the minority teachers suffer most in the high schools. In the elementary schools, the students are still children. They think the accent is cute, and they have the patience for that. In the high school, the students give the minority teachers the worst times. They make fun of their accent. Many are not tolerant or understanding (Espiritu 1995: 102).

The difficulties faced by immigrant employees in various fields because of their non-American accents were discussed in detail in Chapter 4. As we have seen, not only may they experience self-doubt, embarrassment, and frustration because of their own perceived shortcomings in English, or because of the mismatch between their self-image and Anglo-American cultural scripts available to express it, but they also lose the ability to perform their professional role because of how their English is judged.

Burck (2004) succinctly sums up the complex challenges encountered in multilingual negotiations of identity: "Different languages speak us differently"

(Burck 2004: 323). She then outlines the different possible outcomes for speakers who live in two languages: those who live in what she terms "doubleness," and those who establish hybrid identities. Among her interviewees, the former talked about double lived and double selves, such as Angela who explains, "And you live in no man's land, especially language-wise. You're neither one nor the other. And it's quite, it's quite, and in childhood, it's quite an isolating factor in your life. Um. You have this dual personality" (Burck 2004: 330). The latter, meanwhile, found ways to accept and grow their multiple selves: "When individuals 'owned' their sense of multiplicity, despite inherent contradictions, they were more able to find ways to use their different perspectives" (Burck 2004: 331).

Some dualities or "doublenesses" are unresolvable: the Vietnamese refugee engineer will probably never advance past assembly line in America, and that realization is certainly difficult if not impossible to embrace. He or she will likely never have the opportunity to develop English skills commensurate with his or her intelligence and education. In these cases, we must remember, the immigrant has little choice or freedom in reconstructing his or her identity. At other times, even given greater opportunities to advance in the post-migration context, embracing L2 and one's self as expressed in L2 may be emotionally difficult because the old, L1 self cannot be successfully translated. Psychologist Olivia Espín makes the following observation based on her experience researching and counseling immigrant women: "An immigrant's resistance to language learning may be an expression of a desire for self-preservation. Entering the world of a new language may pose a threat to the individual's sense of identity" (Espín 1999: 135). This seems to be the case with young Eva Hoffman, who at first rebels against the new person she is forced to become in Canada, and cannot establish a visceral connection with English. But Espín also points out that "[c]onversely, learning a new language provides the immigrant with the opportunity to 'create a new self'" (Espín 1999: 135). This new self does not have to be seen as separate from the old self, although sometimes this may be the case. Rather, it is possible to blend the L1 and L2 identities through what Burck (2004) calls "owning" one's "sense of multiplicity" (Burck 2004: 331). To return once more to Eva Hoffman's example, it is once she chooses to "own" English, to study in it and write in it, that she is eventually able to construct a blended, hybrid self. The process of constructing the new self that engages with and owns the new language is analyzed, based on first-person immigrant narratives, by Pavlenko and Lantolf (2000), and will be returned to in the final section of this chapter.

7.3 Gender and Sexuality in Immigrant Contexts

Becoming American is not an ethnic transition accomplished separately from other dimensions of one's identity. Gender and sexuality, which as identity categories are salient in every society yet very much culture-specific, stand out as especially important in immigrant identity (re)formation. It is nearly impossible to read an immigrant memoir without encountering references to gender issues, from Maxine Hong Kingston's book title *The Woman Warrior*, to Eva Hoffman's description of her introduction to American make-up and brow-plucking, to Kyoko Mori's conflicted feelings about who she is supposed to be as a Japanese woman living in America in *Polite Lies*.[4] Gender and sexuality have emerged as recurring themes throughout this book because of their rich intersection of with other aspects of immigrant identities: the Sikh turbans are an explicitly masculine ethnic and religious marker (Klein 2009; see Section 3.2), Eddie Huang borrows from AAVE to construct a hybrid masculine self (Huang 2013, see Section 3.3), Latina girls construct their femininities in reference to locally meaningful gender norms that span the spectrum from obedient daughters to gang members (Mendoza-Denton 1997, 2008; Dietrich 1998; see Section 2.4), and several examples of meaning-negotiation through language choice involve the mother-daughter relationship (Williams 2005 in Section 5.1; Wierzbicka 2007 in Section 7.2). In this section, however, I will focus specifically on gender and sexual identities in the context of the immigrant experience, on how they are mediated through language, and on their construction through competing discourses and linguistic practices. I aim to challenge the frequently encountered assumption that national origin or ethnic background figure as primary identity categories through which immigrants define themselves, and to show that the linguistic choices they make are not just responses to their immigrant status and to the pressure to "assimilate," but rather strategic moves in the negotiation of a multiplicity of subject positions as these emerge in immigrant contexts.

A perfect illustration of this point is Kyoko Mori's experience with politeness and femininity in Japanese discourse that I discussed in the previous section. Mori makes a choice not to speak Japanese in the United States, not even with her Japanese colleague at the university, but her language choice is not motivated by national identification, desire to assimilate, or alienation from her homeland – in other words, it is not rooted in strictly ethnolinguistic concerns. Rather, Mori finds that English gives her more opportunity to construct her identity as a woman without adhering to gender norms and hierarchies implicit in Japanese discourse structure. This preference affects her relationship with Japan, which she has fond feelings about, but does not like to visit because she finds it "exhausting to speak Japanese all day, every day" (Mori 1997: 10). She adds, as if to emphasize this apparent mental separation between her homeland and her native language, "What I am afraid of is the language, not the place" (10). Like Mori, many immigrants find that their

[4] Although, as Pavlenko (2001) notes, this is mostly true of women's rather than men's memoirs.

language choices, practices, and preferences are not solely outcomes of feelings about ethnicity or nationality, even though they become available, possible, and relevant because of the immigrant experience. For Mori, the choice between Japanese and English is linked to her feelings about her gender identity as related to other social roles, although this choice is made possible in part because she is an immigrant.

Gender ideologies can also become deeply embroiled in the construction of ethnic-American identities at the level of group or political movements. At the turn of the twentieth century, Norwegian American activists, who portrayed their immigrant group as the standard bearers for the ideals of progress and democracy (see Section 1.2), developed a discourse in which claiming Norwegian ethnicity entailed a duty to support women's suffrage (Peterson 2011). As Peterson explains, "[b]etween 1901 and 1913, Norwegian women won a series of legislative victories, including the universal right to vote" (Peterson 2011: 5), which bolstered Norwegian American women's organizations' assertions both that Norway was intrinsically a nation of progressive-minded people, and that women's equality was a fundamental feature of this progress. As a logical extension of the argument that Norwegian Americans had the duty to promote their progressive ideals in America, groups such as the editors of the Norwegian-language immigrant journal *Kvinden og Hjemmet* (*The Scandinavian Woman and Home*) directly linked Norwegian American identity with feminism (Peterson 2011: 9). The president of the Scandinavian Woman's Suffrage Association in Minneapolis, Nanny Mattson Jaeger, described her organization's primary goal as "inject[ing] 'a little suffrage spice in to the melting pot'" (cited in Peterson 2011: 12). This and other groups worked to promote the cause of women's enfranchisement among Scandinavian American men, women, and legislators, insisting that their support and fight for it constituted an "ethnic duty" (12). The circulation of this discourse in the Norwegian American and broader Scandinavian American community not only contributed to the debate over gender roles and norms in the United States, but also created a particular context within which Scandinavian American women had to negotiate their own gender identities.

Language and the Experience of Sexuality

As we have seen thus far in this chapter, language is intimately bound up with the experience of emotion, of self, and of relationships. Olivia Espín's (1999) collection of interviews with immigrant women in the United States, which she analyzes from her disciplinary perspective as a psychologist, reveals that moving between L1 and L2 can allow for new ways of experiencing sexuality and sex itself, as well as open the possibilities of testing new sexual choices and exploring one's sexual orientation. Not surprisingly, given our discussion in

Section 7.1, Espín finds that for most of her interviewees, the first language remains most closely bound up with intense emotion. Consequently, some women find it more tender and joyful to experience sexual relationships in their L1, but for others, sex in L1 feels like a taboo, whereas English allows them to be freer. Thus for example Cecilia, a sixty-year-old Puerto Rican who came to the US at age sixteen, and who following the dissolution of a heterosexual marriage has been involved in lesbian relationships, appreciates it when her partners try to speak Spanish with her, but her feelings are conflicted:

> [W]henever she uses words or expressions in Spanish, it touches me deeply; the intensity increases. Spanish carries a lot of feeling. But it also carries shame. Sex words in Spanish are dirty; talking about parts of the body in Spanish feels shameful. It is like I have Spanish encapsulated in some part of me; I have "put away" words and feelings in Spanish. But because Spanish carries all this feeling, it is liberating to use Spanish; it is like a sexual eye-opener to use Spanish but it also gives me an insight on how much shame I carry in Spanish (Espín 1999: 88).

A clearer sentiment comes from another Puerto Rican, fifty-year-old Lorena, who left Puerto Rico at age thirty and also identifies as a lesbian. Lorena believes that her sexual orientation can only find full expression in English:

> I can be out in English but not in Spanish. When the plane lands in Puerto Rico it is as if I "shut down" and do not become a lesbian again until I come back to the US. It took me forever to say certain words in English. It is still impossible to say them in Spanish . . . It is not that I think that English is "liberating" or that people are so "free" in this country. It is just that lesbianism is more visible here . . . and, besides, English is much less charged for me, not only about sexuality but about practically anything emotional (Espín 1999: 78).

Many other women also said they prefer to explore and experience their sexuality in English rather than in their L1. Cindy, whose family emigrated from Taiwan when she was two years old, associates speaking Chinese with her parents and therefore avoids sexual relationships with Chinese-speaking partners (Espín 1999: 80). Thai Australian Aurelia, who has lived in the US for ten years, feels that in Thai, she can speak more affectionately and build more trust with her partner, but tellingly, for her, Thai is a second language while English is the first. But others expressed opposite feelings. Cuban immigrant Maritza, after living in the US for two decades, continues to date only Spanish speakers because she "cannot make love in English" (Espín 1999: 76). Peruvian immigrant Cornelia prefers speaking about sex in Spanish than in English, which may be because she never discussed this topic with her family, and instead "learned about sex in Perú 'in the street, from strangers'" (Espín 1999: 109), and as a result did not internalize Spanish vocabulary surrounding sex as shameful and taboo. At the same time, however, Maritza believes that she can be more open with her sexuality in America because of its more liberal gender norms. This view is echoed by thirty-three-year-old Noriko, who immigrated to the US from Japan to pursue college education. Noriko discusses the non-equivalence of emotional expressions such as "I love you" in English and in Japanese, and also observes that as a professional woman, she feels more freedom and can be herself more readily in the United States than in Japan.

Gender Roles and Performances

Gender norms are a site of conflict and struggle for immigrant girls and women, as we saw on the example of Kyoko Mori. But Mori is an adult naturalized US citizen, a published writer and a professor of creative writing, and a single woman living on her own, with her own professional and social life, supporting herself financially. She is in the fortunate position of having the relative freedom to choose her identifications with gender norms, and to announce these choices through her linguistic moves. For others, however, the freedom to make such choices may be more constrained because of their stronger integration within their ethnic communities, which is motivated by valuable kinship and friendship ties sustained in these communities, and by dependence – economic, emotional, and practical – on relatives and friends, as is common in dense and multiplex social networks. Decena et al. (2006) point out that among Dominican immigrants, certain traditional gender roles prevail in part because their transnational networks are older, more established, and denser as compared to some others: "After migration, the relatively denser structure of existing networks for Dominicans offered opportunities for women [to migrate] while exerting greater force in the retention of traditional household dynamics" (Decena et al. 2006: 44). Similarly, in Zentella's (1997) study of Puerto Ricans living on one block (*el bloque*) in New York City, which I discussed in earlier chapters, traditional gender norms structure the lives of young boys and girls, including their respective language practices. These norms, which derive from the traditional cultural norms in Puerto Rico, are maintained post-immigration because they can be reinforced by multiple participants in the dense, multiplex network of *el bloque*. Zentella (1997: 51–55) observed that girls were expected to stay at home helping their mothers with household chores and looking after younger children, they were charged with running errands to local shops and attending traditional religious services, and they spent significant amounts of time in the company of older Spanish-dominant women. Boys, on the other hand, had few such expectations placed on them and enjoyed greater freedom to venture outside the house and *el bloque*. As a result, the girls were exposed to more Spanish than boys and became more fluent speakers.

Traditional ideologies of gender sometimes conflict with the reinvention of gender identities that takes place in immigrant contexts, leading to contradictory messages being conveyed to young immigrant women by their families, and especially by female relatives. Ayala (2006) writes about Latina mother-daughter relationships in which the mothers simultaneously impress upon their daughters the importance of self-reliance and independence from men, and actively police their sexuality to ensure that the daughters do not forfeit their chance for independence by becoming sexually active and pregnant. Independence from men requires economic self-sufficiency, which in turn becomes hard to achieve for a very young mother. Because of these factors, mothers of young women who encourage independence also seek to control and neutralize their daughters' sexuality. But, from the daughters' point of view in particular, the mothers' tactic is contradictory: the independence that they encourage does not seem to extend to control over one's own body.

It is common to find contradictions among immigrants' stated views, the gender ideologies that are reproduced in immigrant discourses, and the realities of immigrant lives, even if these contradictions may be masked by the prevailing stereotypical representations of sending countries as uniformly backward, patriarchal, and oppressive, and of the United States as a haven for immigrant women. Decena et al. (2006) show that many Latin American immigrants living in and around New York City believe that moving to the United States results in changes in gender roles and expectations that benefit women. Their interviewees stated that women claimed greater freedoms due to their financial contribution to the household, exposure to America's more liberal gender norms, and legal frameworks supposedly favorable to women. Women's wage-earning capacity was seen as causing them to expect greater participation in the domestic sphere from men, who reported feeling pressured to comply because of what they perceived as pro-woman American society. One male interviewee asserted that post-immigration, "[the man] becomes submissive to women. At least one obeys. The woman says . . . 'It's your turn to take care of the kids, cook for them, or take them to school.' You are at the same level as a woman. Since the law is in her favor, that changes a person a lot from being a *machista* to being a little submissive" (Decena et al. 2006: 35). As the authors point out, however, the changes in household dynamics do not result from any transformation in men's attitudes, as exemplified by many statements, including one by a husband whose wife quoted his frequent admonition: "Here you and I are at the same level. You think you are worth a lot, but wait until we get back to Mexico" (39).

The threatening tone of that last statement, and the mention of US law in the previous quote, illustrate another theme that emerged in the narratives, namely, that "[m]ale participants linked women's independence and autonomy after migration to legal protections from domestic violence" (41). In a somewhat inflated assessment of the American justice system, a Mexican man explains: "Women are freer here. Here is where woman also adopts the same rights as man, of equals, we are worth the same; or she is worth more. Because the laws protect a woman. A man cannot beat a woman, cannot yell at her, cannot tell her do not do this or do not do that because he will already be in trouble with the law. They (women) are always treated well. They have better standards than men so then, yes, she is better off' (41). However, both the letter of the law and its application are not nearly as supportive of women – and especially of immigrant women – as the men interviewed by Decena and his colleagues believe (cf. Holmquist 2016)[5]. Similarly, the reality of gender dynamics in the home is much more complex than portrayed by the men. Some men continue to refuse to contribute to household chores post-immigration, viewing those as "women's work." Others preempt the issue altogether by leaving their spouses behind in their home countries (Decena et al. 2006: 43). But the men's "perceived invalidation of immigrant masculinities" (43) is also complicated by their subordinate positioning with respect to Anglo-American men, who may be potential employers or representatives of law enforcement (42). Latino men's narratives of passivity and submissiveness post-immigration are products of identity negotiations that extend beyond their relationships with wives or other Latina women. Meanwhile, both men and women tend to police immigrant women's appearance and sexuality according to traditional norms, as evident in the numerous criticisms of both American women's public self-presentation, and of those Latina women who adopt styles of dress, talk, or behavior that are perceived as "American" and thus "too free" (Decena et al. 2006).

Negotiations of gender identity present a challenge for immigrants not just because gender norms in their home countries may conflict with those encountered in the United States – both in the immigrant communities and in wider society – but, crucially, also because gender is discursively constructed, and as such it may not be possible to construct it in the same ways in different languages. Language, as we have seen, is intimately linked to lived experience. In L2 contexts, "the language of the learner becomes an important tool for establishing one's social identity, one's self, in the changing reality within which second language speakers need to function" (Teutsch-Dwyer 2001: 178).

Pavlenko (2001) points out that "the range of subjectivities validated within each community, subculture, or culture is ultimately limited – even though constantly negotiated and reconstituted" (Pavlenko 2001: 135). These subjectivities, meanwhile, are produced and enacted through discourse/language.

[5] Decena et al. (2006) point out that for undocumented immigrants, legal protection is minimal, as women avoid reporting domestic violence because of fear of deportation of either themselves or their partners.

An examination of L2-speakers' narratives leads Pavlenko to conclude that "linguistic devices contribute to changes in gender performance: from changes in pitch and voice quality . . . to modifications of the lexicon, speech acts, and discursive repertoires" (141). We already discussed Kyoko Mori's realization that she cannot perform her identity as an independent, strong, intellectual woman in Japanese as successfully as she can in English. Pavlenko discusses numerous other examples: Richard Watson's failure at learning French because of an internalized association between the sounds of French and effeminate masculinity (147–148); Karen Ogulnick's choice between enacting female subordination and falling short of speaking Japanese "authentically" – as well as her realization that women are objectified through language also in English (146–147); Jerzy Kosinski's bafflement at suddenly being unable to flirt and enact his "eloquent seducer" persona in English in the United States (153); Richard Rodriguez' loss of "real macho Mexican" characteristics upon being socialized into English and dedicating himself to the study of literature (163). Maxine Hong Kingston, similarly, tells the story of reconstructing her gender identity according to American norms – and missing the mark somehow, so that instead she ended up reproducing the common stereotype of the quiet Asian girl: "Normal Chinese women's voices are strong and bossy. We American-Chinese girls had to whisper to make ourselves American-feminine. Apparently we whispered even more softly than the Americans . . . . We invented an American-feminine speaking personality" (Kingston 1989 [1975]: 200, cited in Pavlenko 2001: 150).

The effects of these struggles vary. For some, inhabiting a gendered subjectivity that is enacted in the second language never feels right, and as a result they feel perpetually conflicted, or unable/unwilling to embrace the new language (Pavlenko 2001; Espín 1999). For others, the opposite happens: they reinvent themselves through L2, but "as a result of second language socialization in adulthood, [their] performance of gender in the first language may no longer be seen as authentic" (Pavlenko 2001: 163). And sometimes the reconstituted gender identities emerge as complex new hybrids that "were previously untellable in either language" (143), but can be formed through hybrid language practices: code-switching, language mixtures, translanguaging.

Crucially, reformations of gender identity are complicated by other intersecting discourses, such as those of race and ethnicity. Pavlenko points out that European American immigrants do not face the same challenges in their process of L2 gender socialization as those from non-white backgrounds (Pavlenko 2001: 162). On one hand, the mainstream gender ideologies available to immigrants as "examples" of American norms continue to present predominantly white, non-diverse images. On the other hand, gender and sexuality are racialized while race is sexualized according to circulating race/

gender ideologies in America. An example of this is the stereotype of the quiet Asian female, mentioned above. Similarly, black and Latina sexualities are commonly represented according to the exoticizing white gaze. For instance, Chavez (2008) describes an unfortunate billboard ad for Mexican Tecate beer that appeared in Albuquerque, New Mexico, on Cinco de Mayo 2004. The ad, placed by the company Labatt USA that imports the beer, featured an ice-cold beer bottle with the caption: "Finally, a cold Latina," clearly referring to the stereotype of Latin American women as hypersexual ("hot"), as well as metaphorically equating them with objects for consumption (in this case, beer) (Chavez 2008: 75).

Gloria Anzaldúa's (2012 [1987]) book *Borderlands/La Frontera: The New Mestiza* explores the complexity of race/gender/sexuality in the lives of those who straddle the problematic categories of "immigrant" and "American." Anzaldúa's notion of the "borderlands" encompasses the ambiguities and fluidity of being both Mexican and American, of speaking Spanish and accented English but descending from generations of US citizens dating back to 1848, and of identifying as female, independent, and lesbian both in a rigidly patriarchal Mexican community and in the larger American society that may be more open to feminists and lesbians, but that stereotypically exoticizes Latina women. In the rest of this section, I turn to this intersectionality of immigrant experiences – to the (re)formation of identities in the borderlands.

Multisexual Spaces

In her article about Sudanese refugee women's reconstruction of their post-migration identities through and around language learning, Warriner (2007) argues: " . . . language teaching and learning cannot be examined as isolated, neutral, or individual processes. Instead, the teaching (and learning) of a language – particularly a language of power, prestige, and wider communication like English – is substantially influenced by a variety of cultural, social, economic, and political factors and contexts" (347). Indeed, the women in Warriner's study internalized and articulated the dominant discourses surrounding English language learning in the United States – that knowing English will open educational and employment opportunities, allow for personal growth, and for greater participation in American society – despite the fact that their personal experiences contradicted these expectations (e.g. learning English did not translate into better jobs), and that the quality of English-learning contexts available to them was "not prioritized because the learners themselves are members of marginalized groups" (Warriner 2007: 350; cf. Tollefson 1991). Warriner describes one case in which a refugee invokes English-learning ideologies to assert herself, in English, in front of her prospective supervisor, by unapologetically explaining her circumstance as a mother of young children and someone who intends to make time for studying English, and negotiating the conditions of her employment on this basis (Warriner 2007: 354). But ultimately, Warriner argues that ESL education for immigrants from historically marginalized backgrounds, while propagating the ideology of English as a gateway to social mobility in tandem with the ideology of personal independence and economic self-reliance, in fact channels these immigrants into dead-end, low-skill jobs where little further English learning is likely to happen (cf. Tollefson 1991). This example illustrates how the adult ESL classroom becomes "a site of cultural politics" (Pennycook 1998, cited in Warriner 2007: 356).

The cultural politics enacted and negotiated in the ESL classroom involve aspects of identity and social practice that have hitherto been rendered invisible in ESL education, specifically, sexual identities and orientations. ESL students constitute social groups that are multilingual, transcultural, as well as multisexual (Nelson 2006: 4). For this reason, Nelson (2006) argues, researchers ought to think "of education settings as multisexual spaces" and to acknowledge "that sociosexual meanings infuse language, social interactions, and public discourse (which crisscross national borders and linguistic contact zones)" (4). Such a perspective would hopefully translate into greater awareness of the diversity of sexual identities in the ESL classroom. At present, sexual minority students must negotiate complex maneuvers as they perform and language their identities in their English classes. As Nelson accurately observes, "classroom cohorts and curricula tend to be constructed as domains in which straight people are interacting exclusively with other straight people" (Nelson 2006: 3). Not only are gay and lesbian topics either excluded or treated as external to the student group, but many activities implicitly assume that all the students in the classroom are straight.

For example, Nelson (2010) describes an ESL class she observed in which the topic *lesbian/gay culture*, chosen by the students, was approached by the teacher through discussion questions such as "Do you have friends, know people, or know about people who are gay? If yes . . . How are they different from you?," which presuppose that none of the students themselves are gay or lesbian (Nelson 2010: 442). Pablo, a gay ESL student from Mexico whose case is the subject of Nelson's (2010) article, found himself in a classroom dominated by topics such as marriage and family (e.g. "Do you want to get married? Why or why not?"), in which he could not engage without resorting to coded messages (e.g. "No, because I don't wanna share anything"). Nelson observes: "there is a problem if classroom discourse and curricula focus exclusively on straight social conventions and routinely and unquestioningly presume that all students have, or hope to have, heterosexual relationships" (Nelson 2010: 452–453). She also reports cases where teachers silence students who bring up gay and lesbian themes by redirecting class discussion, ignore discriminatory comments about gays and lesbians made by students, and in some language schools are even expressly prohibited from discussing LGBTQ subject matter in class.

Yet to immigrants such as Pablo, sexuality is at the core of who they are as immigrant Americans. Pablo came to the Unites States in order to live freely as a gay man, which was impossible in his native Mexico without fear for his safety. He is, therefore, a sexual migrant, a category defined as "those migrants seeking 'greater sexual equality and rights,' or at least some distance from sexuality-related discrimination or oppression" (Nelson 2010: 446, citing Carrillo 2004: 59). Pablo's express purpose for learning English is to be able to participate actively in the American gay community: "He considered migration a pathway to gay liberation, and English the passport to a cosmopolitan gay life" (Nelson 2010: 458). At the same time, Pablo's socialization as a gay man in Mexico was specific to his locality; for example, it did not feature such practices as the verbal act of coming out or the explicit self-identification as gay. Pablo has to "learn how to be gay" (Nelson 2010: 459) in America, in and through English. Typical ESL classrooms, however, do not provide an environment that would encourage and facilitate this process. Although they are multisexual spaces, their structure erases non-normative sexualities. And, in addition to sidelining the second-language learning and socialization needs of LGBTQ students, this represents a missed opportunity for engaging all immigrant students in a discussion about "changing discourse conventions associated with a changing social institution like marriage" (Nelson 2010: 457), and with non-normative sexual identities and relationships.

Immigrants such as Pablo, furthermore, negotiate their identities in the borderlands (Anzaldúa 2012): the ideological sites and spaces where gender relations are produced through unfamiliar discourses and a new language, where sexuality is enacted through practices and codes that escape classifications transferred from L1 contexts, and which are characterized by the intersectionality of race, gender, sexuality, and language. The performance of identity in the borderlands cannot proceed according to a fixed, predetermined script. Anzaldúa, herself a Chicana lesbian activist and writer, describes this complex and conflicted experience especially vividly in the following passage:

> For the lesbian of color, the ultimate rebellion she can make against her native culture is through her sexual behavior. She goes against two moral prohibitions: sexuality and homosexuality. Being lesbian and raised Catholic, indoctrinated as straight, I *made the choice to be queer* (for some it is genetically inherent). It's an interesting path, one that continually slips in and out of the white, the Catholic, the Mexican, the indigenous, the instincts. In and out of my head. It makes for *loquería*, the crazies. It is a path of knowledge – one of knowing (and of learning) the history of oppression of our *raza*. It is a way of balancing, of mitigating duality (Anzaldúa 2012: 41; emphasis original).

Decena (2011) similarly describes the lives of gay Dominican immigrant men in New York that are negotiated in what Anzaldúa calls the "borderlands." Although they migrate from a more sexually conservative to an ostensibly more liberal society, they remain connected to and frequently supported by the transnational Dominican networks. Their sexual identities and relationships are often expressed "tacitly," in ways that account for their ongoing participation in the Dominican American community.

Intersectionality of Experience

The concepts of multisexual spaces and borderlands assume the fluidity and intersectionality of identities, even as various institutions that interact with immigrants – the federal and state governments, schools, ESL programs – impose normative, frequently rigid or dichotomous classifications on immigrant groups. We already saw that ESL classrooms marginalize LGBTQ students because they operate on the implicit presumption that LGBTQ identities and themes are not relevant in ESL contexts. Similarly, immigrants are divided up into documented or undocumented, white or non-white, coming from specific national backgrounds, and gay or straight. These categories are made to appear discrete and well defined, and are not usually treated as if they had anything to do with each other. Yet, for gay and lesbian immigrants, they are always intersecting, mutually constitutive, and fluid. Some aspects of immigrant identities may be foregrounded at one time but recede at another.

This point is well illustrated in Viteri's (2014) discussion of the Ecuadorian LGBTQ community in New York City, whose members' "life strategies and identity formations" (121) disrupt the dominant narratives of migration that emphasize heteronormativity and identification with the sending and receiving countries. For the self-identified gay men that Viteri interviewed, the primary reason for migration was finding a place where, as one of them put it, "he could be free and do whatever he wanted" in terms of his sexual identity and relationships (125). The men tended to identify primarily as gay and only second as Ecuadorian, while distancing themselves from the category of "immigrant" and its implied racial, linguistic, and socioeconomic associations. They were all undocumented, but their status derived from overstaying their visas rather than the stereotypical crossing of the border. Viteri's (2014) case study of Renato further complicates the stereotypical image of the undocumented Latino immigrant because Renato owns an apartment in an upscale building in Manhattan and enjoys a high standard of living, in addition to being able to "pass" as white due to his physical appearance. The apartment, crucially, is the result of a long-term relationship with a married man. As Viteri explains, "In the case of Ecuadorians who self-identify as gay, the queer versus ethnic networks translate into groups not necessarily marked by ethnicity and/or place of origin, but by sexual identity which quickly moved them from the enclaves of Ecuadorians and Latinos towards the Manhattan neighborhoods that are not only 'whiter' but have more economic as well as social capital" (Viteri 2014: 122). Since Renato can also be read as white, but speaks with a foreign accent, his acquaintances question his Latin American identity: "You don't look Ecuadorian. You look Russian" (126). Perhaps because he has integrated himself into LGBTQ networks in New York City, Renato does not experience discrimination because of his sexuality, but he claims to have faced discrimination "for having an accent and for being from Latin America" (126), presumably both within and outside the gay community. Yet at the same time, the ability to pass as European accelerates Renato's access to middle class and upper class social circles, which are already more open to him, through his gay relationships, than the traditional networks within his ethnic community. Yet Renato's gay self-identification does not fit clearly delineated mainstream categories, either, because he reports having had relationships with women.

The case of Ecuadorian gay men in New York illustrates the point that "[q]ueer migrants often challenge tidy tales of assimilation that frequently make up the popular imaginaire of migratory journeys to the global north" (Howe 2014: 138). Their social mobility has more to do with their sexual identities than with the trajectory of assimilation conceived in ethnic and national terms. Furthermore, their identities are fluid and complex products of the intersections of race, ethnicity, nationality, gender, sexuality, and language. By contrast, dominant discourses both in their countries of origin and in the United States typically require LGBTQ migrants to conform to rigid norms of behavior and self-presentation. This process is especially highlighted in legal contexts in which sexual orientation and sexual asylum are discursively produced as clearly defined classifications, and which may contrast sharply with the condemnation and thus erasure of non-heterosexual identities in sexual migrants' home countries. As Howe (2014) explains, "Sexual migrants, queer refugees and asylum seekers may very quickly go from living in a context where they have been expected to defer, cover or reject their sexual selves, to, conversely, inhabiting a juridical field demanding that they compress their LGBT-Queerness into a legible, visible and packaged form" (138). Sexual asylum seekers are expected to be "visibly gay" as well as "inherently" so, since sexual refugee status derives from the legal category of those who have a "'well-founded fear' of persecution because of their 'membership in a particular social group'" (Howe 2014: 148); this membership, however, must be innate or otherwise immutable (149). While such a requirement is consistent with the understanding of sexual orientation as an innate quality rather than a "lifestyle choice," Howe reminds us that queer theorists have challenged the view of sexuality as "pre-programmed and essentialized in the ways that the immutability argument demands" because it leaves little room for "a more flexible and fluid definition of sexuality" (150). In reality, not only are sexual migrants unlikely to exhibit a fixed set of highly visible and immutable "gay" characteristics, but they may be apprehensive about visibly highlighting their sexuality as a result of their socialization in oppressively anti-gay environments in their countries and regions of origin.

On the other hand, some immigrants not only reject the heteronormative discourses of their ethnic communities and the mainstream culture, but also the legal formulations of the US immigration system that classify them as undocumented, and thus excluded from citizenship regardless of their integration into US society. Seif (2014) describes how the undocumented LGBTQ youth of color mobilize and reinvent the discourse of "coming out" to claim their place in the United States, to challenge the legal categories that marginalize them as "illegal," and to highlight their intersectional experiences of sexuality, race, and legal status. The Coming Out of the Shadows movement, including its "undocumented and unafraid" slogan, is inspired by LGBTQ rights activism. As one undocumented activist describes, "And the conversation soon said, there is National Coming out of the Closet Day for LGBTQ people, why can't we have something like that? And then, someone else in the room said, 'Gay people come out of the closet, what do immigrants come out of?' And someone said, 'The shadows!' And that's when we started thinking about this" (Interview with a member of the Immigrant Youth Justice League in Chicago, cited in Seif 2014: 100). The idea resulted in the first Coming Out of the Shadows rally in Chicago's Federal Plaza on March 10, 2010 (Seif 2014: 88).[6] The rally has become an annual event and grown into a national movement.[7] At the rallies, undocumented youth tell their stories, openly and in English, thus making themselves visible and challenging negative stereotypes of "illegal aliens" in front of legislators and voters (Seif 2014: 98). This public "coming out" is part of the political strategy of advocating for a path to legal status, but does not, as Seif points out, constitute appropriation of LGBTQ-rights discourse. Rather, "it is rooted in the speech of young organizers from undocumented, LGBTQ, and generally Latina/o social locations" and as such "is a speech tactic that reflects the intersectionality of queer youth of color" (Seif 2014: 94). This point is illustrated by the recent emergence of the term "undocuqueer," created and adopted by undocumented youth who self-identify as LGBTQ, and of groups such as the UndocuQueer project, the Undocumented Queer Youth Collective, and the Queer Undocumented Immigrant Project (QUIP) (Seif 2014: 110). Seif argues that "undocuqueer" "has multiple meanings" and "is used by 1.5-generation immigrants who refuse to tailor their speech and actions for

[6] See also www.iyjl.org/national-coming-out-of-the-shadows-day/, accessed April 10, 2016.

[7] See, for example, www.crln.org/NCOS_2015, accessed April 10, 2016, or Facebook groups such as www.facebook.com/March-is-National-Coming-Out-of-the-Shadows-Month-570795212934089/, accessed April 10, 2016.

acceptability in dominant society" (110), including both dominant American society with its fear of the "illegal alien" – and with its heteronormativity – and the immigrant communities that may be supportive of undocumented youth, but unsympathetic towards non-heterosexual identities and relationships. "Undocuqueer" as a term both forms a linguistic expression of the intersectional experience of LGBTQ undocumented youth, and opens the way for the discursive negotiation of this experience.

7.4 Language Choice and Assimilation

The above discussion of sexuality, with examples such as the New York gay men from Ecuador or youth who identify as undocuqueer, illustrates the challenges of talking about immigrants in terms of assimilation. The early chapters of this book also demonstrate that assimilation is not a straightforward or fixed concept, despite its being presented as such in mainstream discourses that construct it as a positive process, beneficial to both the receiving country and the immigrants themselves. Implied in this representation is the assumption of what immigrants are expected to assimilate to: the norms, values, and identities of those citizens who are of European descent, middle-class, monolingual in "accentless" – that is, MUSE – American English, and Christian, preferably Protestant. This, as we saw in Chapter 2, is what the original proponents of the "melting pot" idea envisioned as the final product to emerge out of the American crucible. And by the early twentieth century the idea that true assimilation or Americanization must proceed from learning English and abandoning heritage languages was actively promoted.

But among immigrants themselves conversations about assimilation have always been complex and conflicted, its meanings contested, and its desirability questioned. For example, many Poles in the late nineteenth century saw themselves as exemplary American citizens but also fundamentally Polish, and duty-bound to teach Polish to their US-born children and to promote Polish cultural and political causes in America (Dziembowska 1977a and 1977b). The same was true of other groups, such as Swedes and Norwegians. Irish intellectuals laid claim to being the original settlers of North American soil, and from the mid-nineteenth century onwards, Irish Americans have established a visible, influential, cohesive group identity that – as St. Patrick's Day celebrations exemplify – has been incorporated into the mainstream idea of American culture. On the other hand, there have been many immigrants who have chosen to blend in as much as possible, convinced that their future depends on successful cultural and linguistic assimilation (Warriner 2007; Antin 1912), and even that this is the only acceptable path for immigrants to take (Rodriguez 1982). Others find that neither choice is satisfactory, and they experience their immigration journey as a state of limbo or non-belonging, of being stuck in a perpetual sense of loss, as Eva Hoffman (1989) did throughout her adolescence, until she reconstructed her subjectivity in her new, English voice (Pavlenko and Lantolf 2000). Faced with the same dilemma, many create hybrid spaces and transnational identities that are only possible in immigrant contexts, but that are also not uniform or fixed: immigrants' relationships with hybrid spaces, hybrid identities, and hybrid languaging are complex, varied, and often fraught with anxiety, as we have seen throughout this book, and in particular in this chapter.

Hegemonic discourses surrounding the idea of true Americanness construct a binary distinction between immigrants and Americans, and produce the "problem" of immigrants "refusing to assimilate" by insisting on maintaining their cultural and linguistic differences. The multiplicity of perspectives and experiences of immigrants themselves, however, reveals a much more complex, fluid, and dynamic relationship between being an immigrant and being American, which also intersects with other aspects of identity, such as – but not only – gender and sexuality discussed above, and which is enacted through language choices and practices. The relationship between immigrants' identities and their linguistic choices and practices, meanwhile, emerges in response to dominant language ideologies circulating in American society, and to US language policies (De Fina and King 2011).

Public and Private Lives

The aggressive promotion of English monolingualism as a benchmark of Americanness in the first half of the twentieth century contributed to the abandonment of heritage languages by many immigrant families. Parents accepted their children's use of English at home in the belief that they were helping them succeed in American society. In families where the heritage language continued to be used, it was often confined to the private, home sphere. The goal was for the new generation to speak American "without an accent." Gloria Anzaldúa, whose Spanish-speaking family, paradoxically, has lived in the Texas area for generations, recalls her mother's admonitions: "I want you to speak English. *Pa' hallar buen trabajo tienes que saber hablar el inglés bien. Qué vale toda tu educación si todavía hablas inglés con un* 'accent'" ("To find a good job you have to know how to speak English well. What good is all your education if you keep speaking English with an *accent*"; Anzaldúa 2012 [1987]: 76).

The dichotomous separation between public and private languages that correspond to public and private lives and identities is presented not only as natural but also desirable in Richard Rodriguez' (1982) memoir *Hunger of Memory*. Rodriguez builds his arguments against bilingual education on the assumption that the public/private split in an individual's bilingual practices is inevitable. Expressing the language ideology in which English figures as the only dominant (public) language, and heritage languages become hidden (private) ones, Rodriguez portrays assimilation as the only sensible choice for an immigrant who hopes to succeed:

> Today I hear bilingual educators say that children lose a degree of "individuality" by becoming assimilated into public society . . . But the bilingualists simplistically scorn the value and necessity of assimilation. They do not seem to realize that there are *two* ways a person is individualized. So they do not realize that while one suffers a diminished sense of *private* individuality by becoming assimilated into public society, such assimilation makes possible the achievement of *public* individuality (Rodriguez 1982: 26; emphasis original).

Rodriguez' argument makes several problematic assumptions, such as that there can only be one public language that cannot be challenged, and that a person cannot achieve both "types" of individuality simultaneously, or that these could overlap and intersect. But, despite presenting his position in this passage in such black-and-white terms, Rodriguez' narrative throughout the book reveals multiple and sometimes conflicted perspectives.

Rodriguez argues that bilingual education keeps immigrant children from embracing their English-speaking "public individuality," and from claiming their right to have a public voice, that is, to participate in public life and to speak English in public spaces. Rodriguez seems to see public life as singular, uniform, and demanding conformity. He writes, "Only when I was able to think of myself as an American, no longer an alien in *gringo* society, could I seek the rights and opportunities necessary for full public individuality" (Rodriguez 1982: 26–27). He accepts and reiterates the notion that becoming American requires letting go of one's "private" heritage that positions one as a minority, and to sideline one's "private" language. But at the same time, Rodriguez' praises of assimilation are brief and academic, in stark contrast to his colorful, emotionally rich, lengthy depictions of the joys of speaking Spanish in the private sphere, at home, and of the pain caused by losing access to this experience once he became English-dominant: "Once I learned public language, it would never again be easy for me to hear intimate family voices" (27).

Surprisingly, however, it turns out that English, too, can provide access to intimacy for Rodriguez. After his parents began speaking English at home as requested by his American Catholic schoolteachers, he observes: "Making more and more friends outside my house, I began to distinguish intimate voices speaking through *English*. I'd listen at times to a close friend's confidential tone or secretive whisper . . . After such moments of intimacy outside my house, I began to trust hearing intimacy conveyed through my family's English" (31–32; emphasis original). It seems that even for Rodriguez, the separation between English as the public language and Spanish as the private language is not as clear-cut as he attempts to portray it.

Other immigrants whose lives were shaped by the monolingualist, assimilationist discourse of the early twentieth century also experience a contrast between public and private domains of language use. Jerre Mangione, professor emeritus of English at the University of Pennsylvania and author of the autobiographical narrative *Mount Allegro* (1942), describes language as enacting the difference between the Italian world of his home, and the American world outside. Unlike Rodriguez' parents, Mangione's mother maintained her home as an Italian-only space. Mangione felt embarrassed when his two linguistic worlds intersected, such as when his American friends heard his mother address him in Italian.

As Carnevale (2009) explains, "This separation between the private and the public was formalized through naming: Mangione was Jerre to his friends, but Gerlando at home" (Carnevale 2009: 97). For immigrants such as Mangione, however, the separation between linguistic and cultural worlds was more complex than a simple compartmentalization of English and the heritage language. Italian immigrants spoke a variety of regional dialects, and it was these dialects, not standard Italian, that connected them to each other and to the old country. While he expresses admiration for what he calls "proper Italian," Mangione observes that the language of his Sicilian relatives and their networks was Sicilian. He seconds his uncle's argument that "the only reason Sicilians ever addressed each other in proper Italian was to show off their schooling and prove to each other that they were not peasants" (Mangione 1942: 57, cited in Carnevale 2009: 97). For Italian immigrants, standard Italian became one of the "public" languages that they encountered in their new communities in America. Meanwhile, the "private" language of the home was also being Americanized. Carnevale writes of families such as Mangione's, "Like many Italian immigrants, they spoke a mixture that included English, other Italian dialects, and Italianized – or Sicilianized – words, including some words from other languages they encountered in the United States" (Carnevale 2009: 97). As we saw in Chapter 5, such translanguaging, mixing, and hybridization is a more common feature of immigrant communities' communicative practices than a maintenance of a "pure" form of the heritage language.

In comparing several early accounts by Italian immigrants, Carnevale demonstrates the diversity in their motivations for learning English and in their feelings about assimilation. Two contrasting examples are the autobiographies by Constantine Panunzio (1928) and Pascal D'Angelo (1924). Panunzio, through all his experiences of exploitation and humiliation, remains dedicated to his goal of becoming an American and sees English as central to this project. He immersed himself in mainstream American society, obtaining formal education, joining the army, and eventually converting to Methodism, which is an especially powerful statement in light of longstanding anti-Catholic sentiments directed at Italian and Irish immigrants in America. Panunzio believes that if Italians adopted the English language, they would "come to understand the advantages of mingling with American people and to develop a wholesome attitude towards America and all things American" (cited in Carnevale 2009: 105). Panunzio embraces assimilation through English with even more eagerness than Rodriguez.

D'Angelo, on the other hand, teaches himself English in an effort to improve his life circumstances. He starts out as an uneducated laborer and becomes a recognized poet writing in English, with a promising literary career cut short by his death at the age of thirty-eight (Carnevale 2009: 99). But while he publishes his work in English, D'Angelo remains connected to his fellow laborers with whom he speaks Italian, and "does not equate his linguistic conversion to English with becoming American" (Carnevale 2009: 99). In a letter to the editor of *The Nation*, he passionately proclaims his continued solidarity with his fellow workers: "I am not deserting the legions of toil to refuge myself in the literary world. No! No! I only want to express the wrath of their mistreatment" (cited in Carnevale 2009: 99). English does, in Rodriguez' terms, become D'Angelo's "public language" in which he reaches a wider American audience, claiming a voice not just for himself but on behalf of his fellow Italians. But unlike Rodriguez, D'Angelo does not begin to inhabit a new, English-speaking and assimilated self. His English world centers on his writing, but his social and cultural world remains Italian. And, arguably, Italian functions as a public language for those immigrants who speak it at work and in their communities, as D'Angelo does with his fellow laborers. For immigrants such as D'Angelo, the heritage language's relevance for constructing identities and forming relationships in a range of social contexts and registers may be much greater than that of English.

Borderlands

Gloria Anzaldúa's concept of the borderlands, described above in Section 7.3, provides a useful metaphor for the negotiations of language choice and assimilation as it occurs in the lives of many immigrants. Anzaldúa's memories of her childhood in Texas in mid-twentieth century include stories of teachers punishing children for speaking Spanish: "I remember being caught speaking Spanish at recess – that was good for three licks on the knuckles with a sharp ruler. I remember being sent to the corner of the classroom for 'talking back' to the Anglo teacher when all I was trying to do was tell her how to pronounce my name. 'If you want to be American, speak "American." If you don't like it, go back to Mexico where you belong'" (Anzaldúa 2012 [1987]: 75). Although

Anzaldúa's family's roots are in Texas, her use of Spanish was construed as indicating foreignness and allegiance to Mexico, as opposed to the United States. It was, additionally, bound up with issues of race, given Anzaldúa's Chicana ethnicity and the resulting reading of her as "belonging" in Mexico.

But Anzaldúa does not make a choice between Spanish or English, or between Mexican or American identity. Instead, she makes new meanings out of the contradictions that she experiences when faced with dominant discourses, both in mainstream society and in her local Texan-Mexican community. She embraces Chicano Spanish, which she describes as "a border tongue which developed naturally . . . *Un lenguaje que corresponde a un modo de vivir*" (a language that corresponds to a way of life), and adds, "And because we are a complex, heterogeneous people, we speak many languages" (Anzaldúa 2012 [1987]: 77). She lists no less than eight languages spoken by her community: standard English, working class and slang English, standard Spanish, standard Mexican Spanish, North Mexican Spanish dialect, Chicano Spanish in its Texas, New Mexico, Arizona, and California variations, Tex-Mex (which she equates with Spanglish), and *pachuco*, a sort of secret dialect that she describes as "the language of the zoot suiters" (78). It is through the creative combination of these different language forms that the borderland identities of Texan Mexican-Americans are enacted. The heterogeneity of identities that Anzaldúa discusses as circulating among her people parallels that of language: *mexicano*, Chicano, Spanish, Hispanic, Spanish-American, Latin-American, Latin, Mexican-American, Indian (84). In the borderlands, there is no clear-cut correspondence between language and either American or foreign identity.

For communities such as Anzaldúa's, for Native Americans and for descendants of Spanish colonizers, the borderlands are both a physical, geographic space as well as a symbolic one. For immigrants of color who cannot go back to their countries of origin, on the other hand, it is the disconnection from a physical place that becomes especially significant. While their phenotype makes them easily classifiable as outsiders in the United States according to dominant ideologies of race, the US is at the same time the only place where they are able to negotiate belonging. Warriner (2007) explains this in reference to the Sudanese refugee women in her study: "For African women refugees, questions of language learning, educational access, identity formation, and belonging are exceedingly complicated – especially given the absence of a physical 'homeland' to return to, the related 'deterritorialization' of their national identities, the unstable relationship they have had with the government of that former (and now imagined) 'homeland,' and their newly minoritized and racialized identities here in the US context" (Warriner 2007: 344). These immigrants' experience in the "borderlands" involves negotiating "the master narrative that equates speaking English with *becoming* and *being* American" (345; emphasis original) that they are exposed to and at least partly internalize, and the reality in which learning English does not translate into better jobs or being accepted as an equal in American society.

A different type of relationship between language and assimilation can be observed in the narratives of Ethiopian immigrants, collected and analyzed by Weldeyesus (2007). Drawing on Bucholtz and Hall's (2005) notion of identity as "the social positioning of the self against other" (Weldeyesus 2007: 2, cf. Bucholtz and Hall 2005: 586), Weldeyesus explains his participants' stories of language learning as constructing an opposition between their newly arrived "former-self" and their present-day, acculturated "current-self" (Weldeyesus 2007: 2). In the narratives, the speakers jokingly recount moments of linguistic and cultural misunderstandings that transpired between themselves and American interlocutors in the early days of their life in the United States. Crucially, while the tone of the narratives is a joking one, the events at the time were not experienced by the speakers as funny. For example, one participant, Teki, describes a time when she was working in a donut shop and a customer asked for a croissant, but, unfamiliar with the word, she assumed he wanted coffee and kept asking him "What size?" At the time, Teki felt embarrassed, especially since she was mocked by a coworker, and ended up crying in the coffee shop's basement. But when telling the story eleven years later in the interview, she does so with laughter, which underscores her current self-perception as "a well-socialized and enlightened individual with good command of the English language, a good paying job, [who] does not appear to have similar problems any more" (4).

Another Ethiopian immigrant, Dawit, recalls applying for a job at the post office shortly after coming to the US in the mid-1990s, and explaining to the employee who took his application that in Ethiopia the year was 1988. The employee replied with "Get out of here" in the idiomatic sense of "I don't believe it," but Dawit understood this literally and began gathering his things. Now, having learned English well, Dawit realizes his mistake and tells the story as an amusing mishap that happened to him prior to his L2 socialization, when he was unfamiliar with both American idioms and culture. Dawit concludes his narrative with the evaluation: "then I thought 'Get out of here' means like 'Don't be kidding me' . . . So from then on . . . I learnt something" (Weldeyesus 2007: 4). Like Teki, in the process of telling his story, Dawit positions his former self, unsocialized in American ways, in contrast to his acculturated self who has gone through a process of learning. This socialization, however, is not equated with assimilation or Americanization, nor does the learning of English require a rejection or marginalization of the immigrants' first language.

Linguistic border crossings

Pavlenko and Lantolf (2000) set out to investigate "what happens to a self when an individual moves from participation in the discursive practices of one culture ... to those of another culture" (Pavlenko and Lantolf 2000: 163), referring to such moves as "linguistic border crossings" (169). Starting from the premise that "a self is a coherent dynamic system ... that is 'in continuous production' ... and which emerges when the individual participates in (most especially, verbal) practices of a culture" (163), the authors argue that agency and intentionality are key components in a person's successful "second language becoming" (167). Based on what is known about the connection between language and emotion, they posit that adults (or adolescents, such as Eva Hoffman) who find themselves living in a new cultural and linguistic context as expatriates or immigrants, and who attempt to become native-like speakers of the new language, experience some form of loss and reconstruction of linguistic identity. They further break these two phases down into a number of stages. The phase of loss consists of loss of linguistic identity, loss of all subjectivities, loss of frame of reference, loss of the inner voice, and first language attrition. The phase of recovery and reconstruction consists of appropriation of others' voices, emergence of one's own voice, translation and reconstruction of one's past, and finally the "continuous growth 'into' new positions and subjectivities" (162–163). Pavlenko and Lantolf emphasize that the stages are continuous and overlapping, even as the reconstruction phase comes later than the loss phase. I would argue that the stages should also be seen as fluid and potentially merging together, rather than categorically separate and sequential.

The key point made by Pavlenko and Lantolf is that individuals who constructed their "self" in one cultural context, and who wish to participate actively in their new linguistic and cultural community, must take conscious steps to embrace this new environment, which involves a reorganization and reconstruction of their life stories "in line with the new set of conventions and social relationships sanctioned by the new community in which they find themselves" (Pavlenko and Lantolf 2000: 172). The authors stress that "while a person may become a functional bilingual either by necessity or by choice, as an adult she or he becomes a bicultural bilingual by choice only" (173). Individuals make sense of the events in their lives by interpreting them as parts of a meaningful storyline, so that the self is constructed along a particular plot. This plot has to be translated into the new language and culture, and in the process it often requires reconfiguration or remaking (Pavlenko and Lantolf 2000: 160). Unsurprisingly, not everyone is eager to remake one's "story of oneself" in a new language and according to new cultural conventions. Some may neither wish to become nativelike speakers of L2, nor aspire to cultural assimilation.

As a result, immigrants have different trajectories: "in one case [they] undertake the construction of new identities, appropriate to the new surroundings, while in another they assume an overarching identity as non-native speakers – legitimate but marginal members of a community" (Pavlenko and Lantolf 2000: 171).

The emphasis on personal agency and choice is key because that is what ultimately allows an immigrant to complete the "linguistic border crossing" and accept both their new social identity and role. Mary Antin, the Russian Jewish immigrant whose influential autobiography *The Promised Land* (1912) was briefly discussed in Chapter 3 (Section 3.1), intentionally commits all her emotional energy towards remaking herself as an English speaker and an American. Eva Hoffman is far more apprehensive, but eventually she, too, decides to allow herself to become socialized in American English. But, we must remember, for many the choice is not a momentary and final decision, nor does it guarantee success. The pain of losing connection with one's L1 self can be traumatizing, as we see on Hoffman's example. Hoffman, furthermore, experiences her Polish-speaking self as irrelevant and meaningless in her new reality, and she chooses to embrace English in order to reclaim the ability to construct her own storyline. She succeeds in this endeavor, but it is a slow process. Others may find that they can never construct a new self in L2 that corresponds to a coherent plot line. For some of those, the alternative may be maintaining most of their social relationships within their ethnic communities, where the reorganized, immigrant self is much more closely embedded within what is familiar. Their L1 changes over time, adjusting to the language of their ethnic enclave, including hybrid forms and borrowings from English that reflect the community's experience in America – but they do not become "full-fledged participants" (Pavlenko and Lantolf 2000: 169) in mainstream American culture.

Finally, it is perhaps important to emphasize that linguistic border crossings are not one-time, bounded events, nor are they irreversible. The linguistic border can be crossed multiple times, and the crossing itself is often an ongoing process – though for some, to be sure, it may be a more linear experience, such as for Mary Antin or Richard Rodriguez. But in contrast to the "master narrative" (Warriner 2007) encountered in mainstream discourses, learning English and assimilation are rarely experienced as equivalent or as unproblematic choices. The immigrant experiences of language learning, "second language becoming" (Pavlenko and Lantolf 2000), and becoming American are diverse and complex, reflecting the creation of "rich, complex, and highly salient identities cutting across borders and going beyond the fixed, geographic, nation-bound binaries" (Sirin and Fine 2008: 131).

Linguistic border crossings may be envisioned as taking place in Anzaldúa's borderlands. This is also where immigrants and their descendants negotiate the overlapping, intersecting, converging categories that structure their lives: American/immigrant, assimilated/foreign, English speaker/non-English speaker, documented/undocumented, monolingual/bilingual, native-speaker/accented speaker, citizen/alien. Even though these categories are often presented as binary, in reality they are fluid and contextualized, as this chapter and this book have aimed to show. The borderlands are the site of self-translation, and consequently of the negotiation between one's internally constructed story of the self, and the identities that one enacts through languaging and translanguaging.

Epilogue

The story of language in immigrant America continues to be made every day, and in recent decades it has been influenced by the sociocultural and political trends brought about by globalization and technological innovations that have made communication and the exchange of ideas more immediate and accessible than ever. In response to these trends and the changes they cause, researchers in the humanities and social sciences have developed theoretical accounts that Arnaut and Spotti (2014) refer to as "superdiversity discourse." The authors describe it as "rest[ing] on the growing awareness that over the past two and a half decades the demographic, socio-political, cultural, and sociolinguistic face of societies worldwide has been changing as a result of (a) ever faster and more mobile communication technologies and software infrastructures, along with (b) ever expanding mobility and migration activity related to major geo-political changes around 1990" (Arnaut and Spotti 2014: 2; cf. Rampton et al. 2015). In sociolinguistics, thinking in terms of superdiversity, or diversification of diversity (Vertovec 2007; Arnaut and Spotti 2014), has led researchers to conceptual shifts away from languages as discrete systems of which people are either native speakers or second-language speakers and learners, and towards languaging and translanguaging, resources and repertoires, hybrid linguistic practices, transculturations, transnational and translocal speech communities, and other related frameworks that emphasize complexity, hybridity, intersectionality, agency, and the mobility of people and ideas.

The concept of superdiversity was suggested by Steven Vertovec (2007) as a way of analyzing new trends in migration in Britain starting in the early 1990s. According to Vertovec, whereas previously most migration consisted of waves of ethnic groups mostly from countries with historical ties to the UK, the "new migration" has been characterized by a great diversification of countries of origin, as well as of other aspects of the migrants' identities: immigration status and related rights, educational and occupational background, gender and age profiles, language, religion, motivations for migration, and geographical distribution of settlement, among others. In Vertovec's definition, "[t]he interplay of these factors is what is meant here, in summary fashion, by the notion of 'super-diversity'" (Vertovec 2007: 1025). As interpreted by sociolinguists, ideas related to Arnaut and Spotti's "superdiversity discourse" are applicable across the world's societies, and include "real" as well as virtual connections and communities (Rampton et al. 2015; Arnaut and Spotti 2014). Some, such as Makoni (2012) and Bolonyai (personal communication), have criticized the superdiversity approach for exaggerating the novelty of modern-day diversity, pointing out for example that "[m]ass movement of populations is not new to Africa, so if diversity is accentuated by migration, then prior to colonialism there was considerable migration; however, it is framed as nomadism!" (Makoni 2012: 193). And, as the main architects of the superdiversity framework themselves observe, the focus on the interaction between language and other sociocultural forms, on the complexity and situatedness of identities, and on the overall necessity to integrate linguistics with ethnography, has for some time already been central to linguistic anthropology as practiced in North America (Rampton et al. 2015: 6).

Nonetheless, the conceptual move away from traditional categorizations and dichotomies, and towards intersectionality and hybridity, is in part a response to the growing interconnectedness of communities and movements of people both in the emerging superdiversity approach (e.g. Blommaert and Backus 2012; Rampton et al. 2015; Blommaert 2010, and others), and in recent work in linguistic anthropology and related fields (e.g. Reyes and Lo 2009; Farr 2006; Sirin and Fine 2008; García and Kleifgen 2010; García and Li 2014). Thus, for example, as we have seen in this book, young Muslim Americans are described as negotiating multidimensional and hybrid identities "at the hyphen" (Sirin and Fine 2008), while Mexican migrants in Chicago maintain a closely connected transnational community between Michoácan and their Chicago neighborhood (Farr 2006), reminding us of Vertovec's observation that "[t]he degrees to and ways in which today's migrants maintain identities, activities and connections linking them with communities outside Britain is unprecedented" (Vertovec 2007: 1043). And, as discussed in the final chapter of this book, ethnicity and national heritage also powerfully intersect with gender and sexuality in the lives of many immigrants, and together they are mediated through language and its emotional significance as shaped by individual experience.

At the same time, however, as pointed out by Makoni (2012) in his critique of superdiversity and related approaches, a celebratory focus on diversity and complexity can lead us to lose sight of the bigger picture and the social inequalities that it reveals. Makoni writes:

> It is the powerful who celebrate the notion of diversity; those of us from other parts of the world feel the idea of diversity is a careful concealment of power differences. When we celebrate mass movements we need to be able to distinguish between those who are

> compelled by circumstances to travel and those who do so willingly. *Superdiversity* contains a powerful sense of social romanticism, creating an illusion of equality in a highly asymmetrical world, particularly in contexts characterized by a search for homogenization . . . I find it disconcerting, to say the least, to have an open celebration of diversity in societies marked by violent xenophobia . . . (Makoni 2012: 192–193; emphasis original).

Along somewhat similar lines, Rampton (2013) urges researchers to pay simultaneous attention to linguistic form, situated discourse, and ideology, warning that when they ignore any of these, "potentially crucial aspects of their informants' social, political, rhetorical or linguistic positioning are obscured, and this lets in the romantic celebration of difference and creative agency that has been so common in sociolinguistics" (Rampton 2013: 3, cited also in Arnaut and Spotti 2014: 7).

Such fascination with diversity and diversification at the expense of exposing social inequality is likewise evident in the conflicting discourses surrounding English and other languages in the US today. Despite the ongoing perpetuation of fears that languages other than English pose a threat to the American way of life, as demonstrated in anti-immigrant political rhetoric, Official English laws, or the dismantling of bilingual education, in some domains multilingualism is being celebrated without being problematized. Thus, for example, Spanish features routinely in children's programming, in extremely commercially successful shows such as Nickelodeon's *Dora the Explorer* and *Go Diego, Go!*, as well as in Sprout Channel's *Good Night Show*, which explicitly incorporate learning Spanish into the structure of each episode.[1] A similar approach is adopted in Nickelodeon's *Ni hao, Kai Lan*, with Mandarin as the target language. In other children's shows, Spanish appears along with bilingual characters who are also portrayed as Latino immigrants, for example in *The Dragon Tales* produced by PBS and running from 1999 to 2005. Crucially, however, these shows portray Spanish and Chinese speakers as completely unaffected by their bilingualism that marks them as non-white and/or immigrant, while learning a language other than English is promoted as important for talking to different kinds of people who may be "visiting" the United States (e.g. in Sprout's *Good Night Show*).

Thus, for example, the young siblings Emmy and Max, protagonists of *The Dragon Tales*, are presented as having an unspecified Latino background, which becomes further decontextualized as they venture into the magical Dragonland where the story is set. In this mythical land, the children befriend a group of young dragons whose own diversity – different-colored scales, dragons with one versus two heads, and so on – is rendered apolitical because

[1] See Banet-Weiser (2007) for an insightful analysis of representations of ethnicity in children's programing on Nickelodeon.

it does not correspond to categories relevant in human societies. Meanwhile, the young dragons' schoolteacher, whose name, Quetzal, suggests Indigenous Mexican roots, is a second-language English speaker whose first language is Spanish. Quetzal is older and wise, and immensely respected by dragon and human children alike. He speaks with a slight Spanish accent, and often uses simple Spanish phrases when addressing the children, such as for example *muy bien, niños!*, which the children appear to understand. Quetzal's social and political status in the Dragonland society, however, remains unclear: Is he an immigrant? If so, from where? Why does he appear to be the only Spanish speaker? The only time migration is engaged with in the show is when Emmy and Max's cousin Enrique arrives from Colombia and finds himself feeling lonely in the culturally unfamiliar world of, presumably, the United States, as well as Dragonland. Enrique speaks Spanish and accented English, and finds support in Quetzal with whom he shares his first language. But we never find out if Enrique migrated alone or with his parents, if he is only visiting or staying permanently, or what may have motivated his move. And in a perhaps accidentally ironic twist, when the children try to make Enrique feel less homesick on his birthday, they organize a celebration that involves a *piñata* – even though the *piñata* is a specifically Mexican tradition unknown in Colombia. Thus, in seeking to normalize ethnic and linguistic diversity, the show also homogenizes Spanish speakers as representatives of a conglomerate, unitary "Hispanic" culture.

I do not wish to detract from children's programming that incorporates Spanish, Chinese, or other languages as suitable alternatives to English, and that presents non-English speakers as unmarked and in all ways equal to English speakers. To be sure, such shows help to normalize multilingualism, non-native accents, and speakers of non-English languages as well as these languages' presence in the United States. The popularity of these shows suggests that early exposure to other languages, bilingualism, and even specific languages such as Spanish, are becoming relevant and valued in the perception of mainstream American public. But it has to be remembered that social inequalities, such as unequal access to resources or racial and linguistic profiling, do not simply disappear once enough harmonious and apolitical diversity is depicted in the media. Moreover, not every celebrant of such diversity is truly interested in tackling inequality; after all, it is one thing to encourage children to learn languages that can one day benefit them, but quite another to allow these languages to challenge the privileged place of English. Thus, the same American children whose parents buy them bilingual *Dora the Explorer* storybooks may be going to kindergarten with immigrant classmates who, thanks to underfunded bilingual education, have little hope of an equal start in school, and end up being not enriched but limited by their experience with Spanish.

It is not a new observation that it is those at the top of the sociopolitical power structure, whose identities are made normative and unmarked, that benefit the most from sampling surrounding diversity. Mathews (2000) describes what he calls the present-day "cultural supermarket," in which "shoppers" can pick and choose from diverse cultural markers to construct their identities. These might include home decor, elements of religious practice (e.g. Buddhist mandala on the wall, or regular yoga practice), or "ethnic" foods. But Mathews points out that it is the educated and affluent who are best positioned to take full advantage of the cultural supermarket, because they have greater access to the available resources, and greater socioeconomic means for appropriating them (Mathews 2000: 21). His analysis highlights how, following decades of pressure to assimilate exerted on immigrants, ethnic markers have been commodified and appropriated by mainstream white Americans as indexes of qualities such as sophistication, cosmopolitan outlook and urban lifestyle. Along similar lines, Halter (2000) observes, "Ethnicity has typically been associated with the lifestyle of the lower classes. However, increasingly, explicit ethnic identification has become an indicator of economic success and integration" (Halter 2000: 10). Second- and third-generation immigrants demonstrate their accomplishment of the American Dream by emphasizing and displaying their ethnic heritage. Halter describes this as "part-time ethnicity" (Halter 2000: 116) or "occasional" ethnicity (Halter 2000: 119), focusing in particular on the marketing and consumption of "ethnic" foods.

Another example of social inequality in access to "fashionable ethnicity," as we might call it, is found among the "new Italians" in the Southeast, described by Fellin (2015), who, despite being first-generation immigrants, reject historically established Italian American identity and do not aspire to assimilation. Unlike their turn-of-the-twentieth-century predecessors, the Italians in Fellin's study are highly educated, work in their professional fields in America, come from various regions of Italy rather than only the South, speak English, and speak Standard Italian rather than the regional vernaculars associated with their hometowns. They place high value on maintaining the Italian language and Italian cultural practices in their families, and explicitly distance themselves from Italian American cultural markers, such as Italian American food, which, despite being associated with Italians in the United States, does not always resemble present-day cuisine found in Italy. They also identify with Italy's artistic and cultural heritage through discourses and practices that are often exclusive to those of higher socioeconomic status. Fellin (2015) stresses that the "new Italians" reject both assimilation and hyphenation, describing their US-raised children as Italian *and* American, rather than Italian-American. Crucially, these new immigrants arrive in the US in a privileged position that affords them the freedom not only to actively enact their non-American ethnic identity, but also to choose and claim the high-prestige aspects of their ethnic background. Italy has by now become a prestigious foreign holiday destination for upper-middle-class Americans, and Italians have been accepted as European and as white. Consequently, highly educated, affluent Italians face few of the pressures encountered by newly arrived migrants from Mexico or refugees from Southeast Asia, the Middle East, or Africa.

The approaches adopted in this book – complex and socially constructed identities, fluidity, hybridity, languaging and translanguaging, continua, and webs in place of binaries – are shared with the superdiversity perspective, or, as Arnaut and Spotti (2014) frame it, are part of superdiversity discourse. As such, they are open to the same critique of presenting a version of social reality that optimistically celebrates diversity while overlooking larger power structures. In this book, I have attempted to maintain a balance between recognizing and examining the diversity, complexity, and creative agency that characterize immigrant America, with a critical assessment of the dominant narrative that produces the normative definitions of terms such as "American," "citizen," and "immigrant." This narrative – of immigration, assimilation, the American Dream, the melting pot, the nation of immigrants – although changing over time, has always worked to naturalize inequality through ideologies of race, ethnicity, gender, sexuality, nationhood, and language. Indeed, the story of language in immigrant America is not a history lesson, but rather a continuous, conflicted and dynamic process that is and will be relevant in the lives of not just immigrants, but of all Americans, for many decades to come. During the 2016 general election campaigns, anti-immigrant rhetoric, aimed primarily at Latinos and Muslims, became particularly aggressive and rather openly racist to the extent not seen in mainstream national politics in a long while. Anti-immigrant legislation, from Arizona's Senate Bill 1070 passed in 2010 that effectively encourages racial profiling to the elimination of bilingual education in several states, the continued portrayal of undocumented immigrants as criminal and alien, and finally President Trump's controversial order, issued a week after his inauguration, banning migration and travel from several predominantly Muslim countries, demonstrates the persisting fear on part of many Americans of having groups "not like us" contribute to the definition of Americanness. At the same time, ethnic, cultural, and linguistic diversity defines the social reality that many Americans inhabit. Hybrid and hyphenated identities are continuously being produced and reinvented. Immigrant America's creative agency has to be described and celebrated, not in the least in the hope of providing a challenge and an alternative to the dominant narrative of "the nation of (assimilated) immigrants." With time, perhaps, this alternative story will have an impact on mainstream attitudes, on dominant media discourse, and on policymaking.

References

Abedi, Jamal (2004) The No Child Left Behind Act and English Language learners: Assessment and accountability issues. *Educational Researcher* 33(1): 4–14.

Abedi, Jamal and C. Lord (2001) The language factor in mathematics tests. *Applied Measurement in Education* 14: 219–234.

Alim, H. Samy and Geneva Smitherman (2012) *Articulate While Black: Barack Obama, Language, and Race in the U.S.* Oxford and New York: Oxford University Press.

Alvarez, Lizette (1998) It's the talk of Nueva York: The hybrid called Spanglish. In Virginia P. Clark, Paul A. Eschholz, and Alfred F. Rosa (Eds.) *Language: Readings in Language and Culture*. New York: St. Martin's Press. 483–488.

Alvarez, Stephanie (2013) Subversive English in *Raining Backwards*: A different kind of Spanglish. *Hispania* 96(3): 444–459.

Alvarez, Steven (2014) Translanguaging *Tareas*: Emergent bilingual youth as language brokers for homework in immigrant families. *Language Arts* 91(5): 326–339.

Ancheta, Angelo N. (2006) *Race, Rights and the Asian American Experience*. New Brunswick, NJ, and London: Rutgers University Press.

Anderson, Benedict (1982) *Imagined Communities: Reflections on the Origin and Spread of Nationalism*. London and New York: Verso.

Anderson, Gary Clayton (2014) *Ethnic Cleansing and the Indian: The Crime That Should Haunt America*. Norman, OK: Oklahoma University Press.

Andresen, Julie Tetel (2014) *Linguistics and Evolution: A Developmental Approach*. Cambridge: Cambridge University Press.

Andresen, Julie Tetel and Philip Carter (2015) *Languages in theWorld: How History, Culture, and Politics Shape Language*. Malden, MA: Wiley Blackwell.

Andrews, Edna (2014) *Neuroscience and Multilingualism*. Cambridge: Cambridge University Press.

Antaki, Charles and Sue Widdicombe (Eds.) (1998) *Identities in Talk*. London: SAGE Publications.

Antieau, Lamont (2003) Plains English in Colorado. *American Speech* 78(4): 385–403.

Antin, Mary (1912) *The Promised Land*. Boston and New York: Houghton Mifflin Company. http://digital.library.upenn.edu/women/antin/land/land.html#10.

Anzaldúa, Gloria (2012 [1987]) *Borderlands/La Frontera: The New Mestiza*. San Francisco: Spinsters/Aunt Lute.

Araujo-Dawson, Beverly (2015) Understanding the complexities of skin color, perceptions of race and discrimination among Cubans, Dominicans, and Puerto Ricans. *Hispanic Journal of Behavioral Sciences* 37(2): 243–256.

Ardila, Alfredo (2005) Spanglish: An Anglicized Spanish dialect. *Hispanic Journal of Behavioral Sciences* 27(1): 60–81.

Arnaut, Karel and Massimiliano Spotti (2014) Superdiversity discourse. Working Papers in Urban Language and Literacies. Working Paper 122.

Asher, Nina (2008) Listening to hyphenated Americans: Hybrid identities of youth from immigrant families. *Theory Into Practice* 47: 12–19.

Auer, Peter (1998) Introduction: Bilingual conversation revisited. In Peter Auer (Ed.) *Code-Switching in Conversation: Language, Interaction and Identity*. New York: Routledge. 1–22.

Auer, Peter (2007) The monolingual bias in bilingualism research, or: Why bilingual talk is (still) a challenge for linguistics. In Monica Heller (Ed.) *Bilingualism: A Social Approach*. Basingstoke, UK and New York: Palgrave Macmillan. 319–339.

Ayala, Jennifer (2006) Confianza, consejos, and contradictions: Gender and sexuality lessons between Latina adolescent daughters and mothers. In Jill Denner and Bianca L. Guzmán (Eds.) *Latina Girls: Voices of Adolescent Strength in the United States*. New York and London: New York University Press. 29–43.

Babbitt, Eugene Howard (1896) The language of the lower classes in New York City and vicinity. *Dialect Notes* 1: 457–464.

Bailey, Benjamin (2000a) The language of multiple identities among Dominican Americans. *Journal of Linguistic Anthropology* 10(2): 190–223.

Bailey, Benjamin (2000b) Social/interactional functions of code switching among Dominican Americans. *Pragmatics* 10(2): 165–193.

Bailey, Benjamin (2001) Dominican-American ethnic/racial identities and United States social categories. *International Migration Review* 35(3): 677–708.

Bailey, Benjamin (2007) Heteroglossia and boundaries. In Monica Heller (Ed.) *Bilingualism: A Social Approach*. Basingstoke, UK and New York: Palgrave Macmillan. 257–274.

Bailey, Richard W. (2003) The foundation of English in the Louisiana Purchase: New Orleans, 1800–1850. *American Speech* 78(4): 363–384.

Bakhtin, Mikhail (1981) *The Dialogic Imagination*. Austin: University of Texas Press.

Banet-Weiser, Sarah (2007) *Kids Rule!: Nickelodeon and Consumer Citizenship*. Durham and London: Duke University Press.

Baptiste, David A. (1987) Family therapy with Spanish-heritage immigrant families in cultural transition. *Contemporary Family Therapy* 9(4): 229–251.

Baptiste, David A. (1993) Immigrant families, adolescents, and acculturation: Insights for therapists. *Marriage and Family Review* 19(3/4): 341–363.

Baquedano-López, Patricia (2001) Creating social identities through *Doctrina* narratives. In Alessandro Duranti (Ed.) *Linguistic Anthropology: A Reader*. Malden, MA: Blackwell. 343–358.

Baran, Dominika (1999) Russian-Uzbek language contact in Tashkent: Code-switching and borrowing in urban colloquial language. Unpublished MA thesis: Harvard University.

Baran, Dominika (2001) English loan words in Polish and the question of gender assignment. *Proceedings from Penn Linguistics Colloquium 25 (PLC 25)* 8.1: 15–28.

Baran, Dominika (2013) Working with adolescents: Identity, power and responsibility in sociolinguistic ethnography. In Isabella Paoletti, Maria Isabel Tomás, and Fernanda Menéndez (Eds.) *Practices of Ethics: An Empirical Approach to Ethics in Social Sciences Research*. 155–176.

Baran, Dominika (2014) Linguistic practice and identity work: Variation in Taiwan Mandarin at a Taipei county high school. *Journal of Sociolinguistics* 18(1): 32–59.

Barker, Chris (2000) *Cultural Studies: Theory and Practice*. London: Sage Publications.

Bartlett, Lesley and Ofelia García (2011) *Additive Schooling in Subtractive Times: Bilingual Education and Dominican Immigrant Youth in the Heights*. Nashville: Vanderbilt University Press.

Bayley, Robert (2004) Linguistic diversity and English language acquisition. In Edward Finegan and John J. Rickford (Eds.) *Language in the USA: Themes for the Twenty-First Century*. Cambridge: Cambridge University Press. 268–288.

Bayley, Robert, Holly Hansen-Thomas, and Juliet Langman (2005). Language brokering in a middle school science class. In James Cohen, Kara T. McAlister, Kellie Rolstad, and Jeff MacSwan (Eds.) *Proceedings of the 4th International Symposium on Bilingualism*. Somerville, MA: Cascadilla Press. 223–232.

Bean, William G. (1934) Puritan versus Celt: 1850–1860. *The New England Quarterly* 7(1): 70–89.

Becker, Alton L. (1991) Language and languaging. *Language and Communication* 11(1/2): 33–35.

Becker, Alton L. (1995) *Beyond Translation: Essays towards a Modern Philology*. Ann Arbor: University of Michigan Press.

Belgum, Kirsten (2015) Accidental encounter: Why John Quincy Adams translated German culture for Americans. *Early American Studies* (Winter 2015): 209–236.

Besemeres, Mary (2002) *Translating One's Self: Language and Selfhood in Cross-Cultural Autobiography*. Oxford: Peter Lang.

Besemeres, Mary (2006) Language and emotional experience: The voice of translingual memoir. In Aneta Pavlenko (Ed.) *Bilingual Minds: Emotional Experience, Expression and Representation*. Clevedon: Multilingual Matters. 34–58.

Besemeres, Mary (2007) Between *żal* and emotional blackmail: Ways of being in Polish and English. In Mary Besemeres and Anna Wierzbicka (Eds.) *Translating Lives: Living with Two Languages and Cultures. St.* Lucia, Queensland: University of Queensland Press. 128–138.

Bhaba, Homi K. (1994) *The Location of Culture*. New York: Routledge.

Bigler, Ellen (1996) Telling stories: On ethnicity, exclusion, and education in Upstate New York. *Anthropology and Education Quaterly* 27(2): 186–203.

Birdsong, David (2006) Age and second language acquisition and processing: A selective overview. *Language Learning* 56: 9–49.

Blegen, Theodore C. (1931) *Norwegian Migration to America 1825–1860*. Northfield, MN: The Norwegian-American Historical Association.

Blommaert, Jan (2010) *The Sociolinguistics of Globalization*. Cambridge: Cambridge University Press.

Blommaert, Jan and Ad Backus (2012) Superdiverse Repertoires and the Individual. Tilburg Papers in Culture Studies. Paper 24.

Blommaert, Jan and Ben Rampton (2011) Language and superdiversity. *Diversities* 13(2): 1–21.

Boas, Hans C. (2009) *The Life and Death of Texas German*. Durham, NC: Duke University Press.

Bobo, Lawrence (1997). The color line, the dilemma, and the dream: American race relations at the close of the 20th century. In John Higham (ed.), *Civil Rights and Social Wrongs: Black–White Relations since World War II*. University Park: Pennsylvania State University Press. 31–55.

Bolonyai, Agnes (2015) "Where are you from?": Immigration stories of accent, belonging, and other experiences in the South. Paper presented at the Language Variety in the South conference (LAVIS IV). Raleigh, NC. April 9–12.

Brimelow, Peter (1995) *Alien Nation: Common Sense about America's Immigration Disaster*. New York: Random House.

Brown, C. L. (2005) Equity of literacy-based math performance assessments for English language learners. *Bilingual Research Journal* 29(2): 337–364.

Brown, Kimberley (1988) American college student attitudes toward non-native instructors. Unpublished PhD Dissertation, University of Minnesota.

Brown, Penelope and Stephen C. Levinson (1987) *Politeness: Some Universals in Language Use*. Cambridge and New York: Cambridge University Press.

Brożek, Andrzej (1972) *Ślązacy w Teksasie: Relacje o najstarszych osadach polskich w Ameryce*. Warsaw and Wrocław: Państwowe Wydawnictwo Naukowe (PWN).

Bryce-LaPorte, Roy S. (1993) Voluntary immigration and continuing encounters between blacks: The post-quincentenary challenge. *Annals, AAPS* 530: 28–41.

Buchanan, Patrick (2002) *Death of the West: How Dying Populations and Immigrant Invasions Imperil Our Country and Civilization*. New York: Thomas Dunne Books.

Buchanan, Patrick (2006) *State of Emergency: The Third World Invasion and the Conquest of America*. New York: Thomas Dunne Books/St. Martin's Press.

Bucholtz, Mary (1999a) You da man: Narrating the racial other in the production of white masculinity. *Journal of Sociolinguistics* 3(4): 443–460.

Bucholtz, Mary (1999b) "Why be normal?": Language and identity practices in a community of nerd girls. *Language in Society* 28: 203–223.

Bucholtz, Mary (2009) Styles and stereotypes: Laotian American girls' linguistic negotiation of identity. In Angela Reyes and Adrienne Lo (Eds.) *Beyond Yellow English: Towards a Linguistic Anthropology of Asian Pacific America*. Oxford: Oxford University Press. 21–42.

Bucholtz, Mary and Kira Hall (2004) Language and identity. In Alessandro Duranti (Ed.) *A Companion to Linguistic Anthropology*. Malden: Blackwell. 369–394.

Bucholtz, Mary and Kira Hall (2005) Identity and interaction: A sociocultural linguistic approach. *Discourse Studies* 7: 585–614.

Burck, Charlotte (2004) Living in several languages: Implications for therapy. *Journal of Family Therapy* 26: 314–339.

Burck, Charlotte (2005) *Multilingual Living: Explorations of Language and Subjectivity*. Basingstoke, UK: Palgrave Macmillian.

Buriel, Raymond, William Perez, Terri L. De Ment, David V. Chavez, and Virginia R. Moran (1998) The relationship of language brokering to academic performance, biculturalism, and self-efficacy among Latino adolescents. *Hispanic Journal of Behavioral Sciences* 20(3): 283–297.

Butler, Judith (1990) *Gender Trouble: Feminism and the Subversion of Identity*. New York and London: Routledge.

Callahan-Price, Erin (2013a) Past tense marking and interlanguage variation in emerging N.C. Hispanic English. Paper presented at the 87th Annual Meeting of the Linguistic Society of America, Boston, Massachusetts, 3–6 January 2013.

Callahan-Price, Erin (2013b) Emerging Hispanic English in the Southeast U.S.: Grammatical Variation in a Triethnic Community. Unpublished PhD dissertation: Duke University.

Cameron, Deborah (1990) Demythologizing sociolinguistics: Why language does not reflect society. In J.E. Joseph and T.J. Taylor (Eds). *Ideologies of Language*. London: Routledge. 79–93.

Cameron, Deborah (1997) Performing gender identity: Young men's talk and the construction of heterosexual masculinity. In Sally Johnson and Ulrike Meinhof (Eds.) *Language and Masculinity*. Oxford: Blackwell. 270–284.

Campano, Gerald (2007) *Immigrant Students and Literacy: Reading, Writing, and Remembering*. New York and London: Teachers College, Columbia University.

Canagarajah, Suresh (2011a) Translanguaging in the classroom: Emerging issues for research and pedagogy. *Applied Linguistics Review* 2: 1–28.

Canagarajah, Suresh (2011b) Codemeshing in academic writing: Identifying teachable strategies of translanguaging. *The Modern Language Journal* 95: 401–417.

Cargile, A.C. and J.J. Bradac (2001) Attitudes toward language: A review of applicant-evaluation research and a general process model. In W.B. Gudykunst (Ed.) *Communication Yearbook 25*. Mahwah, NJ: Lawrence Erlbaum. 347–382.

Cargile, Assron Castelán, Eriko Maeda, Jose Rodriguez, and Marc Rich (2010) "Oh, You speak English so well!": U.S. American listeners' perceptions of "foreignness" among nonnative speakers. *Journal of Asian American Studies* 13(1): 59–79.

Carlson, Lewis H. and George A. Colburn (Eds.) (1972) *In Their Place: White America Defines Her Minorities, 1850–1950*. New York: John Wiley & Sons.

Carnevale, Nancy C. (2009) *A New Language, A New World: Italian Immigrants in the United States, 1890–1945*. Urbana and Chicago: University of Illinois Press.

Carrillo, Hector (2004) Sexual migration, cross-cultural sexual encounters, and sexual health. *Sexuality Research and Social Policy* 1: 58–70.

Carter, Phillip (2007) Phonetic variation and speaker agency: *Mexicana* identity in a North Carolina middle school. *University of Pennsylvania Working Papers in Linguistics* 13(2): 1–14.

Cashman, Holly (2005a) Identities at play: Language preference and group membership in bilingual talk in interaction. *Journal of Pragmatics* 37: 301–315.

Cashman, Holly (2005b) Aggravation and disagreement: A case study of a bilingual, cross-sex dispute in a Phoenix classroom. *Southwest Journal of Linguistics* 24(1 & 2): 31–51.

Chacko, Elizabeth (2003) Identity and assimilation among young Ethiopian immigrants in metropolitan Washington. *Geographical Review* 93(4): 491–506.

Chanbonpin, Kate (2004/2005) How the border crossed us: Filling the gap between *Plume v. Seward* and the dispossession of Mexican landowners in California after 1848. *Cleveland State Law Review* 52: 297–319.

Chavez, Leo R. (2008) *The Latino Threat: Constructing Immigrants, Citizens, and the Nation*. Stanford, CA: Stanford University Press.

Cheryan, Sapna and Benoît Monin (2005) Where are you really from?: Asian Americans and identity denial. *Journal of Personality and Social Psychology* 89(5): 717–730.

Chun, Elaine (2001) The construction of white, black, and Korean American identities through African American Vernacular English. *Journal of Linguistic Anthropology* 11(1): 52–64.

Chun, Elaine (2009) Ideologies of legitimate mockery: Margaret Cho's revoicings of Mock Asian. In Angela Reyes and Adrienne Lo (Eds.) *Beyond Yellow English: Towards a Linguistic Anthropology of Asian Pacific America*. Oxford: Oxford University Press. 261–287.

Chun, Elaine (2015) "She be acting like she's black": Ideologies of language and blackness among Korean American female youth in Texas. Paper presented at the Language Variety in the South conference (LAVIS IV). Raleigh, NC. April 9–12, 2015.

Chung, Haesook Han (2006) Code switching as a communicative strategy: A case study of Korean-English bilinguals. *Bilingual Research Journal* 30(2): 293–307.

Cisneros, Josue (2013) *The Border Crossed Us: Rhetorics of Borders, Citizenship, and Latina/o Identity*. Tuscaloosa, AL: University of Alabama Press.

Citrin, Jack, Beth Reingold, and Evelyn Walters (1990) The "Official English" movement and the symbolic politics of language in the United States. *The Western Political Quarterly* 43(3): 535–559.

Clark, Herbert H. and Deanna Wilkes-Gibbs (1986) Referring as a collaborative process. *Cognition* 22: 1–39.

Combs, Mary Carol, Carol Evans, Todd Fletcher, Elena Parra, and Alicia Jiménez (2005) Bilingualism for the children: Implementing a dual-language program in an English-only state. *Educational Policy* 19(5): 701–728.

Crawford, James (1999) *Bilingual Education: History, Politics, Theory and Practice*. Fourth edition, revised and expanded. Los Angeles, CA: Bilingual Educational Services.

Crawford, James (2004) *Educating English Learners: Language Diversity in the Classroom*. Los Angeles: Bilingual Education Services, Inc.

Crawford, James (2007) *No Child Left Behind: A Failure for English Language Learners*. Tacoma Park, MD: Institute for Language and Education Policy.

Crowley, Tony (2003) *Standard English and the Politics of Language*. New York: Palgrave Macmillan.

Csábi, Szilvia (2001) The concept of America in the Puritan mind. *Language and Literature* 10(3): 195–209.

Cummins, James (1979) Linguistics interdependence and the educational development of bilingual children. *Review of Educational Research* 49(2): 222–251.

Cummins, James (1991) Conversational and academic language proficiency in bilingual contexts. *AILA Review* 8: 75–89.

Cutler, Cecilia (1999) Yorkville Crossing: White teens, hip-hop and African American English. *Journal of Sociolinguistics* 3(4): 428–442.

D'Angelo, Pascal (1924) *Son of Italy*. New York: Macmillan.

Dale, T.C. and G.J. Cuevas (1992) Integrating mathematics and language learning. In P.A. Richard-Amato and M.A. Snow (Eds.) *The Multilingual Classroom: Readings for Content-Area Teachers*. New York: Longman. 330–348.

Daniels, Roger (2002) *Coming to America: A History of Immigration and Ethnicity in American Life* (2nd edition). New York: Harper Perennial.

Dannenberg, Clare (2002) *Sociolinguistic Constructs of Ethnic Identity: The Syntactic Delineation of a Native American English*. Durham, NC: Duke University Press.

De Fina, Anna (2000) Orientation in immigrant narratives: The role of ethnicity in the identification of characters. *Discourse Studies* 2(2): 131–157.

De Fina, Anna (2007) Code-switching and the construction of ethnic identity in a community of practice. *Language in Society* 36: 371–392.

De Fina, Anna (2012) Family interaction and engagement with the heritage language: A case study. *Multilingua* 31: 349–379.

De Fina, Anna and Kendall K. King (2011) Language problem or language conflict? Narratives of immigrant women's experiences in the US. *Discourse Studies* 13(2): 163–188.

De Jongh, Elena (1990) Interpreting in Miami's federal courts: Code-switching and Spanglish. *Hispania* 73(1): 274–278.

De Ment, Terri L., Raymond Buriel, and Christina M. Villanueva (2005) Children as language brokers: A narrative of the recollections of college students. In Farideh Salili and Rumjahn Hoosain (Eds.) *Language in Multicultural Education*. Greenwich, CT: Information Age Publishing. 255–272.

Debes, John L. III (1981) It's time for a new paradigm: Languaging! *Language Sciences* 3(1): 186–192.

Decena, Carlos Ulises (2011) *Tacit Subjects: Belonging and Same-Sex Desire among Dominican Immigrant Men*. Durham and London: Duke University Press.

Decena, Carlos Ulises, Michele G. Shedlin, and Angela Martínez (2006) "Los hombres no mandan aquí": Narrating immigrant genders and sexualities in New York. *Social Text* 24(3): 35–54.

DeGraff, Michel (2003) Against Creole exceptionalism. *Language* 79(2): 391–410.

DeGraff, Michel (2005) Linguists' most dangerous myth: The fallacy of Creole exceptionalism. *Language in Society* 34: 533–591.

Del Torto, Lisa M. (2008) Once a broker, always a broker: Non-professional interpreting as identity accomplishment in multigenerational Italian-English bilingual family interaction. *Multilingua* 27: 77–97.

Delgado-Gaitán, Concha and Enrique Trueba (1991) *Crossing Cultural Borders: Education for Immigrant Families in America*. London and New York: Falmer Press.

Deloria, Philip J. and Neal Salisbury (Eds.) (2002) *A Companion to American Indian History*. Malden, MA: Blackwell.

Dewaele, Jean-Marc (2004a) The emotional force of swearwords and taboo words in the speech of multilinguals. *Journal of Multilingual and Multicultural Development* 25(2/3): 204–222.

Dewaele, Jean-Marc (2004b) Blistering barnacles! What language do multilinguals swear in?! *Estudios de Sociolingüística* 5(1): 83–105.

Dewaele, Jean-Marc (2004c) Perceived language dominance and language preference for emotional speech: The implications for attrition research. In M. Schmid, B. Köpke, M. Kejser, and L. Weilemar (Eds.) *First Language Attrition: Interdisciplinary Perspectives on Methodological Issues*. Amsterdam/Philadelphia: John Benjamins. 81–104.

Dewaele, Jean-Marc (2006) Expressing anger in multiple languages. In Aneta Pavlenko (Ed.) *Bilingual Minds: Emotional Experience, Expression, and Representation*. Clevedon, UK: Multilingual Matters.

Dewaele, Jean-Marc (2007) "Christ fucking shit merge!": Language preferences for swearing among maximally proficient multilinguals. *Sociolinguistic Studies* 4(3): 595–614.

Díaz-Lázaro, Carlos M. (2002) The effects of language brokering on perceptions of family authority structure, problem solving abilities, and parental locus of control in Latino adolescents and their parents. Unpublished PhD Dissertation: State University of New York at Buffalo.

Dick, Hilary (2010) No option but to go: Poetic rationalization and the discursive production of Mexican migrant identity. *Language and Communication* 30: 90–108.

Dick, Hilary Parsons (2011a) Language and migration to the United States. *Annual Review of Anthropology* 40: 227–240.

Dick, Hilary Parsons (2011b) Making immigrants illegal in small-town USA. *Journal of Linguistic Anthropology* 21(S1): 35–55.

Dietrich, Lisa C. (1998) *Chicana Adolescents: Bitches, 'Ho's, and Schoolgirls*. Westport, CT: Praeger.

Dillard, J.L. (1972) Afro-American, Spanglish, and something else: St. Cruzan naming patterns. *Names* 20: 225–230.

Doroszewski, Witold (1938) *Język polski w Stanach Zjedonoczonych A.P.* Warsaw: Towarszystwo Naukowe Warszawskie.

Dubisz, Stanisław (1981) Formy i typy funkcjonalnej adaptacji leksemów amerykańskoangielskich w dialekcie polonijnym Nowej Anglii. In Szliferszteјn, Salomea (Ed.) *Z badań nad językiem polskim środowisk emigracyjnych*. Wrocław: Ossolineum. 51–68.

Dunbar-Ortiz, Roxanne (2014) *An Indigenous People's History of the United States*. Boston: Beacon Press.

Dziembowska, Janina (Ed.) (1977a) *Memoirs of Polish Emigrants: USA* V.1. Warsaw: Książka i Wiedza.

Dziembowska, Janina (Ed.) (1977b) *Memoirs of Polish Emigrants: USA* V.2. Warsaw: Książka i Wiedza.

Easthope, Antony (1998) Bhabha, hybridity and identity. *Textual Practice* 12(2): 341–348.

Ebert, Roger (1982) Chan Is Missing (Reviews). http://www.rogerebert.com/reviews/chan-is-missing-1982.

Eckert, Penelope (1989) *Jocks and Burnouts: Social Categories and Identity in the High School*. New York and London: Teachers College, Columbia University.

Eckert, Penelope (2000) *Linguistic Variation as Social Practice: The Linguistic Construction of Identity at Belten High*. Malden, MA: Blackwell.

Eckert, Penelope and Sally McConnell-Ginet (1992) Think practically and look locally: Gender as a community-based practice. *Annual Review of Anthropology* 21: 461–490.

Eikel, Fred Jr. (1966a) New Braunfels German: Part I. *American Speech* 41: 5–16.

Eikel, Fred Jr. (1966b) New Braunfels German: Part II. *American Speech* 41: 254–260.

Eikel, Fred Jr. (1967) New Braunfels German: Part III. *American Speech* 42: 83–104.

Elías-Olivares, L. (Ed.) (1983) *Spanish in the U.S. Setting: Beyond the Southwest*. Rosslyn, VA: National Clearinghouse for Bilingual Education.

Erikson, Erik H.(1968) *Identity, Youth and Crisis*. New York: W.W. Norton.

Espín, Olivia M. (1999) *Women Crossing Boundaries: A Psychology of Immigration and Transformations of Sexuality*. New York and London: Routledge.

Espinosa, A. (1911) *The Spanish Language in New Mexico and Southern Colorado*. Santa Fe: New Mexican Publishing Company.

Espiritu, Yen Le (Ed.) (1995) *Filipino American Lives*. Philadelphia: Temple University Press.

Fairclough, Norman (2001) *Language and Power*. London and New York: Routledge.

Fan, Jiayang (2015) Hoop dreams. *New Yorker*, January 12. www.newyorker.com/magazine/2015/01/12/hoop-dreams.

Farr, Marcia (2006) *Rancheros in Chicagoacán: Language and Identity in a Transnational Community*. Austin: University of Texas Press.

Fellin, Luciana (2015) The New Italians of the South. Paper presented at the Language Variety in the South conference (LAVIS IV). Raleigh, NC. April 9–12.

Feng, Peter (1996) Being Chinese American, becoming Asian American: *Chan Is Missing*. *Cinema Journal* 35(4): 88–118.

Fishman, Joshua (1966) *Language Loyalty in the United States*. The Hague: Mouton.

Fishman, Joshua (1985) *The Rise and Fall of the Ethnic Revival: Perspectives on Language and Ethnicity*. Berlin: Mouton de Gruyter.

Fishman, Joshua (1991) *Reversing Language Shift: Theoretical and Empirical Foundations of Assistance to Threatened Languages*. Clevedon, UK: Multilingual Matters.

Fishman, Joshua A. (2004) Multilingualism and non-English mother tongues. In Edward Finegan and John J. Rickford (Eds.) *Language in the USA: Themes for the Twenty-First Century*. Cambridge: Cambridge University Press. 115–132.

Fixico, Donald L. (2009) American Indian history and writing from home: Constructing an Indian perspective. *The American Indian Quarterly* 33(4): 553–560.

Fought, Carmen (2003) *Chicano English in Context*. Basinstoke and New York: Palgrave Macmillan.

Fought, Carmen (2006) *Language and Ethnicity*. Cambridge: Cambridge University Press.

Franklin, Vincent P. (1991) Black social scientists and the mental testing movement, 1920–1940. In Reginald L. Jones (Ed.) *Black Psychology*. Berkeley, CA: Cobb & Henry. 207–224.

Freyere, Gilberto (1946 [1933]) *The Masters and the Slaves*. Translated by Samuel Putnam. New York: Knopf.

Freyere, Gilberto (1963 [1959]) *New World in the Tropics*. New York: Vintage

Freyere, Gilberto (1986 [1936]) *The Mansions and the Shanties*. Translated by Harriet de Onis. Berkeley: University of California Press.

Fulger, Diana (2012) The colors of the Cuban diaspora: Portrayal of racial dynamics among Cuban-Americans. *Forum for Inter-American Research* 5(2). http://interamericaonline.org/volume-5–2/fulger/ accessed December 9, 2015.

Gal, Susan (1988) The political economy of code choice. In Monica Heller (Ed.) *Code-Switching: Anthropological and Sociolinguistic Perspectives*. New York: Mouton de Gruyter. 45–264.

Gándara, Patricia and Megan Hopkins (Eds.) (2010) *Forbidden Language: English Learners and Restrictive Language Policies*. New York and London: Teachers College, Columbia University.

Gándara, Patricia, Daniel Losen, Diane August, Miren Uriarte, M. Cecilia Gómez, and Megan Hopkins (2010) Forbidden language: A brief history of U.S. language policy. In Patricia Gándara and Megan Hopkins (Eds.) *Forbidden Language: English Learners and Restrictive Language Policies*. New York and London: Teachers College, Columbia University. 20–33.

Gans, Herbert J. (1979) Symbolic ethnicity: The future of ethnic groups and cultures in America. *Ethnic and Racial Studies* 2(1): 1–20.

García, Ofelia (2009) *Bilingual Education in the 21st Century: A Global Perspective*. Malden, MA, and Oxford: Wiley-Blackwell.

García, Ofelia and Jo Anne Kleifgen (2010) *Educating Emergent Bilinguals: Policies, Programs, and Practices for English Language Learners*. New York and London: Teachers College Press, Columbia University.

García, Ofelia and Li Wei (2014) *Translanguaging: Language, Bilingualism, and Education*. Basingstoke: Palgrave Macmillan.

García, Ofelia, Jo Anne Kleifgen, and Lorraine Falchi (2008) *Equity Matters: Research Review No. 1. From English Language Learners to Emergent Bilinguals.* New York: Teacher College, Columbia University (A Research Initiative of the Campaign for Educational Equity). Available at http://www.equitycampaign.org/i/a/document/6468_Ofelia_ELL__Final.pdf.

Gardner-Chloros, Penelope (1987) Code-switching in relation to language contact and convergence. In Georges Ludi (Ed.) *Devenir bilingue – parler bilingue.* Tubingen: Max Niemeyer Verlag. 99–111.

Gardner-Chloros, Penelope (2009) *Code-Switching*. Cambridge: Cambridge University Press.

Gee, James Paul (1999) *An Introduction to Discourse Analysis: Theory and Method.* London and New York: Routledge.

Geyer, Georgie Anne (1996) *Americans No More: The Death of Citizenship*. New York: Atlantic Monthly Press.

Gilbert, Glenn G. (1963) The German dialect spoken in Kendall and Gillespie Counties, Texas. PhD Dissertation: Harvard University.

Gilbert, Glenn G. (1970) The phonology, morphology, and lexicon of a German text from Fredericksburg, Texas. In Glenn G. Gilbert (Ed.) *Texas Studies in Bilingualism*. Berlin: Walter de Gruyter & Co. 63–104.

Gilbert, Glenn G. (1972) *Linguistic Atlas of Texas German*. Austin: University of Texas Press.

Glenn, Charles L. (2011) *American Indian/First Nations Schooling: From the Colonial Period to the Present*. New York: Palgrave Macmillan.

Gluszek, Agata and John F. Dovidio (2010) Speaking with a nonnative accent: Perceptions of bias, communication difficulties, and belonging in the United States. *Journal of Language and Social Psychology* 29(2): 224–234.

Goddard, Henry H. (1917) Mental tests and the immigrant. *Journal of Delinquency* 2: 243–277.

Goffman, Erving (1961) *Asylums*. Chicago: Aldine Publishing Company.

Goffman, Erving (1979) Footing. *Semiotica* 25: 1–29.

Goldberg, David Theo (1993) *Racist Culture: Philosophy and the Politics of Meaning*. Cambridge, MA: Blackwell.

Golla, Victor (2011) *California Indian Langauges*. Berkeley and Los Angeles: University of California Press.

Gonzalez-Reigosa, F. (1976) The anxiety-arousing effect of taboo words in bilinguals. In C. Spielberger and R. Diaz-Guerrero (Eds.) *Cross-Cultural Anxiety*. Washington, DC: Hemisphere. 89–105.

Goodenough, Florence (1926) Racial differences in the intelligence of school children. *Journal of Experimental Psychology* 9: 388–397.

Granillo, Christina Marie (2011) Language brokering, interactional styles and parental behaviors among Latino families. Unpublished PhD Dissertation: Claremont Graduate University.

Grosjean, François (1989) Neurolinguists, beware! The bilingual is not two monolinguals in one person. *Brain and Language* 36(1): 3–15.

Gruchmanowa, Monika (1979) Badania nad językiem polonii amerykańskiej w świetle metod socjolingwistycznych. *Socjolingwistyka* 2: 95–102.

Gruchmanowa, Monika (1984) O odmianach polszczyzny w Stanach Zjednoczonych A.P. *Polonica* 10: 185–205.

Guillén, Nicolás (1972) *Songoro Cosongo. (Obra poetica, vol. 1.)* La Habana: Instituto Cubano del Libro.

Gumperz, John J. (1982) *Discourse Strategies*. Cambridge: Cambridge University Press.

Gutiérrez González, H. (1993) *El español en El Barrio de Nueva York: estudio léxico*. New York: Academia Norteamericana de la Lengua Española.

Gutiérrez, Kris D., Patricia Baquedano-López, and Carlos Tejeda (1999) Rethinking diversity: Hybridity and hybrid language practices in the third space. *Mind, Culture, and Activity* 6(4): 286–303.

Gutiérrez, M. (1994) Simplification, transference and convergence in Chicano Spanish. *Bilingual Review* 19: 111–121.

Haguen, Einar (1950) The analysis of linguistic borrowing. *Language* 26(2): 210–231.

Hakuta, Kenji (1986) *Mirror of Language: The Debate on Bilingualism*. New York: Basic Books.

Hall, Stuart (1992) The questions of cultural identity. In Stuart Hall, David Held, and Tony McGrew (Eds.) *Modernity and Its Futures*. Cambridge: Polity Press. 273–326.

Halter, Marilyn (2000) *Shopping for Identity: The Marketing of Ethnicity*. New York: Schocken Books.

Hanson, Victor Davis (2003) *Mexifornia: A State of Becoming*. San Francisco: Encounter Books.

Harkins, Jean and Anna Wierzbicka (1997) Language: A key issue in emotion research. *Innovation* 10(4): 319–331.

Harris, C., A. Aiçiçegi, and J. Gleason (2003) Taboo words and reprimands elicit greater autonomic reactivity in a first language than in a second language. *Applied Psycholinguistics* 24(4): 561–579.

Harvey, Sean P. (2015) *Native Tongues: Colonialism and Race from Encounter to the Reservation*. Cambridge, MA, and London: Harvard University Press.

Haugen, Einar (1967) *The Norwegians in America: A Student's Guide to Localized History*. New York: Teachers College Press.

Heath, Shirley Brice (1983) *Ways with Words: Language, Life, and Work in Communities and Classrooms*. Cambridge: Cambridge University Press.

Helms, Janet E. (1994) The conceptualization of racial identity and other "racial" constructs. In Edison J. Trickett, Roderick J. Watts, and Dina Birman (Eds.) *Human Diversity: Perspectives on People in Context*. San Francisco: Jossey-Bass. 285–311.

Higgins, C. (2009) *English as a Local Practice: Post-Colonial Identities and Multilingual Practices*. Bristol: Multilingual Matters.

Hill, Jane H. (1993a) Is it really "no problemo"? Junk Spanish and Anglo racism. *Texas Linguistic Forum* 33(1): 1–12.

Hill, Jane H. (1999) Styling locally, styling globally: What does it mean? *Journal of Sociolinguistics* 3(4): 542–556.

Hill, Jane H. (2001) Language, Race, and White Public Space. In Alessandro Duranti (Ed.) *Linguistic Anthropology: A Reader*. Malden, MA: Blackwell. 450–464.

Hill, Jane H. (2008) *The Everyday Language of White Racism*. Malden, MA: Blackwell.

Hobson, John M. (2012) *The Eurocentric Conception of World Politics: Western International Theory 1760–2010*. Cambridge: Cambridge University Press.

Hoffman, Eva (1989) *Lost in Translation: A Life in a New Language*. New York: Penguin Books.

Holliday, Adrian, Martin Hyde, and John Kullman (2004) *Intercultural Communication: An Advanced Resource Book*. London and New York: Routledge.

Holloway, Joseph and Winifred K. Vass (1993) *The African Heritage of American English*. Bloomington and Indianapolis: Indiana University Press.

Holmes, Janet and Miriam Meyerhoff (1999) The community of practice: Theories and methodologies in language and gender research. *Language in Society* 28: 173–183.

Holmquist, Quinn (2016) Strange Chains: A Microanthropological Study of Non-English Speakers' Courtroom Experience. Unpublished BA thesis: Duke University.

Hopper, Paul (1998) Emergent grammar. In Michael Tomasello (ed.) *The New Psychology of Language: Cognitive and Functional Approaches to Language Structure*. Mahwah, NJ: Lawrence Erlbaum. 155–175.

Hornberger, Nancy (1989) Continua of biliteracy. *Review of Educational Research* 59: 271–296.

Hornberger, Nancy (Ed.) (2003) *Continua of Biliteracy: An Ecological Framework for Educational Policy, Research and Practice in Multilingual Settings*. Clevedon, UK: Multilingual Matters.

Hornberger, Nancy and Holly Link (2012) Translanguaging and transnational literacies in multilingual classrooms: A biliteracy lens. *International Journal of Bilingual Education and Bilingualism*. 15(3): 261–278.

Hornberger, Nancy and E. Skilton-Sylvester (2000) Revisiting the continua of biliteracy: International and critical perspectives. *Language and Education: An International Journal* 14: 96–122.

Hosoda, Megumi and Eugene Stone-Romero (2010) The effects of foreign accents on employment-related decisions. *Journal of Managerial Psychology* 25(2): 113–132.

Hosoda, Megumi, Lam T. Nguyen, and Eugene F. Stone-Romero (2012) The effect of Hispanic accents on employment decisions. *Journal of Managerial Psychology* 27(4): 347–364.

Howe, Cymene (2014) Sexual adjudications and queer transpositions. *Journal of Language and Sexuality* 3(1): 136–155.

Hsu, Hua (2006) Wayne Wang Is Missing. *Slate*, March 30. http://www.slate.com/articles/arts/dvdextras/2006/03/wayne_wang_is_missing.html, accessed March 27, 2015.

Huang, Eddie (2013) *Fresh Off The Boat: A Memoir*. New York: Spiegel & Grau Trade Paperbacks.

Huang, Eddie (2015) Bamboo-Ceiling TV. *Vulture*, February 4. http://www.vulture.com/2015/01/eddie-huang-fresh-off-the-boat-abc.html, accessed May 23, 2017.

Huntington, Samuel (2004) *Who Are We? The Challenges to America's National Identity*. New York: Simon & Schuster.

Irvine, Judith and Susan Gal (2000) Language ideology and linguistic differentiation. In Kroskrity, Paul (Ed.) *Regimes of Language*. Santa Fe, NM: School of American Research Press. 35–83.

Jacquemet, Marco (2005) Transidiomatic practices: Language and power in the age of globalization. *Language and Communication* 25: 257–277.

James, William (1890) *The Principles of Psychology*. New York: H. Holt and Company.

Javier, Rafael and Luis Marcos (1989) The role of stress on the language-independence and code-switching phenomena. Journal of Psycholinguistic Research 18(5): 449–472.

Jespersen, Otto (1922) *Language*. London: George Allen and Unwin.

Jones, Curtis J. and Edison J. Trickett (2005) "Immigrant adolescents behaving as culture brokers" a study of families from the former Soviet Union. *The Journal of Social Psychology* 145(4): 405–427.

Jones, Katharine W. (2001) *Accent on Privilege: English Identities and Anglophilia in the U.S.* Philadelphia: Temple University Press.

Jorae, Wendy Rose (2009) *The Children of Chinatown: Growing Up Chinese American in San Francisco 1850–1920*. Chapel Hill: The University of North Carolina Press.

Jørgensen, J. Normann (2008) Polylingual languaging around and among children and adolescents. *International Journal of Multilingualism* 5(3): 161–176.

Jørgensen, J. Normann (2012) Ideologies, norms, and practices in youth poly-languaging. *International Journal of Bilingualism* 17(4): 525–539.

Jørgensen, J. Normann, M.S. Karrebæk, L.M. Madsen, and J.S. Møller. (2011) Polylanguaging in superdiversity. *Diversities* 13(2): 23–37.

Jozefski, Jeffrey M. (2008) The role of Polish and American identities in the future of the Polish National Catholic Church. *Polish American Studies* 65(2): 27–52.

Kalmar, Tomás Mario (2001) *Illegal Alphabets and Adult Biliteracy: Latino Migrants Crossing the Linguistic Border*. Mahwah, NJ, and London: Lawrence Erlbaum Associates, Publishers.

Kayyal, Mary H. and James A. Russell (2013) Language and emotion: Certain English-Arabic translations are not equivalent. *Journal of Language and Social Psychology* 32(3): 261–271.

Kennedy, John F. (1964) *A Nation of Immigrants*. New York: Harper Perennial.

Kersten, Holger (2006) America's multilingualism and the problem of the literary representation of "pidgin English." *Amerikastudien / American Studies* 51(1): 75–91.

Kim, Ronald I. (2008) California Chinese pidgin English and its historical connections: Preliminary remarks. *Journal of Pidgin and Creole Languages* 23(2): 329–344.

Kingston, Maxine Hong (1989 [1975]) *The Woman Warrior: Memoirs of a Girlhood Among Ghosts*. New York: Vintage International.

Klein, Wendy L. (2009) Turban narratives: Discourses of identification and difference among Punjabi Sikh families in Los Angeles. In Angela Reyes and Adrienne Lo

(Eds.) *Beyond Yellow English: Toward a Linguistic Anthropology of Asian Pacific America*. Oxford: Oxford University Press. 111–130.

Kloss, Heinz (1998) *The American Bilingual Tradition*. Washington, DC: Center for Applied Linguistics.

Knapp, Kiyoko Kamio (1997) Language minorities: Forgotten victims of discrimination? *Georgetown Immigration Law Journal* 11: 747–787.

Kohn, Mary (2008) Latino English in North Carolina: A Comparison of Emerging Communities. Unpublished MA thesis. Raleigh: North Carolina State University.

Kohn, Mary and Hannah Franz (2009) Localized patterns for global variants: The case of quotative systems of African American and Latino speakers. *American Speech* 84: 259–297.

Kosinski, Jerzy (1976) *The Painted Bird*. Boston: Houghton Mifflin.

Kraus, Joe (1999) How *The Melting Pot* stirred America: The reception of Zangwill's play and theater's role in the American assimilation experience. *Multi-Ethnic Literature of the United States (MELUS)* 24(3): 3–19.

Krauss, M. (1998) The condition of Native North American languages: The need for realistic assessment and action. *International Journal of the Sociology of Language* 132: 9–21.

Kruszka, Wacław X. (1905) *Historya Polska w Ameryce*. Milwaukee, WI: Kuryer. 13 vols.

Kubota, Ryuoko and Angel Lin (2006) Race and TESOL: Introduction to concepts and theories. *TESOL Quarterly* 40(3): 471–493.

Kurtz, William B. (2014) "Let us hear no more 'Nativism'": The Catholic press in the Mexican and Civil Wars. *Civil War History* 60(1): 6–31.

Kyratzis, Amy (2010) Latina girls' peer play interactions in a bilingual Spanish-English U.S. preschool: Heteroglossia, frame-shifting, and language ideology. *Pragmatics* 20(4): 557–586.

Labov, William (1966) *The Social Stratification of English in New York City*. Washington, DC: Center for Applied Linguistics.

Labov, William (2010) *Principles of Linguistic Change: Cognitive and Cultural Factors (Vol. 3)*. Oxford: Wiley-Blackwell.

Lakoff, George (2004) *Don't Think of an Elephant!: Know Your Values and Frame the Debate – The Essential Guide for Progressives*. White River Junction, VT: Chelsea Green Publishing.

Lamanna, Scott G. (2012) Colombian Spanish in North Carolina: The Role of Language and Dialect Contact in the Formation of a New Variety of U.S. Spanish. Unpublished Ph.D. Dissertation: Indiana University.

Lanehart, Sonja (2007) If our children are our future, why are we stuck in the past? Beyond the Anglicisms and the Creolists, and toward social change. In H. Samy Alim and John Baugh (Eds.) *Talkin Black Talk: Language, Education, and Social Change*. New York and London: Teachers College, Columbia University. 132–141.

Lave, Jean and Etienne Wenger (1991) *Situated Learning: Legitimate Peripheral Participation*. Cambridge: Cambridge University Press.

Leap, William L. (1981) American Indian languages. In Charles Ferguson and Shirley Brice Heath (Eds.) *Language in the USA*. Cambridge: Cambridge University Press. 116–144.

Lee, Margaret (1998) Out of the Hood and into the News: Borrowed Black Verbal Expressions in a Mainstream Newspaper. Paper presented at the New Ways of Analyzing Variation (NWAV) 27 conference, Athens, Georgia.

Lee, Robert G. (1999) *Orientals: Asian Americans in Popular Culture*. Philadelphia: Temple University Press.

Lee, Stacey J. (1994) Behind the model-minority stereotype: Voices of high- and low-achieving Asian American students. *Anthropology & Education Quarterly* 25(4): 413–429.

Lee, Tiffany S. (2009) Language, identity, and power: Navajo and Pueblo young adults' perspectives and experiences with competing language ideologies. *Journal of Language, Identity, and Education* 8: 307–320.

Leeman, Jennifer (2004) Racializing language: A history of linguistic ideologies in the US Census. *Journal of Language and Politics* 3(3): 507–534.

Leland, Charles G. (1892) *Pidgin-English Sing-Song or Songs and Stories in the China-English Dialect*. London: Kegan Paul, Trench, Trübner, & Co. Ltd.

Lewis, Ronald L. (2008) *Welsh Americans: A History of Assimilation in the Coalfields*. Chapel Hill: The University of North Carolina Press.

Li Wei (2011) Moment analysis and translanguaging space: Discursive construction of identities by multilingual Chinese youth in Britain. *Journal of Pragmatics* 43: 1222–1235.

Li, Juan (2004) Pidgin and code-switching: Linguistic identity and multicultural consciousness in Maxine Hong Kingston's Tripmaster Monkey. *Language and Literature* 13(3): 269–287.

Lindemann, Stephanie (2002) Listening with an attitude: A model of native-speaker comprehension of non-native speakers in the United States. *Language in Society* 31: 419–441.

Lindemann, Stephanie (2003) Koreans, Chinese or Indians? Attitudes and ideologies about non-native English speakers in the United States. *Journal of Sociolinguistics* 7(3): 348–364.

Lindemann, Stephanie (2005) Who speaks "broken English"? US undergraduates' perceptions of non-native English. *International Journal of Applied Linguistics* 15(2): 187–212.

Linton, April (2009) Language politics and policy in the United States: Implications for the immigration debate. *International Journal of the Sociology of Language* 199: 9–37.

Lippi-Green, Rosina (2004) Language ideology and language prejudice. In Edward Finegan and John J. Rickford (Eds.) *Language in the USA: Themes for the Twenty-First Century*. Cambridge: Cambridge University Press. 289–304.

Lippi-Green, Rosina (2012) *English with an Accent: Language, Ideology and Discrimination in the United States* (2nd edition). London and New York: Routledge.

Lipski, John (2014) Is "Spanglish" the third language of the South? Truth and fantasy about US Spanish. In Michael Picone and Catherine Evans Davies (Eds.) *New Perspectives on Language Variety in the South: Historical and Contemporary Approaches*. Tuscaloosa: University of Alabama Press. 657–677.

Lipski, John M. (2008) *Varieties of Spanish in the United States*. Washington, DC: Georgetown University Press.

Liu, Eric (1999) *The Accidental Asian: Notes of a Native Speaker*. New York: Random House.

Liu, Eric (2014). Why I don't hyphenate Chinese American. http://www.cnn.com/2014/07/11/opinion/liu-chinese-american, accessed August 5, 2016.

Lo, Adrienne (1997) Heteroglossia and the Construction of Asian American Identities. *Issues in Applied Linguistics* 8(1): 47–62.

Lo, Adrienne (1999) Codeswitching, speech community membership, and the construction of ethnic identity. *Journal of Sociolinguistics* 3(4): 461–479.

Love, Julia Anne (2007) Theory of mind ability in the preadolescent language broker: Connections between language brokering, social cognition, and academic achievement. Unpublished PhD Dissertation: Claremont Graduate University.

Love, Julia A. and Raymond Buriel (2007) Language brokering, autonomy, parent-child bonding, biculturalism, and depression: A study of Mexican American adolescents from immigrant families. *Hispanic Journal of Behavioral Sciences* 29(4): 472–491.

Luna-Firebaugh, Eileen M. (2002) The border crossed us: Border crossing issues of the indigenous peoples of the Americas. *Wicazo Sa Review* 17(1): 159–181.

Maira, S. (2004) Imperial feelings: Youth culture, citizenship, and globalization. In Marcel Suarez-Orozco and D. Quin-Hilliard (Eds.) *Globalization: Culture and Education in the New Millennium*. Berkeley: University of California Press. 203–234.

Major, Clarence (1994) *Juba to Jive: A Dictionary of African-American Slang*. New York: Penguin Books.

Makoni, Sinfree (2012) A critique of language, languaging and supervernacular. *Muitas Vozes, Ponta Grossa*, 1(2): 189–199.

Makoni, Sinfree and Alastair Pennycook (2005) Disinventing and (re)constituting languages. *Critical Inquiry in Language Studies: An International Journal* 2(3): 137–156.

Mangione, Jerre (1998 [1942]) *Mount Allegro: A Memoir of Italian American Life*. New York: Syracuse University Press.

Martínez-Echazábal, Lourdes (1998) *Mestizaje* and the discourse of national/cultural identity in Latin America, 1845–1959. *Latin American Perspectives* 25(3): 21–42.

Mathews, Gordon (2000) *Global Culture/Individual Identity: Searching for Home in the Cultural Supermarket*. London: Routledge.

Matsuda, M. (1991) Voices of America: Accent, antidiscrimination law, and a jurisprudence for the last reconstruction. *Yale Law Journal* 100(5): 1329–1407.

Maulucci, Maria S. Rivera (2008) Intersections between immigration, language, identity and emotions: a science teacher candidate's journey. *Cultural Studies of Science Education* 3: 17–42.

McCarty, Teresa L. (2002) *A Place to Be Navajo: Rough Rock and the Struggle for Self-Determination in Indigenous Schooling*. Mahwah, NJ: Lawrence Erlbaum Associates.

McCarty, Teresa L. (2010) Native American languages in the USA. In Kim Potowski (Ed.) *Language Diversity in the USA*. Cambridge: Cambridge University Press. 47–65.

McGee, ThomasD'Arcy(1852) *A history of the Irish settlers in North America, from the earliest period to the census of 1850*. Boston: Office of the "American Celt." https://archive.org/details/historyofirishse00mcge.

McQuillan, Jeff and Lucy Tse (1995) Child language brokering in linguistic minority communities: Effects on cultural interaction, cognition and literacy. *Language and Education* 9(3): 195–215.

McRobbie, Angela (2005) *The Uses of Cultural Studies*. London: Sage Publications.
Medvedeva, Maria (2012) Negotiating languages in immigrant families. *International Migration Review* 46(2): 517–545.
Mendoza-Denton, Norma (1997) Chicana/Mexicana Identity and Linguistic Variation: An Ethnographic and Sociolinguistic Study of Gang Affiliation in an Urban High School. Ph.D. Dissertation, Stanford University.
Mendoza-Denton, Norma (2008) *Homegirls: Language and Cultural Practice among Latina Youth Gangs*. Malden, MA: Blackwell.
Meyerhoff, Miriam (1999) *Sorry* in the Pacific: Defining communities, defining practices. *Language in Society* 28: 225–238.
Miller, Stuart Creighton (1969) *The Unwelcome Immigrant: The American Image of the Chinese, 1785–1882*. Berkeley: University of California Press.
Milroy, James (1999) The consequences of standardization in descriptive linguistics. In Tony Bex and Richard J. Watts (Eds.) *Standard English: The Widening Debate*. London and New York: Routledge. 16–39.
Milroy, Lesley and Li Wei (1995) A social network approach to code-switching: The example of a bilingual community in Britain. In Lesley Milroy and Peter Muysken (Eds.) *One Speaker, Two Languages: Cross-Disciplinary Perspectives on Code-Switching*. Cambridge: Cambridge University Press. 136–157.
Miodunka, Władysław (1990) Wstęp. In Władysław Miodunka (Ed.) *Język polski w świecie*. Warsaw-Kraków: Państwowe Wydawnictwo Naukowe (PWN). 9–20.
Mizutani, Satoshi (2013) Hybridity and history: A critical reflection on Homi K. Bhabha's post-historical thoughts. *Ab Imperio* 4: 27–47.
Montes-Alcalá, Cecilia (2009) Hispanics in the United States: More than Spanglish. *Camino Real* 1(1): 97–105.
Mora, G.Cristina (2014) *Making Hispanics: How Activists, Bureaucrats, and Media Constructed a New American*. Chicago: The University of Chicago Press.
Morales, Ed (2002) *Living in Spanglish: The Search for Latino Identity in America*. New York: St. Martin's Press.
Morgan, Marcyliena (1998) More than a mood or an attitude: Discourse and verbal genres in African-American culture. In Salikoko Mufwene, John R. Rickford, Guy Bailey, and John Baugh (Eds.) *African-American English: Structure, History and Use*. London and New York: Routledge. 251–281.
Morgan, Marcyliena (2002) *Language, Discourse and Power in African American Culture*. Cambridge: Cambridge University Press.
Mori, Kyoto (1997) *Polite Lies: On Being a Woman Caught Between Two Cultures*. New York: Ballantine Publishing Group.
Mufwene, Salikoko (2000) Creolization is a social, not a structural, process. In Ingrid Neumann-Holzschuh and Edgar Schneider (Eds.) *Degrees of Restructuring in Creole Languages*. Amsterdam: John Benjamins. 65–84.
Mufwene, Salikoko (2001) *The Ecology of Language Evolution*. Cambridge: Cambridge University Press.
Mufwene, Salikoko (2008) *Language Evolution: Contact, Competition and Change*. London and New York: Continuum.
Mulroy, Martin John (1906) Culdees & Irland It Milka: The Irish in America one thousand years before Columbus. http://www.aughty.org/pdf/culdees_irland_mikla.pdf

Myers-Scotton, Carol (1992) Comparing codeswitching and borrowing. *Journal of Multilingual & Multicultural Development* 13(1–2), 19–39.

Myers-Scotton, Carol (1993) *Duelling Languages: Grammatical Structure in Codeswitching*. Oxford: Clarendon Press.

Myhill, William N. (2004) The state of public education and the needs of English language learners in the era of "No Child Left Behind." *Journal of Gender, Race and Justice* 8(2): 393–419.

Nash, Rose (1970) Spanglish: Language contact in Puerto Rico. *American Speech* 45: 223–233.

Nelson, Cynthia D. (2006) Queer inquiry in language education. *Journal of Language, Identity, and Education* 5(1): 1–9.

Nelson, Cynthia D. (2010) A gay immigrant student's perspective: Unspeakable acts in the language class. *TESOL Quarterly* 44(3): 441–464.

Newlin-Łukowicz, Luiza (2012) TH-stopping in New York City: Substrate effect turned ethnic marker? Poster presented at the New Ways of Analyzing Variation (NWAV) 41 conference, Bloomington, Indiana, October 25–28.

Newlin-Łukowicz, Luiza (2014) From interference to transfer in language contact: Variation in voice onset time. *Language Variation and Change* 26: 359–385.

Newman, Michael (2003) New York City English. *LanguageMagazine* (August). https://www.languagemagazine.com/archives/.

Newman, Michael (2010) Focusing, implicational scaling, and the dialect status of New York Latino English. *Journal of Sociolinguistics* 14: 207–239.

Newton, Lina (2008) *Illegal, Alien, or Immigrant: The Politics of Immigration Reform*. New York and London: New York University Press.

Nicholas, Sheilah E. (2009) "I live Hopi, I just don't speak it" – The critical intersection of language, culture, and identity in the lives of contemporary Hopi youth. *Journal of Language, Identity, and Education* 8: 321–334.

Niehaus, Kate and Gerda Kumpiene (2014) Language brokering and self-concept: An exploratory study of Latino students' experiences in middle and high school. *Hispanic Journal of Behavioral Sciences* 36(2): 124–143.

Niklewicz, Franciszek (1938) *Historia pierwszej polskiej parafii w Ameryce*. Green Bay.

Oh, Janet S. and Andrew J. Fuligni (2010) The role of heritage language development in the ethnic identity and family relationships of adolescents from immigrant backgrounds. *Social Development* 19(1): 202–220.

Olesch, Reinhold (1970) The West Slavic languages in Texas with special regard to Sorbian in Serbin, Lee County. In Glenn G. Gilbert (Ed.) *Texas Studies in Bilingualism*. Berlin: Walter de Gruyter & Co. 151–162.

Opotow, Susan (1990) Moral exclusion and injustice: An overview. *Journal of Social Issues* 46(1): 1–20.

Opotow, Susan (1995) Drawing the line: Social categorization, moral exclusion, and the scope of justice. In B.B. Bunker and J.Z. Rubin (Eds.) *Conflict, Cooperation, and Justice*. San Francisco: Jossey-Bass. 347–369.

Orellana, Marjorie Faulstich (2009) *Translating Childhoods: Immigrant Youth, Language and Culture*. New Brunswick, NJ: Rutgers University Press.

Ornstein-Galicia, Jacob (1984) *Form and function in Chicano English*. Rowley, MA: Newbury House Publishers.

Ortiz, Fernando (1947) On the social phenomenon of "transculturation" and its importance in Cuba. In *Cuban Counterpoint: Tobacco and Sugar*. Translated by Harriet de Onfs. New York: Knopf. 97–102.

Orzell, Laurence (1979) A minority with a minority: The Polish National Catholic Church, 1896–1907. *Polish American Studies* 36(1): 5–32.

Osofsky, Gilbert (1975) Abolitionists, Irish immigrants, and the dilemmas of romantic nationalism. *American Historical Review* 80(4): 889–912.

Otheguy, Ricardo and Ana Celia Zentella (2012) *Spanish in New York: Language Contact, Dialectal Leveling, and Structural Continuity*. Oxford: Oxford University Press.

Otheguy, Ricardo, Ana Celia Zentella, and David Livert (2007) Language and dialect contact in Spanish in New York: Toward the formation of a speech community. *Language* 83: 770–802.

Otsuji, E. and Alastair Pennycook (2010) Metrolingualism: Fixity, fluidity and language in flux. *International Journal of Multilingualism* 7: 240–253.

Page, Jake (2004) *In the Hands of the Great Spirit: The 20,000-year History of American Indians*. New York, London, Toronto, Sydney: Free Press.

Palmer, Deborah K. (2009) Code-switching and symbolic power in a second-grade two-way classroom: A teacher's motivation system gone awry. *Bilingual Research Journal* 32: 42–59.

Palmer, Deborah K., Ramón Antonio Martínez, Suzanne G. Mateus, and Kathryn Henderson (2014) Reframing the debate on language separation: Toward a vision for translanguaging pedagogies in the dual language classroom. *The Modern Language Journal* 98(3): 757–772.

Pan, Barbara Alexander (1995) Code negotiation in bilingual families: "My body starts speaking English." *Journal of Multilingual and Multicultural Development* 16(4): 315–327.

Panayiotou, Alexia (2004) Switching codes, switching code: Bilinguals' emotional responses in English and Greek. *Journal of Multilingual and Multicultural Development* 25(2 & 3): 124–139.

Panek, P. (1898) *Emigracyja Polska w Stanach Zjednoczonych Ameryki Północnej*. Lwów: Nakładem redakcji Przeglądu Wielkopolskiego.

Pantos, Andrew J. and Andrew W. Perkins (2012) Measuring implicit and explicit attitudes toward foreign accented speech. *Journal of Language and Social Psychology* 32(1): 3–20.

Panunzio, Constantine (1928) *The Soul of an Immigrant*. New York: Arno Press.

Pavlenko, Aneta (2001) "How am I to become a woman in an American vein?" Transformations of gender performance in second language learning. In Aneta Pavlenko, Adrian Blackledge, Ingrid Piller, and Marya Teutsch-Dwyer (Eds.) *Multilingualism, Second Language Learning, and Gender*. The Hague: Mouton de Gruyter. 133–174.

Pavlenko, Aneta (2002) "We have room for but one language here": Language and national identity in the US at the turn of the 20th century. *Multilingua* 21: 163–196.

Pavlenko, Aneta (2005) *Emotions and Multilingualism*. Cambridge: Cambridge University Press.

Pavlenko, Aneta and James P. Lantolf (2000) Second language learning as participation and the (re)construction of selves. In James P. Lantolf (Ed.) *Sociocultural Theory and Second Language Learning*. Oxford: Oxford University Press. 155–177.

Pearce, Roy Harvey (1965) *The Savages of America: A Study of the Indian and the Idea of Civilization*. Baltimore: The Johns Hopkins Press.

Peñalosa, Fernando (1980) *Chicano Sociolinguistics: A Brief Introduction*. Rowley, MA: Newbury House.

Pennycook, Alastair (1998) *English and the Discourses of Colonialism*. New York: Routledge.

Pennycook, Alastair (2010) *Language as a Local Practice*. London and New York: Routledge.

Peterson, Anna (2011) Making women's suffrage support an ethnic duty: Norwegian American identity constructions and the women's suffrage movement, 1880–1925. *Journal of American Ethnic History* 30(4): 5–23.

Phillips, R. (1967) Los Angeles Spanish: A description analysis. Unpublished PhD dissertation: University of Wisconsin.

Phillipson, Robert (1992) *Linguistic Imperialism*. Oxford: Oxford University Press.

Platt, Warren C. (1977) The Polish National Catholic Church: An inquiry into its origins. *Church History* 46(4) 474–489.

Polkinghorne, Donald E. (1988) *Narrative Knowing and the Human Sciences*. Albany, NY: State University of New York Press.

Pomerantz, Anita (1984) Agreeing and disagreeing with assessments: some features of preferred/dispreferred turn shapes. In M. Atkinson, J. Heritage (Eds.), Structures of Social Action: Studies in Conversation Analysis. Cambridge University Press, Cambridge. 57–101.

Poplack, Shana (1978) Dialect acquisition among Spanish-English bilinguals. *Language in Society* 7: 89–103.

Poplack, Shana (1980) "Sometimes I'll start a sentence in Spanish *y termini en español*": Toward a typology of code-switching. *Linguistics* 18(7): 581–618.

Poplack, Shana and David Sankoff (1987) The Philadelphia story in the Spanish Caribbean. *American Speech* 62: 291–314.

Poplack, Shana and Sali Tagliamonte (1989) There's no tense like the present: Verbal *-s* inflection in Early Black English. *Language Variation and Change* 1: 47–84.

Poplack, Shana, David Sankoff, and Christopher Miller (1988) The social correlates and linguistic processes of lexical borrowing and assimilation. *Linguistics* 26(1): 47–104.

Poplack, Shana, Susan Wheeler, and Anneli Westwood (1990) Distinguishing language contact phenomena: Evidence from Finnish-English bilingualism. In Rodolfo Jacobson (Ed.) *Codeswitching as a Worldwide Phenomenon*. New York: Peter Lang Publishing. 185–218.

Porges, A. (1949) The influence of English on the Spanish of New York. Unpublished MA thesis, University of Florida.

Portes, Alejandro and Lingxin Hao (2002) The price of uniformity: language, family and personality adjustment in the immigrant second generation. *Ethnic and Racial Studies* 25(6): 889–912.

Portes, Alejandro and Rubén G. Rumbaut (2001) *Legacies: The Story of the Immigrant Second Generation*. Berkeley and New York: University of California Press and Russell Sage Foundation.

Portes, Alejandro and Rubén G. Rumbaut (2006) *Immigrant America: A Portrait*. Berkeley: University of California Press.

Potowski, Kim (2011) Linguistic and cultural authenticity of "Spanglish" greeting cards. *International Journal of Multilingualism* 8(4): 324–344.

Potowski, Kim (Ed.) (2010) *Language Diversity in the USA*. Cambridge: Cambridge University Press.

Preston, Dennis R. (2011) The power of language regard – discrimination, classification, comprehension, and production. *Dialectologia* 2: 9–33.

Prifti, Elton (2014) *Italoamericano: Italiano e Inglese in Contatto negli USA*. Berlin/Boston: Walter de Gruyter.

Pulte, William, Jr. (1970) An Analysis of Selected German Dialects of Northern Texas and Oklahoma. In Glenn G. Gilbert (Ed.) *Texas Studies in Bilingualism*. Berlin: Walter de Gruyter & Co. 105–141.

Purchas, Richard Haklyut (1614) *Haklyutus Posthumus, or Purchas His Pilgrimes*. William Stansby: London. Available at https://archive.org/details/purchashispilgri00purc. Quoted in Pearce, Roy Harvey (1965) The Savages of America: A Study of the Indian and the Idea of Civilization. Baltimore: The Johns Hopkins Press, p. 8.

Rampton, Ben (1995) *Crossing: Language and Ethnicity Among Adolescents*. London and New York: Longman.

Rampton, Ben (2013) Drilling down to the grain in superdiversity. *Working Papers in Urban Language and Literacies*, paper 98. www.kcl.ac.uk/ldc.

Rampton, Ben, Jan Blommaert, Karel Arnaut, and Massimiliano Spotti (2015) Superdiversity and sociolinguistics. *Working Papers in Urban Language and Literacies*, paper 152. 1–13.

Ravitch, Diane (2010) *The Death and Life of the Great American School System: How Testing and Choice are Undermining Education*. New York: Basic Books.

Rell, Amy (2004) An exploration of Mexican-American Spanglish as a source of identity. *Mester* 33(1): 143–157.

Reyes, Angela (2005) Appropriation of African American slang by Asian American youth. *Journal of Sociolinguistics* 9(4): 509–532.

Reyes, Angela (2009) Asian American stereotypes as circulating resource. In Angela Reyes and Adrienne Lo (Eds.) *Beyond Yellow English: Towards a Linguistic Anthropology of Asian Pacific America*. Oxford: Oxford University Press. 43–62.

Reyes, Angela and Adrienne Lo (Eds.) (2009) *Beyond Yellow English: Towards a Linguistic Anthropology of Asian Pacific America*. Oxford: Oxford University Press.

Reyes, Sharon Adelman and Trina Lynn Vallone (2007) Toward an expanded understanding of two-way bilingual immersion education: Constructing identity through a critical, additive bilingual/bicultural pedagogy. *Multicultural Perspectives* 9(3): 3–11.

Reyhner, Jon and Jeanne Eder (2004) *American Indian Education: A History*. Norman: University of Oklahoma Press.

Reynolds, Jennifer F. and Marjorie Faulstich Orellana (2015) Translanguaging within enactment of Quotidian interpreter-mediated interactions. *Journal of Linguistic Anthropology* 24(3): 315–338.

Rickford, John and Russell Rickford (2000) *Spoken Soul: The Story of Black English*. New York: John Wiley & Sons, Inc.

Rickford, John R. (1998) The creole origins of African-American Vernacular English: Evidence from copula absence. In Salikoko Mufwene, John R. Rickford, Guy Bailey, and John Baugh (Eds.) *African-American English: Structure, History and Use*. London and New York: Routledge. 154–200.

Riley, Philip (2007) *Language, Culture and Identity: An Ethnolinguistic Perspective*. London and New York: Continuum.

Roca, A. and John M. Lipski (Eds.) (1993) *Spanish in the United States: Linguistic Contact and Diversity*. Berlin: Mouton de Gruyter.

Rodriguez, Richard (1982) *Hunger of Memory: The Education of Richard Rodriguez*. Boston: D.R. Godine.

Roizblatt, Arturo and Daniel Pilowsky (1996) Forced migration and resettlement: Its impact on families and individuals. *Contemporary Family Therapy* 18(4): 513–521.

Romaine, Suzanne (1995) *Bilingualism* (2nd Edition). Malden, Massachusetts: Blackwell.

Roosevelt, Theodore (1919) *Newer Roosevelt Messages: Speeches, Letters and Magazine Articles Dealing with the War, Before and After, and Other Vital Topics, Volume 3*. Edited by William Griffith. New York: The Current Literature Publishing Company.

Rouse, Roger (1988) Migración al suroeste de Michoacán durante el Porfiriato: El caso de Aguililla. In Thomas Calvo and Gustavo López (Eds.) *Movimientos de población en el occidente de México*. Zamora and Mexico City: El Colegio de Michoacán and Centre d'Etudes Mexicaines et Centraméricaines. 231–250.

Rubin, Donald L. (1992) Nonlanguage factors affecting undergraduates' judgments of nonnative English-speaking teaching assistants. *Research in Higher Education* 33(4): 511–531.

Rubin, Donald L. and K. A. Smith (1990) Effects of accent, ethnicity, and lecture topic of undergraduates' perceptions of non-native English speaking teaching assistants. *International Journal of Intercultural Relations* 14: 337–353.

Rubinstein-Avila, Eliane (2002) Problematizing the "Dual" in a Dual-Immersion Program: A Portrait. *Linguistics and Education* 13(1): 65–87.

Rubinstein-Ávila, Eliane (2007) From the Dominican Republic to Drew High: What counts as literacy for Yanira Lara? *Reading Research Quarterly* 42(4): 568–589.

Sacks, Karen Brodkin (1994) How Did Jews Become White Folks? In Steven Gregory and Roger Sanjek (Eds.) *Race*. New Brunswick, NJ: Rutgers University Press. 78–102.

Safire, William (1978) *Safire's Political Dictionary*. New York: Random House.

Salmons, Joseph C. and Felecia A. Lucht (2006) Standard German in Texas. In Glenn G. Gilbert, Janet M. Fuller, and Linda L. Thornburg (Eds.) *Studies in Contact Linguistics: Essays in Honor of Glenn G. Gilbert*. New York: Peter Lang. 148–186.

Sanjek, Roger (1994) The enduring inequalities of race. In Steven Gregory and Roger Sanjek (Eds.) *Race*. New Brunswick, NJ: Rutgers University Press. 1–17.

Sankoff, David and Shana Poplack (1981) A formal grammar for code-switching. *Papers in Linguistics* 14: 3–46.

Sankoff, David, Shana Poplack, and Swathi Vanniarajan (1990) The case of the nonce loan in Tamil. *Language Variation and Change* 2(1): 71–101.

Sankoff, Gilian (1979) The genesis of a language. In Kenneth C. Hill (Ed.) *The Genesis of Language*. Ann Arbor: Karoma. 23–47.

Santa Ana, Otto (1993) Chicano English and the nature of the Chicano language setting. *Hispanic Journal of Behavioral Sciences* 15(1): 3–35.

Sayer, Peter (2008) Demystifying language mixing: Spanglish in school. *Journal of Latinos and Education* 7(2): 94–112.

Schecter, Sandra R. and Robert Bayley (1997) Language socialization practices and cultural identity: Case studies of Mexican-descent families in California and Texas. *TESOL Quarterly* 31(3): 513–541.

Schieffelin, Bambi B. (2003) Language and place in children's worlds. *Texas Linguistics Forum (SALSA)* 45: 152–166.

Schlegloff, Emanuel (1982) Discourse as an interactional achievement: Some uses of "uh huh" and other things that come between sentences. In Deborah Tannen (Ed.) *Analyzing Discourse: Text and Talk*. Washington, DC: Georgetown University Press. 71–93.

Schmid, Carol L. (2001) *The Politics of Language: Conflict, Identity, and Cultural Pluralism in Comparative Perspective*. Oxford: Oxford University Press.

Schmidt, Ronald, Sr. (2000) *Language Policy and Identity Politics in the United States*. Philadelphia: Temple University Press.

Schmidt, Ronald, Sr. (2002) Radicalization and language policy: The case of the United States. *Multilingual* 21: 141–161.

Seals, Corinne A. (2013) Te Espero: Varying child bilingual abilities and the effects on dynamics in Mexican immigrant families. *Issues in Applied Linguistics* 19: 119–142.

Searle, John (1995) *The Construction of Social Reality*. London: Penguin.

Sears, David O. and P.J. Henry (2003) The origins of symbolic racism. *Journal of Personality and Social Psychology* 85(2): 259–275.

Seif, Hinda (2014) "Layers of humanity": Interview with undocuqueer artivist Julio Salgado. *Latino Studies* 12: 300–309.

Sessions, Gene (1987) "Years of struggle": The Irish in the village of Northfield, 1845–1900. *Vermont History* 1987: 69–95.

Shannon, Sheila M. (1990) English in the barrio: The quality of contact among immigrant children. *Hispanic Journal of Behavioral Sciences* 12(3): 256–276.

Shreve, Bradley G. (2011) *Red Power Rising: The National Indian Youth Council and the Origins of Native Activism*. Norman: University of Oklahoma Press.

Shuck, Gail (2006) Racializing the Nonnative English Speaker. *Journal of Language, Identity, and Education* 5(4): 259–276.

Silverstein, Michael (1979) Language structure and linguistic ideology. In R. Cline, William Hanks, and C. Hofbauer (Eds.) *The Elements: A Parasession of Linguistic Units and Levels*. Chicago: Chicago Linguistic Society. 193–247.

Silverstein, Michael (2013) How language communities intersect: Is "superdiversity" an incremental or transformative condition? Paper presented at the conference Language and Super-diversity: Explorations and Interrogations. Jyväskylä: June 5–7, 2013.

Simić, Andrei (2007) Understanding hyphenated ethnicity: The Serbian-American case. *Serbian Studies: Journal of the North American Society for Serbian Studies* 21(1): 37–54.

Simon, Rita J. (1985) *Public Opinion and the Immigrant: Print Media Coverage, 1880–1980*. Lexington, MA, and Toronto: Lexington Books.

Sirin, Selcuk R. and Michelle Fine (2008) *Muslim American Youth: Understanding Hyphenated Identities through Multiple Methods*. New York and London: New York University Press.

Skilton-Sylvester E (2003) Legal discourse and decisions, teacher policymaking and the multilingual classroom: Constraining and supporting Khmer/English biliteracy in the United States. In A. Creese and P. Martin (Eds.) *Multilingual Classroom Ecologies: Inter-Relationships, Interactions, and Ideologies*. Clevedon, UK: Multilingual Matters. 8–24.

Skutnabb-Kangas, Tove (1981) Guest worker or immigrant? Different ways of reproducing the underclass. *Journal of Multilingual and Multicultural Development* 2(2): 89–115.

Smedley, Audrey and Brian Smedley (2011) *Race in North America: Origin and Evolution of a Worldview*. Boulder, CO: Westview Press.

Smith, Patrick (2002) "Ni a Pocha Va a Llegar": Minority Language Loss and Dual Language Schooling in the U.S.-Mexico Borderlands. *Southwest Journal of Linguistics* 21(1): 165–183.

Smitherman, Geneva (1986) *Talkin and Testifyin: The Language of Black America*. Detroit: Wayne State University Press.

Smitherman, Geneva (1998) Word from the hood: the lexicon of African-American vernacular English. In Salikoko Mufwene, John R. Rickford, Guy Bailey, and John Baugh (Eds.) *African-American English: Structure, History and Use*. London and New York: Routledge. 203–225.

Smitherman, Geneva (2000) *Black Talk: Words and Phrases from the Hood to the Amen Corner*. Boston and New York: Houghton Mifflin Company.

Solomos, John and Les Back (1995) *Race, Politics and Social Change*. London and New York: Routledge.

Song, John Huey-Long, John Dombrink, and Gil Geis (1992) Lost in the melting pot: Asian youth gangs in the United States. *Gang Journal* 1: 1–12.

Spears, Arthur K. (1998) African-American language use: Ideology and so-called obscenity. In Salikoko Mufwene, John R. Rickford, Guy Bailey, and John Baugh (Eds.) *African-American English: Structure, History and Use*. London and New York: Routledge. 226–250.

Stasiewicz-Bieńkowska, Agnieszka (2011) *Kształtowanie tożsamości etnicznej dzieci imigrantów szwedzkich w USA według Augustana Book Concern (1889–1962)*. Kraków: Wydawnictwo Uniwersytetu Jagiellońskiego.

Stavans, Ilan (2003) *Spanglish: The Making of a New American Language*. New York: Harper Collins Publishers.

Stave, Bruce M. (2010) Coming to Connecticut: Immigrants in the land of unsteady habits. *Connecticut History* 2010: 201–210.

Stepick, A., C. Stepick, E. Eugene, D. Teed, and Y. Labissiere (2001) Shifting identities and intergenerational conflict: Growing up Haitian in Miami. In R. Rumbaut and A. Portes (Eds.) *Ethnicities: Children of immigrants in America*. Berkeley, CA: University of California Press. 229–266.

Suárez-Orozco, Carola and Marcelo M. Suárez-Orozco (2001) *Children of Immigration*. Cambridge: Harvard University Press.

Sue, Derald Wing (2010) *Microaggressions in Everyday Life: Race, Gender, and Sexual Orientation*. Hoboken, NJ: Wiley.

Sue, Derald Wing, Christina M. Capodilupo, Gina C. Torino, Jennifer M. Bucceri, Aisha M.B. Holder, Kevin L. Nadal, and Marta Esquilin (2007) Racial Microaggressions in Everyday Life: Implications for Clinical Practice. *American Psychologist* 62(4): 271–286.

Takagi, Dana Y. (1994) Post-Civil Rights Politics and Asian-American Identity: Admissions and Higher Education. In Steven Gregory and Roger Sanjek (Eds.) *Race*. New Brunswick, NJ: Rutgers University Press. 229–242.

Tannen, Deborah (1989) *Talking Voices: Repetition, Dialogue, and Imagery in Conversational Discourse*. Cambridge: Cambridge University Press.

Tannenbaum, Michal (2012) Family language policy as a form of coping or defence mechanism. *Journal of Multilingual and Multicultural Development* 33(1): 57–66.

Terrio, Susan J. (2015) Dispelling the Myths: Unaccompanied, Undocumented Child Migrants in U.S. Immigration Custody. Presentation at the Unaccompanied Child Migration Symposium, The Keenan Institute for Ethics, Duke University, Durham, North Carolina. February 23.

Teuton, Sean Kicummah (2008) *Red Land, Red Power: Grounding Knowledge in the American Indian Novel*. Durham and London: Duke University Press.

Teuton, Sean Kicummah (2013) Cities of Refuge: Indigenous Cosmopolitan Writers and the International Imaginary. *American Literary History* 25(1): 33–53.

Teutsch-Dwyer, Marya (2001) (Re)constructing masculinity in a new linguistic reality. In Aneta Pavlenko (Ed.) *Multilingualism, Second Language Learning, and Gender*. Berlin and New York: Mouton de Gruyter.

Thao, Nguyen Thi Thu (2007) Difficulties for Vietnamese when pronouncing English final consonants. Unpublished manuscript, Dalarna University College, Sweden.

Thorne, S. and James Lantolf (2007) A linguistics of communicative activity. In Sinfree Makoni and Alastair Pennycook (Eds.) *Disinventing and Reconstituting Languages*. Clevedon: Multilingual Matters. 170–195.

Tollefson, James (1991) *Planning Language, Planning Inequality: Language Policy in the Community*. London and New York: Longman.

Tracy, James (1988) The Rise and Fall of the Know-Nothings in Quincy. *Historical Journal of Massachusetts* 16(1): 1–19.

Trickett, Edison J. and Curtis J. Jones (2007) Adolescent culture brokering and family functioning: A study of families from Vietnam. *Cultural Diversity and Ethnic Minority Psychology* 13(2): 143–150.

Trudgill, Peter (1986) *Dialects in Contact*. Oxford and New York: Blackwell.

Tse, Lucy (1995) Language brokering among Latino adolescents: Prevalence, attitudes, and school performance. *Hispanic Journal of Behavioral Sciences* 17(2): 180–193.

Tse, Lucy (1996a) Who decides?: The effects of language brokering on home-school communication. *The Journal of Educational Issues of Language Minority Students* 16: 225–234.

Tse, Lucy (1996b) Language brokering in linguistic minority communities: The case of Chinese- and Vietnamese-American students. *Bilingual Research Journal* 20 (3/4): 485–498.

Tseng, Vivian and Andrew J. Fuligni (2000) Parent-adolescent language use and relationships among immigrant families with East Asian, Filipino, and Latin American backgrounds. *Journal of Marriage and the Family* 62: 465–476.

Tuan, Luu Trong (2011) Vietnamese EFL learners' difficulties with English consonants. *Studies in Language and Literature* 3(2): 56–67.

Tuan, Mia (1999) *Forever Foreigners or Honorary Whites? The Asian Ethnic Experience Today*. New Brunswick, NJ: Rutgers University Press.

Turner, Jonathan H. (2002) *Face to Face: Toward a Sociological Theory of Interpersonal Behavior*. Stanford, CA: Stanford University Press.

Urciuoli, Bonnie (1995) Language and borders. *Annual Review of Anthropology* 24: 525–546.

Urciuoli, Bonnie (1996) *Exposing Prejudice: Puerto Rican Experiences of Language, Race, and Class*. Boulder, CO: Westview Press.

Uriarte, Miren, Rosann Tung, Nicole Lavan, and Virginia Diez (2010). Impact of restrictive language policies on engagement and academic achievement of English learners in Boston Public Schools. In Patricia Gándara and Megan Hopkins (Eds.) *Forbidden Language: English Learners and Restrictive Language Policies*. New York and London: Teachers College, Columbia University. 65–85.

Valdés, Guadalupe (2001) *Learning and Not Learning English: Latino Students in American Schools*. New York and London: Teachers College Press, Columbia University.

Valdés, Guadalupe (2003) *Expanding Definitions of Giftedness: The Case of Young Interpreters From Immigrant Communities*. Mahwah, NJ, and London: Lawrence Erlbaum Associates, Publishers.

Valenzuela, Angela (1999) *Subtractive Schooling: U.S.-Mexican Youth and the Politics of Caring*. Albany: State University of New York Press.

Vasconcelos, José (1979 [1925]) *The Cosmic Race/La raza cósmica*. Edited by Didien T. Jaén. Los Angeles: Pace.

Vertovec, Steven (2007) Super-diversity and its implications. *Ethnic and Racial Studies* 30(6): 1024–1054.

Vigil, James D. (2012) *From Indians to Chicanos: The Dynamics of Mexican-American Culture*. Long Grove, IL: Waveband Press.

Vile, John R. (2013) *The Men Who Made the Constitution: Lives of the Delegates to the Constitutional Convention*. Lanham: The Scarecrow Press, Inc.

Viteri, María Amelia (2014) Citizenship(s), belonging and xenophobia: Ecuador and NYC. *Journal of Language and Sexuality* 3(1): 121–135.

Voake, Steve (2011) *Daisy Dawson at the Beach*. Somerville, MA: Candlewick Publishers.

Vološinov, V.N. (1973) *Marxism and the Philosophy of Language*. New York: Seminar Press.

Vought, Hans (1994) Division and reunion: Woodrow Wilson, immigration, and the myth of American unity. *Journal of American Ethnic History* 13(3): 24–50.

Vought, Hans P. (2004) *The Bully Pulpit and the Melting Pot: American Presidents and the Immigrant 1897–1933*. Macon, GA: Mercer University Press.

Wade, Peter (2005) Rethinking *Mestizaje*: Ideology and lived experience. *Journal of Latin American Studies* 37(2): 239–257.

Warriner, Doris S. (2007) Language learning and the politics of belonging: Sudanese women refugees *becoming* and *being* "American." *Anthropology and Education Quarterly* 38(4): 343–359.

Weber, David (2003) *Foreigners in Their Native Land: Historical Roots of the Mexican Americans*. Albuquerque: University of New Mexico Press.

Weinreich, Uriel (1953) *Languages in Contact: Findings and Problems*. The Hague: Mouton Publishers.

Weisgerber, Leo (1966) Vorurteile und Gefahren der Zweisprachigkeit. *Wirkendes Wort* 16: 73–89.

Weisskirch, Robert S. (2006) Emotional aspects of language brokering among Mexican American adults. *Journal of Multilingual and Multicultural Development* 27(4): 332–343.

Weldeyesus, Weldu Michael (2007) Narrative and identity construction among Ethiopian immigrants. *Colorado Research in Linguistics* 20: 1–10.

Wierzbicka, Anna (1998) Angst. *Culture and Psychology* 4(2): 161–188.

Wierzbicka, Anna (1999) Emotional universals. *Language Design: Journal of Theoretical and Experimental Linguistics*. 2: 23–69.

Wierzbicka, Anna (2004) Preface: Bilingual lives, bilingual experience. *Journal of Multilingual and Multicultural Development* 25(2&3): 94–104.

Wierzbicka, Anna (2007) Two languages, two cultures, one (?) self: Between Polish and English. In Mary Besemeres and Anna Wierzbicka (Eds.) *Translating Lives: Living with Two Languages and Cultures*. St. Lucia, Queensland: University of Queensland Press. 96–113.

Wierzbicka, Anna (2008) A conceptual basis for research into emotions and bilingualism. *Bilingualism: Language and Cognition* 11(2): 193–195.

Wiese, Ann-Marie and Eugene Garcia (2001) The Bilingual Education Act: Language minority students and US federal educational policy. *International Journal of Bilingual Education and Bilingualism* 4(4): 229–248.

Wiesskirch, Robert S. and Sylvia Alatorre Alva (2002) Language brokering and the acculturation of Latino children. *Hispanic Journal of Behavioral Sicences* 24(3): 369–378.

Wiley, Terrence G. (2004) Language policy and English-only. In Edward Finegan and John J. Rickford (Eds.) *Language in the USA: Themes for the Twenty-First Century*. Cambridge: Cambridge University Press. 319–338.

Wiley, Terrence G. (2005) *Literacy and Language Diversity in the United States*. Washington, DC: Center for Applied Linguistics.

Wiley, Terrence G. (2014) Diversity, super-diversity, and monolingual language ideology in the United States: Tolerance or intolerance? *Review of Research in Education* 38: 1–32.

Wilkerson, Isabel (2011) *The Warmth of Other Suns: The Epic Story of America's Great Migration*. New York: Random House.

Willey, Day Allen (1909) Americans in the making: New England's method of assimilating the alien. *Putnam's Monthly and the Reader* 5: 456–463.

Williams, Ashley M. (2005) Fighting words and challenging expectations: Language alternation and social roles in a family dispute. *Journal of Pragmatics* 37: 317–328.

Williams, Ashely M. (2008) Brought-along identities and the dynamics of ideology: Accomplishing bivalent stances in a multilingual interaction. *Multilingua* 27: 37–56.

Willis, Paul (1977) *Learning to Labour: How Working Class Kids Get Working Class Jobs*. New York: Columbia University Press.

Witcomb, Andrea (2007) Growing up between two languages/worlds: Learning to live without belonging to a *terra*. In Mary Besemeres and Anna Wierzbicka (Eds.)

Translating Lives: Living with Two Languages and Cultures. St. Lucia, Queensland: University of Queensland Press. 83–95.

Wolfram, Walt (1974) *A Sociolinguistic Study of Assimilation: Puerto Rican English in New York City*. Washington, DC: Center for Applied Linguistics.

Wolfram, Walt (2003) Reexamining the development of African American English: Evidence from isolated communities. *Language* 79: 282–316.

Wolfram, Walt and Clare Dannenberg (1999) Dialect identity in a tri-ethnic context: The case of Lumbee American Indian English. *English World-Wide* 20(2): 179–216.

Wolfram, Walt and Natalie Schilling (2016) *American English* (3rd edition). Malden, MA: Blackwell.

Wolfram, Walt, Phillip Carter, and Beckie Moriello (2004) Emerging Hispanic English: New dialect formation in the American South. *Journal of Sociolinguistics* 8(3): 339–358.

Wolfram, Walt, Mary E. Kohn, and Erin Callahan-Price (2011) Southern-bred Hispanic English: An emerging socioethnic variety. In Jim Michnowicz and Robin Dodsworth (Eds.) *Selected Proceedings of the 5th Workshop on Spanish Sociolinguistics*. Somerville, MA: Cascadilla Proceedings Project. 1–13.

Wong, Jock (2007) East meets West, or does it really? In Mary Besemeres and Anna Wierzbicka (Eds.) *Translating Lives: Living with Two Languages and Cultures*. St. Lucia, Queensland: University of Queensland Press. 70–82.

Wood, Peter H. (2003) *Strange New Land: Africans in Colonial America*. Oxford: Oxford University Press.

Wright, Russell O. (2008) *Chronology of Immigration in the United States*. Jefferson, NC: McFarland & Company.

Wright, Wayne E. and Xiaoshi Li (2006) Catching up in math? The case of newly-arrived Cambodian students in a Texas intermediate school. *TABE Journal* 9(1): 1–22.

Wright, Wayne E. and Xiaoshi Li (2008) High-stakes math tests: How *No Child Left Behind* leaves newcomer English language learners behind. *Language Policty* 7: 237–266.

Wu, Frank H. (2002) Where are you really from? Asian Americans and the perpetual foreigner syndrome. *Civil Rights Journal Winter* 2002: 14–22.

Wytrwal, Joseph Anthony (1982) *Polish-black encounters: a history of Polish and black relations in America since 1619*. Detroit, MI: Endurance Press.

Ye, Zhengdao [Veronica] (2007) Returning to my mother tongue: Veronica's journey continues. In Mary Besemeres and Anna Wierzbicka (Eds.) *Translating Lives: Living with Two Languages and Cultures*. St. Lucia, Queensland: University of Queensland Press. 56–69.

Young, Linda Wai Ling (1982) Inscrutability revisited. In John J. Gumperz (Ed.) *Language and Social Identity*. Cambridge: Cambridge University Press. 72–84.

Zapf, Harald (2006) Ethnicity and performance: Bilingualism in Spanglish verse culture. *American Studies* 51(1): 13–27.

Zentella, Ana Celia (1997) *Growing Up Bilingual: Puerto Rican Children in New York*. Malden, MA: Blackwel.

Zentella, Ana Celia (1998) Multiple codes, multiple identities: Puerto Rican Children in New York City. In S.M. Hoyle and C.T. Adger (Eds.) *Kids Talk: Strategic Language Use in Later Childhood*. Oxford, UK: Oxford University Press. 95–111.

Zentella, Ana Celia (2003) "José, can you see?": Latin@ responses to racist discourse. In Doris Sommer (Ed.) *Bilingual Games: Some Literary Investigations*. New York: Palgrave Macmillan. 51–66.
Zentella, Ana Celia (2004) Spanish in the Northeast. In Edward Finegan and John J. Rickford (Eds.) *Language in the USA: Themes for the Twenty-First Century*. Cambridge: Cambridge University Press. 182–204.
Zentella, Ana Celia (2008) Preface. In Mercedes Niño-Murcia and Jason Rothman (Eds.) *Spanish at the Crossroads with Other Languages*. Amsterdam and Philadelphia: John Benjamins. 3–10.

Index